Honour of Empire Glory of Sport

THE HISTORY OF ATHLETICS
AT THE COMMONWEALTH GAMES

By Bob Phillips

WITH A FOREWORD BY DAVID MOORCROFT O.B.E.

The Parrs Wood Press
MANCHESTER

First Published in 2000

THE PARRS WOOD PRESS
St Wilfrid's Enterprise Centre,
Royce Road, Manchester, M15 5BJ
www.parrswoodpress.com

© Bob Phillips 2000

ISBN: **1 903158 09 5**

This book was produced by Andrew Searle, Bob Wells and Ruth Heritage of The Parrs Wood Press and was printed in Great Britain by:

Fretwell Print and Design
Healey Works
Golbourne Street
Keighley
West Yorkshire BD21 1PZ

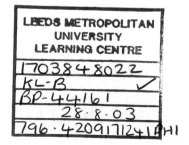

This book is dedicated to Norris and the late Ross McWhirter, whose innovative writing in the early 1950s fired the enthusiasm of so many young track "nuts"; to Neil Allen, whose authoritative column in "World Sports" magazine provided a rare, often unique, insight into international athletics; to Roberto Quercetani, the maestro of athletics statisticians whose passion for the sport began in the 1930s; and, by no means least, to my wife, Daphne, for her continuing encouragement and support.

"We declare that we are all loyal subjects of His Majesty the King Emperor and will take part in the British Empire Games in the true spirit of sportsmanship, recognising the rules which govern them and desirous of participating in them for the honour of our Empire and for the glory of sport."

This was the oath of allegiance taken on behalf of all the competitors at the 1934 Games by R.L. 'Bonzo' Howland, England team captain and shot-putt record-holder. It was reported at the time that *"in full accordance with such delightful principles, the Games proceeded."*

ABOUT THE AUTHOR

Born in Lewisham, in South London, and educated - more or less - at a minor public school in St Albans, in Hertfordshire, in the 1950's, my interest in athletics was first seriously roused by the sight of Gordon Pirie beating an American named Wes Santee in the Emsley Carr mile at the White City Stadium, in London, in 1953. That initial enthusiasm became an obsession after going to see the Empire Games in Cardiff in 1958 and the Olympic Games in Rome in 1960, with Herb Elliott's majestic victories at both remaining an abiding memory to this day. A peripatetic youthful experience in the labour market as a farm labourer, carpenter's mate, postman and insurance clerk led me by curious chance to a career in journalism and then public relations.

As a member of BBC Radio 5's athletics commentary team, I have had the pleasure of attending all the major championships of recent years, and the enjoyment of many a meeting has been further enhanced by endless discussions afterwards with fellow-members of the National Union of Track Statisticians (yes, the acronym of "NUTS" is singularly appropriate) about all manner of performances past and present. A long and exceedingly modest competitive career with various clubs has included such "highlights" as winning the Watford Harriers 100 yards title (slow gun, quick start), coming last in the Coventry Godiva Harriers cross-country championship, finishing 777th in the first London Marathon in 2:50:08 (quite proud of that), and more recently - since the knees and hamstrings started to suffer the effects of 60 miles running a week - turning to cycle time-trials and racing against Chris Boardman, among others, though he could be forgiven for not noticing. Other interests pursued with unbridled vigour include modern literature, jazz, cinema, wine and travel, and a current project is writing a biography of the 1936 Olympic relay gold-medallist, Bill Roberts, which is also to be published shortly in Manchester by The Parrs Wood Press.

CONTENTS:

INDEX OF PHOTOGRAPHS

FRONT COVER PHOTOGRAPH:

1998. Four continents represented in one graphic image which epitomises the far-reaching appeal of the Commonwealth Games - Africa, the Americas, Europe and Oceania. Mozambique, newly accepted into the Commonwealth, competed for the first time in the 1998 Games and the women's 800 metres was won by their former World champion, Maria Mutola. Here she leads in her semifinal in characteristically forthright fashion from Mardrea Hyman, of Jamaica (left), with Diane Modahl for England, Toni Hodgkinson for New Zealand and Tamsyn Lewis for Australia among the pursuers.

ACKNOWLEDGEMENTS

No one could write about any aspect of the Commonwealth Games without making some reference to the work of the foremost authority on the subject of Commonwealth athletics, Stan Greenberg. I've known Stan for more years than either of us care to remember and as always he has been infectiously enthusiastic and selflessly helpful. I've also made use of work done by Daniel Schamps, Peter Matthews, Peter Lovesey, Norris McWhirter and the late Ross McWhirter, Ian Buchanan, David Thurlow, Roger Gynn, Mel Watman, Les Crouch and many other members of the National Union of Track Statisticians and the Association of Track & Field Statisticians, and I've pored over the columns of "Athletics Weekly", "Athletics World", "Athletics Today", "Athletics International", "The Times" and the "Sporting Chronicle". Some of my research has been carried out at the National Centre for Athletics Literature at Birmingham University and at the Manchester Reference Library, and I am grateful to the respective staffs for their help. I have also had access to the astonishingly comprehensive private collection of books and magazines built up by Dave Terry, whose knowledge and guidance has been invaluable. All this has enabled much new material to be discovered and the first comprehensive list of Games results to be compiled. For space reasons the results listed in this book are restricted to the finals, but fuller details will be published in "Track Stats", the quarterly publication of the National Union of Track Statisticians which I have the pleasure of editing. My particular thanks are directed, also, to Andy Searle, without whose support this project would not have gone ahead, and it's especially gratifying for me that it should be a Manchester publisher backing this venture as the 2002 Games - the 17th in the series - draw near.

PREFACE

From 1930 to 1966 events run on the track were at imperial distances rather than metric. For guidance equivalent measures are listed as follows: 100 yards = 91.44 metres, 100 metres = 109 yards 1 foot 1 inch, 120 yards = 109.728 metres, 110 metres = 120 yards 10fl inches, 200 metres = 218 yards 2 feet 2 inches, 220 yards = 201.168 metres, 400 metres = 437 yards 1 foot 4 inches, 440 yards = 402.336 metres, 800 metres = 874 yards 2 feet 8 inches, 880 yards = 804.672 metres, 1500 metres = 1640 yards 1 foot 3 inches, 1 mile = 1609.344 metres, 3 miles = 4828.032 metres, 5000 metres = 3 miles 188 yards 2 inches, 6 miles = 9656.064 metres, 10,000 metres = 6 miles 376 yards 5 inches. The time factors for conversion are generally accepted by track & field statisticians as being as follows: 100 yards to 100 metres + 0.85sec, 220 yards to 200 metres - 0.1sec, 440 yards to 400 metres - 0.3sec, 880 yards to 800 metres - 0.7sec, 3 miles to 5000 metres + 28sec, 6 miles to 10,000 metres + 58sec. Field events measurements were made in feet and inches through to 1966 but are usually given here in metric form for consistency.

THE COMPETING COUNTRIES

At the 1926 Imperial Conference the six existing Dominions of the British Empire, which were Australia, Canada, the Irish Free State, Newfoundland, New Zealand and South Africa, had been established as "autonomous communities within the British Empire, equal in status, in no way subordinate to one another in any aspect of their domestic or external affairs, although united by a common allegiance to the Crown and freely associated as Members of the British Commonwealth of Nations". The Statute of Westminster 1931 gave this declaration legal standing. Subsequently, no less than 87 countries, some in different guises, have taken part in the Games, and the abbreviations used for them are as follows, indicating the year in which they first competed:

Aden 1962 Ade (South Arabia in 1966), Anguilla 1998 Ang, Antigua & Barbuda 1966 Ant, Australia 1930 Aus, Bahamas 1954 Bah, Bangladesh 1978 Ban, Barbados 1958 Bar, Bermuda 1930 Ber, British Guiana 1930 BG (Guyana from 1966), British Honduras 1962 BH (Belize from 1973), Belize 1978 Blz (formerly British Honduras), Botswana 1974 Bot, Brunei 1994 Bru, British Virgin Islands 1990 BVI, Canada 1930 Can, Cameroon 1998 Cam, Cayman Islands 1978 Cay, Ceylon 1938 Cey (Sri Lanka from 1972), Cook Islands 1974 CkI, Cyprus 1978

Cyp, Dominica 1994 Dom, England 1930 Eng, Falkland Islands 1990 Fal, Fiji 1950 Fij, Gambia 1970 Gam, Ghana 1958 Gha (formerly Gold Coast), Gibraltar 1958 Gib, Gold Coast 1954 GC (Ghana from 1957), Grenada 1970 Gre, Guernsey 1970 Gue, Guyana 1966 Guy (formerly British Guiana), Hong Kong`1954 HK, India 1934 Ind, Ireland 1930 Ire, Irish Free State 1934 IFS, Isle of Man 1958 IoM, Jamaica 1934 Jam, Jersey 1958 Jer, Kenya 1954 Ken, Lesotho 1974 Les, Malawi 1970 Mlw, Malaya 1950 Mal (Malaysia from 1965), Malaysia 1966 Mal, Maldives 1994 Mld, Malta 1994 Mlt, Mauritius 1958 Mau, Montserrat 1994 Mon, Mozambique 1998 Moz, Namibia 1994 Nam, Nauru 1994 Nau, Newfoundland 1930 NF (Canada from 1949), New Zealand 1930 NZ, Nigeria 1950 Nig, Norfolk Islands 1990 Nor, North Borneo 1958 NB (Malaya from 1963), Northern Ireland 1934 NI, Northern Rhodesia 1954 NR (Zambia from 1964), Pakistan 1954 Pak, Papua New Guinea 1966 PNG, Rhodesia 1934 Rho (Northern Rhodesia from 1954), Rhodesia & Nyasaland 1962 Rho (Zambia from 1964), St Helena 1962 StH, St Kitts & Nevis 1978 StK, St Lucia 1958 StL, St Vincent & the Grenadines 1958 StV, Sarawak 1958 Sar (Malaya from 1963), Scotland 1930 Sco, Seychelles 1990 Sey, Sierra Leone 1958 SL, Singapore 1958 Sin, Solomon Islands 1982 Sol, South Africa 1930 SA, South Arabia 1966 SAr (formerly Aden), Southern Rhodesia 1934 SR (Zimbabwe from 1980), Sri Lanka 1972 SriL (formerly Ceylon), Swaziland 1970 Swa, Tanganyika 1958 Tan (Tanzania from 1964), Tanzania 1970 Tan (formerly Tanganyika), Tonga 1974 Ton, Trinidad & Tobago 1934 Tri, Turks & Caicos Islands 1978 TCI, Uganda 1954 Uga, Vanuatu 1982 Van, Wales 1934 Wal, Western Samoa 1974 WS, Zambia 1966 Zam (formerly Northern Rhodesia), Zimbabwe 1982 Zim (formerly Southern Rhodesia).

THE GAMES VENUES

The dates listed refer to the opening and closing days of competition for all Games sports and the venues are those for the athletics events.

Ist Civic Stadium, Hamilton, Ontario, CANADA, 16-23 August 1930
IInd White City Stadium, London, ENGLAND, 4-11 August 1934
IIIrd Cricket Grounds, Sydney, AUSTRALIA, 5-12 February 1938
IVth Eden Park, Auckland, NEW ZEALAND, 4-11 February 1950
Vth Empire Stadium, Vancouver, CANADA, 30 July-7 August 1954
VIth Cardiff Arms Park, Cardiff, WALES, 17-26 July 1958
VIIth Perry Lakes Stadium, Perth, AUSTRALIA, 21 November-1 December 1962
VIIIth National Stadium, Kingston, JAMAICA, 4-13 August 1966

IXth Meadowbank Stadium, Edinburgh, SCOTLAND, 16-25 July 1970
Xth Queen Elizabeth II Park, Christchurch, NEW ZEALAND, 24 January-2 February 1974
XIth Commonwealth Stadium, Edmonton, CANADA, 3-12 August 1978
XIIth Queen Elizabeth II Stadium, Brisbane, AUSTRALIA, 30 September-9 October 1982
XIIIth Meadowbank Stadium, Edinburgh, SCOTLAND, 24 July-2 August 1986
XIVth Mount Smart Stadium, Auckland, NEW ZEALAND, 24 January-3 February 1990
XVth Centennial Stadium, Victoria, British Columbia, CANADA, 18-28 August 1994
XVIth Bukit Jalil National Stadium, Kuala Lumpur, MALAYSIA, 11-21 September 1998
XVIIth Eastlands, Manchester, ENGLAND, 25 July-3 August 2002

Bob Phillips

Willaston, South Wirral, and Boutieres, France, 2000.

FOREWORD

By David Moorcroft O.B.E.
Chief Executive, UK Athletics

THE COMMONWEALTH GAMES hold especially fond memories for me, though not entirely so, I have to say. In 1974 the Games were held in New Zealand right at the beginning of the year, and so the trials for the England team took place the previous September, when I was still at Loughborough College and just starting out on my international career. I led the 1500 trial for the first two laps, perhaps unwisely, and when it came to the final rush for the tape I was left well adrift. It was neither the first nor the last time that I would finish behind everyone else in a race, and as an athlete you remember those occasions as vividly as you do the wins. Incidentally, a certain Brendan Foster was England's first choice for the 1500, and as he broke the British record in New Zealand but still came 7th it was perhaps just as well I hadn't somehow scraped a place in the team!

By the time the 1978 Commonwealth Games came round I had also, coincidentally, come 7th in a championship 1500 metres race - the 1976 Olympic final in Montreal - and so I was very much older and wiser. The Commonwealth meeting was also in Canada, at Edmonton, in Alberta - but it was by no means a case of everything going smoothly. After qualifying comfortably in the heats I was summoned for a random dope test, which involved providing a urine sample under medical supervision. In my dehydrated state this turned out to be a very time-consuming process. I did not get back to the athletes' village until 11pm and then lay awake all night after a hurried meal.

I hardly dared look at the clock during the race because Filbert Bayi, the Tanzanian who had won in 1974 with a World record time which still stood four years later, was setting such a fast pace, but as we came into the final straight there was that glorious certainty in my mind that it was going to be gold and I was scarcely even aware of crossing the finishing line. When

I got back to my room Brendan Foster had stuck a notice on the door: "Congratulations, Dave - now wash your socks". It was an old joke between us from training together that if you threw your socks against the wall afterwards, and they stuck there, they needed washing!

The next Commonwealth Games, in Brisbane in 1982, came at a very opportune time for me. I had broken the World record for 5000 metres in Oslo during the summer but had then lost to the German, Thomas Wessinghage, in the European Championships, so that going to Brisbane in October gave me a rare chance late in the season to redeem myself. There was a very amiable atmosphere at the Games, as there always is when the Commonwealth athletes get together, and the title of 'The Friendly Games' is one that is genuinely deserved. The competition is still fierce, though, and stimulated by that, or whatever, I managed to win the 5000, and so ended the year on a high note.

I haven't mentioned any specific times for any of these races I've talked about because I feel that when it comes to competition between individuals it doesn't matter very much what the previous performances might have been. Of course, someone who's run 13 minutes for 5000 metres is most probably going to beat someone who's run 13:30, but I can't get very excited about the differences between, say, 13:01 and 13:02. One person I know who can - and does so very often in his capacity as a BBC radio Broadcaster - is Bob Phillips, the author of this book, who happily admits to being called a track 'nut'. The organisation to which such enthusiasts in Britain belong is even called the National Union of Track Statisticians (NUTS, for short), and they live up to the title!

But I've known Bob for a long time, ever since he was a member of my Club, Coventry Godiva Harriers, when he was working for the local newspaper in the city, and he's one of those people who can bring the facts and figures of athletics to life and give them a real meaning. I've had the pleasure of working with him and his colleagues, John Rawling and Mike Whittingham, in the BBC Radio commentary team on many occasions. They really do enjoy their athletics and can communicate that passion to the listeners.

I'm sure you will get the same impression when you read this book.

1.

A Victorian sporting concept is realised, and against all the odds it continues to hold good into the 21st Century

THE MOST REMARKABLE FEATURE of the Commonwealth Games is that they should exist at all. Having taken an inordinately long time to be created in the first place, they have survived when a torrent of political and economic issues ought, in any realistic assessment, to have swept them brutally away. Their failure has been anticipated more than once as they experience their eighth decade in existence, and yet they still find an established place both in the sporting calendar and in the hearts and minds of the fans, the competitors, officialdom, politicians and - not least in importance in this marketing-orientated day and age - financial backers.

Now it is the alternative and often irresistible allure of the high-paying Grand Prix athletics circuit which is cited as a spectre at the funeral of the Commonwealth Games, and it has to be said straight away that with all due respect to the other sports - to the swimmers, the boxers, the cyclists, and now the cricketers and the hockey and rugby players - it is athletics which is at the heart of the Games and which is the corner-stone of its popular appeal and commercial viability. It is the sprinters from the Caribbean, Britain and Canada and the distance-runners from Africa and Australia who bolster the TV ratings which, however regrettable it might be, feed the life-blood of so many sports.

In earlier times the Games have faced other potential breaking-points. It was an astonishing achievement that they should have begun at all, as they did in 1930 in the midst of a World economic depression. The home countries had shown no great enthusiasm for the original idea, and

1

then when the Empire delegates met at the 1932 Olympics to decide the venue for the second Games in 1934 they courageously concluded that their original choice of South Africa would have to be changed because of the likely attitude there towards ethnic minorities. England stepped in despite their earlier apathy but dominated the athletics events in London with far too much ease for the comfort of the other participants, even if the packed crowds at the White City stadium were happy enough. In 1938, and again in 1950 after wartime disruption, there were the problems for many countries of long and expensive journeys to Australia and New Zealand.

Then, even as the British Empire was crumbling and political obligations were being severely realigned, came what can now be seen as a Golden Era. From 1954, when it was back to Canada and the year of Bannister and Landy's "Miracle Mile", through to 1958 and the resplendence of Cardiff Arms Park, all hywl and hubris, and at further celebrations in Australia, Jamaica, Scotland, New Zealand, Canada and again Australia in 1982, the Games flourished, bejewelled by some of the greatest of athletes - Elliott, Snell, Halberg, Keino, Lynn Davies, Ron Clarke, Don Quarrie, Marjorie Jackson-Nelson, Raelene Boyle, Mary Peters. New cultures, new influences, a new and unaccustomed independence for so many emerging nations ought really to have dictated otherwise, but the Games pragmatically moved with the times to accommodate a changing World, even if it seemed to be little more than a cosmetic altering of the title from "British Empire Games", as it had been from 1930 to 1950, to "British Empire & Commonwealth Games", as it became from 1954 to 1966, and then further modification to "British Commonwealth Games" in 1970 and 1974 , and simply to "Commonwealth Games" from 1978.

South Africa had taken its leave of the Commonwealth after 1958 but still exercised an influence to the extent that the Games seemed to have finally given way in Edinburgh in 1986 under the weight of political opportunism. A proposed South African rugby-union tour of New Zealand fired up a host of countries to withdraw, and a typically grey and windswept midsummer at Meadowbank, playing gloomy host to what was little more than a match between the Home Countries, Canada and Australasia, was discouraging for all - even if the likes of Steve Cram, Rob de Castella, Lisa Martin, Daley Thompson and a certain Ben Johnson did produce World-class performances in spite of everything. A tawdry closing ceremony reached its nadir when the benefactor who had apparently saved the Games from financial disaster made a self-important appearance on the track to a sychophantic introduction. The patron was Robert Maxwell.

Yet if he had not stepped in with someone's money to underwrite the affair we might not now be looking forward to the return of the Games to England for the first time in 68 years. Certainly, it was all refreshingly exhilarating when the likes of Linford Christie, Douglas Wakiihuri, Merlene Ottey and Liz McColgan cheerfully turned up out-of-season in Auckland in the January of 1990 to give their blessing and their golden presence to the Games and help restore the status of a major athletics fixture. Then on to another marvellously hospitable and scenic venue in that most sublime of cities - Victoria, British Columbia - in 1994, and even though Merlene made her excuses and the Kenyans only sent their reserve team it didn't really matter. Linford was there, and so was Frankie Fredericks, and there was a wonderfully graceful and supremely athletic Aboriginal lady named Cathy Freeman, a Sioux Indian local heroine called Angela Chalmers, and the beauteous and feline Denise Lewis all lending their infinite charm to captivating winning performances. To cap it all, the exuberant young Kenyan distance-runners selected by the old master, Kip Keino, were still mostly better than anyone else, anyway.

The gregarious and wildly enthusiastic citizens of Kuala Lumpur in 1998 provided a first infusion of Asian culture for the Games, even though their political masters were working to another agenda entirely and had really built their monumentally breathtaking sporting complexes in the interests of the longer-term grandiose scheme of hosting an eventual Olympic Games sometime into the 21st Century. A few of the athletics events were a bit thin on the ground, and the sparse gaggle of marathon runners gathering before dawn in a deserted city-centre square presented something of a forlorn sight, though even on that seemingly inauspicious occasion there was an historic reward for the patient few spectators as a sinewy little man from the Southern African nation of Lesotho won his country's first ever gold medal. Those who considered the introduction of team games to be a pandering to base popularity would surely have been won over by the bizarre spectacle at the Rugby Union sevens of the great Jonah Lomu shaking off brave but puny would-be tacklers from the Cook

Islands like raindrops off a cape, or of spindly Malaysian hockey players desperately trying to stop the bronzed and battle-hardened Aussies running rings round them. Athletics is the Commonwealth Games, and it is for that reason that this book has been written, but the other sports give the Games a broad dimension which make them far far more than just another track meeting.

Now Manchester faces the challenge of hosting a Commonwealth Games bound to be once again assailed by all manner of commercial pressures being placed on the potential stars, and with the additional burden of ensuring that the first such Games to be held in England in almost seven decades are worthy of their immediate predecessors. Of course, there is a profusion of imponderables: Will the big names come? Will it rain? Will the public give the competitors the support they deserve? Well, just so long as no one - organisers, commercial backers, athletes - expects to make too much money out of it, and provided that Mancunians readily familiar with sporting endeavour of the very highest level on their doorsteps most Saturday afternoons recognise the Commonwealth Games for what they are in all truth - an unassuming and friendly family gathering of sportsmen and sportswomen, most of them virtually unknown outside their native lands - the whole affair will work beautifully. As a matter of curious interest, it's not as if it is the first time the Games have been to Manchester, though there won't be many who recall attending the day of cycle-racing at Fallowfield which formed part of the Games of 1934 because London did not have a suitable track for the events.

So how did it all start? There is no doubt as to who deserves the credit for first devising a practical plan for a British Empire Games. There had been proposals put forward as early as the 1890s without anyone taking up the idea seriously, even though the Olympic Games had been revived in 1896 and were held in London in 1908, with athletes from Britain, Australia, Canada and South Africa among the prominent winners at these early celebrations. There had been a competition between countries of the Empire in London in 1911, and matches involving teams from the USA and the British Empire had become established as post-Olympic fixtures in the 1920s, but it took the singular energy of a man named Bobby Robinson to persuade the establishment that an Empire Games should be held. He was manager of the Canadian athletics team at the 1928 Olympics in

Amsterdam and by profession was sports editor of the local newspaper in Hamilton, Ontario. He had apparently been approached to publicise and promote the project by the Canadian Amateur Athletic Union, which had passed an enterprising resolution in 1924 supporting the idea of an Empire Games, and so it seemed logical that his local knowledge and connections should lead to Hamilton becoming the first venue in 1930. It was not without considerable effort on his part, though, that this eventually came about, and the decisive factor in his argument was his brilliantly inventive idea to persuade the public authorities in Hamilton to contribute towards the travelling expenses of the teams. The city fathers put up $30,000, and all credit to them for doing so in such straitened economic times. Robinson's idea was finally approved at a meeting of Empire representatives in London in January 1930 and the inaugural British Empire Games opened barely seven months later.

In a perceptive reference in his book, "Sport and the British: A Modern History", Richard Holt, of Stirling University, points out that in the 1920s *"the loosening of the formal bonds of Empire came at the same time as new economic pressures were being placed upon the relationships between the Dominions and Britain."* Whilst a mere sporting event was not going to replace such close political ties *"the pervasiveness of imperial propaganda between the wars created a climate where the members of the relevant sporting bodies - many of whom were active in other areas of public life - were increasingly inclined to consider organising a specifically imperial event. Growing criticism of the stridency and chauvinism of the Olympic Games also played a part. Imperial athletes sought an affirmation of the 'fair play' spirit, and significantly it was the Dominions which most fervently advocated this ideal."*

Bobby Robinson may not have thought about it in quite those erudite terms, but there was no doubt that he was a public-spirited man with a strong sense of colonial pride and his hopes were enshrined in a bold statement of intent which he approved for those first Empire Games of 1930. Compared to the Olympics, the Empire Games *"should be merrier and less stern and will substitute the stimulus of novel adventure for the pressure of international rivalry."* And so the novel adventure began.

5

2.

The supreme fulfilment of
Bobby Robinson's dream

CIVIC STADIUM, HAMILTON, ONTARIO, CANADA
16-23 AUGUST 1930

THE UNFLAGGING ENTHUSIASM of Bobby Robinson and the generosity of Hamilton's civic leaders had paid handsome dividends. More than 400 competitors from 11 countries made the journey to Canada for the inaugural British Empire Games to contest six sports - athletics, bowls, boxing, rowing, swimming and wrestling. Admittedly, of the 131 entrants for the track and field programme almost three-quarters came from Canada (52) and England (42), but there were others from Australia, Bermuda, British Guiana, Ireland, Newfoundland, New Zealand, Scotland and South Africa. There were no women's events in athletics, though these had been controversially introduced at the Olympic Games two years previously, and despite the fact that there <u>were</u> women taking part in the swimming competition in Hamilton. Much the most famous names on the athletics starting-lists were those of Percy Williams, Canada's reigning Olympic champion at 100 and 200 metres, and the imposingly-titled David George Brownlow Cecil, Lord Burghley, who had won the 400 metres hurdles for Great Britain at the same Games.

Among the Hamilton competitors there were altogether 18 members of the British team at the 1928 Olympics and 13 of the Canadian team, and for many of them there would have been little or no international competition in between. The domestic season in Britain began with the

Oxford-v-Cambridge Inter-Varsity match in unseasonable March and continued with the Inter-Counties' Championships, the various regional championships in the North of England, the South, the Midlands, Scotland and Wales in June, and concluded - to all intents and purposes - with the AAA Championships in July. Even for the select few there was no more than a single opportunity each year of representing Great Britain, and that was in the series of international matches against France which had begun in 1921, had continued in non-Olympic years throughout the 1920s, and was to go on thus until 1938. It was not until 1929 that a second match was arranged, against Germany, and not until 1933 that the fixture with Germany every other year became established. The European Championships were not to be inaugurated until 1934, and even then Britain sent no team to that meeting because it was felt that the Empire Games that year would provide quite enough competition.

The only notable absentees in Hamilton were two World-class sprinters - Daniel Joubert, of South Africa, and Jim Carlton, of Australia - and every member nation of the Empire with any sort of established athletics reputation was represented, with the exceptions of India, Jamaica and - somewhat oddly - Wales. The local response of the public was equally fervent, and more than 20,000 people packed into the Civic Stadium on Saturday 16 August for the official opening of the Games by the Governor-General of Canada, Lord Willingdon. Percy Williams read the oath of allegiance on behalf of the athletes but rather surprisingly did not reappear for the heats of the 220 yards which formed part of that afternoon's programme and for which, of course, he would have been the gold-medal favourite.

In Williams's absence the three heats were won by the South Africans, Bill Walters and Werner Gerhardt, who had the fastest pre-Games performances of 21.4 and 21.6 respectively to their credit, and by the 20-year-old Yorkshireman, Stanley Engelhart, whose 22.0 clocking was the best of the series and equalled his winning time in the AAA Championships the previous month. The final was held later in the day and despite his earlier form the Englishman was still the somewhat unexpected winner in 21.8 from Johnny Fitzpatrick, of Canada, who had been 5th in the 1928 Olympic final, while Walters was 3rd. The six miles race began at 5 p.m. with 11 runners - four each from Canada and England, two Scots and a

New Zealander - and was almost ruined by a light-fingered official who turned over one card too many on the lap-counter board and sent the leader, New Zealand's Bill Savidan, off on a 'last lap' sprint only for him to discover after he thought he had finished that he still had another 440-yard circuit to cover. Fortunately for Savidan, his advantage was so substantial that he still won by 10 seconds from England's Ernie Harper and 20-year-old Tom Evenson. It was Savidan's first-ever six-mile race and he finished in such an exhausted state that he had to ask someone in the dressing-room afterwards whether or not he had won.

All three medallists in the six miles were to go on to perform with great credit in the Olympic Games, and this was a pattern which would regularly repeat itself over the years at the Empire Games. Savidan was 4th at both 5000 and 10,000 metres and Evenson 2nd in the steeplechase at the 1932 Olympics in Los Angeles, while Harper was 2nd in the 1936 marathon in Berlin.

The first field-events gold medal was won by a Canadian, Gordon ("Spike") Smallacombe, in the hop step and jump (later renamed the triple jump) with a leap of 48ft 5in (14.76m) which was to rank as the ninth best in the World for 1930. Only one competitor needed to be eliminated in the 440 yards hurdles heats and Lord Burghley duly won the subsequent final by a dozen yards in 54.4 with the other Englishmen in the next three places. From the two heats of the 880 yards eight men qualified for the following week's final, including most notably Phil Edwards, competing for his native British Guiana, who had placed 4th for Canada in the 1928 Olympic 800 metres, and England's bespectacled AAA champion, Tommy Hampson.

The second day of athletics competition did not take place until the following Thursday, 21 August, and gold medals were decided for the 880 yards, three miles, marathon, high jump, shot putt and hammer throw. Hampson won the 880 by a huge margin in 1min 52.4sec, which was to be the equal fastest time in the World for the year, with his team-mate, Reg Thomas, 2nd and Canada's Alex Wilson 3rd. Hampson and Wilson were both to figure in an historic Olympic 800 metres final two years later when they took the gold and silver medals respectively and became the first men to run under 1min 50sec for the distance. For the three miles there was no Savidan, presumably still suffering the after-effects of his traumatic six miles, and this left as clear favourite Australia's Alex Hillhouse, who had run a time of 14:25.5 on the same Hamilton track 20 days earlier which was bettered throughout 1930 only by the greatest of all the Flying Finns, Paavo Nurmi. But there were again four Englishmen in the race, and it was actually one of the lesser regarded of them, Stan Tomlin, who prevailed in a desperately close finish by two-tenths of a second from Hillhouse as all the first six men home finished within 15 yards of each other. Tomlin, who had placed only 3rd in the GB v France match at the beginning of the month, later became a noted athletics writer and magazine editor.

Among the 15 runners in the marathon there was a wealth of competitive experience as seven of them had taken part in the 1928 Olympic race in Amsterdam. England's Sam Ferris, 8th in those Games, had also placed 5th in the 1924 Olympics; Duncan McLeod Wright, running for Scotland and 20th in Amsterdam, was the current AAA champion; and Canada's Johnny Miles had won the annual Boston classic in 1929. McLeod Wright led Ferris by 30secs at 10 miles, was four minutes ahead at 18 miles, and continued to pull away, completing two of the closing three laps round the track before Ferris entered the stadium, and so winning the first Empire marathon title as comfortably as the arduous event would allow. Ferris, who always ran with a broad smile on his face, cheerfully shook McLeod Wright's hand in congratulations as they passed on the track. England's hopes had originally lain with Harry Payne, who had run a World best 2:30:57.6 the previous year, but he had been knocked down by a car while training and was not fit to make a proper challenge. At the 1932 Olympics both Ferris and McLeod Wright ran superbly: Ferris 2nd and McLeod Wright 4th. Coincidentally, the Northern Ireland-born Ferris and his steeplechase team-mate, Vernon Morgan, also become eminent sports journalists later in life

In the field events there were wins for two impressively versatile South Africans: Johannes ("Snaar") Viljoen in the high jump and the prolific Hendrik ("Harry") Hart in the shot. It has to be said, though, that Empire standards in the jumps and throws then, and for many years afterwards, only occasionally matched the best international level. Viljoen's high jump, for example, was 27th best in the World for the year and Hart's shot 29th, though relatively unnoticed in 4th place in the former event was a 19-year-old US-trained Canadian, Duncan McNaughton, who was to win the Olympic title in 1932. It is also worth noting that the hammer

9

champion, Malcolm Nokes, had been the bronze-medallist at the 1924 Olympics and excelled himself in Hamilton with a season's best to beat the favoured Irishman, Bill Britton, with a 48-year-old Canadian, Jack Cameron, who had taken part in the 1920 Olympics, in 3rd place.

The attention of the Canadian spectators was naturally most closely focussed on the great Percy Williams, at long last stepping on to the track for the 100 yards heats, and his performance readily matched expectations. Anticipation was specially heightened because he had set a World record of 10.3 for 100 metres in Toronto 12 days before, and he displayed comparable form by winning his qualifying round in a wind-assisted 9.6. Ernie Page, of England, was only one-tenth slower in his heat, and the other qualifiers for the final two days later were the 220 medallists, Engelhart and Fitzpatrick, and the South Africans, Gerhardt and Billy Legg (the AAA title-winner the previous month). The heats of the 440 yards provided no surprises, and nor was there great excitement in the 120 yards hurdles except that one of the Canadians, Bill Pierdon, did not get to race at all because he was disqualified for two false starts, and another, Art Ravensdale, was eliminated in accordance with the rules then in existence as he knocked down two barriers.

On the closing day, Saturday 23 August, it was cool and wet for the remaining 11 finals: 100 yards, 440 yards, one mile, 120 yards hurdles, steeplechase, 4 x 110 and 4 x 440 relays, pole vault, long jump, discus and javelin. So far, England had won five gold medals, South Africa two, and Canada, New Zealand and Scotland one each.

The 100 yards final held hopes of a World record, which had been set three months earlier at 9.4 by the American, Frank Wykoff, and the deceptively frail-looking Williams was clearly heading for a very fast time at halfway, but he then suffered a severe thigh-muscle strain and only managed to somehow stumble the last 30 yards to the line, still winning decisively in 9.9. Though he ran in the 1932 Olympics, that was Williams's last major achievement on the track at the age of only 23, and he became reclusive in later life and sadly eventually committed suicide in 1982.

The 440 yards final brought together a World-class field. Jimmy Ball, of Canada, had won the Olympic silver in 1928; his team-mate, Alex Wilson, already 3rd at 880 yards, had reached the Olympic semi-finals; and the Australians, George Golding and Herbert Bascombe, had run times of

48.3 and 48.6 at the beginning of the year. Wilson won in 48.8, but by no more than a yard from the South African, Bill Walters, who had also appeared in the 100 yards heats and placed third at 220. Golding was 3rd and only a week later in Toronto recorded the fastest time in the World for the year at 47.9.

The 10 starters in the mile included the 880 silver-medallist, Reg Thomas, who had won the AAA mile title seven weeks earlier in 4:15.2. Thomas was actually the Welsh champion and record-holder, but Wales had entered no athletes for these Games so he opted for England instead and won rather easily by 15 yards in a time of 4:14.0 which was the third fastest in the World for the year. Next was Australia's intriguingly named "Tickle" Whyte, who had been a 1928 Olympic 1500 metres finalist, and 3rd was Jerry Cornes, who became the Olympic silver-medallist two years later. In 5th place was the ubiquitous Phil Edwards, who had already contested the 440 and 880 at these Games and during his long career took part in the Olympics of 1928, 1932 and 1936, reaching seven finals and winning five bronze medals at 800 metres, 1500 metres and the 4 x 400 relay!

Lord Burghley, whose best time of 14.5 earlier in the year was only one-tenth slower than the World record, won a second title at 120 yards hurdles, and the small number of teams in the relays gave further opportunities for potential multiple medallists. Canada's Johnny Fitzpatrick, with medals at 100 and 220, was in the winning 4 x 110 relay team, and his compatriot, Alex Wilson, added 4 x 440 silver to his earlier medals in the individual 440 and 880. But neither of them matched the staying power of the South African, Walters, who had won medals at 220 and 440 and added bronze in both relays, while Lord Burghley was the most successful of them all with a third gold at 4 x 440.

The distance covered in the steeplechase final was some 80-to-100 yards short of two miles, and the winner was George Bailey, a Salford Harriers clubmate of the bronze medallist at six miles, Tom Evenson. Bailey, Evenson and two other distance runners at these Games, Ernie Harper and Jack Winfield, were all gritty cross-country specialists from the North of England, brought up in a time-honoured tradition of racing nine or 10 miles across ploughed fields and through flooded streams, with as likely as not no more than a tin bath of cold water in a wooden shed with which to refresh themselves afterwards, so a few laps of a firm cinder track held no

11

fears for them. Harper ran for the Yorkshire club, Hallamshire, and Winfield for the equally renowned Derby & County, and all of them figured in one or more of England's winning cross-country teams in the International Championships against the other home countries, Belgium and France from 1930 onwards. Curiously, Bailey and Evenson were involved in another steeplechase of unconventional duration when all the competitors ran a lap too far in the 1932 Olympics and in the course of an additional 460 metres Evenson gained a medal, moving to 2nd place, and Bailey lost one, slipping to 5th. Both Britons were working-class men: Bailey a quarryman in Buxton, in Derbyshire, and Evenson a carpenter in Manchester.

The field events provided further medals for the South Africans, Viljoen and Hart, but the two champions of undoubted international class were Vic Pickard, of Canada, and Stan Lay, of New Zealand. Pickard, whose brother had run in the 880 final, won the pole vault, having placed 5th and 4th in the two previous Olympic finals, while Lay - who was to become one of the most durable of Games athletes - won the javelin and was ranked 17th best in the World for the year. Two years previously, at the AAA Championsips at Stamford Bridge, in London, Lay had thrown a remarkable 222ft 9in (67.89m), which was only two metres short of the World record held, inevitably, by a Finn, Eino Penttila, but he missed qualifying for the Amsterdam Olympic final less than three weeks later by one place. Pickard competed regularly in the USA indoors and out during the intervening period between the Olympics and the Empire Games, and as the Americans had 15 of the 20 best vaulters in the World in 1929 he was in his element, whereas Lay had had to make do with what were virtually "exhibition" appearances in his far-distant homeland in the interim.

Altogether, the final day brought England's total of gold medals to nine, followed by six for Canada, three for South Africa, two for New Zealand and one for Scotland. There were no wins for any of the other competing countries, but Australia's team of five earned four medals between them, while British Guiana's two-man team included the high-jump silver-medallist, Colin Gordon, who was also the AAA champion, and from the three-man Irish team Bill Britton was another silver winner in the hammer. In any case, no one was bothering too much with medal tables and as commendable a performance as any was that of the Scotsman, Robbie Sutherland, a Lance-Sergeant in the 3rd Carabiniers Regiment, who made his long journey worthwhile by contesting the mile, the three miles and the six miles ... but then the previous March he had taken part in the Scottish and English national cross-country championships, the Army championships, and then the International Championships, each over 10 miles, and all within the space of 15 days! Yet the athlete who earned more public acclaim than any other, even though he only came 4th in his event, was the English javelin-thrower, Robert Turner. Out on a pre-Games stroll through the streets of Hamilton he witnessed an armed bank-raid and coolly noted down the registration number of the getaway car and a description of the robbers, leading to their arrest But then he would have regarded that as no more than being all in the line of duty; he was a Birkenhead police officer by profession.

There was no doubt that the Games had been a success. Most importantly, for their long-term future, they had been staged in a relaxed manner which, as had been hoped, contrasted with much of the bombast and xenophobia which was already characterising the Olympics, and a delighted Bobby Robinson, as Chairman of the Games, concluded that *"it had been proved that the members of the Empire family can meet in competition"*. He received enthusiastic support from the Australians, who had long been advocates for the Empire Games. The Australian team manager, Hugh Weir, stated unequivocally: *"One cannot speak too highly of the work performed by the British Empire Games Committee of Canada, headed by Mr Robinson, in staging the Games at Hamilton. No one who was not present could properly appreciate the tremendous amount of organisation necessary, firstly to interest the nations, and then to put into operation one of the largest schemes ever undertaken in Canada. It was a remarkable achievement for Canada to conduct a set of Games outrivalled in magnitude only by the Olympic Games. Many difficulties were met and overcome with such tenacity that the Games from every angle were a brilliant success."*

Two years later, at the Los Angeles Olympics, the British Empire Games Federation was formed, and how gratified, and maybe astonished, would those worthy pioneers surely feel if they were to know that much of that family spirit was to survive into the next century.

RESULTS 1930

100 YARDS (23 Aug): 1 Percy Williams (Can) 9.9, 2 Ernie Page (Eng) 10,2, 3 Johnny Fitzpatrick (Can), 4 Billy Legg (SA), 5 Werner Gerhardt (SA), 6 Stanley Engelhart (Eng).

220 YARDS (16 Aug): 1 Stanley Engelhart (Eng) 21.8, 2 Johnny Fitzpatrick (Can), 3 Bill Walters (SA), 4 Roy Hamilton (Sco), 5 Jimmy Ball (Can), 6 Werner Gerhardt (SA).

440 YARDS (23 Aug): 1 Alex Wilson (Can) 48.8, 2 Bill Walters (SA) 48.9, 3 George Golding Aus), 4 Kenneth Brangwin (Eng), 5 Jimmy Ball (Can), 6 Herbert Bascombe (Aus).

880 YARDS (21 Aug): 1 Tommy Hampson (Eng) 1:52.4, 2 Reg Thomas (Eng) 1:55.5e, 3 Alex Wilson (Can) 1:55.6e, 4 John Chandler (SA), 5 Phil Edwards (BG), 6 Stuart Townend (Eng). Also ran - Mike Gutteridge (Eng), Percy Pickard (Can).

1 MILE (23 Aug): 1 Reg Thomas (Eng) 4:14.0, 2 William "Tickle" Whyte (Aus) 4:17.0e, 3 Jerry Cornes (Eng), 4 Jack Walters (Can), 5 Phil Edwards (BG), 6 Robbie Sutherland (Sco), 7 Russell McDougall (Aus). Also ran - Harry Hedges (Eng), Stuart Townend (Eng).

3 MILES (21 Aug): 1 Stan Tomlin (Eng) 14:27.4, 2 Alex Hillhouse (Aus) 14:27.6e, 3 Jack Winfield (Eng) 14:28.0e, 4 Robbie Sutherland (Sco) 14:29.0e, 5 Tom Evenson (Eng) 14:29.0e, 6 Brian Oddie (Eng) 14:29.8e. Also ran - George Ball (Can), Walter Hornby (Can), Fred Sargeant (Can).

6 MILES (16 Aug): 1 Bill Savidan (NZ) 30:49.6, 2 Ernie Harper (Eng) 31:01.6e, 3 Tom Evenson (Eng), 4 Jimmy Woods (Sco), 5 Robbie Sutherland (Sco), 6 Billy Reynolds (Can), 7 Jack Winfield (Eng), 8 Wilf McCluskey (Can), 9 George Irwin (Can), 10 Harold Webster (Can). Did not finish - Stan Tomlin (Eng).

STEEPLECHASE (23 Aug): 1 George Bailey (Eng) 9:52.0, 2 Alex Hillhouse (Aus), 3 Vernon Morgan (Eng), 4 Art Wilkins (Can), 5 Bill Reid (Can), 6 Pete Suttie (Can).

MARATHON (21 Aug): 1 Duncan McLeod Wright (Sco) 2:43:43.0, 2 Sam Ferris (Eng) 2:47:13e, 3 Johnny Miles (Can), 4 Percy Wyer (Can), 5 Bert Bignall (Eng), 6 Norman Dack (Can), 7 Silas McLellan (Can), 8 Ronald O'Toole (NF), 9 Jack O'Reilly (Ire), 10 Ezra Lee (Can). Did not finish - Johnny Cuthbert (Can), William Mulrooney (NF), Harry Payne (Eng), Stan Smith (Eng), Clifford Stone (NF).

120 YARDS HURDLES (23 Aug): 1 Lord Burghley (Eng) 14.6, 2 Howard Davies (SA) 14.7e, 3 Fred Gaby (Eng), 4 Johannes Viljoen (SA), 5 Roly Harper (Eng), 6 Harry Hart (SA).

440 YARDS HURDLES (16 Aug): 1 Lord Burghley (Eng) 54.4, Roger Leigh-Wood (Eng) 55.9e, 3 Douglas Neame (Eng), 4 Wilfred Tatham (Eng), 5 Walter Connolly (Can), 6 John Hickey (Can).

4 x 110 YARDS RELAY (23 Aug): 1 Canada (Jim "Buster" Brown, Leigh Miller, Ralph Adams, Johnny Fitzpatrick) 42.2, 2 England (John Hanlon, James Cohen, John Heap, Stanley Engelhart) 42.7e, 3 South Africa (Howard Davies, Werner Gerhardt, Billy Legg, Bill Walters). 3 teams competed.

4 x 440 YARDS RELAY (23 Aug): 1 England (Roger Leigh-Wood, Stuart Townend, Lord Burghley, Kenneth Brangwin) 3:19.4, 2 Canada (Art Scott, Stan Glover, Jimmy Ball, Alex Wilson) 3:19.8e, 3 South Africa (Billy Legg, Werner Gerhardt, John Chandler, Bill Walters). 3 teams competed.

HIGH JUMP (21 Aug): 1 Johannes Viljoen (SA) 1.90, 2 Colin Gordon (BG) 1.88, 3 William Stargratt (Can) 1.85, 4 Duncan McNaughton (Can), 5 Edward Bradbrooke (Eng), 6 Geoffrey Turner (Eng). Also competed - Jack Portland (Can), Reg Revans (Eng), Gordon Smallacombe (Can).

POLE VAULT (23 Aug): 1 Vic Pickard (Can) 3.73, 2 Howard Ford (Eng) 3.73, 3 Robert Stoddard (Can), 4 Alf Gilbert (Can), 5 Laurence Bond (Eng), 6 Bernard Babington-Smith (Eng), 7 Fred Foley (Eng).

LONG JUMP (23 Aug): 1 Len Hutton (Can) 7.20, 2 Reg Revans (Eng) 6.96, 3 Johannes Viljoen (Sa) 6.96, 4 Chester Smith (Can) 6.79, 5 Gordon Smallacombe (Can) 6.61, 6 James Cohen (Eng), 7 Fred Foley (Eng).

TRIPLE JUMP (16 Aug): 1 Gordon Smallacombe (Can) 14.76, 2 Reg Revans (Eng) 14.29, 3 Len Hutton (Can) 13.90, 4 George Sutherland (Can) 13.75, 5 Gregory Powers (NF) 13.44, 6 Roger Johnson (NZ) 13.16.

SHOT (21 Aug): 1 Harry Hart (SA) 14.58, 2 Robert Howland (Eng) 13.46, 3 Charlie Herman (Can) 12.98, 4 Abe Zvonkin (Can) 12.63, 5 Howard Ford (Eng) 12.44, 6 Kenneth Pridie (Eng) 12.40. Also competed - Jack Cameron (Can), Fred Foley (Eng), Archie Stewart (Can).

DISCUS (23 Aug): 1 Harry Hart (SA) 41.43, 2 Charlie Herman (Can) 41.22, 3 Abe Zvonkin (Can) 41.18, 4 Kenneth Pridie (Eng) 39.22, 5 Malcolm Nokes (Eng), 6 Howard Ford (Eng). Also competed - Robert Howland (Eng), Archie Stewart (Can), George Sutherland (Can).

HAMMER (21 Aug): 1 Malcolm Nokes (Eng) 47.13, 2 Bill Britton (Ire) 46.90, 3 Jack Cameron (Can) 44.46, 4 Alexander Smith (Sco) 44.30, 5 Alex Murray (Sco) 42.70, 6 Archie McDiarmid (Can) 42.44. Also competed - W. Coldfield (NF), Harry Hart (SA), Charlie Herman (Can), Kenneth Pridie (Eng), George Sutherland (Can), Johannes Viljoen (SA).

JAVELIN (23 Aug): 1 Stan Lay (NZ) 63.13, 2 Doral Pilling (Can) 55.94, 3 Harry Hart (SA) 53.22, 4 Robert Turner (Eng), 5 Leslie Snow (Eng), 6 Archie Stewart (Can).

3.

Lovelock's legend lights up
a grey summer's afternoon

SURPRISINGLY, THERE WERE NOT that many more male athletes entered for the 1934 Empire Games than there has been in Canada four years previously - 154 as against 131 - but there was the significant bonus of 53 women making their debut. England's contingent of 87 athletes was inevitably much the biggest, and even though there were only four countries involved in the women's events there were 16 teams altogether, including for the first time India, Jamaica, Rhodesia, Trinidad and Wales. Of the champions in Hamilton only four - McLeod Wright in the marathon, Bailey in the steeplechase, Hart in the shot and discus and Nokes in the hammer - were defending their titles, and none of the Empire's three Olympic champions in Los Angeles two years earlier took part: Hampson and McNaughton had retired, and there was no event for 50km walker, Tommy Green.

The White City Stadium had been refurbished in 1932 after lying almost unused since the 1908 Olympics, but the AAA Championships held there three weeks before the opening of the Empire Games had been a distinctly lacklustre curtain-raiser. Much had been expected of the mile final in which Jack Lovelock, the Oxford University Rhodes Scholar from New Zealand who had set a World record of 4:07.6 in the USA the previous year, met the 19-year-old prodigy from Blackheath Harriers, Sydney Wooderson, but Lovelock won in only 4:26.6 after a pedestrian early pace. Yet there were

17

huge crowds for the Empire Games events with 50,000 attending the opening ceremony, and that was not at all uncommon for athletics meetings at the White City in the 1930s.

The athletics events were held over three days - Saturday, Monday and Tuesday 4-6-7 August. Seven finals were decided on the first day, and England began well by winning three of them, as Australia, Scotland and South Africa provided the other champions, and the first two women's gold-medallists naturally attracted much attention. The South African, Marjorie Clark, who had broken the World high-jump record as a 17-year-old in 1927 and again a year later at London's Stamford Bridge, won that event with 5ft 3in (1.60m), which may seem undistinguished by today's standards but was achieved with a primitive "scissors" technique which entailed crossing the bar in a seated position and, in any case, was only five centimetres below the current World record and was to last as a Games best for 20 years. A modest javelin competition, contested only by four Englishwomen, was won by Gladys Lunn, and both she and Marjorie Clark were to figure prominently again in the next few days.

Marthinus Theunissen, of South Africa, was the notional favourite for the 100 yards, having run 9.7 the previous April, but it was the Irish-born Englishman, Arthur Sweeney, who won by a foot, having also finished 1st in his heat and semi-final earlier in the afternoon. Of historical significance in hindsight was the first appearance of a sprinter from Jamaica, though Arthur Jones failed to survive his qualifying heat. The three miles included a Trinidad runner in the line-up, but he was a non-finisher as the English, again led by a hardened Northern cross-country specialist, Walter Beavers, of York Harriers, took the first three places. At 440 yards hurdles the surprise winner was an awkward-looking but effective Scot, Alan Hunter, who was the son of the Games Federation secretary.

Much the best performance of the opening day came from one of the very finest British Empire athletes of the 1930s, and provided the first of what would become a multitude of gold medals for Australia over the years. The winning effort of 51ft 3 1/2 in (15.63m) in the triple jump by 22-year-old Jack Metcalfe was only nine centimetres short of the World record set by Chuhei Nambu, of Japan, at the Los Angeles Olympics, and the following year Metcalfe himself became World record-holder with 15.78m. In a long and distinguished involvement with the sport Metcalfe went on to place 3rd in the 1936 Olympics, successfully defend his Empire title in 1938, and serve as Australian team manager at the 1948 Olympics in London. All credit, also, to the 2nd-placed athlete, who was a prodigiously talented 16-year-old Canadian, Sam Richardson, for whom even greater success was to come.

Harry Hart won the discus again for his third gold medal, and a first Empire Games medal in any athletics event for a Caribbean athlete was achieved here by Bernard Prendergast, who was Jamaican-born of British descent and was studying medicine in London and later represented Great Britain in the Berlin Olympics. The fastest qualifier in the 880 heats was a Scot, James Stothard, known as "Hamish", but the triple bronze-medallist from Los Angeles, Phil Edwards, also went through without difficulty.

The 880 was one of nine finals featured on the second day's competition, together with the six miles, 120 yards hurdles, high jump, pole vault and shot for men and the 100 yards, 880 and a sprint relay for women. Harry Hart predictably won his fourth gold medal in the shot, with the resplendently-named England team captain, Bonzo Howland, a distant 2nd, as he had been to Hart in 1930. The favourite for the six miles was the AAA champion, Jack Holden, from another famous cross-country club, Tipton Harriers, but he was well beaten by his team-mate, Arthur Penny, of the London club, Belgrave Harriers, and who could possibly have thought then that Holden would finally win an Empire Games gold medal 16 years later? Phil Edwards led all the way to win the 880 with the Englishmen, Jack Cooper and Jack Powell, who had both run 1:52.2 for 800m in Paris the previous weekend, well beaten, but Don Finlay duly won the high hurdles for England - and not surprisingly as he was the Olympic bronze-medallist of 1932 and silver-medallist in 1936 and, like Holden, would be back at the Empire Games in 1950.

Yet in the six men's track finals so far decided at the 1934 Empire Games not a single winning performance had been better than that of 1930, though a typically rainswept English midsummer and the White City's notoriously heavy and unhelpful cinders were hardly conducive to record-breaking. The field-events competitors fared rather better with the lanky Edwin Thacker retaining the high-jump title for South Africa, equalling the Games best, and 19-year-old Syl (short for "Sylvanus") Apps, who later became an outstanding ice-hockey player, beating his Canadian compatriot, Alf Gilbert, in a jump-off for the pole-vault gold and silver at 12ft 9in (3.88m).

Gladys Lunn, versatile captain of the Birchfield Harriers ladies' team, remarkably added the 880 title to the javelin she had won the previous Saturday, and she did so in the very respectable time of 2:19.4. What is more, it was something of an achievement that the event had been held at all. The Olympic establishment had included an 800m when women's athletics events were introduced at the 1928 Games but had dropped it afterwards because of alleged scenes of distress among competitors at the finish, and for whatever reason the 880 did not figure again at an Empire Games until 1962. Eileen Hiscock, who had unofficially equalled the World record of 11.0 for 100 yards three years earlier, won that event and was also a member of the English team which took the first of two curious relay races, involving in this instance three successive stages of 110 yards, 220 yards and 110 yards. The same afternoon the fleet Miss Hiscock, who had won an Olympic relay bronze in 1932, ran the fastest 220 heat time of 25.4.

The final day contained the 12 remaining track and field finals, plus the marathon, and it was largely a triumph for England's sprinters even if it was the mile which had been anticipated as being the race of the Games and which lived up fully to its billing. Arthur Sweeney beat Theunissen at 220 by much the same margin as in the 100 and then anchored the 4 x 110 relay team to victory. Eileen Hiscock was even more impressive, winning the 220 in a World record time of 25.0, though mystifyingly this was never officially ratified, but the Canadians - coached by the 1928 Olympic 4 x 100m gold-medallist, Fanny Rosenfeld - caused an upset by beating an England team including Hiscock in a second relay race made up of 2 x 220 and 2 x 110. Marjorie Clark won her second title at 80m hurdles and Phyllis Bartholomew was England's winner in the long jump.

Godfrey Rampling, who had been a member of Britain's silver-medal team in the 1932 Olympic 4 x 400 relay, won the 440 yards and was actually the first track champion of these Games to run faster than his 1930 predecessor. In fact, Rampling's time of 48.0 on soggy cinders was of the very highest order, ranking equal seventh in the World for the year and beating the British record which had stood since 1908! England took all the medals in the event, with Bill Roberts, of Salford Athletic Club, seemingly content to finish 2nd, and later in the day Rampling and bronze-medallist Crew Stoneley (though not Roberts, inexplicably) contributed to England's 4 x 440 win. Stan Scarsbrook led another England 1-2-3 in the steeplechase, and it was actually a 1-2-3-4 with the next three finishers - Tom Evenson, defending champion George Bailey and Pat Campbell - all, remarkably, from Salford Harriers. Another winner from 1930, Duncan McLeod Wright, was beaten into 3rd place in the marathon, won by the 39-year-old Canadian, Harold Webster, who had placed 10th in Hamilton, while the 5th finisher was a team-mate, Percy Wyer, who was apparently 50 years old and was still sprightly enough to run almost exactly the same time again in the Berlin Olympics two years later! Webster, who had been born in Derbyshire, moved to the front at 12 miles on the out-and-back course, was three minutes ahead at 20 miles, and increased his advantage to over four minutes at the finish. The field events provided a nice contrast in generations as 16-year-old Sam Richardson, already silver-medallist in the triple jump, won the long jump, while Malcolm Nokes, 21 years his senior, defended his title in the hammer. Young Richardson leaped 24ft 11in (7.59m) the following year, but in his one other international appearance was only 14th at the Berlin Olympics.

The mile had been the first track final of the afternoon at 2.45 p.m., a quarter-of-an-hour after the marathon men had been led out on to the streets of West London by a Newfoundland runner, Tom Kelly. The principal mile finalists, following largely inconsequential heats the previous day, were Jack Lovelock for New Zealand and Sydney Wooderson for England, together with Jerry Cornes, Horace Craske and Aubrey Reeve (all of England), Les Wade (Canada), Bobby Graham (Scotland) and Ken Harris (Wales). Craske, who had been 4th in the AAA Championships, led the first lap in a time of 59.5sec, which was so fast that it was either foolhardiness on his part or was the basis of a devious English plot to unsettle Lovelock, but then slowed to 2:06 at the half-mile. Cornes, the 1932 Olympic silver-medallist at 1500m, continued at the same pace, reaching the bell in 3:12.5, and led Wooderson and Lovelock into the last bend, but when the New Zealander began his drive for home 100 yards out the race was quickly decided and he went on to win by six yards in 4:12.8. Of course, Lovelock was already a famous figure and widely regarded as being English-trained and nurtured, but he proudly carried New Zealand's

21

flag at the opening ceremony, lost no opportunity to wear the familiar and now fearsome all-black uniform and silver fern emblem of his native land, reinforced his legendary status that dull day at the White City, and consolidated it for ever when he won the Olympic 1500m in World record time two years later.

Even so, these 1934 Games were equally important for establishing some degree of women's franchise, even if their programme of events was limited and their performances not always of international standard. This was a formative year for women's athletics with the World Games, which had been held by the Women's World Federation (FSFI) since 1922 as an alternative to the Olympics, starting at the White City immediately after the Empire Games. Marjorie Clark, who had set national records in the high jump and hurdles at the Empire Games, added three more at 100m, long jump and javelin in the FSFI meeting, and Eileen Hiscock (3rd at 100m), Gladys Lunn (3rd at 800m) and Canada's Betty Taylor (2nd at 80m hurdles) were among the medallists.

England had won 13 of the 18 Empire Games track events, which delighted the packed crowds, but the traditional apathy of perfidious Albion towards the more technical disciplines meant that they won only three of the 11 field events, and British Guiana, New Zealand, Canada, Scotland and South Africa each took their place at the top of the victory dais. It was from the same spot that Bonzo Howland, the Union Jack flag grasped firmly in his hand, had declared at the opening ceremony on behalf of the athletes that *"we are all loyal subjects of His Majesty the King Emperor and will take part in the British Empire Games in the spirit of true sportsmanship, recognising the rules which govern them and desirous of competing in them for the honour of our Empire and for the glory of sport".* Brave words, inevitably sounding a shade outmoded almost 70 years later, but prophetically summarising the singular nature of the place in sport occupied by the Empire Games as the shadow of Hitler's Olympics began to loom.

RESULTS 1934

MEN

100 YARDS (4 Aug): 1 Arthur Sweeney (Eng) 10.0, 2 Marthinus Theunissen (SA) 10.0e, 3 Ian Young (Sco) 10.1e, 4 George Saunders (Eng), 5 Robin Murdoch (Sco), 6 Howard Yates (Aus).

220 YARDS (7 Aug): 1 Arthur Sweeney (Eng) 21.9, 2 Marthinus Theunissen (SA) 22.0e, 3 Walter Rangeley (Eng) 22.1e, 4 Robin Murdoch (Sco), 5 Ian Young (Sco), 6 Frank Nicks (Can).

440 YARDS (7 Aug): 1 Godfrey Rampling (Eng) 48.0, 2 Bill Roberts (Eng) 48.5e, 3 Crew Stoneley (Eng) 48.6e, 4 Bill Fritz (Can), 5 Joe Addison (Can), 6 Alan Hunter (Sco).

880 YARDS (6 Aug): 1 Phil Edwards (BG) 1:54.2, 2 Willie Botha (SA) 1:55.0, 3 Hamish Stothard (Sco) 1:55.1, 4 Jack Powell (Eng), 5 Jerry Sampson (Can), 6 Jack Cooper (Eng).

1 MILE (7 Aug): 1 Jack Lovelock (NZ) 4:12.8, 2 Sydney Wooderson (Eng) 4:13.4e. 3 Jerry Cornes (Eng) 4:13.6e, 4 Aubrey Reeve (Eng), 5 Bobby Graham (Sco), 6 Les Wade (Can). Also ran - Horace Craske (Eng), Ken Harris (Wal).

3 MILES (4 Aug): 1 Walter Beavers (Eng) 14:32.6, 2 Cyril Allen (Eng) 14:37.8, 3 Alex Burns (Eng) 14:35.4, 4 Bob Rankine (Can), 5 Jack Parker (NI), 6 Harold Thompson (SA) 7 Jackie Laidlaw (Sco), 8 Lloyd Longman (Can), 9 James Caie (Sco), 10 Len Tongue (Wal). Did not finish - Mannie Dookie (Tri).

6 MILES (6 Aug): 1 Arthur Penny (Eng) 31:00.6, 2 Bob Rankine (Can) 31:03.0e, 3 Arthur Furze (Eng) 31:04.0e, 4 Jack Holden (Eng), 5 John Potts (Eng), 6 Ray Oliver (Can), 7 Lloyd Longman (Can). Did not finish - Mannie Dookie (Tri).

2 MILES STEEPLECHASE (7 Aug): 1 Stan Scarsbrook (Eng) 10:23.4, 2 Tom Evenson (Eng) 10:25.8e, 3 George Bailey (Eng), 4 Pat Campbell (Eng), 5 Earl Moore (Can), 6 Walter Gunn (Sco).

MARATHON (7 Aug); 1 Harold Webster (Can) 2:40:36, 2 Donald McNab Robertson (Sco) 2:45:08, 3 Duncan McLeod Wright (Sco) 2:56:20; 4 Harold Wood (Eng) 2:58:41, 5 Percy Wyer (Can) 3:00.40, 6 Wilf Short (Wal) 3:02:56, 7 Reg Nicholls (Eng) 3:05:23. Did not finish - Alex Burnside (Can), Tom Kelly (NF), Bert Norris (Eng), Ross Sutherland (Sco), Laurie Weatherill (Eng).

120 YARDS HURDLES (6 Aug): 1 Don Finlay (Eng) 15.2, 2 Jim Worrall (Can) 15.5e, 3 Ashleigh Pilbrow (Eng) 15.7e, 4 Art Ravensdale (Can), 5 John Gabriel (Eng). Did not finish - Johannes Viljoen (SA).

440 YARDS HURDLES (4 Aug): 1 Alan Hunter (Sco) 55.2, 2 Charles Reilly (Aus) 55.8e, 3 Ralph Brown (Eng) 56.0e, 4 Jim Worrall (Can), 5 John Stone (Eng), 6 Ashleigh Pilbrow (Eng).

4 x 110 YARDS RELAY (7 Aug): 1 England (Everard Davis, George Saunders, Walter Rangeley, Arthur Sweeney) 42.2, 2 Canada (Bert Pearson, Frank Nicks, Allan Poole, Bill Christie) 42.5e, 3 Scotland (Archie Turner, David Brownlee, Robin Murdoch, Ian Young) 43.0e, 4 Australia (Noel Dempsey, Fred Woodhouse, Jack Horsfall, Howard Yates), 5 Bermuda (Stan Gascoigne, Buddy Card, Frank Peniston, Richard Freisenbruch), 6 India (Gyan Prakash Bhalla, Jehangir Khan, Ronald Vernieux, Niranjan Singh).

4 x 440 YARDS RELAY (7 Aug): 1 England (Denis Rathbone, Geoff Blake, Crew Stoneley, Godfrey Rampling) 3:16.8, 2 Canada (Bill Fritz, Joe Addison, Art Scott, Ray Lewis) 3:17.4e, 3 Scotland (Ronnie Wallace, Ronald Wylde, Hamish Stothard, Alan Hunter). 3 teams competed.

HIGH JUMP (6 Aug): 1 Edwin Thacker (SA) 1.90, 2 Joe Haley (Can) 1.90, 3 John Michie (Sco) 1.90, 4 Jack Metcalfe (Aus) 1.88, 5 Arthur Gray (Eng) 1.85, 6= Bill Land (Eng), Joe McKenzie (Jam), Stanley West (Eng) 1.83. Frank Whitcutt (Wal) failed at opening height (1.73).

POLE VAULT (6 Aug): 1 Syl Apps (Can) 3.81 (3.88 in jumpoff), 2 Alf Gilbert (Can) 3.81, 3 Fred Woodhouse (Aus) 3.66, 4 Andries du Plessis (SA) 3.66, 5 Frank Phillipson (Eng) 3.66, 6 Patrick Ogilvie (Eng) 3.50. Also competed - Abdul Safi Khan (Ind), Alfred Kinally (Eng), J.H. Walker (Eng), Dick Webster (Eng).

LONG JUMP (7 Aug): 1 Sam Richardson (Can) 7.17, 2 Johann Luckhoff (SA) 7.10, 3 Jack Metcalfe (Aus) 6.93, 4 Sandy Duncan (Eng) 6.91, 5 Ray Cooper (Can) 6.83, 6 Leslie Butler (Eng) 6.79. Also competed - Harold Brainsby (NZ), R.C.

Crombie (Eng), Alf Gilbert (Can), Jack Horsfall (Aus), Niranjan Singh (Ind), George Pallett (Eng), Bobby Robertson (Sco), Bertie Shillington (NI), Maurice Tait (NI).

TRIPLE JUMP (4 Aug): 1 Jack Metcalfe (Aus) 15.63, 2 Sam Richardson (Can) 14.65, 3 Harold Brainsby (NZ) 14.62, 4 Edward Boyce (NI) 13.80, 5 Jack Higginson (Eng) 13.73, 6 Bertie Shillington (NI) 13.69. Also competed - Leslie Butler (Eng), Ray Cooper (Can), Alf Gilbert (Can), Arthur Gray (Eng), Niranjan Singh (Ind), George Sutherland (Can), F. Turner (Eng).

SHOT (6 Aug): 1 Harry Hart (SA) 14.67, 2 Robert "Bonzo" Howland (Eng) 13.53, 3 Kenneth Pridie (Eng) 13.43, 4 George Walla (Can) 13.23, 5 Harry Reeves (Eng) 12.76, 6 Anthony Watson (Eng) 12.18. 7 A.W. "Tiny" Lewis (Wal) 11.70, 8 George Sutherland (Can).

DISCUS (4 Aug): 1 Harry Hart (SA) 41.53, 2 Douglas Bell (Eng) 40.44, 3 Bernard Prendergast (Jam) 40.24, 4 George Walla (Can) 39.40, 5 Bill Land (Eng) 39.34, 6 Kenneth Pridie (Eng) 37.79, 7 George Sutherland (Can). Also competed - Pat Bermingham (IFS), Johann Luckhoff (SA), A. Spurling (Ber), Bob Waters (Can).

HAMMER (7 Aug): 1 Malcolm Nokes (Eng) 48.25, 2 George Sutherland (Can) 46.25, 3 William Mackenzie (Sco) 42.50, 4 Bob Waters (Can) 39.88, 5 Douglas Bell (Eng) 38.78, 6 Norman Drake (Eng) 35.80. Also competed - W. Coldfield (NF), Harry Reeves (Eng).

JAVELIN (7 Aug): 1 Bob Dixon (Can) 60.02, 2 Harry Hart (SA) 58.28, 3 Johann Luckhoff (SA) 56.50, 4 Stanley Wilson (Eng) 54.74, 5 Joseph Heath (Eng) 53.42, 6 George Walla (Can) 52.16. Also competed - Charles Bowen (Eng), John Duus (Eng), Jehangir Khan (Ind).

WOMEN

100 YARDS (6 Aug): 1 Eileen Hiscock (Eng) 11.3, 2 Hilda Strike (Can) 11.5e, 3 Lillian Chalmers (Eng) 11.6e, 4 Elsie Maguire (Eng), 5 Ethel Johnson (Eng), 6 Audrey Dearnley (Can).

220 YARDS (7 Aug): 1 Eileen Hiscock (Eng) 25,0, 2 Aileen Meagher (Can) 25.4e, 3 Nellie Halstead (Eng) 25.6e, 4 Lillian Palmer (Can), 5 Hilda Cameron (Can), 6 Ethel Johnson (Eng).

880 YARDS (6 Aug): 1 Gladys Lunn (Eng) 2:19.4, 2 Ida Jones (Eng) 2:21.0e, 3 Dorothy Butterfield (Eng) 2:21.4e, 4 Constance Furneaux (Eng), 5 Doris Morgan (SA), 6 Violet Smith (Can), 7 Mildred Storrar (Sco).

80 METRES HURDLES (7 Aug): 1 Marjorie Clark (SA) 11.8, 2 Betty Taylor (Can) 11.9e, 3 Elsie Green (Eng) 12.2e, 4 Roxy Atkins (Can), 5 Alda Wilson (Can), 6 Phyllis Goad (Eng).

440 YARDS RELAY - 220y, 110y, 110y - (6 Aug): 1 England (Nellie Halstead, Eileen Hiscock, Elsie Maguire) 49.4, 2 Canada (Aileen Meagher, Audrey Dearnley, Hilda Strike), 3 Rhodesia (Dorothy Ballantyne, Cynthia Keay, Mollie Bragge), 4 South Africa (Doris Morgan, Barbara Burke, Marjorie Clark), 5 Scotland (Sheila Dobbie, Cathie Jackson, Barbara Barnetson). 5 teams competed.

660 YARDS RELAY - 2 x 220, 2 x 110 - (4 Aug): 1 Canada (Lillian Palmer, Betty White, Aileen Meagher, Audrey Dearnley) 1:14.4, 2 England (Nellie Halstead, Eileen Hiscock, Ethel Johnson, Ivy Walker), 3 Scotland (Joan Cunningham, Sheila Dobbie, Cathie Jackson, Margaret Mackenzie). 3 teams competed.

HIGH JUMP (4 Aug): 1 Marjorie Clark (SA) 1.60, 2 Eva Dawes (Can) 1.57, 3 Margaret Bell (Can) 1.52, 4 Mary Milne (Eng) 1.52 (Bell 1.57, Milne 1.55 in jumpoff for third place), 5 Isabella Miller (Can) 1.47, 6 Marjorie Okell (Eng) 1.45, 7 Hilda Thorogood (Can), 8 Elsie Harris (Eng), 9 Mollie Bragge (Rho).

LONG JUMP (7 Aug): 1 Phyllis Bartholomew (Eng) 5.47, 2 Evelyn Goshawk (Can) 5.42, 3 Violet Webb (Eng) 5.23, 4 Mary Frizzell (Can) 5.21, 5 Doris Razzell (Eng) 5.18, 6 Margaret Fitzpatrick (Can) 4.94., 7 Mollie Bragge (Rho), 8 Beatrice Proctor (Rho).

JAVELIN (4 Aug): 1 Gladys Lunn (Eng) 32.19, 2 Edith Halstead (Eng) 30.94, 3 Margaret Cox (Eng) 30.08, 4 Louise Fawcett (Eng) 29.28. 4 competed. Note: Edith and Nellie Halstead, who ran in the 220 yards and 660 yards relay, were sisters, though Edith was later pronounced to have been male from birth and as Eddie Halstead became a father.

4.

"Dashing Dessie" is the maiden who bowls them over

CRICKET GROUNDS, SYDNEY, AUSTRALIA
5 - 12 FEBRUARY 1938

GEOGRAPHICAL CONSIDERATIONS DICTATED the number and variety of competitors in the formative years of the Empire Games. As hosts in 1938 Australia fielded a team of 75 athletes, compared with a mere seven in London four years previously, whilst England, whose team of 87 had been much the largest in 1934, sent just 25 to Sydney. Only 11 countries entered athletics in 1938 - the same number as in 1930 - and there were inevitably some prominent absentees. The long winter-time voyage to Australia meant that many athletes from the home countries could not afford to take the time off, and these included Godfrey Brown and Godfrey Rampling, the Berlin Olympic 4 x 400 gold-medallists, as well as Arthur Collyer (the AAA champion at 880), Sydney Wooderson (who had set a World mile record of 4:06.4 in 1937) and Don Finlay (the Olympic 110m hurdles silver-medallist). Yet there were still 184 athletes in attendance and among the six medallists from Berlin were Bill Roberts, who had been 2nd in the 1934 Empire 440 yards, and Jack Metcalfe, the defending champion in the triple jump. Even so, Roberts had given up his job as a timber-yard manager in Salford to compete after his employers refused him time off. The Canadians, who like the Britons were away from home for almost three months, still sent 37 athletes, and most prominent of them was the Berlin 400m hurdles silver-medallist, John Loaring.

Rather against expectations the close-cropped grass of the Sydney

Cricket Grounds provided what transpired to be a brilliant setting for athletics, beginning on Saturday 5 February with finals at 100 yards, three miles, 440 yards hurdles, high jump and javelin for men and at 100 yards and relay for women. Both sprints promised much with Cyril Holmes, of Manchester University, taking on formidable opposition, and Decima Norman for Australia against Barbara Burke, who was running for South Africa though she had won an Olympic 4 x 100 silver for Great Britain in Berlin. Holmes and the South African, Tom Lavery, faced four Australians in the final, and Holmes - who had run 9.7 in a handicap race in Sydney a fortnight earlier - showed marvellous form considering that it was out-of-season for him, winning again in 9.7. Norman won her first-round heat by six yards in 11.1, repeated that time in her semi-final (equalled in the other semi-final by Burke), and then ran yet another 11.1 to win the final by two yards from her team-mate, Joyce Walker, with Burke beaten into 4th place.

The clear favourites for the three miles were the Cambridge University graduate, Peter Ward, and a New Zealander, Cecil Matthews. Both had run without much success in the 1936 Olympics, but the following year they had each set excellent new national records: Ward 14:02.0 in a close race with the great Finn, Taisto Maki, and Matthews an unexpected 14:07.0 in easily winning his country's Games trial. Their encounter produced a wonderful race - perhaps the most enthralling yet seen at the Empire Games. On the lop-sided D-shaped track Matthews took the lead early on and passed two miles almost precisely on a 14-minute schedule at 9:20.5. He then spiritedly resisted Ward's challenges on the last lap and drew away to win by some 30 yards in 13:59.6, only nine seconds outside the World record held by Finland's 1936 Olympic 5000m champion, Lauri Lehtinen. This was magnificent running, and there was more to come.

There were only six competitors in the 440 hurdles, but the event produced yet another startling performance on this stirring first day of athletics competition. John Loaring had not apparently taken part in a hurdles race since winning the Olympic silver medal 18 months previously and yet he came out and ran 52.9, which was to remain the fastest time in the World for the year. Also a fine performer on the flat, having reached the 400m final in Berlin, Loaring was an athlete of quite exceptional ability who like so many others lost some of the best years of his competitive life to the war. In 1942, while serving with the Canadian forces in England, he made a brief appearance at a meeting in Portsmouth and despite little specialised training ran the 440 hurdles in 53.4!

To underline the quality of the Games another relatively little-known New Zealander, Pat Boot, broke Tommy Hampson's Games record for 880 yards with 1:52.3 in his heat and South Africa's Edwin Thacker retained his high-jump title with a clearance of 6ft 5 1/8in (1.96m). Decima Norman, colourfully known as "Dashing Dessie", or even more improbably "The Flying Handful", further delighted her Aussie supporters by sharing in a comfortable win over England in the 660 yards relay.

The second day's events were held on Monday 7 February, with finals at 880, the marathon and discus for men and the 440 yards relay and long jump for women. Bizarrely, there were several false starts before the half-mile got under way, but Pat Boot made no mistake, winning in majestic style fully 20 yards ahead of England's Frank Handley and in a time of 1:51.2, which was only beaten by two other men in the World during 1938 - one of them being Sydney Wooderson, who set World records of 1:48.4m/1:49.2y in a specially-framed handicap race the following August. What a pity that Boot and Wooderson did not meet in Sydney! The marathon entrants included five men who had run in the Berlin Olympics: the South Africans, Johannes Coleman and Jackie Gibson, who had finished 6th and 8th; the 1934 Empire silver-medallist, McNab Robertson, who was 7th; Jimmy Bartlett, of Canada, 15th; and England's Bert Norris, a non-finisher. The conditions were almost ideal - bright and sunny but with a cooling breeze - and at 10 miles the South Africans (54:32) were already a full two minutes ahead, and soon afterwards Coleman broke away, winning by more than seven minutes in the second fastest time in the World for the year. It was his seventh win in nine marathons, and he carried this sort of form through to many years after, placing 4th in the 1948 Olympics at the age of 38.

Yet it was Dashing Dessie who stole the hearts of the spectators and the headlines in the newspapers, winning her third gold medal in the long jump with 19ft 0 1/4in (5.79m), a distance which was to be beaten by only four other women (all of them German) during 1938, and then anchoring the Australian team to predictable success in the 440 yards relay. The best sprint performances of the day, though, actually came in the men's 220 yards heats where Australians John Mumford and Ted Best each ran 21.6 before England's Bill Roberts excelled himself with a new Australian all-comers' record of 21.5.

So on to Thursday 10 February and six more finals: 220, six miles, 4 x 110, long jump and hammer for men and javelin for women. In the 220 semi-finals Larry O'Connor, of Canada, beat Roberts by half-a-yard in 21.5 and then the 100 yards winner, Cyril Holmes, won by a foot from Best and Howard Yates in 21.3 to set up a thrilling final. Improving with every race Holmes was slowly away but soon into his rhythmic stride to complete the sprint double with another personal best of 21.2 ahead of the impressive Mumford, 21.3. The full measure of Holmes's performance is that only two other athletes, both of them American, ran faster during 1938, and that no other British sprinter has ever subsequently won outright both events at Empire & Commonwealth level - or, for that matter, Olympic, World or European. His majestic running and his gentlemanly manner made him one of the favourites of the Sydney spectators.

The first four men in the three miles - Matthews, Ward, Canada's Bob Rankine and South Africa's Wally Hayward - appeared again for the six miles, together with the marathon winner, Johannes Coleman, and the race began in sensational style. Coleman set off at a blistering speed - 4:46 for the first mile, which was 28:36 pace compared with the existing World record of 29:08.4! - and only the inexperienced Noel Stanford, of Trinidad, went in pursuit. The two of them battled for the lead, literally, and Stanford was apparently knocked to the ground and out of the race in the sixth lap. Coleman was heartily booed by the crowd and he was subsequently disqualified by the officials when he retired from the race just before halfway, apparently having completed pacemaking duties on behalf of his compatriot, Hayward. As had been the case with his predecessor, Bill Savidan, in 1930, Matthews was making his debut at six miles but confidently led Ward, also a novice at the distance, through halfway in 15:12 and then increased the pace and went on to win by 180 yards from Rankine as the Englishman dropped out. Matthews's final time was still not at all comparable to the World record for 10,000m set at 30:02.0 by Taisto Maki, of Finland, that year, but he amply merited the soubriquet of "New Zealand's Nurmi" bestowed upon him by "The Times" and was undoubtedly a great talent never fully realised.

Distance-runners of the 1930s had learned something from the intense commitment of the Flying Finns, and particularly Nurmi, but they still did not train with anything like the intensity of the succeeding generations who copied the examples of the Swedish milers of the early 1940s and the great Czech, Emil Zatopek. Matthews had achieved 4:20 for the mile while still at school, which was exceptional for those days, and may well have trained harder than most. He is known to have been a pioneer of interval training on the track, running repeatedly at speed over distances as short as 300 and 600 yards. By contrast, Laurie Weatherill, of South London Harriers, who did not do himself full justice in his Empire Games appearances of 1934 and 1938 but was three times Southern cross-country champion and twice in England's winning international team, is reputed to have put in two 10-mile runs during a typical week's training and then run 30 miles on Saturday and walked 30 miles on Sunday!

The men's 440 yards heats were extravagantly fast with the South African, Dennis Shore, who had run 47.5 at altitude the previous year, breaking Godfrey Rampling's Games record with 47.9 in the first heat, and then Bill Roberts coming very close with 48.1 in the third heat. Only three countries contested the 4 x 110 relay, but it was a cracking race with a mere three yards between them all and Canada winning with a team which included the highly versatile hurdlers, Loaring and O'Connor, and in addition Canadians won the long jump and hammer. Hal Brown leaped 24ft 4 3/4in (7.43m), which was astounding because he had come to Sydney as a javelin thrower and had never previously beaten even 23ft in the long jump, for which his twin brother, Wally, had been selected. [Hal Brown, incidentally, briefly re-emerged in 1945 when he appeared at a military sports in Taunton, Somerset, while serving with the Canadian forces in England and proceeded to long jump 24ft 5 1/2in (7.45m)!]. Canada's other winner was George Sutherland, who enthusiastically contested a variety of events and had finished 3rd in the discus three days before and 2nd in the hammer in 1934, setting a new Games record this time in the hammer. The one women's event of the day, the javelin, was won by yet another Canadian, Robina Higgins, who beat the Empire record holder, Toni Robertson, of South Africa, with the defending champion, Gladys Lunn, 3rd, and later in the year improved the Empire record to 131ft 11 1/4in (40.21m), ranking a respectable 17th in the World.

The closing day was Saturday 12 February, completing the programme with finals at 440, the mile, 120 yards hurdles, 4 x 440, pole vault, triple jump and shot for men and 220, hurdles and high jump for women, and in sultry weather 30,000 people packed the arena. The 440 brought together Shore and Roberts as the favourites, with the 220 silver-medallist, John Mumford, plus the Canadians, Bill Fritz and John Loaring, and the New Zealander, Harold Tyrie, who had enjoyed the luck of the draw, qualifying in heat two in 49.3 when the Canadian, Jack Orr, had already been eliminated in heat one in 48.4. Roberts, Fritz and Loaring had finished 4th, 5th and 6th respectively in the Berlin Olympic final, and Fritz had also placed 4th in the 1934 Empire final behind Roberts's 2nd place. The race truly reflected the ability and experience of the competitors and to the immense excitement of the crowd Roberts, who led into the home straight by two yards, was passed by Fritz, and then responded to win on the line. Roberts was given the verdict by inches over Fritz, both running 47.9, and Shore was only two yards back in 3rd place.

The mile finalists included only one survivor from the 1934 Games - Bobby Graham, of Scotland - and the winner seemed likely to be Pat Boot, on the strength of his runaway 880 success, and particularly as in the absence of Sydney Wooderson the only other home countries' representatives were Bernard Eeles (England) and James William Llewellyn Alford (Wales), with modest personal bests of 4:16.4 and 4:17.1 respectively. But Jim Alford was determined to do better than he had in the half-mile, where he was so disappointed with his 4th place that he had written a letter of apology afterwards to his coach back in Wales, and he astonishingly unleashed a 61sec last lap, passing Boot and the Australian, Gerald Backhouse, in the final 220 yards and recording 4:11.5 - an improvement of almost six seconds on his previous best and better than Jack Lovelock's Games record. Alford went on to an illustrious coaching career, including being in charge of the Welsh team at the 1958 Empire Games and still at the age of 84 advising a Commonwealth Games silver-medallist 40 years later!

The 4 x 440 was a renewal of rivalries between England and Canada. England's team was somewhat makeshift with Brian MacCabe and Frank Handley, both primarily half-milers, joining Harry Pack, a City of London policeman, and the individual gold-medallist, Bill Roberts, and Canada looked rather the stronger with Bill Fritz and John Loaring partnering Bill Dale, the runner-up at 880, and Jack Orr, the 18-year-old who unluckily missed the 440 final. Canada won quite comfortably by 15 yards in 3:16.9, but the careers of Roberts and Fritz had regularly intertwined over a five-year period, and they had even unusually figured in the same World record-breaking team in 1936 when the British Empire (Roberts, Rampling, Fritz and Brown) beat the USA at 4 x 440 in the traditional post-Olympic relays meeting. Their time of 3:10.6 had not been ratified because of the mixture of nationalities involved.

There was no Don Finlay for England at 120 yards hurdles, but a World-class race was promised and duly delivered. Tom Lavery, of South Africa, who had already run in the 100 yards final, had recorded 14.2 in Sydney a few days before the Games began, while Canada's Larry O'Connor had been 4th at 220 and had also run a 14.2 hurdles the previous year. After heats of 14.4 and 14.6 respectively, the two of them blazed away in the final and the times were sensational: 14.0 for Lavery and an estimated 14.2 for O'Connor only a yard or so behind. Claims have been made that the race was wind-assisted - beyond the favourable two metres per second which is the maximum allowed for record purposes - but this was a matter of subjective judgment in those days rather than automatic measurement, and there is in any case no doubt of the supreme quality of Lavery's hurdling. Jack Metcalfe retained his triple-jump title to achieve Australia's one and only men's victory of the Games and the pole vault went to the South African, Andries du Plessis, at 13ft 6in (4.11m), which was a huge improvement on the Games record. The shot, won by the prolific Harry Hart at the two previous Games, went to another South African, Louis Fouche,

Dashing Dessie ended the Games as she had begun them - with another superlative gold-medal performance. Two days earlier she had set the tone for the 220 yards final by establishing new Games records of 24.9 in her heat and 24.5 in the semi-finals, and she needed "only" 24.7 to win the final easily from her team-mate, Jean Coleman, who had also been a member of both winning relay teams. The 80m hurdles was won very narrowly by the Anglo-South African, Barbara Burke, and the high jump provided the only success for a member of the England women's team as Dorothy Odam equalled the Games best. She had won the Olympic silver two years previously at the age of 16, was Olympic silver-medallist again in 1948, Empire Games champion once more in 1950 as Mrs Tyler, and 2nd in 1954 at the same height as she had cleared 16 years before!

Against the odds, these Sydney Games had turned out to be by far the best yet. There had been World-class performances in every men's track event, and the occasion was witness to the flowering of talents such as Holmes, Mumford, Roberts, Fritz, Boot, Alford, Matthews, Coleman, Lavery, Loaring and Metcalfe. Even above all else there was the uninhibited athleticism of Decima Norman, and the shame of it all was that, while a handful of them were able to resume their athletics careers in peacetime a decade later, for the vast majority of the 184 competitors in Sydney this was their last great day in the sun. In all innocence the publishers of the official programme had printed a heartening slogan: *"Whether We Win Or Lose TODAY, We Will Play The Game Again TOMORROW"*.

RESULTS 1938

MEN

100 YARDS (5 Feb): 1 Cyril Holmes (Eng) 9.7, 2 John Mumford (Aus) 9.8e, 3 Ted Best (Aus) 9.9e, 4 Tom Lavery (SA) 9.9e, 5 Teddy Hampson (Aus) 10.0e, 6 Howard Yates (Aus) 10.1e.

220 YARDS (10 Feb): 1 Cyril Holmes (Eng) 21.2, 2 John Mumford (Aus) 21.3e, 3 Ted Best (Aus) 21.4e, 4 Larry O'Connor (Can) 21.6e, 5 Howard Yates (Aus) 21.7e, 6 Bill Roberts (Eng) 21.7e.

440 YARDS (12 Feb): 1 Bill Roberts (Eng) 47.9, 2 Bill Fritz (Can) 47.9e, 3 Dennis Shore (SA) 48.1e, 4 John Mumford (Aus), 5 John Loaring (Can), 6 Harold Tyrie (NZ).

880 YARDS (7 Feb): 1 Pat Boot (NZ) 1:51.2, 2 Frank Handley (Eng) 1:53.5e, 3 Bill Dale (Can) 1:53.6e, 4 Jim Alford (Wal), 5 Theo Allen (NZ), 6 Brian MacCabe (Eng), 7 Gerald Backhouse (Aus), 8 Niklaas "Klasie" Wessels (SA).

1 MILE (12 Feb): 1 Jim Alford (Wal) 4:11.5, 2 Gerald Backhouse (Aus) 4:12.2, 3 Pat Boot (NZ) 4:12.6, 4 Art Clarke (Can) 4:14.4e, 5 Bernard Eeles (Eng) 4:15.2e, 6 Bill Pullar (NZ). Did not finish - Theo Allen (NZ), Bobby Graham (Sco).

3 MILES (5 Feb): 1 Cecil Matthews (NZ) 13:59.6, 2 Peter Ward (Eng) 14:05.6, 3 Bob Rankine (Can), 14:24.0e, 4 Wally Hayward (SA) 14:24.4, 5 Stan Nicholls (Aus), 6 Laurie Weatherill (Eng), 7 Alan Geddes (NZ). Did not finish - Art Clarke (Can), Fred Colman (Aus), Keith Faulkner (Aus), Bobby Graham (Sco), Lloyd Longman (Can), Walter Weightman (Aus).

6 MILES (10 Feb): 1 Cecil Matthews (NZ) 30:14.5, 2 Bob Rankine (Can), 3 Wally Hayward (SA), 4 Alan Geddes (NZ), 5 Laurie Weatherill (Eng), 6 Jackie Gibson (SA), 7 Milton Wallace (Can), 8 Fred Bassed (Aus), 9 Stan Millington (Aus), 10 Brendan Doyle (Aus). Did not finish - Lloyd Longman (Can), Noel Stanford (Tri), Peter Ward (Eng). Disqualified - Johannes Coleman (SA).

MARATHON (7 Feb): 1 Johannes Coleman (SA) 2:30:49.8, 2 Bert Norris (Eng) 2:37:57.0, 3 Jackie Gibson (SA) 2:38:20.0, 4 Donald McNab Robertson (Sco)

2:42:40.0; 5 Jimmy Bartlett (Can) 2:50:51.0, 6 Lloyd Longman (Can) 2:54:54.0, 7 Walter Young (Can) 2:59:05.0, 8 Dick Crossley (Aus) 3:12.50.0, 9 John Wood (Aus) 3:19:47.0. Did not finish - Alf Hayes (Aus), William Liddle (Aus), Ernest Jolly (Aus), James Patterson (Aus), Noel Stanford (Tri).

120 YARDS HURDLES (12 Feb); 1 Tom Lavery (SA) 14.0, 2 Larry O'Connor (Can) 14.2e, 3 Sid Stenner (Aus) 14.4e, 4 Don McLardy (Aus) 14.6e, 5 Sidney Kiel (SA) 14.7e, 6 Philip Sharpley (NZ) 15.0e.

440 YARDS HURDLES (5 Feb): 1 John Loaring (Can) 52.9, 2 John Park (Aus) 54.6e, 3 Alan McDougall (Aus) 55.2e, 4 Alf Watson (Aus), 5 Arnold Anderson (NZ), 6 Paul Magee (Aus).

4 x 110 YARDS RELAY (10 Feb): 1 Canada (Jack Brown, Pat Haley, John Loaring, Larry O'Connor) 41.6, 2 England (Ken Richardson, Sandy Duncan, Lawrence Wallace, Cyril Holmes) 41.8e, 3 Australia (Ted Best, Alf Watson, Teddy Hampson, Howard Yates) 41.9e. 3 teams competed.

4 x 440 YARDS RELAY (12 Feb): 1 Canada (Jack Orr, Bill Dale, Bill Fritz, John Loaring) 3:16.9, 2 England (Frank Handley, Harry Pack, Brian MacCabe, Bill Roberts) 3:19.2, 3 New Zealand (Arnold Anderson, Alan Sayers, Graham Quinn, Harold Tyrie) 3:22.0, 4 Australia (John Park, Hugh Johnson, Athol Jones, Vernon Wallace). 4 teams competed.

HIGH JUMP (5 Feb): 1 Edwin Thacker (SA) 1.96, 2 Robert Heffernan (Aus) 1.88, 3 Doug Shetliffe (Aus) 1.88, 4 Peter Tancred (Aus) 1.86, 5 John Newman (Eng) 1.86, 6 Joe Haley (Can) 1.86, 7 Jack Metcalfe (Aus) 1.82, 8 Henry Perera (Cey) 1.82, 9 Pat Haley (Can) 1.78, 10 Jim Panton (Can), 11 Tracket Ashmead (Tri) 1.73. Note: Joe and Pat Haley were brothers.

POLE VAULT (12 Feb): 1 Andries du Plessis (SA) 4.11, 2 Les Fletcher (Aus) 3.97, 3 Stuart Frid (Can) 3.88, 4 Dick Webster (Eng) 3.88, 5 Ted Winter (Aus) 3.88, 6 Ian Barrett (Rho) 3.77, 7 Fred Woodhouse (Aus) 3.77, 8 Bill Cartwright (Aus) 3.50, 9 Arthur Dep (Cey) 3.50. John Clarke (NI) failed at opening height.

LONG JUMP (10 Feb): 1 Hal Brown (Can) 7.43, 2 Jim Panton (Can) 7.25, 3 Basil Dickinson (Aus) 7.15, 4 Harry Gould (Aus) 7.12, 5 Jack Metcalfe (Aus) 7.08, 6 Walter Tambimuttu (Cey) 6.95, 7 Bertie Shillington (NI) 6.85, 8 Ray Graf (Aus) 6.85, 9 Harry Lister (Eng) 6.84, 10 Wally Brown (Can) 6.63, 11 Sandy Duncan (Eng) 6.61. Note: Hal and Wally Brown were twin brothers.

TRIPLE JUMP (12 Feb): 1 Jack Metcalfe (Aus) 15.49, 2 Lloyd Miller (Aus) 15.41, 3 Basil Dickinson (Aus) 15.28, 4 Ray Graf (Aus) 14.62, 5 Hal Brown (Can) 14.08, 6 Bertie Shillington (NI) 13.94, 7 Jim Panton (Can) 13.37, 8 Wally Brown (Can) 12.23.

SHOT (12 Feb): 1 Louis Fouche (SA) 14.48, 2 Eric Coy (Can) 13.96, 3 Francis Drew (Aus) 13.80, 4 William Plummer (Aus) 13.55, 5 Harry Wilson (Aus) 13.19, 6 William MacKenzie (Aus) 12.84, 7 Jim Courtright (Can) 12.11, 8 George Sutherland (Can) 11.99.

DISCUS (7 Feb): 1 Eric Coy (Can) 44.76, 2 David Young (Sco) 43.05, 3 George Sutherland (Can) 41.47, 4 Harry Wilson (Aus) 40.61, 5 Keith Pardon (Aus) 39.73, 6 William MacKenzie (Aus) 39.31, 7 Adrian Button (Aus) 38.30, 8 Jack Morgan (NZ) 36.56, 9 Jim Courtright (Can) 30.22.

HAMMER (10 Feb): 1 George Sutherland (Can) 48.71, 2 Keith Pardon (Aus) 45.13, 3 Jim Leckie (NZ) 44.34, 4 Pat McNamara (Aus) 42.61, 5 Myer Rosenblum (Aus) 41.39, 6 Les Graham (Aus) 40.07.

JAVELIN (5 Feb): 1 Jim Courtright (Can) 62.80, 2 Stan Lay (NZ) 62.21, 3 Jack Metcalfe (Aus) 55.53, 4 Hal Brown (Can) 53.31, 5 James Barlow (Aus) 51.53, 6 David Goode (Aus) 50.32, 7 Bert Sheiles (Aus) 49.95, 8 John Clarke (NI) 49.65.

WOMEN

100 YARDS (5 Feb): 1 Decima Norman (Aus) 11.1, 2 Joyce Walker (Aus) 11.3e, 3 Jeanette Dolson (Can) 11.4e, 4 Barbara Burke (SA) 11.5e, 5 Joan Woodland (Aus) 11.5e, 6 Barbara Howard (Can) 11.6e.

220 YARDS (12 Feb): 1 Decima Norman (Aus) 24.7, 2 Jean Coleman (Aus) 25.1e, 3 Eileen Wearne (Aus) 25.3e, 4 Aileen Meagher (Can) 25.5e, 5 Barbara Burke (SA), 6 Irene Talbot (Aus).

80 METRES HURDLES (12 Feb): 1 Barbara Burke (SA) 11.7, 2 Isobel Grant (Aus) 11.7, 3 Rona Tong (NZ) 11.8e, 4 Clarice Kennedy (Aus), 5 Thelma Peake (Aus). Did not finish - Kathleen Tiffin (Eng). This race is considered to be wind-assisted.

440 YARDS RELAY - 220, 110, 110 - (7 Feb): 1 Australia (Jean Coleman, Eileen Wearne, Decima Norman) 49.1, 2 Canada (Aileen Meagher, Jeanette Dolson,

Barbara Howard) 49.5, 3 England (Kathleen Stokes, Dorothy Saunders. Winifred Jeffrey) 51.3, 4 New Zealand (Mary Mitchell, Doris Strachan, Rona Tong). 4 teams competed.

660 YARDS RELAY - 2 x 220, 2 x 110 - (5 Feb): 1 Australia (Jean Coleman, Decima Norman, Thelma Peake, Joan Woodland) 1:15.2, 2 England (Kathleen Stokes, Ethel Raby, Dorothy Saunders, Winifred Jeffrey) 1:17.2e, 3 Canada (Violet Montgomery, Barbara Howard, Aileen Meagher, Jeanette Dolson) 1:19.0e. 3 teams competed.

HIGH JUMP (12 Feb): 1 Dorothy Odam (Eng) 1.60, 2 Dora Gardner (Eng) 1.57, 3 Betty Forbes (NZ) 1.57, 4 Margaret Bell (Can) 1.57, 5 Doris Carter (Aus) 1.55, 6 Elsie Poore (Aus) 1.42, 7 Isabella Miller (Can) 1.37.

LONG JUMP (7 Feb): 1 Decima Norman (Aus) 5.80, 2 Ethel Raby (Eng) 5.66, 3 Thelma Peake (Aus) 5.55, 4 Evelyn Goshawk (Can) 5.38, 5 Mary Holloway (Eng) 5.22, 6 Doris Strachan (NZ) 5.20, 7 Dora Gardner (Eng) 5.14, 8 Thelma Norris (Can) 5.12, 9 Isabella Miller (Can) 4.88, 10 Enid Evans (Aus) 4.83, 11 Yvonne Dingley (Can) 4.58, 12 Nell Gould (Aus) 4.51.

JAVELIN (10 Feb): 1 Robina Higgins (Can) 38.28, 2 Antonia "Toni" Robertson (SA) 36.98, 3 Gladys Lunn (Eng) 36.41, 4 Mary Mitchell (NZ) 35.98, 5 Elsie Jones (Aus) 31.00, 6 Lena Mitchell (Aus) 30.56, 7 Clarice Kennedy (Aus) 29.66.

5.

Barefoot in the rain,
Jack's a winner after 16 years

EDEN PARK, AUCKLAND, NEW ZEALAND
4-11 FEBRUARY 1950

THE TASK OF REVIVING THE EMPIRE GAMES after a 12-year hiatus fell to the New Zealanders, and though this had to be an austerity-conscious affair, as had been the case at the London Olympics two years previously, it was a resounding success which attracted huge crowds and was marred only by occasional lapses in organisation. The home countries and their overseas partners were still recovering from the affects of the Second World War, and not surprisingly there were prominent athletes unable to spare the time for a winter adventure which would start for the Britons with a sea voyage well before Christmas 1949, enlivened by whist drives, sing-songs, deck quoits, Horlicks and sandwiches to finish off the day, and all in bed by 10.30 p.m. There were training sessions at Curacao and at a US military base in Panama City on New Year's Eve as the "S.S. Tamaroa" wended its leisurely way across the oceans. Roger Bannister and Bill Nankeville, England's leading milers, were among those who had regretfully turned down their invitations, while the AAA six miles champion, who was a displaced person from Estonia named Valdu Lillakas, and Europe's leading sprinter, Trinidad-born Emmanuel McDonald Bailey, were sadly never asked at all. Disappointingly, there was also a clash of fixtures with the Central American & Caribbean Games, which meant that the great Jamaican quarter-milers, Herb McKenley and George Rhoden, were otherwise engaged, and also missing was their compatriot, Arthur Wint, the

39

Olympic 400m champion. The saddest loss of all had been that of New Zealand's greatest athlete, Jack Lovelock, whose death at the age of 39 as a result of falling under a New York subway train had been reported two months before the Games opened.

There was one Olympic gold-medallist present - the Australian high jumper, John Winter - as well as five silver-medallists, and there were seven men and one woman among the entries who had competed in the prewar Empire Games. Most remarkable of all was the presence of Stan Lay, the javelin winner from 1930, making a nostalgic return in his home country at the age of 43, and not much his junior were Jack Holden, 42, who had run in the 1934 six miles, as well as Don Finlay, 40, and Tom Lavery, 38, the 120 yards hurdles champions from London and Sydney. Keith Pardon and Jim Leckie, 2nd and 3rd in the 1938 hammer, also reappeared, and among the favourites for a title was Duncan White, of Ceylon, who had run in the Sydney sprints as a teenager and then won the 400m hurdles silver medal at the 1948 Olympics. The solitary lady in this company, and much the youngest, was Dorothy Tyler (nee Odam), a mere 29, with an Empire gold, two Olympic silvers and two World records already to her credit and much more to come.

The citizens of Auckland responded to the Games with boundless enthusiasm - not least among them a group of a dozen leading businessmen who clubbed together to raise the £50,000 the Games were expected to cost - and the four sessions of athletics each attracted attendances of over 40,000. The opening day was Saturday 4 February and blessed with glorious sunshine for the finals at 100 yards, six miles and high jump for men and 100 yards for women. Without the West Indian sprinters, Australia's John Treloar seemed to be the 100 yards favourite and he produced the fastest first-round time of 9.7, set a personal-best 9.6 in the semi-finals, and then won the final in 9.7, with only a fiery little Canadian named Don Pettie, who managed to talk his way out of being disqualified for two false starts and delayed the final for an hour in the process, preventing an Australian sweep of the medals. There was never much doubt that Australia would also win the women's 100 yards as their team included 18-year-old Marjorie Jackson, who had equalled the World record of 10.8 the previous month, and Shirley Strickland, who had won the Olympic 100m bronze in 1948, but what was a surprise was that on the grass track laid out at Auckland's famous rugby football ground, and admitted by New Zealanders themselves to be outdated, Jackson should run 10.8 again in the very first heat at 3.10 in the afternoon. She was scarcely any slower in the semi-final with a time of 10.9, and that was equalled by Strickland, but in the final Jackson got a marvellous start and won again in 10.8 with two yards to spare over her Australian team-mate. It was obvious that the teenager from Geelong was going to be just as much a star of these Games as Dashing Dessie Norman had been in 1938.

New Zealand's six milers had a lot to live up to with Bill Savidan and Cecil Matthews having won prewar titles, but again they found the man for the occasion as Harold Nelson, who had finished down the field in the 1948 Olympic 10,000m and had only been 2nd in his national championships, gallantly held off the challenges of a Scotsman, Andrew Forbes, happily telling everyone afterwards that the cheering had been so loud in the last half-mile that he felt as if he was being carried along on a wave of sound. For Forbes a silver medal was adequate recompense to his benefactor, Sir Alexander King, who had paid the air fares to New Zealand for both him and the high-jump silver-medallist, Alan Paterson, because they could not afford to be away for the 2 fi months entailed in the sea voyage. In the high jump John Winter had become the first man to add an Empire title in a field event to an earlier Olympic gold, but the most intriguing feature was the debut of the Nigerians, and the joint 2nd place gained alongside Paterson by Joshua Majekodunmi seemed to herald a new and exciting development of the event. In the 880 heats the New Zealander, Doug Harris, who had been the fastest man in the World three years earlier, pulled out after a lap with a leg injury and the winners were Bill Parnell (Canada) and John Parlett (England).

The finals on the second day - Tuesday 7 February - were at 880, three miles, 440 hurdles, long jump and discus for men and the high jump for women. The half-mile was a disappointment with Parlett emerging in the last 50 yards of a disjointed and ill-tempered race to win in a time a full second slower than he had run in qualifying, and the three miles was no more distinguished with Len Eyre, of England, who had been sent to Auckland as a miler, overtaking the six-mile champion, Harold Nelson, in the last furlong to win in a time which was 24secs slower than Cecil Matthews's record from 1938. However, the courageous hurdling of the

Ceylonese, Duncan White, who had beaten the Games record with 52.8 in his heat the previous Saturday, made much amends. White hit a hurdle hard early on in the final and almost fell but recovered to catch the New Zealander, John Holland (inevitably nicknamed "Dutch"), and win in 52.5, and but for his mishap he might well have broken the World record of 52.2. In the discus the Games record was beaten in curious circumstances by Ian Reed, of Australia, who won the competition at 156ft 7in (47.72m) and was then allowed an extra throw, with which he improved to 158ft 0 3/4in (48.17m), because of some unexplained fault in the throwing circle. Dorothy Tyler beat her team-mate, Bertha Crowther, on countback of failures for her second high-jump title, while four of the men's 100 yards finalists came through the early rounds of the 220 and again no sprinter from the home countries reached the final.

Thursday 9 February was the third day of competition with finals at 220, 120 hurdles, triple jump, shot and women's 220, hurdles and javelin. The respective Australian winners at 100 yards duly succeeded again in the longer sprint: John Treloar by three yards from his 18-year-old team-mate, David Johnson, in an unspectacular time of 21.5, and Marjorie Jackson in the most marvellous fashion with a World record-equalling 24.3 not that far ahead of Shirley Strickland, who ran 24.5. The 120 yards hurdles final brought together the prewar winners, Lavery and the silver-haired Finlay, and two outstanding Australians, Peter Gardner and Ray Weinberg, and it was another 1-2 for Australia, with Gardner winning in 14.3. Later in the month he recorded a 14.2 and this was a time beaten by only five other men in the World, all of them American, during the year. The Australians, enjoying a resoundingly successful day, then took 1-2-3 in the triple jump, as 20-year-old Brian Oliver produced another performance of the very highest calibre at 51ft 2 1/2in (15.60m), which was to be the World's fourth best in 1950 though still short of the great Jack Metcalfe's Games record of 16 years before. Of no consequence so far as distances were concerned, but providing great enjoyment for the spectators, was the unexpected shot-putt win for a genial Fijian, Mataika Tuicakau, in the absence of England's John Savidge who had thrown over a metre further only a couple of months previously. Then there were yet more Australian golds for Charlotte MacGibbon in the javelin and for Shirley Strickland at 80m hurdles.

The remaining finals at Eden Park - 440, mile, 4 x 110 and 4 x 440 relays, pole vault, hammer and javelin for men and two sprint relays and the long jump for women - were held in pouring rain on Saturday 11 February, but the performance of the day came in the marathon out on Auckland's suburban roads. Jack Holden, who had not matched up to expectations when he missed out on an Empire Games medal at six miles back in 1934 and again when he dropped out of the Olympic marathon in 1948, took the lead at seven miles and gradually pulled away to win by over four minutes, but nothing is ever quite as simple as that when it comes to marathon-racing and Holden experienced rather more drama than he would have cared for. He threw away his sodden canvas shoes and ran the last 10 miles barefoot, blistered and bleeding, fending off a Great Dane which lunged at him in the closing stages, and received one of the greatest ovations of the Games on his final lap of the stadium. The one-man Welsh team in Auckland, 39-year-old Tom Richards, was expected to be Holden's main rival as he had won the Olympic silver in 1948 but finished more than nine minutes behind.

Inevitably, the mile final was eagerly awaited, and even without an obvious World-beater in the field it did not disappoint. Len Eyre, who had already won the three miles and in the absence of Roger Bannister and Bill Nankeville was England's No.1 miler, made most of the pace after a 59sec first lap and led by more than 10 yards into the final straight but was caught and passed by the 880 bronze medallist from Canada, Bill Parnell, whose time of 4:11.0 beat Jim Alford's Games best and was a fine achievement on a waterlogged track. At 440 yards the 21-year-old Australian, Edwin Carr, who had equalled his own national record of 47.6 the previous New Year's Eve and whose father had been an Olympic semi-finalist at 100 and 200m in 1924, was considered favourite without the presence of the great Jamaican trio, and even described as a "dead certainty", but he was given a desperately close race in drenching rain and through ankle-deep pools of surface water by England's Les Lewis. The 41,000 spectators roared their approval as Carr, throwing himself at the tape, equalled the Games record of 47.9 and Lewis, whose leading leg appeared to have crossed the line in front, was adjudged 2nd in 48.0. The two of them met again in the 4 x 440 relay, which Australia won rather comfortably, and Lewis turned out for a third time that afternoon in the 4 x 110, but again England were beaten by

Australia and John Treloar won his third gold medal.

It would have been nothing short of sensational if the Australian women had managed to lose either of the sprint relays, and Marjorie Jackson and Shirley Strickland added two more golds apiece, though this was the last occasion on which two such similar events were held before the standard 4 x 110 was brought in four years later. The one other women's final produced one of the finest performance of a Games which had already seen a profusion of records broken as 20-year-old Yvette Williams delighted her home crowd with a long-jump win over the favoured Judy Canty, of Australia, at 19ft 4 5/8in (5.90m), and, even though this beat the 20-year-old Empire record and would turn out to be the second best performance in the World for the year, the measurement did not by any means do Miss Williams justice. The rain had deadened the run-up and made the takeoff slippery, and according to the officials at the long-jump pit she lost the best part of 12 inches when her feet slid in the wet sand and she fell backwards. An adept all-rounder who also placed 2nd in the javelin the same afternoon, Yvette Williams was destined to become one of the greatest of women athletes from the British Empire.

Duncan McDougall Munro Clark - who, of course, could only possibly be Scottish with a name such as that - won the hammer throw with yet another Games record, as Keith Pardon repeated his 2nd place of 12 years before, and a few days later Clark threw a British record of 180ft 1 1/8in (54.89m) which ranked 10th in the World for the year, but the men's pole vault and javelin, admittedly hampered by the weather, were only of mediocre standard. This, though, was a much rarer occurrence than in previous Games, and the most heartening aspect of the four days of competition was aptly expressed in a detailed and perceptive 100-page post-Games report published in the magazine, "The New Zealand Sportsman", which concluded that *"of a welter of lasting memories of top-line achievements, perhaps the most vivid were the amazing performances of the women".* A hauntingly lyrical view of the Games was taken by the poet, Neil McKinnon, who composed a tribute in verse for the "Auckland Star" newspaper which contained the following opening lines:

> *Taut as a screaming wire*
> *Is the tension.*
> *The runners crouch*

In poised tableau,
Vibrant and tremulous,
Translating for
Eternal seconds
The grace and poignance
Of man's aspiration
For perfection.

RESULTS 1950

MEN

100 YARDS (4 Feb): 1 John Treloar (Aus) 9.7, 2 Bill de Gruchy (Aus) 9.8, 3 Don Pettie (Can) 9.9, 4 Alastair "Scotchy" Gordon (Aus) 9.9, 5 Peter Henderson (NZ) 9.9, 6 Clem Parker (NZ) 10.0.

220 YARDS (9 Feb): 1 John Treloar (Aus) 21.5, 2 David Johnson (Aus) 21.8, 3 Don Jowett (NZ) 21.8, 4 Alastair "Scotchy" Gordon (Aus) 21.9, 5 Don Pettie (Can) 21.9, 6 Clem Parker (NZ) 22.2.

440 YARDS (11 Feb): 1 Edwin Carr (Aus) 47.9, 2 Les Lewis (Eng) 48.0, 3 David Batten (NZ) 48.8, 4 Derek Pugh (Eng), 5 Ross Price (Aus), 6 Jack Sutherland (NZ).

880 YARDS (7 Feb): 1 John Parlett (Eng) 1:53.1, 2 Jack Hutchins (Can) 1:53.4, 3 Bill Parnell (Can) 1:53.4, 4 David White (Aus) 1:53.7, 5 Tom White (Eng) 1:53.9, 6 Colin Simpson (NZ) 1:56.0, 7 Schalk Booysen (SA), 8 Noel Wilson (NZ).

1 MILE (11 Feb): 1 Bill Parnell (Can) 4:11.0 , 2 Len Eyre (Eng) 4:11.8, 3 Maurice Marshall (NZ) 4:13.2, 4 John Marks (Aus) 4:14.8, 5 Tom White (Eng) 4:15.0, 6 Jack Sinclair (NZ) 4:20.6, 7 Don Macmillan (Aus), 8 Jack Hutchins (Can).

3 MILES (7 Feb): 1 Len Eyre (Eng) 14:23.6, 2 Harold Nelson (NZ) 14:27.8, 3 Tony Chivers (Eng) 14:28.1, 4 Alan Merritt (Aus) 14:34.0, 5 Ken MacDonald (Aus) 14:35.9, 6 Colin Lousich (NZ) 14:41.0, 7 Les Perry (Aus). Also ran - Andrew Forbes (Sco), George Hoskins (NZ), Noel Taylor (NZ). Did not finish - Bill Emmerton (Aus), Rich Ferguson (Can).

6 MILES (4 Feb): 1 Harold Nelson (NZ) 30:29.6, 2 Andrew Forbes (Sco) 30:31.9, 3 Noel Taylor (NZ) 30:31.9, 4 John Davey (Aus) 30:34.7, 5 Alan Merritt (Aus) 30:46.3, 6 Tony Chivers (Eng) 31:15.2, 7 Jack Holden (Eng), 8 Sid Luyt (SA), 9 John Pottage (Aus), 10 Paul Collins (Can), 11 George Norman (Can), 12 Walter Fedorick (Can). Did not finish - Colin Lousich (NZ).

MARATHON (11 Feb): 1 Jack Holden (Eng) 2:32:57.0, 2 Sid Luyt (SA) 2:37:02.2, 3 Jack Clarke (NZ) 2:39:26.4, 4 Gordon Stanley (Aus) 2:40:49.0, 5 Tom Richards (Wal) 2:42:10.6, 6 Paul Collins (Can) 2:45:01.4, 7 Bill Bromily

(NZ) 2:46:51.0, 8 George Norman (Can) 2:47:49.8, 9 Bob Prentice (Aus) 2:48:53.8, 10 Walter Fedorick (Can) 2:51:28.6, 11 Gerard Cote (Can) 2:51:51.6, 12 Arthur Lydiard (NZ) 2:51:58.8, 13 Lionel Fox (NZ) 2:57:47.2, 14 Jack Paterson (Sco) 3:00:58.8. Did not finish - Bill Emmerton (Aus), John Pottage (Aus).

120 YARDS HURDLES (9 Feb): 1 Peter Gardner (Aus) 14.3, 2 Ray Weinberg (Aus) 14.4, 3 Tom Lavery (SA) 14.6, 4 Don Finlay (Eng) 14.7, 5 John Holland (NZ), 6 Lionel Smith (NZ).

440 YARDS HURDLES (7 Feb): 1 Duncan White (Cey) 52.5, 2 John Holland (NZ) 52.7, 3 Geoff Goodacre (Aus) 53.1, 4 George Lubbe (SA), 5 Harry Whittle (Eng), 6 George Gedge (Aus).

4 x 110 YARDS RELAY (11 Feb): 1 Australia (Bill de Gruchy, David Johnson, Alastair "Scotchy" Gordon, John Treloar) 42.2, 2 England (Les Lewis, Brian Shenton, Nick Stacey, Jack Archer) 42.5, 3 New Zealand (Clem Parker, Peter Henderson, Kevin Beardsley, Arthur Eustace) 42.6, 4 Ceylon (Sumana Navaratnam, John de Saram, Oscar Wijayasinghe, Duncan White). 4 teams competed.

4 x 440 YARDS RELAY (11 Feb): 1 Australia (Ross Price, George Gedge, James Humphreys, Edwin Carr) 3:17.8, 2 England (Terry Higgins, John Parlett, Derek Pugh, Les Lewis) 3:19.3, 3 New Zealand (John Holland, David Batten, Derek Steward, Jack Sutherland) 3:20.0, 4 Ceylon (John de Saram, Oscar Wijayasinghe, A. Sompala, Duncan White) 3:22.8, 5 Canada (Bill La Rochelle, Bill Parnell, Don Pettie, Jack Hutchins). 5 teams competed.

HIGH JUMP (4 Feb): 1 John Winter (Aus) 1.98, 2= Joshua Majekodunmi (Nig) & Alan Paterson (Sco) 1.95, 4 John Borland (NZ) 1.95, 5 Peter Wells (Eng) 1.93, 6 Ron Pavitt (Eng) 1.90, 7 John Vernon (Aus) 1.90, 8 Doug Stuart (Aus) 1.88, 9 Mervyn Peter (Aus) 1.88, 10 Art Jackes (Can) 1.85, 11= Christiaan de Jongh (SA), Ray McKenzie (NZ) & Lloyd Valberg (Mal) 1.83, 14= Orisi Dawai (Fij), Boniface Guobadia (Nig), Eric Rhodes (NZ) & Roy Woolley (NZ) 1.75.

POLE VAULT (11 Feb): 1 Tim Anderson (Eng) 3.96, 2 Stan Egerton (Can) 3.96, 3 Peter Denton (Aus) 3.88, 4 Wallace Heron (NZ) 3.88, 5 Ron Miller (Can) 3.81, 6 George Martin (NZ) 3.73, 7 Doug Robinson (Can) 3.73, 8 Mervyn Richards (NZ) 3.67, 9 Joshua Olotu (Nig). Note: Olotu may not have cleared a height.

LONG JUMP (7 Feb): 1 Neville Price (SA) 7.31, 2 Bevan Hough (NZ) 7.20, 3 David Dephoff (NZ) 7.08, 4 Keith Forsyth (NZ) 7.08, 5 Harry Whittle (Eng) 6.91, 6 Karim Olowu (Nig) 6.91, 7 Mohamed Sheriff (Cey) 6.55.

TRIPLE JUMP (9 Feb); 1 Brian Oliver (Aus) 15.61, 2 Les McKeand (Aus) 15.28, 3 Ian Polmear (Aus) 14.67, 4 Roger Johnson (NZ) 14.51, 5 Keith Forsyth (NZ) 14.22, 6 Graeme Jeffries (NZ) 14.09, 7 Neville Price (SA) 14.00, 8 Alan Lindsay (Sco) 13.97, 9 Colin Kay (NZ) 13.91, 10 Harry Whittle (Eng) 12.89.

SHOT (9 Feb): 1 Mataika Tuicakau (Fij) 14.63, 2 Harold Moody (Eng) 13.92, 3 Leo Roininen (Can) 13.68, 4 Doug Herman (NZ) 13.41, 5 Jack Morgan (NZ) 13.36, 6 C.L. "Tiny" Main (NZ) 12.60, 7 Duncan McDougall Clark (Sco) 12.07, 8 Manasa Nukuvou (Fij) 11.93.

DISCUS (7 Feb): 1 Ian Reed (Aus) 47.72, 2 Mataika Tuicakau (Fij) 43.96, 3 Svein Sigfusson (Can) 43.48, 4 Keith Pardon (Aus) 41.10, 5 Gus Redmond (NZ) 40.44, 6 Ronald Trangmar (Rho) 39.27, 7 Harold Moody (Eng) 39.06, 8 Max Carr (NZ) 38.63. Note: because of unexplained irregularities in the circle Reed was allowed an extra throw which was 48.17 and was accepted as a Games record.

HAMMER (11 Feb): 1 Duncan McDougall Clark (Sco) 49.94, 2 Keith Pardon (Aus) 47.84, 3 Herb Barker (Aus) 45.62, 4 Norman Drake (Eng) 44.78, 5 Alan Fuller (NZ) 43.65, 6 Max Carr (NZ) 42.85, 7 Jim Leckie (NZ) 41.62, 8 Keith Allen (Aus) 41.31, 9 John Brown (NZ) 41.23, 10 Svein Sigfusson (Can) 37.25.

JAVELIN (11 Feb): 1 Leo Roininen (Can) 57.11, 2 Luke Tunabuna (Fij) 56.02, 3 Doug Robinson (Can) 55.60, 4 Anthony Hignell (Eng) 55.34, 5 Claude Clegg (NZ) 53.62, 6 Stan Lay (NZ) 53.44, 7 Les McKeand (Aus) 50.29.

WOMEN

100 YARDS (4 Feb): 1 Marjorie Jackson (Aus) 10.8, 2 Shirley Strickland (Aus) 11.0, 3 Verna Johnston (Aus) 11.1, 4 Doris Parker (NZ) 11.2, 5 Shirley Hardman (NZ) 11.3, 6 Ann Shanley (Aus) 11.4. Note: Doris Parker was the sister of relay bronze-medallist Clem Parker.

220 YARDS (9 Feb): 1 Marjorie Jackson (Aus) 24.3, 2 Shirley Strickland (Aus) 24.5, 3 Daphne Robb (SA) 24.7, 4 Doris Parker (NZ) 24.8, 5 Verna Johnston (Aus) 25.3, 6 Lesley Rowe (NZ).

80 METRES HURDLES (9 Feb): 1 Shirley Strickland (Aus) 11.6, 2 June Schoch (NZ) 11.6, 3 Joan Shackleton (NZ) 11.7, 4 Noeline Gourlay (NZ) 11.9, 5 Ann May Stalder (Aus) 11.9, 6 Pixie Fletcher (NZ).

440 YARDS RELAY - 220, 110, 110 - (11 Feb): 1 Australia (Marjorie Jackson, Shirley Strickland, Verna Johnston) 47.9, 2 New Zealand (Lesley Rowe, Shirley Hardman, Doris Parker) 48.7, 3 England (Sylvia Cheeseman, Margaret Walker, Dorothy Manley) 50.0, 4 Canada (Eleanor McKenzie, Gerry Bemister, Peggy Moore). 4 teams competed.

660 YARDS RELAY - 2 X 220, 2 X 110 - (11 Feb): 1 Australia (Shirley Strickland, Verna Johnston, Marjorie Jackson, Ann Shanley) 1:13.4, 2 England (Margaret Walker, Doris Batten, Sylvia Cheeseman, Dorothy Manley) 1:17.5, 3 Canada (Eleanor McKenzie, Gerry Bemister, Pat Jones, Elaine Silburn). New Zealand (Doris Parker, Lesley Rowe, Ruth Dowman, Shirley Hardman), 2nd in 1:16.8, disqualified for dropping baton. 4 teams competed.

HIGH JUMP (7 Feb): 1 Dorothy Tyler (Eng) 1.60, 2 Bertha Crowther (Eng) 1.60, 3 Noeline Swinton (NZ) 1.55, 4 Dorothy Manley (Eng) 1.52, 5= Beverley Brewis (NZ) & Shirley Gordon (Can) 1.47, 7= Joan Morrison (Aus), Elaine Silburn (Can) & Rosella Thorne (Can) 1.47, 10 Jacqueline Baumann (Aus) 1.47. Note: Tyler nee Odam.

LONG JUMP (9 Feb): 1 Yvette Williams (NZ) 5.91, 2 Judy Canty (Aus) 5.77, 3 Ruth Dowman (NZ) 5.74, 4 Verna Johnston (Aus) 5.54, 5 Elaine Silburn (Can) 5.35, 6 Edith Anderson (Sco) 5.23, 7 Rosella Thorne (Can) 5.21, 8 Dorothy Tyler (Eng) 5.08, 9 Bertha Crowther (Eng) 4.97, 10 Jean Desforges (Eng) 4.96, 11 June Schoch (NZ) 4.66.

JAVELIN (9 Feb): 1 Charlotte MacGibbon (Aus) 38.84, 2 Yvette Williams (NZ) 37.97, 3 Cleo Rivett-Carnac (NZ) 34.43, 4 Dorothy Tyler (Eng) 32.85, 5 Bertha Crowther (Eng) 26.02. 5 competed.

6.

The "Bannister & Landy" Show
but a strong supporting cast

EMPIRE STADIUM, VANCOUVER, CANADA
30 JULY-7 AUGUST 1954

TO HAVE MERELY DESCRIBED IT AS the "Mile Of The Century" would have been gross devaluation. To call it the "Mile Of The Millenium" seemed neither pretentious then in the introverted days of the mid-1950s, nor does it pall by comparison with all the other much lauded record-breaking mile races which have taken place since. It was a promoter's dream which would have earned the chief participants a King's ransom in a later generation, but Roger Bannister and John Landy were two gentlemen of the track perfectly content to run for their expenses and the honour of representing their countries. If it was an altogether different era to what has followed later, it also marked a major change from just four years before, and this was no better illustrated than by the fortunes of the 1950 mile champion, Bill Parnell.

Having won so surprisingly in Auckland, Parnell had only marginally improved in the interim to a best of 4:09.6 and now found himself in the unenviable position of defending his title in front of his fellow citizens against Bannister, who had run his historic first sub-four-minute mile at Oxford the previous May, and Landy, who had come desperately close to four minutes on numerous occasions, and invariably in adverse conditions in his native Australia, and had then achieved 3:57.9 in Finland in June. Times, indeed, were changing, and Parnell was one of only five athletes attempting a second successive Empire Games win. Not only Bannister and Landy had set World records in the months leading up to the Vancouver gathering: the Australian sprinter, Hec Hogan, had sped to a 9.3 100 yards on grass; Jim Peters had run the fastest-ever marathon for the fourth time in two years; and the marvellous New Zealand all-rounder, Yvette Williams, had long jumped 6.28 to beat a record which had been held by the great Fanny Blankers-Koen for over 10 years. Furthermore, Williams had won Olympic gold in 1952, as had Marjorie Jackson (now Mrs Nelson) at 100 and 200 metres.

Empire records had also been regularly surpassed during the first half of 1954 in field events long regarded as Second Division, and in some cases the amendments were long overdue. Geoff Elliott, of England, had already beaten Vic Pickard's pole-vault best after 23 years and had made five further improvements to 4.26 on the eve of the Vancouver Games. Neville Price, of South Africa, had set his first Empire long-jump record in 1949, beating a mark held by the Irishman, Peter O'Connor, since 1901 (!), and had progressed further to 7.67 in Texas in April. John Savidge, of England, who had missed out on the 1950 Games, had bettered the Empire shot record six times, culminating with a 16.83 in May. Another Englishman, Mark Pharaoh, had achieved a discus best of 49.68 virtually unnoticed because it was the same night as Bannister's sub-four-minute mile, and a Canadian, Gino Roy Pella, had easily beaten that with 52.28 only eight days later. The South African hammer-thrower, Vic Dreyer, had apparently removed another ancient record, dating from 1911, with a throw of 56.81, but it was disallowed because of sloping ground. Yvette Williams had equalled her shot record of 13.33, first set in the 1952 Olympics, and had thrown the discus 46.18.

Whereas there had been 193 competitors from 12 countries in Auckland in 1950, there were 252 from 23 countries in Vancouver. Bermuda, Fiji and Northern Rhodesia sent women athletes for the first time, and among the men's teams were the Bahamas, Gold Coast, India, Jamaica, Kenya, Nigeria, Pakistan, Trinidad and Uganda. It had taken almost a quarter-of-a-century to achieve, but at long last the Games were beginning to reflect the true ethnic mix of the Empire, and the first appearance of one of those newcomers was to have particularly far-reaching repercussions that no one could possibly have foreseen. The international debut of the Kenyan distance-runners at the AAA Championships a month before the Empire Games had seemed no more than an exotic interlude at the time: a 19-year-old named Lazaro Chepkwony led the six miles for 11 laps and only retired because he had apparently dislocated his knee; and then a barefoot Tisii tribesman, Nyandika Maiyoro, ran the first mile of the three miles seven seconds inside World-record pace and still finished 3rd. Oh, well, we thought as we watched agog, the poor lads don't know what they're doing. Of course, what they knew and we didn't was that all our pre-conceived Western ideas of distance races being run with civilised restraint and careful judgment were merely sophisticated inhibitions.

In perfect summer's weather, but with only 11,400 people in attendance apparently as a reaction to high ticket prices, the first day's competition on Saturday 31 July featured finals for the 100 yards, six miles and high jump and for the women's 100 yards and shot. In the six miles the England team captain, Jim Peters, led at four miles and with four laps to go his team-mates, Peter Driver and Frank Sando, started to pull away. Driver, coached by the 1938 Empire mile champion, Jim Alford, won with a blazing 58.6 last lap and Sando and Peters completed the first clean sweep in any Games track event for men since England had done the same at 440, three miles and the steeplechase 20 years earlier. Chepkwony, amazingly recovered from his AAA ordeal, was a commendable 7th. Yvette Williams easily won the shot with a new Empire record of 45ft 9 (13.96), and the sprint finals both produced new Games records, but the undoubted star of the day was a 19-year-old Nigerian, Emmanuel Arinze Ifeajuna, who was only 5ft 7 (1.70) tall but set another new Empire record - the first ever by a black African athlete - of 6ft 8 (2.03) in the high jump with what was described as *"quite breath-taking raw spring"*. In the men's 100 yards it was apparent from the first round onwards that the Australian, Hec Hogan, was not in his World-record form, and it was the equally powerful but much more elegant Mike Agostini, of Trinidad, who won in 9.6, setting another precedent by becoming the first West Indies champion at the Empire Games. Needless to say, Marjorie Nelson sustained her reputation as the World's leading woman sprinter by winning her event in 10.7 from the delightfully-named Winsome Cripps, who had been 4th in both sprints at the 1952 Helsinki Olympics, and Northern Rhodesia's Edna Maskell, who had competed for South Africa in those Games. Another record went in the

440 hurdles heats when 18-year-old David Lean, of Australia, ran 52.3.

Tuesday 3 August was cloudy, cool and occasionally rainy for the finals at 880, three miles, 440 hurdles, triple jump, discus and women's high jump, and English runners were again 1-2-3 in two of the events. The Kenyan novice, Maiyoro, was still with the leaders at the bell in the three miles but was outkicked as Chris Chataway, who had helped pace Bannister to his mile record and had then shared a World record at three miles in the AAA Championships though beaten by Freddie Green, won from Green and Sando, but still the Kenyan's performance, improving another 11secs to finish 4th, would be seen in retrospect as the most significant of them all. At 880 the astonishingly versatile Derek Johnson, whose talents ranged from 100 yards to the steeplechase during his career, held off Brian Hewson in a Games record 1:50.7, while the hurdles title went to Lean, who had only taken up the event earlier in the year, but he misjudged his pace and was slower than in his heat. A tired 6th in this event was England's Ken Wilmshurst, for whom the start of the race had been delayed while he became the first winner from the home countries in the triple jump, with only an inch to spare from Paul Esiri, of Nigeria. The title-holder Brian Oliver, an officer in the Royal Australian Air Force, grounded in 3rd position but was destined to achieve the unique feat for such a field-event specialist of winning further bronze medals in both relays later in the Games.

The women's high jump, remarkably, included three past or future World record-holders over a 17-year span: Dorothy Tyler, now 34, with 1.66 from 1939; Sheila Lerwill, with 1.72 from 1951; and Thelma Hopkins, who was to clear 1.74 in 1956. Hopkins, 18, and Yorkshire-born though representing Northern Ireland, won handily at the second best height in the World for the year of 5-6 (1.68), using the straddle technique which was much more efficient than the antiquated "scissors", and another defending champion (from both 1938 and 1950), Dorothy Tyler, was 2nd. In the discus the two Empire record-breakers, Pharaoh and Pella, were well beaten by a South African, Stephanus du Plessis, and in 5th place was an enterprising Welshman, Hywel Williams, who had paid his own way to the Games while on RAF service in Kenya.

The third day - Thursday 5 August - included finals at 220, 120 hurdles, long jump, shot, javelin and women's 220, hurdles and javelin, plus the mile heats, which attracted an extra 6,000 spectators. Bannister and Landy qualified without troubling themselves too much, but the title-holder, Bill Parnell, went out (as did a future Olympic steeplechase champion, Chris Brasher) and five runners in the first heat beat the Canadian's Games record. The most appealing competition of the day was in the men's javelin in which the unheralded Pakistanis, Muhammad Nawaz and Jalal Khan, were the leaders into the last round before James Achurch, of Australia, produced a final winning throw of 224-9 1/2 (68.51). Though still modest by World standards, both this throw and the earlier effort of 223-4 1/2 (68.08) by Nawaz beat the Empire record which had astonishingly (and depressingly) been set no less than 36 years earlier by Stan Lay, and there was further evidence of slow but steady progress with an English record of 216ft 7 (66.01) by Dennis Tucker. The shot title went at last to the Empire record-holder, 6ft7in (2.01) tall Royal Marine John Savidge, and the long jump to Ken Wilmshurst - the first man to win both horizontal jumps - ahead of two more Nigerians, Karim Olowu and Sylvanus Williams, with the Empire record-holder, Neville Price, not among the entries presumably because of commitments to the US university where he was studying.

Continuing the theme of this being the Games with a difference, none of the 100 yards medallists also figured in the first three at 220. Hec Hogan, Canada's Harry Nelson and Welshman Ken Jones had all run in the 100 final, and Jones got 3rd at 220 in his last international appearance at the age of 32, while the bronze-medallist from 1950, New Zealand's Don Jowett, won by a foot from Brian Shenton, of England. Jowett also progressed through the heats and semi-finals of the 440 in which Kevan Gosper, a US-based Australian, impressively but unnecessarily won his heat by a dozen yards in a Games record of 47.1. Marjorie Nelson, who had equalled the Games 220 record of 24.3 two days earlier despite slowing to a jog at the finish, won the final as she had done in 1950 and set a World record - again just as she had done in Auckland - with 24.0, though by all accounts not looking as impressive as in qualifying. Less predictably, another World record was equalled when Edna Maskell won the 80m hurdles final in 10.9 and became Northern Rhodesia's first Games champion, though the time was subsequently declared to be wind-assisted.

For the last day of competition - Saturday 7 August - it was again high summer, with the temperature 75 degrees in the shade, if any was to be found, and 35,500 people at last packing the Empire Stadium for the eagerly anticipated mile final, plus the 440, both relays, pole vault, hammer, marathon and women's long jump, discus and relay. No allowance had been made for the weather or the well-being of the 16 marathon competitors in sending them off at 12.30 p.m., but the English duo of Jim Peters and Stan Cox, who had both run exceptionally well in the six-mile track race earlier, seemed to be coping and Peters passed 20 miles in a brisk 1hr 48min (around 2:23 pace) with Cox about a quarter-of-a-mile behind. Yet half of the starters had already dropped out, and unbeknown to the enthralled crowd in the stadium watching the milers come to their marks at 2.30 p.m. the conditions and the severely hilly course were about to take their toll of the few remaining survivors.

The line-up for the mile was Landy, of Australia; Baillie and Halberg, of New Zealand; Ferguson, of Canada; Milligan, of Northern Ireland; and Bannister, Boyd and Law, all of England and all closely associated with Oxford University - Bannister and Law as graduates and 20-year-old undergraduate Boyd, who had placed 3rd in the Empire Games 880 though only 4th in the Inter-Varsity match earlier in the year! Baillie and Law led briefly before Landy, with his characteristic clipped stride, went ahead and at the end of the first lap (58.2) was five yards in front of Bannister, who had rightly already sensed the danger. Landy, clearly determined to make the pace so fast that Bannister would lack the reserves for his famous finishing sprint, went on through the half-mile in 1:58.2 and increased his lead to 10 yards, but in the third lap Bannister, with the patience of a stalking lion, steadily reduced the margin to no more than a couple of strides at the bell (2:58.4). To the wild excitement of the spectators Landy held his lead round the final curve of the track and just as he glanced over his left shoulder to see how he was getting on Bannister swept by on his right and strode majestically on to win by four or five yards. It was the most memorable of races, and remains so to this day. The time for Bannister, as it happens, was 3:58.8, and almost half-a-century later 800 or so other runners can now claim to have beaten four minutes for the mile, and there is realistic prospect that 3mins 40secs might be achieved not long into the 21st Century. Yet in the minds of all who saw them, and of those who have assiduously studied the statistics and history of the sport ever since,

55

Bannister and Landy still stand alongside Elliott, Snell, Ryun, Walker, Coe, Cram, Ovett, Morceli and El Guerrouj in the pantheon of Miracle Milers who have so radically improved on those times since.

Out on the marathon course the exhausted Stan Cox had been told of Bannister's win as he was taken off to hospital by ambulance after collapsing on the climb of Powell Street at 25 miles, and Peters was now 15 minutes in front of the stragglers but unaware that he was dangerously dehydrated. On the steep ramp down into the stadium his sense of balance went and he collapsed repeatedly as he tried to cover the remaining lap of the track. After 10 minutes or so of this harrowing spectacle the England team manager mercifully intervened and Peters was taken away to the same hospital as his team-mate, Cox, spending the next seven hours in an oxygen tent but thankfully surviving eventually unscathed. He never competed again.

Though close to the stadium the next runner in the race - Joe McGhee, of Scotland - had stopped and was waiting for an ambulance when he heard that Peters and Cox had failed to finish. So he climbed back to his feet and plodded on to finish 1st. The most surprised, surprising and courageous winner of the Games, McGhee was a 24-year-old RAF officer whose only previous performance of any real note had been a modest 50th place in the International cross-country championship earlier in the year. His winning time of 2:39:36 was only four minutes or so slower than what he had achieved in the Scottish championship to qualify for the Games, and the 22-year-old South African, Jackie Mekler, who finished 2nd just over a minute later, had to be carried out on a stretcher to the victory dais and supported by McGhee himself during the medal ceremony because his feet were so blistered. Only four others completed the course.

Of course, all else paled into insignificance compared to this Shakespearean drama, and yet there were more fine performances and Games records galore. Kevan Gosper won the 440 for Australia as expected, but the 220 champion, Don Jowett, ran him close with his fastest ever time. Geoff Elliott, the muscular blond-haired decathlete from England, equalled his own Empire record of 14ft (4.27) in the pole vault. There was a first Games gold for Pakistan as a 6ft 3in (1.90m) tall Army infantryman, Muhammad Iqbal, won the hammer (and a week later in London broke the Empire record with 193-3/58.90). Yvette Williams collected her third and fourth gold medals in the long jump and discus. Then the relays provided a perfect climax to the Games with three immensely exciting races: Canada's men beat Nigeria by the proverbial thickness of a vest at 4 x 110, both recording 41.3 to tie the Empire record, with a makeshift Australian team which contained only one genuine sprinter an enterprising 3rd; Australia's women, overwhelming favourites at the same distance, were saved embarassment by the incomparable Marjorie Nelson, who in her last race before retirement made up three yards on England's Ann Pashley on the anchor leg to register her seventh win and her seventh record in seven Empire Games finals; and England, with the 880 yards champion, Derek Johnson, running the last leg, just got home at 4 x 440 ahead of a Canadian team of which the oldest member was only 21.

A mere four Games records that remained unbeaten were at 220 yards, 120 yards hurdles, the marathon and triple jump (still Jack Metcalfe from 1934) for men. Much more meaningful than this for the coming of age of the Games was the fact that Trinidad, Jamaica, Nigeria, Pakistan and Northern Rhodesia had won gold medals and athletes from British Guiana, Kenya, Uganda, Southern Rhodesia and the Gold Coast had achieved honourable top-six placings in finals. Everyone's memories were tinged, of course, with sadness at the fate of Jim Peters, but even he had unwittingly written himself into the history-books. The British magazine, "Athletics Weekly", proclaimed prophetically in the stiff-upper-lip manner of the day: *"Don't feel you have let the Old Country down, Jim. We think just as much of you now as we should have done if you'd won the race in World record time. No one could have put up a better show of British 'guts' and we're proud of you."*

RESULTS 1954

MEN

100 YARDS (31 Jul): 1 Mike Agostini (Tri) 9.6, 2 Don McFarlane (Can) 9.7, 3 Hec Hogan (Aus) 9.7, 4 Edward Ajado (Nig) 9.7, 5 Harry Nelson (Can) 9.7, 6 Ken Jones (Wal) 9.8.

220 YARDS (5 Aug): 1 Don Jowett (NZ) 21.5, 2 Brian Shenton (Eng) 21.5, 3 Ken Jones (Wal) 21.9, 4 Harry Nelson (Can) 22.0, 5 Hec Hogan (Aus) 22.0, 6 George Ellis (Eng) 22.2.

440 YARDS (7 Aug): 1 Kevan Gosper (Aus) 47.2, 2 Don Jowett (NZ) 47.4, 3 Terry Tobacco (Can) 47.8, 4 Peter Fryer (Eng) 48.4, 5 Jim Rogers (BG) 48.5, 6 Alan Dick (Eng) 48.6.

880 YARDS (3 Aug): 1 Derek Johnson (Eng) 1:50.7, 2 Brian Hewson (Eng) 1:51.2, 3 Ian Boyd (Eng) 1:51.9, 4 Bill Baillie (NZ) 1:52.5, 5 Rich Ferguson (Can) 1:52.7, 6 Jimmy Hamilton (Sco) 1:52.7, 7 Bill Parnell (Can) 1:53.8, 8 Doug Clement (Can) 1:54.9. Did not finish - Jim Bailey (Aus).

1 MILE (7 Aug): 1 Roger Bannister (Eng) 3:58.8, 2 John Landy (Aus) 3:59.6, 3 Rich Ferguson (Can) 4:04.6, 4 Victor Milligan (NI) 4:05.0, 5 Murray Halberg (NZ) 4:07.2, 6 Ian Boyd (Eng) 4:07.2, 7 Bill Baillie (NZ) 4:11.0. Did not finish - David Law (Eng).

3 MILES (3 Aug): 1 Chris Chataway (Eng) 13:35.2, 2 Freddie Green (Eng) 13:37.2, 3 Frank Sando (Eng) 13:37.4, 4 Nyandika Maiyoro (Ken) 13:43.8, 5 Peter Driver (Eng) 13:47.0, 6 Geoff Warren (Aus) 13:50.0, 7 Ian Binnie (Sco) 13:59.6, 8 Laurie King (NZ) 14:03.4, 9 Ernest Haskell (NZ) 14:07.0, 10 Allan Lawrence (Aus) 14:16.0, 11 Henry Kennedy (Can) 14:20.0, 12 Lazaro Chepkwony (Ken) 14:27.0, 13 Selwyn Jones (Can) 14:33.0, 14 Jim Daly (NZ) 14:41.0. Did not finish - Lyle Garbe (Can), Doug Kyle (Can).

6 MILES (31 Jul): 1 Peter Driver (Eng) 29:09.4, 2 Frank Sando (Eng) 29:10.0, 3 Jim Peters (Eng) 29:20.0, 4 Geoff Warren (Aus) 29:42.6, 5 Stan Cox (Eng) 30:11.4, 6 Ian Binnie (Sco) 30:15.2, 7 Lazaro Chepkwony (Ken) 30:16.2, 8 Allan Lawrence (Aus) 30:18.8, 9 Laurie King (NZ) 31:01.9, 10 Selwyn Jones (Can)

31:05.0, 11 Ernest Haskell (NZ) 31:41.0. Did not finish - Doug Kyle (Can), Neil Robbins (Aus).

MARATHON (7 Aug): 1 Joe McGhee (Sco) 2:39:36.0, 2 Jackie Mekler (SA) 2:40:57.0, 3 Jan Barnard (SA) 2:51:49.8, 4 Barry Lush (Can) 2:52:47.4, 5 George Hillier (Can) 2:58:43.4, 6 Robert Crossen (NI) 3:00:12.2. Did not finish - Gerard Cote (Can), Stan Cox (Eng), Keith Dunnett (Can), Rowland Guy (Aus), John Kay (NR), Allan Lawrence (Aus), Kevin MacKay (Aus), George Norman (Can), Jim Peters (Eng), Leslie Stokell (Can).

120 YARDS HURDLES (5 Aug): 1 Keith Gardner (Jam) 14.2, 2 Chris Higham (Eng) 14.9, 3 Norm Williams (Can) 14.9, 4 Jack Parker (Eng) 15.0, 5 David Lean (Aus) 15.1. Did not finish - Ken Doubleday (Aus).

440 YARDS HURDLES (3 Aug): 1 David Lean (Aus) 52.4, 2 Harry Kane (Eng) 53.3, 3 Bob Shaw (Wal) 53.3, 4 David Fleming (NZ) 53.9, 5 Murray Gaziuk (Can) 55.5, 6 Ken Wilmshurst (Eng) 56.3.

4 x 110 YARDS RELAY (7 Aug): 1 Canada (Don McFarlane, Don Stonehouse, Harry Nelson, Bruce Springbett) 41.3, 2 Nigeria (Edward Ajado, Karim Olowu, Abdul Karim Amu, Muslim Arogundade) 41.3, 3 Australia (Kevan Gosper, Brian Oliver, Hec Hogan, David Lean) 41.7, 4 England (Ken Box, Alan Lillington, George Ellis, Brian Shenton) 41.9, 5 Pakistan (Abdul Khaliq, Muhammad Sharif Butt, Muhammad Aslam, Abdul Aziz) 42.0, 6 Jamaica (Les Laing, Ronald Horsham, Frank Hall, Keith Gardner).

4 x 440 YARDS RELAY (7 Aug): 1 England (Peter Higgins, Alan Dick, Peter Fryer, Derek Johnson) 3:11.2, 2 Canada (Laird Sloan, Doug Clement, Joe Foreman, Terry Tobacco) 3:11.6, 3 Australia (Brian Oliver, Don Macmillan, David Lean, Kevan Gosper) 3:16.0, 4 Kenya (Kipkorir Boit, Kiptalam Keter, Korigo Barno, Charles Musembi) 3:17.6, 5 Gold Coast (John Quartey, Edward Nyako, Henry Ofori-Nyako, Richard Ampadu) 3:18.6, 6 Jamaica (Louis Gooden, Richard Estick, Keith Gardner, Les Laing) 3:19.0.

HIGH JUMP (31 Jul): 1 Emmanuel Ifeajuna (Nig) 2.03, 2 Patrick Etolu (Uga) 1.99, 3 Nafio Osagie (Nig) 1.99, 4 Peter Wells (NZ) 1.95, 5 Doug Stuart (Aus) 1.93, 6 John Vernon (Aus) 1.93, 7 Derek Cox (Eng) 1.88, 8 Kiprono Maritim (Ken) 1.88, 9 Murray Jeffries (NZ) 1.88, 10 Jonathan Lenemuria (Ken) 1.83, 11 Ajit Singh (Ind) 1.83, 12 Kevin McMahon (Aus) 1.83, 13 David Blair (Can) 1.83, 14 Bob Adams (Can) 1.83, 15 Victor Cassis (Can) 1.78, 16 Ian Hume (Can) 1.78.

Note: Peter Wells had competed for England in 1950; Murray Jeffries was the brother of Graeme Jeffries, 6th in the 1950 triple jump.

POLE VAULT (7 Aug): 1 Geoff Elliott (Eng) 4.27, 2 Ron Miller (Can) 4.20, 3 Andries Burger (SA) 4.13, 4 Bob Adams (Can) 3.96, 5 Mervyn Richards (NZ) 3.96, 6 Orland Anderson (Can) 3.96, 7 Bruce Peever (Aus) 3.81, 8 Peter Denton (Aus) 3.81, 9 Bob Reid (Can) 3.81.

LONG JUMP (5 Aug): 1 Ken Wilmshurst (Eng) 7.54, 2 Karim Olowu (Nig) 7.39, 3 Sylvanus Williams (Nig) 7.22, 4 Derek Cox (Eng) 7.21, 5 Hec Hogan (Aus) 7.06, 6 Gerald Brown (SR) 7.05, 7 Benjamin Laryea (GC) 6.76, 8 Graham Turnbull (Can) 6.74, 9 Keith Gardner (Jam) 6.66, 10 Ben Brooks (Can) 6.57, 11 David Stafford (Can) 6.47, 12 Lenwood Goodine (Can) 6.38.

TRILE JUMP (3 Aug): 1 Ken Wilmshurst (Eng) 15.27, 2 Paul Esiri (Nig) 15.25, 3 Brian Oliver (Aus) 15.14, 4 George Armah (GC) 14.41, 5 Robert McLaughlin (Can) 14.34, 6 Laurence Ogwang (Uga) 14.13, 7 Jack Smyth (Can) 13.56, 8 Victor Cassis (Can) 13.28, 9 Tom Skimming (Can) 13.24.

SHOT (5 Aug): 1 John Savidge (Eng) 16.77, 2 John Pavelich (Can) 14.95, 3 Stephanus du Plessis (SA) 14.93, 4 Stan Raike (Can) 14.67, 5 Lionel Whitman (Can) 14.54, 6 Mark Pharoah (Eng) 14.27, 7 Parduman Singh (Ind) 13.88, 8 Geoff Elliott (Eng) 13.75, 9 Eric Coy (Can) 13.37, 10 Derek Cox (Eng) 12.60, 11 Hywel Williams (Wal) 12.29. Note: Eric Coy was the only Vancouver male competitor to have also taken part in the 1938 Games.

DISCUS (3 Aug): 1 Stephanus du Plessis (SA) 51.71, 2 Gino Roy Pella (Can) 49.54, 3 Mark Pharoah (Eng) 47.85, 4 Stan Raike (Can) 45.72, 5 Hywel Williams (Wal) 45.18, 6 Ken Swalwell (Can) 44.85, 7 Svein Sigfusson (Can) 43.63, 8 Mesulame Rakuro (Fij) 42.71, 9 John Savidge (Eng) 41.86, 10 Parduman Singh (Ind) 41.37.

HAMMER (7 Aug): 1 Muhammad Iqbal (Pak) 55.38, 2 Vic Dreyer (SA) 54.75, 3 Ewan Douglas (Sco) 52.80, 4 Don Anthony (Eng) 52.19, 5 Peter Allday (Eng) 51.92, 6 Alex Valentine (Sco) 51.53, 7 Jim Lally (NI) 47.88, 8 Max Carr (NZ) 47.86. Note: this was the first Empire Games field event to have a separate qualifying event and therefore not to be contested as a straight final.

JAVELIN (5 Aug): 1 James Achurch (Aus) 68.51, 2 Muhammad Nawaz (Pak) 68.08, 3 Jalal Khan (Pak) 67.50, 4 Dennis Tucker (Eng) 66.01, 5 Johnny Veitch

(SA) 62.34, 6 Maboria Tesot (Ken) 61.89, 7 Kevin Flanagan (NI) 61.68, 8 Viliame Liga (Fij) 60.88, 9 Semi Qio (Fij) 59.36, 10 William Donawa (Tri) 55.51, 11 John Roberts (Wal) 55.05, 12 Tito Elo (Fij) 53.87, 13 Ian Hume (Can) 52.16, 14 Ted Cadell (Can) 48.25.

WOMEN

100 YARDS (31 Jul): 1 Marjorie Nelson (Aus) 10.7, 2 Winsome Cripps (Aus) 10.8, 3 Edna Maskell (NR) 10.8, 4 Ann Pashley (Eng) 10.9, 5 Gerry Bemister (Can) 10.9, 6 Heather Armitage (Eng) 11.0. Note: Nelson nee Jackson.

220 YARDS (5 Aug): 1 Marjorie Nelson (Aus) 24.0, 2 Winsome Cripps (Aus) 24.5, 3 Shirley Hampton (Eng) 25.0, 4 Ann Johnson (Eng) 25.2, 5 Heather Armitage (Eng) 25.3, 6 Gerry Bemister (Can) 25.5.

80 METRES HURDLES (5 Aug): 1 Edna Maskell (NR) 10.9, 2 Gwen Hobbins (Can) 11.2, 3 Jean Desforges (Eng) 11.2, 4 Pam Seaborne (Eng) 11.3, 5 Shirley Eckel (Can) 11.3, 6 Yvette Williams (NZ) 11.4.

4 x 110 YARDS RELAY (7 Aug): 1 Australia (Gwen Wallace, Nancy Fogarty, Winsome Cripps, Majorie Nelson) 46.8, 2 England (Shirley Hampton, Shirley Burgess, Heather Armitage, Ann Pashley) 46.9, 3 Canada (Margery Squires, Dorothy Kozak, Annabelle Murray, Gerry Bemister) 47.8. 3 teams competed.

HIGH JUMP (3 Aug): 1 Thelma Hopkins (NI) 1.68, 2 Dorothy Tyler (Eng) 1.60, 3 Alice Whitty (Can) 1.60, 4 Sheila Lerwill (Eng) 1.57, 5= Carol Bernoth (Can) & Noeline Swinton (NZ)1.55, 7 Ruth Hendron (Can) 1.47, 8 Heather Walker (Can) 1.47, 9 Marlene Middlemiss (Aus) 1.42. Note: Tyler nee Odam.

LONG JUMP (7 Aug): 1 Yvette Williams (NZ) 6.08, 2 Thelma Hopkins (NI) 5.84, 3 Jean Desforges (Eng) 5.84, 4 Rosella Thorne (Can) 5.44, 5 Ann Johnson (Eng) 5.42, 6 Annabelle Murray (Can) 5.40, 7 Gwen Wallace (Aus) 5.30, 8 Margery Squires (Can) 5.30, 9 Thelma Jones (Ber) 5.25, 10 Edna Maskell (NR) 5.07, 11 Dorothy Tyler (Eng) 5.06, 12 Terry Thornhill-Fisher (NR) 4.98, 13 Betty Blackburn (NZ) 4.89, 14 Sainiana Sorowale (Fij) 4.75.

SHOT (31 Jul): 1 Yvette Williams (NZ) 13.96, 2 Jackie McDonald (Can) 12.98, 3 Magdalena Swanepoel (SA) 12.81, 4 Val Lawrence (Aus) 12.31, 5 Terry Thornhill-Fisher (NR) 12.30, 6 Suzanne Allday (Eng) 11.96, 7 Mary Lawrence (Can) 10.41, 8 Heather Walker (Can) 9.32, 9 Helen Metchuk (Can) 8.65.

DISCUS (7 Aug): 1 Yvette Williams (NZ) 45.02, 2 Suzanne Allday (Eng) 40.02, 3 Marie Anne Depree (Can) 38.66, 4 Helen Metchuk (Can) 36.52, 5 Val Lawrence (Aus) 31.86, 6 Shirley Couzins (Can) 28.00.

JAVELIN (5 Aug): 1 Magdalena Swanepoel (SA) 43.83, 2 Terry Thornhill-Fisher (NR) 41.97, 3 Shirley Couzins (Can) 38.98, 4 Mary Lawrence (Can) 35.18, 5 Dorothy Tyler (Eng) 32.93, 6 Suzanne Allday (Eng) 28.30.

7.

Gert and Herb:
four-letter words spelling out "G-O-L-D"

THE 1956 OLYMPICS HAD BEEN HELD in Melbourne and among the stars had been the great Australian sprinters, Betty Cuthbert, winning the 100m and 200m, and Shirley Strickland (now Mrs de la Hunty), winning the hurdles, with both of them also sharing in relay success. Their closest challenge had come from Great Britain in the 4 x 100m and there had been totally unexpected victories by an English-born New Zealander, Norman Read, in the longest event of all, the 50 kilometres walk, and by a British Guiana-born Briton, Chris Brasher, in the steeplechase. There were silver medals for two reigning Empire champions, Derek Johnson and Thelma Hopkins, among others, and Australia had won 12 medals in all and Britain seven, with only the political and athletic super-powers, the USA and the USSR, inevitably doing better. In the afterglow of this elevated performance on the World stage, the prospects were alluring for the VIth British Empire & Commonwealth Games, as they were now entitled, to be staged at another famous rugby ground, Cardiff Arms Park.

A new track prepared by Archie McTaggart, the green-fingered groundsman at Motspur Park, in South London, where Sydney Wooderson had broken pre-war World records, was laid around the hallowed turf, and the entries came flooding in: a total of 353 men and 84 women from 32 countries, including the Bahamas, Gibraltar, Hong Kong, the Isle of Man, Jersey, Mauritius, North Borneo, Sarawak, Singapore and St Vincent. There were so many declarations for the men's 100 yards (59 in all) and 440 yards (42) that extra rounds had to be added the day before the Games even officially opened. Disappointingly, the programme of events was still limited: no opportunity for Norman Read or Chris Brasher because their events were not included; nothing for the all-rounders; and still no race further than 220 yards for women. Leading up to the Games there had been a further spate of Commonwealth records, and most encouragingly in the field events in particular. Hendrik Kruger, of South Africa, had taken the pole-vault record up to 4.42; Arthur Rowe, a brawny Yorkshire blacksmith, improved his shot record to 17.30 at the AAA Championships; the discus title-holder, Stephanus ("Fanie") du Plessis, threw 54.90; Mike Ellis, of England, exceeded the hammer record six times during 1957, with a best of 64.56; and Colin Smith, also of England, had thrown the javelin 75.16. Valerie Sloper was established as a most worthy successor in New Zealand to the great Yvette Williams, with six shot records between 1955 and 1957, culminating in 16.29, and she was also one of three record-breakers in the discus in which Suzanne Allday, of England, had eventually thrown 47.70. Albie Thomas, one of the new breed of Australian distance-runners, had set a World record of 13:10.8 for three miles, and two hurdlers had matured to the highest class - Keith Gardner, Jamaica's Empire champion at 120 yards hurdles, running 13.9 in the USA in May, and Gerhardus ("Gert") Potgieter, of South Africa, setting a 400 metres hurdles best of 50.0 in Germany in early July.

Most impressive of all, though, had been those Australian women sprinters. The previous March the World record for 100 yards of 10.4, held by Marjorie Nelson, had been equalled by Betty Cuthbert, with Marlene Willard (nee Mathews) probably also running 10.4 though not getting credit for it, and the following week Cuthbert had improved the 220 record to 23.5. Then at the national championships a fortnight later Willard had won both races from Cuthbert in new record times of 10.3 and 23.4.

Gardner and du Plessis were in Cardiff to defend their titles, as were Mike Agostini (100 yards), Kevan Gosper (440 yards), David Lean (440 hurdles), Geoff Elliott (pole vault), Ken Wilmshurst (long and triple jumps), Muhammad Iqbal (hammer), Thelma Hopkins (high jump) and Magdalena Swanepoel (javelin), and the very first race on the pre-opening day gave a clear indication that the track was fast and this was going to be a Games where the unexpected would happen. Tom Robinson, a powerfully-built 20 year-old sprinter from the Bahamas, practically unknown even to the most knowledgable of athletics fans, came charging home in heat one of the 100 yards with a Games and British all-comers' record of 9.5, unmatched by any of the other heat winners, including Agostini (now a Canadian citizen) and the versatile Gardner.

The Games were formally opened by the Duke of Edinburgh on Friday 18 July and the Queen delighted the 25,000 crowd by sending a message that she intended to invest Prince Charles with the title of Prince of Wales. The next day - which was very sunny and warm - there was an even bigger attendance of 32,000 to watch the remaining three rounds of the 100 yards, the six miles, high jump, javelin and women's shot. Times were being taken as usual on hand-held watches, but automatic recordings were also being made by the Racecourse Technical Services Company and there were to be, as one would expect in allowing for the tendency of human timekeepers to anticipate finishes, some significant discrepancies. The variations are illustrated by the fact that Robinson ran 9.6 (9.81 automatic) and Gardner 9.5 (9.69) in the second round and then Robinson was given 9.5 (9.70 automatic) and Gardner 9.6 (9.74) in winning the semi-finals. In the final the pair of them, both familiar with frenetic 60-yard racing indoors in the USA, got the best starts, but the wiry Jamaican was a couple of feet up at halfway and just managed to resist Robinson's final lunge for the tape. Even the automatic timer could only separate the two of them by 3/100ths of a second - 9.66 to 9.69 - with the defending champion, Agostini, a yard further back in 3rd place.

The six milers suffered from the heat, even though their race did not start until 5.30 p.m. and the favoured Englishman, Stan Eldon, did his cause no further good by running the first mile at way inside World-record schedule. Australia's aptly-named Dave Power took up the lead at halfway and held off the spirited challenges of the 22-year-old Welshman, John Merriman, over a last lap, which naturally brought the spectators to a fever pitch of excitement. The Kenyans continued their advance with Arere Anentia winning their first Games medal and Kanuti Sum placing 6th. The high jump, with 27 competitors, went on for most of the day - six hours in all - but the winner, Ernle (yes, ERNLE not ERNIE) Haisley, of Jamaica, still had the stamina and skill to clear 6-9 (2.06) and there were four

Africans in the top six. Colin Smith won the javelin for England, as had been considered likely, and the 5ft 11in (1.80) tall Valerie Sloper easily took the shot. Both qualifying rounds of the 440 hurdles produced Games records for Gert Potgieter, and Marlene Willard was fastest of the women in the 100 yards heats with 10.7 (10.85 automatic).

Another near-capacity crowd of 32,000 turned out for the third session of competition - Tuesday 22 July - and it can be justifiably described as one of the most memorable days in the history of the Games. The highlight was a new World record at 440 yards hurdles by Potgieter (pronounced "Poch-reeter"), but there was much else besides of the very highest order as the other finals to be decided were the 880 yards, three miles, long jump, discus and women's 100 yards and high jump. The three miles field included the World record-holder, Thomas, and the Games six-mile champion, Power, for Australia; the World record-holders at one mile and 3000m (and both of them Olympic 5000m medallists), Derek Ibbotson and Gordon Pirie, for England; the other six-mile medallists, Merriman and Anentia; and the New Zealanders, Murray Halberg and Bill Baillie, who had both taken part in the epic Bannister-Landy mile in Vancouver. At two miles Thomas led a group of eight, but then Halberg suddenly raced to the front and ran right away from the rest, covering the last three-quarters-of-a-mile in 3:11.4. Halberg was handicapped by a withered left arm as the result of a childhood rugby-football accident but was a ferociously determined competitor who would subsequently win Olympic gold and break Thomas's three-mile record.

For the half-mile England had not selected the defending champion, Derek Johnson, but still had four qualifiers, though Ted Buswell had to withdraw after discovering he had run his heat with a broken bone in his right foot, and among the three who came to the line were Brian Hewson, the AAA champion and silver-medallist from the 1954 Games, and Mike Farrell, who had reached the Olympic final in 1956. The first lap was ridiculously slow with the Scot, Les Locke, the reluctant leader in 58.8 before the 20-year-old Australian prodigy, Herb Elliott, took off and ran the second circuit in 50.5. Hewson, understandably, could never quite get on terms with this searing pace and a full dozen yards behind in 3rd place was Mike Rawson, who was to win the European 800m title three weeks later. A chilly wind sprang up for the 440 hurdles final, but 21-year-old Potgieter

- in lane five with the holder, Lean, outside him - ignored it and ran a monumental race, catching his man before halfway, and storming on to a World record time of 49.7 (49.73, to be precise) which was worth better than the metric equivalent set by Glenn Davis, of the USA. In the 1956 Olympic final, won by Davis, the then teenage Potgieter had been in the bronze-medal position until falling at the last barrier.

Another South African, Fanie du Plessis, wrapped up the discus from the first round, setting a new Commonwealth record of 183ft 6 1/2in (55.94) with his fourth throw, and Marlene Willard secured Australia's fourth successive Games win at 100 yards, with yet another Games and British all-comers' record of 10.6 (10.70), but England's Heather Young and 17-year-old Madeleine Weston both beat Betty Cuthbert. All three women's high-jump medallists were also teenagers and 5ft 8in (1.73) tall Australian Michele Mason, 19, who was still employing the uneconomic "scissors" style, beat 5ft 3in (1.60) New Zealander Mary Donaghy, 18, on fewer failures at a Games record 5-7 (1.70). Donaghy's clearance, using the "Western Roll" technique, at four inches above her own head represented the best such differential ever achieved by a woman, according to the authoritative account by Mel Watman in the magazine, "Athletics Weekly". Even the qualifying times on this Day of Days were extraordinary: Tom Robinson and the South African, Ed ("Judge") Jefferys, ran 20.86 and 20.95 respectively in the 220 semi-finals, both credited with a Games record 20.9, and the second round of the 440 - maybe benefiting from a swirling breeze at track level - was simply amazing. For example, Ted Sampson was only the third-ranked Englishman but broke the European record with 46.8 (46.90), having previously never run faster than 47.6, while the heats which followed were won in 46.71 (Malcolm Spence, of South Africa), 46.78 (Terry Tobacco, of Canada, who had been bronze-medallist in 1954) and 47.05 (Milkha Singh, of India). Even the leading women sprinters, though required to run two rounds of the women's 220 after the 100 final, were irrepressible: the hand times for Cuthbert (23.94) and Willard (24.04) both officially equalling Marjorie Nelson's Games record of 24.0.

Thursday 24 July was again sunny and very windy. The crowd figure was up to 32,800 for finals at 220, 440, 120 hurdles, triple jump and shot, the marathon race, and the women's 220 and javelin. As in Vancouver the mile heats were a major added attraction. In a wind-affected 220 final Tom Robinson reversed the finishing positions from the other sprint final, winning a thrillingly close race in which only 7/100ths separated the first three, and the weather slowed all the 440 runners except for the marvellously fluent Milkha Singh, who won in 46.6 (46.71) from Spence and Tobacco, after Ted Sampson had been bumped firmly back to reality by being eliminated in the semi-finals (48.18). Keith Gardner coped more than adequately with three races at 120 hurdles, as well as the 220 final, and retained his title in 14.0 (14.20), though the South African, Jacobus Swart, was pressing him hard until hitting the last hurdle. Then in the field events Arthur Rowe set another Commonwealth record of 17.57 in the shot to compare favourably with the Americans, of whom only four would rank ahead of him in the World standings at the year's end, and the unpredictable variations of the breeze may well have decided the title in the triple jump. Luckless Jack Smyth, of Canada, cleared a legal 51-5 3/4 (15.69) in the first round to beat Jack Metcalfe's 24-year-old Games record, but Australia still won the gold because at the fourth attempt Ian Tomlinson reached two inches further (15.74) with the only wind-assisted jump of the 48 which were taken throughout the final. Smyth was more than three inches ahead of Tomlinson's legal best, but the rules could make no allowance for such vagaries in an otherwise satisfyingly cosmopolitan competition also involving athletes from Nigeria, North Borneo, Singapore and Uganda.

This was another World record day for the Games, though it came as much more of a surprise than in the 440 hurdles. Anna Pazera was a 21-year-old born in Poland and only recently qualified for Australia who came to the Games with a best javelin throw of 164ft 5 1/2 (50.13) and went back to her new home as not only the Empire & Commonwealth champion but also the World record-holder at 188-4 (57.40)! This enormous throw came in the fourth round, at which stage Pazera had been in 2nd place more than six feet behind the title-holder, Magdalena Swanepoel, and was apparently boosted by a tailwind of six metres per second (around 12 m.p.h.), but unlike the sprints, hurdles and jumps no restriction is imposed on wind assistance for record acceptance purposes in the javelin. Mrs Pazera never approached that distance again in the years that followed, but there is no doubt of her talent: as Anna Wojtaszek in her native Poland she had already ranked 20th in the World when still only 17. No records in the women's 220, though the 23.65 clocking for Marlene Willard, drawn in the outside lane and winning from Betty Cuthbert, was excellent in the conditions.

The marathon-men enjoyed the breeze almost as much as Mrs Pazera had as they set out along the Cardiff-to-Newport road at 2.40 p.m. in what would otherwise have been testing 70-degree temperatures, and the first move of any consequence came at six miles when a Welshman, Rhys Davies, no doubt inspired by the cheers of the bystanders at the sight of his familiar scarlet vest, went ahead with Dave Power, making his marathon debut and running his third distance race in five days. Power led Jan Barnard, of South Africa, by 10 seconds at 15 miles as Davies dropped back with cramp and, curiously for a race which is so often marked by high drama in the closing stages, nothing much changed for the rest of the way home. Power won by nearly the same margin from Barnard, insisting afterwards that he would never run a marathon again (he was wrong), and the first eight finishers beat the 1938 Games record.

The final day's events were on Saturday 26 July, and despite incessant rain all morning there was another full house for the finals of the mile, the pole vault, the hammer, the women's hurdles, long jump and discus, and the three relays. Three Australians (Elliott, Thomas and Merv Lincoln), three Englishmen (Hewson, Pirie and Mike Blagrove), two New Zealanders (Halberg and Neville Scott) and one Cheshire-domiciled Scotsman (Mike Berisford) had qualified for the mile, and it was Scott who for no obvious reason led through two steady laps to reach halfway in 2:03.4. Then Elliott went ahead and irresistibly drew further and further away: five yards up on Pirie at the bell after a 58.9 third lap; 10 yards ahead into the last turn; 20 yards clear at the finish, with Lincoln and Thomas coming through for an Australian 1-2-3 and England again failing to get a medal, as had been the case at three and six miles. Elliott, totally imperious, had run the last half-mile in an estimated 1:55.4 for a final time of 3:59.0, just short of Roger Bannister's Games record, and this was only the start of one of the greatest sequences of performances in the history of middle-distance running. On 4 August at the White City Stadium he ran the year's fastest 880 yards of 1:47.3 ... two evenings later in Dublin's Santry Stadium he made the largest single improvement on the World mile record since 1882 when he set a time of 3:54.5 ... on 28 August in Gothenburg he took more than two seconds off the 1500 metres record with 3:36.0 ... back in London on 3 September he ran another mile race in 3:55.4. In between times he won several other ultra-fast events, and his incomparable career reached its climax at the Rome Olympics two years later when he became the Olympic 1500-metre champion in another World record of 3:35.6.

There <u>was</u> an English win over Australia that day, and it was an outstanding one. With Willard and Cuthbert in their relay team the Australians seemed sure-fire winners, but England's elegant and efficient quartette of Madeleine Weston, Dorothy Hyman, June Paul and Heather Young were half-a-second faster in the heats and outclassed the opposition in the final with a World record of 45.3 (45.37 on the electronic timer). England's men also won at 4 x 110 with a Commonwealth record 40.72, but the South Africans took the 4 x 440, beating a Commonwealth record set by the great Jamaican Olympic gold medal team of 1952, as their anchor runner, Malcolm Spence, was timed at 45.1. Jamaica did get 3rd place on this occasion with the tireless Keith Gardner taking part in his eighth Empire & Commonwealth Games final. The women's hurdles went to Norma Thrower, of Australia, by inches over England's Carole Quinton, while in the men's field events Geoff Elliott retained his pole-vault title, but another 1954 champion, Muhammad Iqbal, lost an absorbing hammer contest to Mike Ellis. In the women's discus Suzanne Allday won the battle of the three Commonwealth record-breakers and completed a nice domestic double as husband Peter had placed 3rd in the hammer final which had opened the day's proceedings.

Mel Watman, as assiduous a reporter then as he still is now, had been keeping a careful tally of facts and figures for "Athletics Weekly" and in addition to the World records he reckoned that there had been 27 Commonwealth records, 37 British all-comers' records, 64 British records and 144 Games records! In spirit as much as in cold statistics this had been unquestionably the greatest athletics meeting ever seen in Britain, the cradle of the modern sport, and it was far and away the best so far in the Empire & Commonwealth Games series. For those of us who had sat enraptured in the stands for those five days in Cardiff in the summer of '58 it was to remain an unforgettable experience.

A PERSONAL POSTSCRIPT TO THE GAMES

The 1958 Empire & Commonwealth Games and the 1960 Olympic Games were the first of many great championships meetings which I have had the privilege of attending, and as a lifelong self-confessed athletics "nut" I readily admit that they continue to hold a special place in my affections. There was a profusion of great performances both in Cardiff, as related beforehand, and in Rome, but the unquestioned supreme champion of both, to my mind, was Herb Elliott. Having seen in action every great miler since Sydney Wooderson, with the exception of Hagg and Andersson, the wartime record-breakers from Sweden, I still have no doubt that Elliott remains the most accomplished of them all, even allowing for all the wonderful achievements of his illustrious successors. He was not a classic stylist, but he was a beautifully balanced runner, rather in the mould of Coe and El Guerrouj, with a rapid and raking stride, and he was a masterly strategist. He had the strength, stamina and confidence to start his finishing effort just as every other normal mortal was briefly gathering his resources for the traditional last-lap dash, and his sustained speed over the closing 700 metres or so, relative to such opposition as remained by that juncture, is unparalleled to this day.

He had been an outstanding junior athlete, setting World best performances for a 16-year-old, and in 1956 he joined the training group master-minded by the eccentric Percy Cerutty, who famously urged on his young proteges to spend spartan weekends running interminable repetitions barefoot up mountainous sand dunes and along twisting trails through the bush. It was the flamboyant Cerutty, three times Elliott's age and once aptly described as looking like a cross between Svengali and Salvador Dali, who according to legend leapt out of his seat in Rome and waved a white towel at Elliott to signify surrender - for the eight other runners in the final, that is. Well, I can vouch for the accuracy of the tale because Cerutty did just that right in front of my position on the back straight, but as to whether Elliott really had need of such a signal is another matter entirely. He seemed to run by glorious natural instinct, and on this occasion he simply loped away from the rest - a future World mile record-holder among them - and won in a time which remained unbeaten for

71

seven years. These days at least 40 men a year run faster than that as they chase the cash prizes on the lucrative Grand Prix circuit, but Elliott retired from international competition at the age of 22 because he had other things to do. We will never know what times he might have run had he persevered, but he had no need to because he had achieved everything in athletics there was to achieve. It is, of course, better that way. The legend of Herb Elliott remains pure and unsullied.

RESULTS 1958

MEN

100 YARDS (19 Jul): 1 Keith Gardner (Jam) 9.66, 2 Tom Robinson (Bah) 9.69, 3 Mike Agostini (Can) 9.79, 4 Peter Radford (Eng) 9.80, 5 Jimmy Omagbemi (Nig) 9.86, 6 Gordon Day (SA) 9.87.

220 YARDS (24 Jul): 1 Tom Robinson (Bah) 21.08, 2 Keith Gardner (Jam) 21.11, 3 Gordon Day (SA) 21.15, 4 Stan Levenson (Can) 21.51, 5 John Scott-Oldfield (Eng) 21.90. Did not finish - Ed Jefferys (SA). Note: the race was officially declared wind-assisted.

440 YARDS (24 Jul); 1 Milkha Singh (Ind) 46.71, 2 Malcolm Spence (SA) 46.90, 3 Terry Tobacco (Can) 47.05, 4 John Salisbury (Eng) 47.15, 5 John Wrighton (Eng) 47.24, 6 Jim MacIsaac (Sco) 48.82.

880 YARDS (22 Jul): 1 Herb Elliott (Aus) 1:49.32, 2 Brian Hewson (Eng) 1:49.47, 3 Mike Rawson (Eng) 1:50.94, 4 Terry Sullivan (NR) 1:51.24, 5 Donal Smith (NZ) 1:51.59, 6 Mike Farrell (Eng) 1:51.85, 7 Les Locke (Sco) 1:54.83. Note: Ted Buswell (Eng) qualified but did not start.

1 MILE (26 Jul): 1 Herb Elliott (Aus) 3:59.03, 2 Merv Lincoln (Aus) 4:01.80, 3 Albie Thomas (Aus) 4:02.77, 4 Gordon Pirie (Eng) 4:04.01, 5 Murray Halberg (NZ) 4:06.65, 6 Mike Berisford (Sco) 4:06.77, 7 Mike Blagrove (Eng) 4:07.78, 8 Brian Hewson (Eng) 4:10.95, 9 Neville Scott (NZ) 4:12.06.

3 MILES (22 Jul): 1 Murray Halberg (NZ) 13:14.75, 2 Albie Thomas (Aus) 13:24.37, 3 Neville Scott (NZ) 13:26.06, 4 Gordon Pirie (Eng) 13:29.45, 5 Peter Clark (Eng) 13:41.41, 6 John Merriman (Wal) 13:32.06, 7 Dave Power (Aus) 13:37.37, 8 Arere Anentia (Ken) 13:39.47, 9 Bill Baillie (NZ) 13:40.92, 10 Derek Ibbotson (Eng) 13:44.18, 11 Mike Bullivant (Eng) 13:45.67, 12 Nyandika Maiyoro (Ken), 13 David Richards (Wal), 14 Ian Binnie (Sco), 15 Barry Magee (NZ), 16 Joe Connolly (Sco), 17 William McCue (NI), 18 Kanuti Sum (Ken), 19 George de Peana (BG), 20 Mubarak Shah (Pak) 21 Abdul Wahab Salleh (Sar). Did not finish - Chepsiror Chepkwony (Ken), John Disley (Wal), Alastair Wood (Sco).

6 MILES (19 Jul): 1 Dave Power (Aus) 28:48.16, 2 John Merriman (Wal) 28:48.84, 3 Arere Anentia (Ken) 28:51.48, 4 Martin Hyman (Eng) 28:58.59, 6

Fred Norris (Eng) 29:44.0, 7 Joe Connolly (Sco) 30:20.4, 8 Barry Magee (NZ) 30:27.2, 9 Stan Eldon (Eng) 30:30.0, 10 Mubarak Shah (Pak) 31:03.2, 11 Hugh Foord (Eng) 31:03.2, 12 Ray Puckett (NZ) 31:57.2, 13 George de Peana (BG) 32:00.0. Did not finish - David Dodds (NR), Alastair Wood (Sco).

MARATHON (24 Jul): 1 Dave Power (Aus) 2:22:45.6, 2 Jan Barnard (SA) 2:22:57.4, 3 Peter Wilkinson (Eng) 2:24:42.0, 4 Eddie Kirkup (Eng) 2:27:31.2, 5 Gordon Dickson (Can) 2:28:42.2, 6 Colin Kemball (Eng) 2:29:17.2, 7 Alex McDougall (Sco) 2:29:57.2, 8 Kanuti Sum (Ken) 2:30:49.6, 9 Rhys Davies (Wal) 2:30:54.6, 10 Ron Franklin (Wal) 2:31:24.6, 11 John Russell (Aus) 2:34:56.2, 12 Arthur Keily (Eng) 2:34:59.4, 13 Marthinus Wiid (SA) 2:36:07.2, 14 Ray Puckett (NZ) 2:38:58.8, 15 Dyfrig Rees (Wal) 2:39:17.2, 16 David Dodds (NR) 2:45:20.0, 17 William Kelly (IoM) 2:50:36.2, 18 Tom Wood (Wal) 2:53:42.0, 19 Jimmy Todd (NI) 3:01:28.0, 20 John Henning (NI) 3:07:51.0, 21 Walter Dass (BG) 3:08:58.0. Did not finish - Jack Dawson (NI), Seki Etwaroo (BG), Harry Fenion (Sco), Hugo Fox (Sco).

120 YARDS HURDLES (24 Jul): 1 Keith Gardner (Jam) 14.20, 2 Jacobus Swart (SA) 14.30, 3 Ghulam Raziq (Pak) 14.32, 4 Peter Stanger (Can) 14.42, 5 Peter Hildreth (Eng) 14.50, 6 Beresford ("Berry") Primrose (Aus) 14.97. Note: assisting wind of 3.5m.

440 YARDS HURDLES (22 Jul): 1 Gert Potgieter (SA) 49.73, 2 David Lean (Aus) 50.59, 3 Bartonjo Rotich (Ken) 51.75, 4 John Metcalf (Eng) 52.35, 5 Chris Goudge (Eng) 52.39, 6 George Shepherd (Can) 52.69.

4 x 110 YARDS RELAY (26 Jul): 1 England (Peter Radford, Roy Sandstrom, Dave Segal, Adrian Breacker) 40.72, 2 Nigeria (Smart Akraka, Thomas Obi, Victor Odofin, Jimmy Omagbemi) 41.05, 3 Australia (Terry Gale, Kevan Gosper, Jim McCann, Hec Hogan) 41.64, 4 Canada (Peter Stanger, Mike Agostini, Stu Cameron, Stan Levenson) 41.74, 5 Wales (Ron Jones, John Morgan, David Roberts, Nick Whitehead) 42.13, 6 Uganda (Erasmus Amukun, S.G.Bwowe, Benjamin Nduga, Ignatius Okello) 42.17.

4 x 440 YARDS RELAY (26 Jul): 1 South Africa (Gordon Day, Gerald Evans, Gert Potgieter, Malcolm Spence) 3:08.21, 2 England (Ted Sampson, Derek Johnson, John Wrighton, John Salisbury) 3:09.61, 3 Jamaica (Gerald James, Mal Spence, George Kerr, Keith Gardner) 3:10.08, 4 Canada (Doug Clement, Joe Mullins, George Shepherd, Terry Tobacco) 3:12.72, 5 India (Alex Silveira, Daljit Singh, Wahid Usmani, Milkha Singh) 3:15.39, 6 Kenya (Samuel Chemweno, Kiptalam Keter, Kipkorir Kibet, Bartonjo Rotich) 3:16.72.

HIGH JUMP (19 Juil): 1 Ernle Haisley (Jam) 2.06, 2 Charles Porter (Aus) 2.03, 3 Robert Kotei (Gha) 2.01, 4= Julius Chigbolu (Nig), Patrick Etolu (Uga) & Joseph Leresae (Ken) 2.00, 7 Crawford Fairbrother (Sco) 1.98, 8 Ken Money (Can) 1.98, 9 Leslie Scipio (Tri) 1.96, 10 Gordon Miller (Eng) 1.96, 11 Nagalingam Ethirveerasingham (Cey) 1.93.

POLE VAULT (26 Jul): 1 Geoff Elliott (Eng) 4.16, 2 Bob Reid (Can) 4.16, 3 Mervyn Richards (NZ) 4.16, 4 Allah Ditta (Pak) 4.06, 5 Ian Ward (Eng) 3.96, 6 Wadi Khan (Pak) 3.96, 7 Rex Porter (Eng) 3.81, 8 Glen Cividin (Can) 3.81.

LONG JUMP (22 Jul): 1 Paul Foreman (Jam) 7.47, 2 Deryck Taylor (Jam) 7.47, 3 Muhammad Ramzan Ali (Pak) 7.32, 4 Ian Tomlinson (Aus) 7.30, 5 Roy Cruttenden (Eng) 7.27, 6 Roy Williams (NZ) 7.26, 7 Jack Smyth (Can) 7.15, 8 Dave Norris (NZ) 7.15, 9 Keith Parker (Eng) 7.09, 10 Victor Odofin (Nig) 7.08, 11 Ken Wilmshurst (Eng) 7.07, 12 Ram Mehar (Ind) 7.03, 13 Lawrence Ogwang (Uga) 6.98, 14 Desmond Luke (SL) 6.96, 15 Karim Olowu (Nig) 6.96, 16 Bryan Woolley (Wal) 6.46.

TRIPLE JUMP (24 Jul): 1 Ian Tomlinson (Aus) 15.74, 2 Jack Smyth (Can) 15.69, 3 Dave Norris (NZ) 15.45, 4 Morrie Rich (Aus) 15.45, 5 Ken Wilmshurst (Eng) 15.40, 6 Gabuh bin Piging (NB) 15.10, 7 Lawrence Ogwang (Uga) 15.10, 8 Tan Eng Yoon (Sin) 14.86, 9 Paul Engo (Nig) 14.63, 10 Solomon Akpata (Nig) 14.30. Note: Tomlinson's performance was the only one that was wind-assisted.

SHOT (24 Jul): 1 Arthur Rowe (Eng) 17.57, 2 Martyn Lucking (Eng) 16.49, 3 Barry Donath (Aus) 15.79, 4 Hannes Botha (SA) 15.61, 5 Nick Morgan (Eng) 15.56, 6 Mike Lindsay (Sco) 15.41, 7 Les Mills (NZ) 15.26, 8 Stan Raike (Can) 15.00, 9 Derek McCorquindale (Eng) 14.13, 10 Parduman Singh (Ind) 14.10, 11 Howard Payne (NR) 13.74, 12 Hywel Williams (Wal) 13.38, 13 Louis Ogbogu (Nig) 13.31, 14 John Davies (Wal) 12.99, 15 Gerry Harrison (Jer) 12.73.

DISCUS (22 Jul): 1 Stephanus du Plessis (SA) 55.94, 2 Les Mills (NZ) 51.72, 3 Gerry Carr (Eng) 51.62, 4 Mike Lindsay (Sco) 49.08, 5 Mesulame Rakuro (Fij) 48.00, 6 Stan Raike (Can) 46.60, 7 Hywel Williams (Wal) 45.78, 8 Peter Isbester (Sco) 46.28, 9 Muhammad Ayub (Pak) 45.44, 10 Balkar Singh (Ind) 45.12, 11 Eric Cleaver (Eng) 43.96, 12 Parduman Singh (Ind) 43.90, 13 Malcolm Pemberton (Wal) 41.70, 14 Howard Payne (NR) 41.30, 15 Benjamin Ovbiagele (Nig) 41.12.

HAMMER (26 Jul): 1 Mike Ellis (Eng) 62.90, 2 Muhammad Iqbal (Pak) 61.70, 3 Peter Allday (Eng) 57.58, 4 Howard Payne (NR) 56.38, 5 Don Anthony (Eng)

55.02, 6 Charley Morris (Aus) 55.00, 7 Charlie Koen (SA) 52.48, 8 Malik Noor (Pak) 50.94, 9 Ewan Douglas (Sco) 50.22, 10 Lawrie Hall (Wal) 48.72, 11 Robert Scott (Sco) 45.68. Alex Valentine (Sco) three invalid throws.

JAVELIN (19 Jul): 1 Colin Smith (Eng) 71.28, 2 Jalal Khan (Pak) 70.82, 3 Hans Moks (Can) 70.40, 4 Dick Miller (NI) 66.96, 5 Viliame Liga (Fij) 66.90, 6 Peter Cullen (Eng) 66.90, 7 Ray Davies (Eng) 66.48, 8 Muhammad Nawaz (Pak) 66.12, 9 Nick Birks (Aus) 65.28, 10 Clive Loveland (Eng) 64.16, 11 Kevin Flanagan (NR) 62.90, 12 Brian Sexton (Wal) 62.82, 13 Malcolm Hahn (NZ) 62.42, 14 Norman Watkins (Wal) 60.00, 15 Patrick Ozieh (Nig) 55.48. Note: Kevin Flanagan competed for Northern Ireland in the 1954 Games.

WOMEN

100 YARDS (22 Jul): 1 Marlene Willard (Aus) 10.70, 2 Heather Young (Eng) 10.73, 3 Madeleine Weston (Eng) 10.81, 4 Betty Cuthbert (Aus) 10.84, 5 June Paul (Eng) 10.93, 6 Anne Shaw (SA) 11.09. Note; Young nee Armitage.

220 YARDS (24 Jul): 1 Marlene Willard (Aus) 23.65, 2 Betty Cuthbert (Aus) 23.77, 3 Heather Young (Eng) 23.90, 4 June Paul (Eng) 24.14, 5 Magdel Myburgh (SA) 24.51, 6 Eleanor Haslam (Can) 24.63.

80 METRES HURDLES (26 Jul): 1 Norma Thrower (Aus) 10.72, 2 Carole Quinton (Eng) 10.77, 3 Gloria Wigney (Aus) 10.94, 4 Margaret Stuart (NZ) 11.18, 5 Wendy Hayes (Aus) 11.21, 6 Heather Young (Eng) 11.34.

4 x 110 YARDS RELAY (26 Jul): 1 England (Madeleine Weston, Dorothy Hyman, June Paul, Heather Young) 45.37, 2 Australia (Betty Cuthbert, Kay Johnson, Wendy Hayes, Marlene Willard) 46.12, 3 Canada (Diane Matheson, Eleanor Haslam, Maureen Reever, Freyda Berman) 47.21, 4 New Zealand (Marise Chamberlain, Mary Donaghy, Margaret Stuart, Beverly Weigel) 48.34, 5 Scotland (Isobel Bond, Moira Campbell, Mary Symon, Doris Tyndall) 48.56, 6 Northern Ireland (Thelma Hopkins, Maeve Kyle, Mary Peters, Bridgett Robinson) 50.43. Note: Heather Young was the second woman to have appeared in all track finals at one Games: Shirley Strickland (Aus) had done so in 1950 (five events).

HIGH JUMP (22 Jul): 1 Michele Mason (Aus) 1.70, 2 Mary Donaghy (NZ) 1.70, 3 Helen Frith (Aus) 1.65, 4 Dorothy Shirley (Eng) 1.65, 5 Mary Bignal (Eng) 1.61, 6 Audrey Bennett (Eng) 1.62, 7 Jean Card (Eng) 1.57m, 8 Thelma Hopkins (NI) 1.57, 9 Violet Odogwu (Nig) 1.57, 10= Alix Jamieson (Sco) & Amelia Okoli (Nig)

1.47, 12 Mary Peters (NI) 1.47, 13 Jestina Ashwood (SL) 1.47. Floretta Iyo (Nig) failed at opening height of 1.47.

LONG JUMP (26 Jul): 1 Sheila Hoskin (Eng) 6.02, 2 Mary Bignal (Eng) 5.97, 3 Beverley Watson (Aus) 5.97, 4 Jean Whitehead (Eng) 5.77, 5 Mary Donaghy (NZ) 5.77, 6 Marian Needham (Eng) 5.70, 7 Thelma Hopkins (NI) 5.55. Beverly Weigel (NZ) no valid jumps.

SHOT (19 Jul): 1 Valerie Sloper (NZ) 15.54, 2 Suzanne Allday (Eng) 14.44, 3 Jackie Gelling (Can) 14.03, 4 Magdalena Swanepoel (SA) 13.17, 5 Jennifer Thompson (NZ) 12.79, 6 Iris Mouzer (Eng) 12.40, 7 Jo Cook (Eng) 12.29, 8 Mary Peters (NI) 11.21, 9 Edith Okoli (Nig) 9.75.Note: Suzanne Allday was the wife of Peter Allday, 3rd in the hammer; Gelling nee McDonald; Amelia Okoli (10th= in the high jump) and Edith Okoli may have been sisters.

DISCUS (26 Jul): 1 Suzanne Allday (Eng) 45.90, 2 Jennifer Thompson (NZ) 45.30, 3 Valerie Sloper (NZ) 44.94, 4 Marie Anne Depree (Can) 42.92, 5 Sylvia Needham (Eng) 42.52, 6 Lois Jackman (Aus) 40.84, 7 Anna Fick (SA) 39.08, 8 Diana Will (Sco) 38.20, 9 Jackie Gelling (Can) 36.00, 10 Rosemary Charters (Sco) 34.96, 11 Antonia Ireland (Sco) 33.12, 12 Edith Okoli (Nig) 31.40, Maya Giri (Eng) no valid throws. Note: Sylvia Needham was not related to the long jumper, Marian Needham, but did have a sister, Hazel, who was also a Women's AAA champion, as a walker.

JAVELIN (24 Jul): 1 Anna Pazera (Aus) 57.40, 2 Magdalena Swanepoel (SA) 48.72, 3 Averil Williams (Eng) 46.76, 4 Sue Platt (Eng) 45.36, 5 Margaret Callender (Eng) 44.30, 6 Myra Tadd (Eng) 41.58, 7 Elizabeth Davenport (Ind) 40.52, 8 Bridgett Robinson (NI) 36.66.

8.

Middle-distance majesty of
Peter Snell and Dixie Belle

ATHLETICS CHANGED ENORMOUSLY IN THE LATE 1950s. Admittedly, such innovations as World Championships, World and European Cups, the Grand Prix series, and even women's races beyond 800 metres, were all still well into the future, but there was already in place a very firmly established programme of top-class competition thoughout Europe, and it was surely the seductive thought of travelling on to star-studded invitation meetings on balmy August evenings in Scandinavia that had encouraged many Commonwealth athletes to make Cardiff a port-of-call in 1958. A protracted excursion to Western Australia a month before Christmas might not seem such an attractive proposition four years later.

Still, it was in-season, though a shade on the early side, for two new World record-holders - Peter Snell and Dixie Willis. Snell had been the most surprising of winners in the Rome Olympic 800 metres in 1960, and then within the space of a week on grass tracks at home in New Zealand in early 1962 he had set three marvellous new standards. On 27 January, in Wanganui, he beat Herb Elliott's mile time of 3:54.5 by just one-tenth, and then on 3 February, in Christchurch, he ran 1:44.3 for 800 metres and 1:45.1 for 880 yards in the same race, beating the existing records by massive margins of 1.4sec and 1.7sec respectively. Dixie Willis, only 20, had upgraded shamefully ill-considered events when she set a Commonwealth record of 53.9 for 440 yards in Adelaide in February and then - much more significantly - emulated Snell on 3 March with a World-record double of 2:01.2 for 800 metres and 2:02.0 for 880 yards on a grass track in Perth, barely beating New Zealand's Marise Chamberlain (2:01.4/2:02.3). This brilliant performance improved the official World record for 800 metres by over three seconds and brought much-needed attention to the event, which had been reintroduced to the Olympics in Rome in 1960 after an unjustifiable 32-year break and was to figure belatedly at the Empire & Commonwealth Games for the first time since 1934.

Snell, Elliott and Murray Halberg had all won gold medals in Rome, and yet this maybe disguised the fact that the overall contribution by Commonwealth athletes had not matched up to the 1956 Games. Great Britain again had the third highest number of medals (eight), but the rest of the Commonwealth had only won 10 between them. History exactly repeated itself when an Olympic champion was denied the chance of adding a Commonwealth title because the decision was once again made not to include a walking race in the Perth schedule; this despite the fact that not only had Don Thompson won the 50 kilometres for Great Britain in Rome but six different Commonwealth countries (including India) placed walkers in the top 15 in one or other of the two Olympic competitions!

The overall entry for Perth was down on Cardiff - 262 men and 66 women from 29 countries - but not drastically so, and the most notable absentee was South Africa, which had withdrawn from the Commonwealth. Apart from Snell, Willis and Halberg two other recent World record-breakers to put in an appearance were the sprinters, Dennis Johnson (Jamaica) and Harry Jerome (Canada), who had run 9.3 and 9.2 respectively for 100 yards. There had also been some encouraging progress in the field events with the Australians, Tony Sneazwell (2.11) and Colin Ridgway (2.14), improving the Commonwealth high-jump record, and an Italian-born Canadian, Gerry Moro, pole-vaulting 4.49. John Baguley triple-jumped 16.36 for another record which had now been shared by three Australians over a 31-year period, and Nick Birks (also of Australia) had become the first 80-metre javelin-thrower from the Commonwealth with a throw of exactly 81 metres. Intriguingly, an Indian hurdler named Gurbachan Singh had set an unofficial best in the decathlon, but that event would not get Games status for another four years. Three Australian women - Robyn Woodhouse, Helen Frith and the defending champion, Michele

Mason - had all cleared 1.75 for further Commonwealth records in the high jump, and Valerie Young (nee Sloper) waited until a warm-up meeting a week before the Games opened to set new Commonwealth records and strike fear into the hearts of her opponents with 16.59 in the shot and 53.77 in the discus. Together with Mason and Sloper the defending champions returning were Tom Robinson (220), Murray Halberg (three miles), Dave Power (six miles and marathon), Ian Tomlinson (triple jump), Colin Smith and Anna Pazera (javelin).

Though entries were down there were still 48 starters for the men's 100 yards, which entailed an additional round the day before the official Games opening, just as in Cardiff, and with the temperature 96degF (35degC) and an assisting wind gusting up to almost twice the official two metres-per-second limit the sprinters enjoyed themselves hugely.. Harry Jerome, Tom Robinson, Australia's Mike Cleary and Kenya's Seraphino Antao were all credited with 9.4 (electronic times ranging from 9.43 for Antao to 9.58 for Robinson), and the spectating 1954 champion, Mike Agostini, wryly remarked to the seasoned Australian writer, Bernie Cecins, who was covering the Games for "Athletics Weekly": *"I've seen and run a few 9.4s myself, but this is the first time I've seen them as a package deal."*

The first full day of competition, Saturday 24 November, was even hotter: 98degF (36degC) in the early afternoon shade and still 85degF (29degC) when the six milers got under way in the evening. The other finals were in the 100 yards, the steeplechase (restored after a ridiculous 28-year absence), the high jump, the javelin and the women's shot. There was a respectable 18,000 crowd in the Perry Lakes Stadium, which had been constructed for the Games on reclaimed marshland, and they got value for money and an early home winner as Trevor Vincent set a personal best 8:43.4 in the steeplechase despite the temperature to get the better of England's Maurice Herriott, whose immaculate hurdling technique could not quite compensate for his lack of basic speed on this occasion but would suffice for an Olympic silver medal two years later. An Australian again triumphed over an Englishman as both Alf Mitchell and the title-holder, Colin Smith, set personal bests in the javelin ahead of the Commonwealth record-holder, Nick Birks, and there was a third success for the host country when Percy Hobson cleared 6ft 11in (2.11) in the high jump. His compatriot, Charles ("Chilla") Porter finished 2nd, as in 1958, and 3rd

1930. Awaiting the victory ceremony the marathon
medallists strike a surprisingly nonchalant pose on the
makeshift podium, considering their exertions earlier in
the afternoon. Only their bedraggled clothing and scuffed
gym shoes give some clue to what they have just endured.
The winner was Duncan Mcleod Wright, of Scotland
(centre), with Sam Ferris, of England (right), in 2nd
place and Johnny Miles, of Canada, 3rd. All three were
vastly experienced runners who between them made
seven Olympic appearances

1930. Stan Lay, of New Zealand, in acrobatic action after releasing the javelin. He was the only exponent of the event in the British Empire to achieve true international class in the 1920s and 1930s. In 1928 he had thrown within two metres of the World record, and after winning the Empire title in Hamilton he made a sentimental return to the Games in his homeland in 1950 at the age of 43 to become one of a select group of seven athletes to compete both before and after World War II.

1934. The heats of the mile. Aubrey Reeve and Sydney Wooderson, of England, lead from Harold Thompson (South Africa), Jackie Laidlaw (Scotland) and Les Wade (Canada), with the World record-holder from New Zealand, Jack Lovelock, content to follow them at a distance despite the slow pace. Reeve won in 4:26.0 by five yards from Wooderson with Lovelock and Wade also qualifying.

1934. The final of the mile. The smoke from the starter's pistol still hangs in the air as the runners start out. The line-up, from the left, is Les Wade (Canada), Jerry Cornes (England), Aubrey Reeve (England), Ken Harris (Wales), Sydney Wooderson (England), Bobby Graham (Scotland), Jack Lovelock (New Zealand) and Horace Craske (England). Lovelock won in 4:12.8 from Wooderson, Cornes and Reeve, and two years he later achieved immortal fame with his Olympic Games 1500 metres victory in World record time. Both Lovelock (in 1933) and Wooderson (in 1937) also set World mile records.

LEFT: 1934. George Bailey was one of the stalwart English cross-country runners who achieved such success in the distance track races at the early Empire Games celebrations. He won the steeplechase in 1930, and though beaten into 3rd place in 1934 (pictured here) he shared in a remarkable display of domination as Stan Scarsbrook, of Surrey Athletic Club, led home his three England team-mates - all of whom were members of the same Salford Harriers club

RIGHT: 1938. Pat Boot, of New Zealand, is one of those intriguing and shadowy figures of pre-war athletics who showed only tantalising glimpses of their real potential. He won the 880 yards at the 1938 Empire Games by a huge margin from the more strongly fancied home countries' runners and also came 3rd in the mile. His erratic career had begun with him beating a school record held by Jack Lovelock and ended with an obscure but valiant attempt on the World record for the 4 x 1 mile relay in 1940 before his tragic early death.

1938. The 14 competitors in the marathon race start out on their long journey. Six of them were from the host country, Australia, but the gold and bronze medals went to South Africa and the silver to England. Johannes Coleman was the winner and it was almost another 50 minutes before the 9th and last finisher came home. Among those who retired was Noel Stanford, of Trinidad, who was involved in a fracas with Coleman during the six miles race three days later. The line-up (from the left) is Young, Norris, Crossley, Longman, Stanford, McNab Robertson, Wood, Liddle, Patterson, Bartlett, Jolly, Coleman, Gibson and Hayes, and full details are given in the results section.

1938. The first two home in the marathon. South Africa's Johannes Coleman, in the dark clothing, and England's Bert Norris each look impressively composed as they pass a checkpoint in the latter stages of the race, but Coleman was much the superior on the day, winning by a margin of over seven minutes, which has never been matched by any other man in Empire & Commonwealth Games history. A decade after his triumph in Sydney Coleman placed 4th in the Wembley Olympics.

1950. The clothing of the era might seem utilitarian rather than decorative but there is no doubting the athleticism of competitors in the women's 80 metres hurdles, walking back across the grass of Auckland's Eden Park after contesting their final. From the left they are Janet Shackleton, Noeline Gourlay, June Schoch, Pixie Fletcher (all of New Zealand), Shirley Strickland and Ann May Stalder (both of Australia). Miss Strickland (later Mrs de la Hunty) was the winner, and with a total of five medals at these Games and seven more in Olympic competition she remains one of the greatest of all women athletes.

1950. The New Zealand tradition at long-distance running which had been established at prewar Games by Bill Savidan and Cecil Matthews was sustained, somewhat unexpectedly, by Harold Nelson in the Auckland six miles. Nelson, who had finished in the minor placings in the 1948 Olympic 10,000 metres, found himself "carried along on a wave of sound" from the excited spectators in the last few laps of the race to win from the Scotsman, Andrew Forbes. It was a pity, though, that no place could be found at the Games for an Estonian refugee, Valdu Lillakas, who had won the AAA title the previous year in much faster time.

1954. Some of the most versatile women athletes in history have graced the Empire &
Commonwealth Games - Mary Rand, Mary Peters, Denise Lewis most prominent
among them. Still regarded, though, as one of the outstanding all-round talents ever is
Yvette Williams, of New Zealand, who achieved the exceptional feat of winning titles in
both the jumps and the throws. In Vancouver she was champion in the long jump, shot
and discus and she had also won the long jump at the 1952 Olympics.

1954. The Mile of the Century. Its defining moment. John Landy, of Australia, had led from early on in the race and Roger Bannister, of England, had gradually closed the gap between them. Entering the home straight, with less than 100 yards to run, Landy glanced briefly to his left to check the situation and at that instant Bannister passed him on his right and went on to win by several yards in 3:58.8. Bannister had run the first sub-four-minute mile the previous May in 3:59.4 and Landy had beaten that record with 3:57.9 the following month. This was Bannister's last race, though Landy went on to win the Olympic 1500 metres bronze medal in 1956.

1958. Grace and determination personified. England's June Paul exhorts
Heather Young to yet greater efforts after passing on the baton at the last
changeover in the 4 x 110 yards relay. England, for which Madeleine Weston
and Dorothy Hyman had run the first two stages, won by a resounding margin from Australia in a World record time of 45.37 secs. Madeleine Weston
(as Mrs Cobb) reappeared 12 years later in the England team at the
Edinburgh Games which lost narrowly to Australia at 4 x 100 metres.

1958. Three of the finest sprinters in Commonwealth history share places on the victory rostrum after the 100 yards final. Jamaica's Keith Gardner (centre) won both that event and the 120 yards hurdles in Cardiff, having also been champion in the latter event four years earlier, and collected five medals in all. Mike Agostini (left) achieved the unusual feat of winning the gold for Trinidad in 1954 and the bronze for Canada on this occasion. Tom Robinson, of the Bahamas, was the surprise silver-medallist in Cardiff and finished in the same position again in 1962 and in 1966.

1958. Herb Elliott's double victory at 880 yards and the mile in Cardiff and his Rome Olympic 1500 metres win two years later in World record time suffice to establish him as one of the very finest of all middle-distance runners. Though failing to match his best form in Cardiff, placing 4th in both the mile and the three miles, the late Gordon Pirie broke seven World records during his tempestuous career and his reputation survives as a great distance-running pioneer of the 1950s. Neither Elliott (pictured left here) nor Pirie were at all averse to competing for fun far from the public spotlight and this photograph shows them chatting amiably after a cross-country match between South London Harriers and Cambridge University. Pirie came 1st and Elliott 8th.

1962. Brian Kilby, of England, leads at the halfway turn in the marathon, and he went on to win from Australia's defending champion, Dave Power. Here his pursuers are John Stephen (Tanzania), Mel Batty (England) and Bruce Kidd (Canada). Stephen finished 6th and deserves to be remembered as the first black African to gain such a placing in a major championships marathon. Batty was 5th, but Kidd - the precocious six miles winner at the age of 19 - dropped out. Kilby had also won the European title earlier in 1962 and he went on to establish a great marathoning tradition for his club, Coventry Godiva Harriers.

RIGHT: 1962. Peter Snell, of New Zealand, repeated Herb Elliott's achievement of four years earlier in winning both the half-mile and mile in Perth. An unlikely-looking middle-distance runner, with his barrel chest, broad thighs and rolling gait, as this photo of him winning a race at London's White City Stadium suggests, he remains a legend to this day with three Olympic gold medals and individual World records at 800 metres, 880 yards, 1000 metres and the mile.

1966. Australia's Ron Clarke broke 19 World records on the track between 1963 and 1968 at two miles, three miles, 5000 metres, six miles, 10,000 metres, 10 miles, 15 kilometres, 20 kilometres and one hour. Yet he never won a major title. Most famously, hc was beaten into 3rd place when he was favourite for the 1964 Olympic 10,000 metres, and he was also runner-up in the Commonwealth Games on four separate occasions. On a happier occasion for him, with his nearest rival barely in sight, this photo shows him winning the 1965 AAA three miles in a World record 12:52.4.

place was taken remarkably by the one-man team from Barbados, Anton Norris, using the old-fashioned "scissors" style.

Valerie Young was nowhere near her record-breaking form of the previous week but still won the shot with ease. Also in this event was a Liverpool-born young lady from Northern Ireland competing in her second Games, finishing a largely unnoticed 4th , and still a decade away from her greatest achievement. Her name? Mary Peters.

Three more rounds of the 100 yards, and all into the wind which had changed direction overnight, meant that the final would be the survival of the fittest as much as the speediest. Though Jerome, Johnson and Robinson all made it to the last six, it was the tall, slim, moustachioed Antao, the double AAA champion, who led from gun to tape and recorded a highly impressive 9.5 into a 1.8m wind. His electronic time was not taken for some reason, but Robinson finished over a yard back in 9.63 so Antao must have run close to 9.50. Aged 25, Antao had been born in the former Portugese possession of Goa, on the Indian sub-continent, and had got to the Rome Olympic 100m semi-finals, but it was still a major upset that the West Indians and Australians should be beaten by an Afro-Asian sprinter. The remaining men's final, the six miles, brought together a World-class field: the holder, Power, and the former Boy Wonder of Australian middle-distance running, Ron Clarke; John Merriman and Arere Anentia, the other medallists from Cardiff; New Zealand's Olympic marathon bronze-medallist, Barry Magee; and a 19-year-old Canadian "kid" named Bruce Kidd, who had run fast times but was surely far too young for this experienced company. As you may have guessed from the teasing introduction, Kidd proved himself an adult by leading at halfway (14:15.0) and then making the two decisive breaks of the race - on the 18th and 22nd laps of the 24 - to go away <u>with</u> Dave Power and then <u>from</u> Power to win with some ease. Merriman, the Watford Harrier from Wales, again proved himself best of the British with another Games medal in 3rd place.

Peter Snell won his heat and semi-final at 880 yards and Jamaica, Australia, Kenya, Wales and England provided the other qualifiers for a truly international final. Betty Cuthbert, holder of three Olympic gold medals and 12 World records, was only 5th in her 100 yards semi-final but said she wouldn't retire - which was just as well because she still had another Olympic gold medal to come. Olympic gold was also to be the destiny for

81

the comely 20-year-old who was 5th in the other 100 yards semi-final. That was Ann Packer.

Monday 26 November was a little cooler but still very windy for seven more finals: 880, three miles, 440 hurdles, long jump, discus and women's 100 yards and high jump. The Kenyan, Peter Francis, led the first lap of the half-mile but in a relatively slow 54.2 before Snell decisively increased the tempo with a 26sec third furlong and then held off the Jamaican, George Kerr, who had been the Olympic bronze-medallist behind him, along the home straight. Murray Halberg, as in Rome and again on the same day, made it a double for New Zealand as only the young six-mile champion, Kidd, made any real effort to test the title-holder in the three miles after a moderately-paced first eight laps, and Halberg's 53.8 last lap - just four-tenths slower than Snell's - was far too quick for anyone, though Australia's Ron Clarke was a sound runner-up. Athletes from Central Africa took silver and bronze at 440 hurdles, won by Ken Roche, of Australia, in a time almost two seconds slower than Gert Potgieter in Cardiff, and the host country took another gold in the discus through Warwick Selvey, who was a left-handed thrower and benefited most from the wind direction.

The long jump final dragged on for more than three hours because the organisers curiously decided not to have a separate qualifying round, and a total of 75 efforts were made by 19 competitors at the mercy of a wildly fluctuating wind. As the six finalists prepared for their last jumps Dave Norris, of New Zealand, led with 7.74, but only just from Jamaiaca's Wellesley Clayton, 7.73, and Welshman Lynn Davies, who had set a new British record of 7.72, and Davies's was maybe intrinsically the best of them because his was the only performance not wind-assisted. He ended up out of the medals, though, because the hugely talented but completely untutored Ghanaian, Mike Ahey, then produced an 8.05 (26ft 5in) closing effort, again with a wind too strong for record purposes (2.74 m) at his back.

The women's high jump was marvellous, with 19-year-old Robyn Woodhouse leading a clean sweep for Australia, setting three Commonwealth records and achieving the third best leap of all time. Woodhouse had already ranked in the top 30 in the World at the age of 14 and her ultimate "scissors" clearance of 1.78 (5ft 10in) overcame the bronze- and gold-medallists from 1958, Helen Frith and Michele Mason. These three and England's 16-year-old Linda Knowles, beaten on countback for 3rd place, all ranked in the World's top 10 for the year. No Englishwoman had won the 100 yards since 1934, and the time was the slowest since then, but there was good reason because Dorothy Hyman, who had gained a valiant silver behind the great Wilma Rudolph in the Rome Olympic 100m, was battling a 5.8m headwind without which she would probably have run 10.6 rather than 11.2. Again the leading women sprinters were also required to run 220 heats and Hyman got through the semi-finals to face four Australians (including Betty Cuthbert), but Ann Packer just missed out in 4th place.

After the pulsating heat a temperature of 72degF (22degC) and rain showers was positively welcome for many on the fourth day of athletics - Thursday 29 November - with finals in the men's 220, 440, 120 hurdles, shot and triple jump and the women's 220 and javelin, plus the marathon race for men. The rain was heavy enough to interrupt the shot competition for a while, but England's Dr Martyn Lucking, who had been 2nd to Arthur Rowe in Cardiff, broke Rowe's Games record by almost two feet and Mike Lindsay, for Scotland, and Dave Steen, for Canada, both came very close to snatching the gold. Back in 8th place Yovan Ochola, of Uganda, threw a very respectable 50ft-plus (15.37) and Imbert Roberts, from the Caribbean island of St Lucia, was by no means last at the reported age of 40. Ian Tomlinson retained his title in a triple jump competition in which the Games record was surpassed four times and a British record of 16.03 (52ft 7in) by Fred Alsop prevented Australia taking all three medals. Anna Pazera, the World record-breaking champion in Cardiff, was well beaten in the javelin by Sue Platt, England's first winner in the event since Gladys Lunn in 1934.

The winner, Seraphino Antao, and the bronze-medallist, Mike Cleary, were the only 100 yards survivors in the 220 final and Antao, running in lane two, had it all his own way to become the fourth man to complete the Games sprint double. He won by a very clear margin from Dave Jones, of England, and his time of 21.28 would have been substantially faster but for a 2.5m adverse wind. Memories of the great Jamaican triumvirate of McKenley, Rhoden and Wint were revived as three Jamaicans - the 880 silver-medallist, George Kerr, and the 26-year-old twins, Mel and Mal Spence - went to the 440 start line, though it was the new European 400m champion, Robbie Brightwell, who led at halfway. Kerr came up to him in the straight and won a shade more easily than the times suggested, and the enormous potential of African athletes was graphically demonstrated by the 25-year-old Ugandan, Amos Omolo, who finished 3rd in only his sixth ever race at the distance, having successively improved from 49sec-plus before the Games to 47.29, 46.96 and 46.88. Ghulam Raziq, 3rd in 1958, won Pakistan's first track gold in the high hurdles and Dorothy Hyman took the women's 220 as easily as Antao had the men's to maintain the unbroken sequence of six double sprint champions in women's events at the Games.

The wet weather suited the marathon-men. The favourite seemed to be the European champion, Brian Kilby, who was an excellent six-miler on the track and had been encouraged to take up the marathon by his elder Coventry Godiva Harriers clubmate, Dyfrig Rees, who had run for Wales in the 1958 Games. But among Kilby's opposition there was a fair amount of experience: Dave Power was back despite his "retirement" after winning in Cardiff; Peter Wilkinson, 3rd in Cardiff, was one of Kilby's England team-mates; Jeff Julian was the sole NZ nomination in the absence of the Olympic bronze-medallist, Barry Magee, whose feet had been badly blistered in the Games six miles the previous weekend; and Gordon Dickson, of Canada, had placed 5th in Cardiff. Equally, there were a few notable novices who had run in the Games six miles, including the winner, Bruce Kidd, and three other top-six finishers, John Merriman, Mel Batty and Martin Hyman. Kilby led at 10 miles (54:36), with 14 of the 20 starters still close behind, and made his break just before the 20-mile mark which he passed in 1:48:00 to hold half-a-minute's advantage over Batty. Looking fresh and confident the Coventrian maintained his pace to the finish and was almost a minute ahead of Power, who thus won his fourth Games medal. Of note in hindsight was the fact that John Stephen, a barefoot Tanganyikan, became the first black athlete to place in the leading six in this Games event.

On the closing day - Saturday 1 December - the remaining finals were for the mile, pole vault and hammer for men, together with the 880, hurdles, long jump and discus for women, and the three relays. The mile, of course, was expected to be the highlight of the day for the 40,000 crowd, with Peter Snell and John Davies for New Zealand facing, among others, Albie Thomas, 3rd in Cardiff, and the European 5000 metres champion, Bruce Tulloh, but the first lap was only 65 and all hope of a fast time was immediately dispelled. Tulloh (2:06.0) and his England team-mate, Stan Taylor (3:09.0), only marginally lifted the pace, and the New Zealanders ran away with the race over the last lap, with only the Rhodesian, Terry Sullivan, challenging them. Snell's last 440 en route to his second gold medal was covered in around 55sec.

Peter Snell looked more like a rugby player than a miler - barrel-chested, powerful thighs, and with a rolling sort of gait. Yet he was both quick - he had run in the 4 x 440 heats the morning of the mile final - and immensely strong, having been brought to prominence by the innovative training methods of Arthur Lydiard, who had taken part in the 1950 Empire Games marathon. Lydiard believed in long-distance running as part of the pre-season preparation even for half-milers, and Snell would regularly accompany Murray Halberg and Bill Baillie on Sunday-morning training stints of 20 miles or more through the hills round Auckland. At the 1964 Tokyo Olympics Snell won a memorable 800/1500 double and he further reduced the World mile record to 3:54.1 the same year. He remains one of the very great half-milers and milers.

With only seven entries the women's half-mile was run as a straight final, but two of the starters were Dixie Willis and Marise Chamberlain, who had shared in the World record race elsewhere in Perth earlier in the year. The pace was made by Chamberlain and was not as fast (61sec at the bell), and when Willis broke away strongly at the beginning of the back straight the outcome was decided. The Australian went on to win by at least a dozen yards, and the victory made some considerable amends for her unnerving Rome Olympic experience of two years earlier when she had suffered a crisis of confidence and abandoned the race in the home straight after leading for much of the way. Unfortunately, she was unwell at the time of the 1964 Olympics when Ann Packer won her famous victory and Marise Chamberlain took the bronze. Chamberlain, incidentally, had doggedly persevered with a career which had included World records ranging from 440 yards to 1500 metres and the mile (in Perth a week after the Games 880 final) and an appearance in the NZ team which was 4th in the 4 x 110 yards relay in Cardiff, and she deserves recognition as one of the unsung heroines of the revival in women's middle-distance running. Other notable Perth finalists were a 15-year-old Canadian, Abigail ("Abby") Hoffman, who did rather better in the 1966 Games, went on to reach the 1968 and 1972 Olympic 800m finals, and become one of that rare species, a woman member of the International Olympic Committee, and Joy Jordan, breaking the British record in her last race before retirement at the age of 27.

Pam Kilborn, only 5ft 2in (1.57m) tall, won the 80m hurdles into a 7m-per-second headwind from Betty Moore, also Australian-born but running for England, who had equalled the World record of 10.5 earlier in the year, and the winning time of 11.07 was assuredly worth close to 10.40. Kilborn then completed a double, beating the high-jump silver-medallist, Helen Frith, in the long jump, with Australians also 3rd and 4th, and Valerie Young won her third Games gold in the discus (with more to come four years later). Betty Cuthbert, with only a 5th place to show from the individual sprints, ran a magnificent last leg of the 4 x 110 relay for Australia, making up four yards on Betty Moore to win on the line, after teenagers Joyce Bennett (17), Glenys Beasley and Brenda Cox (both 18) had run the first three stages ... and Ann Packer had led off for England.

In the men's field events an ex-Rhodesian - Howard Payne, who had placed 4th in Cardiff and had actually been born in South Africa - won the hammer for England, and an ex-South African - the Oxford University graduate, Danie Burger - came second in the pole vault for Rhodesia & Nyasaland: the latter six-hour-long event being won to the delight of the crowd by a 19-year-old Western Australian, Trevor Bickle, with a new Commonwealth record of 14ft 9in (4.50m) aided by use of one of the fibre-glass poles which were rapidly replacing metal and transforming standards in the event [the World record was to be improved on 10 occasions during 1963 from 4.93m to 5.20m]. Both the English and Ghanaian quartets were credited with equalling the Games 4 x 110 record of 40.6, though England were over a tenth-of-a-second ahead on electronic timing, and the Spence twins made history by contributing to Jamaica's 4 x 440 victory, presenting George Kerr with a handsome 10-yard lead on the anchor leg. The latter event was also notable for the participation of the first four finishers in the Olympic 800m two years later: Snell, Crothers, Kiprugut and Kerr.

"A pretty good show," remarked Jimmy Green, the editor of

"Athletics Weekly" in a phlegmatic post-Games summing-up, and that seemed fair enough comment. The athletes dispersed for their Christmas hols, maybe a bit of indoor running, and hard training in preparation for 1963.

RESULTS 1962

MEN

100 YARDS (24 Nov): 1 Seraphino Antao (Ken) 9.5, 2 Tom Robinson (Bah) 9.63, 3 Mike Cleary (Aus) 9.78, 4 Gary Holdsworth (Aus) 9.78, 5 Dennis Johnson (Jam) 9.97, 6 Harry Jerome (Can) 10.05. Note: no automatic time was recorded for Antao.

220 YARDS (29 Nov): 1 Seraphino Antao (Ken) 21.28, 2 Dave Jones (Eng) 21.59, 3 Johann du Preez (Rho) 21.70, 4 Mike Okantey (Gha) 21.83, 5 Mike Cleary (Aus) 21.94, 6 Jeff Smith (Rho) 22.07. Note: headwind of 2.5m.

440 YARDS (29 Nov): 1 George Kerr (Jam) 46.74, 2 Robbie Brightwell (Eng) 46.86, 3 Amos Omolo (Uga) 46.88, 4 Ken Roche (Aus) 47.69, 5 Mal Spence (Jam) 47.73, 6 Mel Spence (Jam) 47.79.

880 YARDS (26 Nov): 1 Peter Snell (NZ) 1:47.64, 2 George Kerr (Jam) 1:47.90, 3 Tony Blue (Aus) 1:48.99, 4 Peter Francis (Ken) 1:49.92, 5 Mike Fleet (Eng) 1:49.95, 6 Tony Harris (Wal) 1:52.43.

1 MILE (1 Dec): 1 Peter Snell (NZ) 4:04.58, 2 John Davies (NZ) 4:05.12, 3 Terry Sullivan (Rho) 4:06.61, 4 Tony Blue (Aus) 4:09.30, 5 Albie Thomas (Aus) 4:11.19, 6 Tony Harris (Wal) 4:11.89, 7 Stan Taylor (Eng) 4:12.81, 8 Jim Irons (Can) 4:17.52, 9 Bruce Tulloh (Eng) 4:22.1.

3 MILES (26 Nov): 1 Murray Halberg (NZ) 13:34.15, 2 Ron Clarke (Aus) 13:35.92, 3 Bruce Kidd (Can) 13:36.37, 4 Bruce Tulloh (Eng) 13:37.91, 5 Albie Thomas (Aus) 13:40.64, 6 Eddie Strong (Eng) 13:41.23, 7 Pat Clohessy (Aus) 13:42.91, 8 Derek Ibbotson (Eng) 13:43.97, 9 John Anderson (Eng) 13:44.69, 10 Arere Anentia (Ken) 13:48.10, 11 Kipchoge Keino (Ken) 13:50.70, 12 Tony Cook (Aus) 14:17.0, 13 Anthony Ngatia (Ken) 14:33.0, 14 Alistair Fyfe (Gib) 15:47.0. Did not finish - Mubarak Shah (Pak).

6 MILES (24 Nov): 1 Bruce Kidd (Can) 28:26.13, 2 Dave Power (Aus) 28:33.53, 3 John Merriman (Wal) 28:40.26, 4 Barry Magee (NZ) 28:40.53, 5 Martin Hyman (Eng) 28:41.43, 6 Mel Batty (Eng) 28:47.15, 7 Arere Anentia (Ken) 29:04.55, 8 Roy Fowler (Eng) 29:44.0, 9 Mike Bullivant (Eng) 29:46.0, 10 Jeff

Julian (NZ) 29:50.0, 11 James Wahome (Ken) 30:03.4, 12 Bob Vagg (Aus) 30:10.0, 13 John Stephen (Tan) 31:08.0. Did not finish - Bill Baillie (NZ), Ron Clarke (Aus), Tony Cook (Aus), Alistair Fyfe (Gib), Pascal Mfyomi (Tan).

3000 METRES STEEPLECHASE (24 Nov): 1 Trevor Vincent (Aus) 8:43.4, 2 Maurice Herriott (Eng) 8:45.0, 3 Ron Blackney (Aus) 9:00.6, 4 Ian Blackwood (Aus) 9:04.0, 5 David Chapman (Eng) 9:05.6, 6 Edward O'Keefe (NZ) 9:05.8, 7 John Coyle (Aus) 9:15.0, 8 Hylke van der Wal (Can) 9:26.0, 9 Ludovic Amukun (Uga) 9:32.0, 10 Mubarak Shah (Pak) 9:41.0, 11 Dilbagh Singh Kler (NB) 9:45.0. Note: automatic timing not in operation.

MARATHON (29 Nov): 1 Brian Kilby (Eng) 2:21:17.0, 2 Dave Power (Aus) 2:22:15.4, 3 Rod Bonella (Aus) 2:24:07.0, 4 Keith Ollerenshaw (Aus) 2:24:59.0, 5 Mel Batty (Eng) 2:25:51.0, 6 John Stephen (Tan) 2:28:39.0, 7 Jeff Julian (NZ) 2:30:13.0, 8 Peter Wilkinson (Eng) 2:30:51.0, 9 Martin Hyman (Eng) 2:32:06.2, 10 Muhammad Gul (Pak) 2:38:26.0, 11 Deogratias Rwabugwene (Uga) 2:42:28.0, 12 Gordon Dickson (Can) 2:44:17.0. Did not finish - Bruce Kidd (Can), John Merriman (Wal), Pascal Mfyomi (Tan), Vinancio Okwere (Uga), Ian Sinfield (Aus), Alastair Wood (Sco), Muhammad Yousuf (Pak).

120 YARDS HURDLES (29 Nov): 1 Ghulam Raziq (Pak) 14.34, 2 David Prince (Aus) 14.48, 3 Laurie Taitt (Eng) 14.81, 4 Mick Devlin (Aus) 14.93, 5 Mick Daws (Aus) 14.94, 6 Bob Birrell (Eng) 15.30. Note: headwind of 2.2m.

440 YARDS HURDLES (26 Nov): 1 Ken Roche (Aus) 51.5, 2 Kimaru Songok (Ken) 51.9, 3 Benson Ishiepai (Uga) 52.3, 4 Gary Knoke (Aus) 52.5, 5 Mick Devlin (Aus) 52.6, 6 Chris Surety (Eng) 53.3. Note: automatic timing not in operation.

4 x 110 YARDS RELAY (1 Dec): 1 England (Peter Radford, Len Carter, Alf Meakin, Dave Jones) 40.62, 2 Ghana (Mike Ahey, Bonner Mends, Bukari Bashiru, Mike Okantey) 40.74, 3 Wales (Dave England, Ron Jones, Berwyn Jones, Nick Whitehead) 40.80, 4 Rhodesia & Nyasaland (Roy Collins, Jeff Smith, Danie Burger, Johann du Preez) 42.80, 5 Australia (Bob Lay, Dennis Tipping, Gary Holdsworth, Mike Cleary) 44.79. Note: Australia dropped baton at first exchange; Sarawak (William Liam Lee, Kuda Ditta, Joseph Lee Gut Hing, William Chai Ah Lim) disqualified after finishing fifth in 43.94.

4 x 440 YARDS RELAY (1 Dec); 1 Jamaica (Laurie Kahn, Mal Spence, Mel Spence, George Kerr) 3:10.2, 2 England (Adrian Metcalfe, Bob Setti, Barry Jackson, Robbie Brightwell) 3:11.2, 3 Ghana (James Addy, Ebenezer Quartey, Fred

Owusu, John Asare-Antwi) 3:12.3, 4 Australia (Brian Waters, Peter Quiggan, John Randall, Ken Roche) 3:12.9, 5 Kenya (Kimaru Songok, Seraphino Antao, Peter Francis, Wilson Kiprugut) 3:15.0, 6 Canada (George Shepherd, Bill Crothers, Lynn Eves, Don Bertoia) 3:20.6. Note: automatic timing not in operation.

HIGH JUMP (24 Nov): 1 Percy Hobson (Aus) 2.11, 2 Charles Porter (Aus) 2.08, 3 Anton Norris (Bar) 2.03, 4 Gordon Miller (Eng) 2.03, 5 Joseph Leresae (Ken) 2.03, 6 Lawrie Peckham (Aus) 2.03, 7 Tony Sneazwell (Aus) 2.01, 8 Crawford Fairbrother (Sco) 1.98, 9 Patrick Etolu (Uga) 1.98, 10 Edward Laboran (PNG) 1.93.

POLE VAULT (1 Dec): 1 Trevor Bickle (Aus) 4.50, 2 Danie Burger (Rh) 4.42, 3 Ross Filshie (Aus) 4.42, 4 Gerry Moro (Can) 4.34, 5= John Pfitzner (Aus) & Bob Watson (Can) 4.27, 7= Allah Ditta (Pak), Kevin Gibbons (NZ), Alf Groom (Can), Bernard McGonagle (NZ), Rex Porter (Eng) & David Stevenson (Sco) 3.96, 13 Robin Barclay (PNG) 3.81. Ohene Asa Akuffo (Gha) failed at opening height (3.66).

LONG JUMP (26 Nov): 1 Mike Ahey (Gha) 8.05, 2 Dave Norris (NZ) 7.74, 3 Wellesley Clayton (Jam) 7.73, 4 Lynn Davies (Wal) 7.72, 5 John Baguley (Aus) 7.64, 6 Ian Tomlinson (Aus) 7.47, 7 Paul Odhiambo (Uga) 7.41, 8 John Howell (Eng) 7.38, 9 Fred Alsop (Eng) 7.37, 10 William Kamanyi (Uga) 7.30, 11 Sev Obura (Uga) 7.25, 12 Allan Crawley (PNG) 7.23, 13 Victor Brooks (Jam) 7.23, 14 Jim McCann (Aus) 7.04, 15 John Blackmore (Aus) 7.04, 16 Roy Collins (Rho) 6.97, 17 Gabuh bin Piging (NB) 6.88, 18 Joseph Lee Gut Hing (Sar) 6.85, 19 Leroy Lucas (BH) 6.64. Note: the performances of all competitors were wind-assisted except for Davies, Tomlinson, Crawley, Blackmore and Collins.

TRIPLE JUMP (29 Nov): 1 Ian Tomlinson (Aus) 16.21, 2 John Baguley (Aus) 16.08, 3 Fred Alsop (Eng) 16.03, 4 Graham Boase (Aus) 15.77, 5 Mahoney Samuels (Jam) 15.50, 6 Dave Norris (NZ) 15.41, 7 Paul Odhiambo (Uga) 14.92, 8 Kevin Rule (Aus) 14.90, 9 Lawrence Ogwang (Uga) 14.86, 10 Gabuh bin Piging (NB) 14.47, 11 Lynn Davies (Wal) 14.47, 12 John Howell (Eng) 14.33, 13 Leroy Lucas (BH) 13.90.

SHOT (29 Nov): 1 Martyn Lucking (Eng) 18.08, 2 Mike Lindsay (Sco) 18.05, 3 Dave Steen (Can) 17.90, 4 Warwick Selvey (Aus) 16.62, 5 Merv Kemp (Aus) 16.02, 6 Les Mills (NZ) 15,81, 7 Warren Ryan (Aus) 15.75, 8 Yovan Ochola (Uga) 15.37, 9 John Cochrane (Aus) 15.02, 10 David Davidson (NI) 14.60, 11 John Sheldrick (Eng) 14.36, 12 Robin Tait (NZ) 14.22, 13 Imbert Roberts (SL) 13.33, 14 Roy Hollingsworth (Eng) 13.30, 15 Lawrie Hall (Wal) 13.18, 16 John McSorley (Eng) 11.89.

DISCUS (26 Nov): 1 Warwick Selvey (Aus) 56.48, 2 Mike Lindsay (Sco) 52.58, 3 John Sheldrick (Eng) 50.67, 4 Robin Tait (NZ) 50.51, 5 Les Mills (NZ) 49.38, 6 Len Vlahov (Aus) 48.28, 7 Roy Hollingsworth (Eng) 48.07, 8 Len Chinnery (Eng) 47.93, 9 Alan Waugh (Aus) 46.40, 10 Muhammad Ayub (Pak) 45.01, 11 Martyn Lucking (Eng) 41.77, 12 Imbert Roberts (SL) 36.03.

HAMMER (1 Dec): 1 Howard Payne (Eng) 61.64, 2 Dick Leffler (Aus) 59.83, 3 Bob Brown (Aus) 57.64, 4 Charley Morris (Aus) 56.78, 5 Lawrie Hall (Wal) 54.41, 6 Mike Edwards (Aus) 54.41, 7 Dave Leech (NZ) 50.74.

JAVELIN (24 Nov): 1 Alf Mitchell (Aus) 78.10, 2 Colin Smith (Eng) 77.89, 3 Nick Birks (Aus) 75.07, 4 Muhammad Nawaz (Pak) 73.66, 5 Reg Spiers (Aus) 69.70, 6 Viliame Liga (Fij) 64.44, 7 Dick Miller (NI) 63.49, 8 Ivaharia Oe (PNG) 61.12, 9 John McSorley (Eng) 57.97, 10 Joe Hart (Aus) 57.82, 11 George Heriot (PNG) 53.63.

WOMEN

100 YARDS (26 Nov): 1 Dorothy Hyman (Eng) 11.2, 2 Doreen Porter (NZ) 11.3, 3 Brenda Cox (Aus) 11.4, 4 Christiana Boateng (Gha) 11.6, 5 Daphne Arden (Eng) 11.6, 6 Betty Moore (Eng) 11.7. Note: automatic timing not in operation; headwind of 5.8m.

220 YARDS (29 Nov): 1 Dorothy Hyman (Eng) 24.00, 2 Joyce Bennett (Aus) 24.21, 3 Margaret Burvill (Aus) 24.42, 4 Brenda Cox (Aus) 24.48, 5 Betty Cuthbert (Aus) 24.80, 6 Doreen Porter (NZ) 24.81. Note: headwind of 3.0m.

880 YARDS (1 Dec): 1 Dixie Willis (Aus) 2:03.85, 2 Marise Chamberlain (NZ) 2:05.66, 3 Joy Jordan (Eng) 2:05.96, 4 Phyllis Perkins (Eng) 2:09.45, 5 Joan Beretta (Aus) 2:12.36, 6 Jackie Barnett (Wal) 2:14.86, 7 Abby Hoffman (Can) 2:21.8.

80 METRES HURDLES (1 Dec): 1 Pam Kilborn (Aus) 11.07, 2 Betty Moore (Eng) 11.40, 3 Avis McIntosh (NZ) 11.47, 4 Pat Nutting (Eng) 11.70, 5 Margot Evans (Aus) 11.87, 6 Ann Packer (Eng) 11.91. Note: headwind of 7.0m.

4 x 110 YARDS RELAY (1 Dec): 1 Australia (Joyce Bennett, Glenys Beasley, Brenda Cox, Betty Cuthbert) 46.71, 2 England (Ann Packer, Dorothy Hyman, Daphne Arden, Betty Moore) 46.81, 3 NZ (Nola Bond, Avis McIntosh, Yvonne Cowan, Doreen Porter) 46.93, 4 Jamaica (Ouida Walker, Carmen Smith, Carmen Williams, Adlin Mair) 48.72, 5 Ghana (Christiana Boateng, Rose Hart, Matilda Adjei, Victoria Chinery) 49.11. 5 teams competed.

HIGH JUMP (26 Nov): 1 Robyn Woodhouse (Aus) 1.78, 2 Helen Frith (Aus) 1.73, 3 Michele Mason (Aus) 1.73, 4 Linda Knowles (Eng) 1.73, 5 Frances Slaap (Eng) 1.70, 6 Carolyn Wright (Aus) 1.70, 7 Dorothy Shirley (Eng) 1.68, 8 Lorraine Curtis (NZ) 1.65, 9 Thelma Hopkins (NI) 1.65, 10 Pam Burnett (NZ) 1.60.

LONG JUMP (1 Dec): 1 Pam Kilborn (Aus) 6.27, 2 Helen Frith (Aus) 6.24, 3 Janet Knee (Aus) 6.13, 4 Ieva Kampe (Aus) 5.89, 5 Sheila Parkin (Eng) 5.87, 6 Thelma Hopkins (NI) 5.72, 7 Pat Nutting (Eng) 5.59, 8 Janette Neil (Sco) 5.45, 9 Christiana Boateng (Gha) 5.28, 10 Dorothy Yates (Jam) 4.99. Note: the performances of all competitors were wind-assisted except for Parkin. This was the first time since the men's triple jump in 1938 that the first four places in any event for men or women were taken by athletes all from the same country.

SHOT (24 Nov): 1 Valerie Young (NZ) 15.23, 2 Jean Roberts (Aus) 14.52, 3 Suzanne Allday (Eng) 13.56, 4 Mary Peters (NI) 13.31, 5 Mary Breen (Aus) 13.20, 6 Larraine Hillier (Aus) 12.89, 7 Rosslyn Williams (Aus) 12.85, 8 Sue Platt (Eng) 11.53. Note: Young nee Sloper.

DISCUS (1 Dec): 1 Valerie Young (NZ) 50.20, 2 Rosslyn Williams (Aus) 46.66, 3 Mary McDonald (Aus) 46.23, 4 Suzanne Allday (Eng) 43.97, 5 Mary Breen (Aus) 42.77, 6 Helen Thayer (NZ) 41.27, 7 Pat Dobie (Can) 39.90.

JAVELIN (29 Nov): 1 Sue Platt (Eng) 50.25, 2 Rosemary Morgan (Eng) 49.62, 3 Anna Pazera (Aus) 48.68, 4 Maureen Wright (Aus) 47.36, 5 Pat Dobie (Can) 44.44, 6 Pam Telfer (Aus) 41.11,

9.

Tropical track carnival rocks
to a distinctive reggae beat

NATIONAL STADIUM, KINGSTON, JAMAICA
5-13 AUGUST 1966

THE DECISION TO AWARD THE VIIIth British Empire &
Commonwealth Games to Jamaica was an ambitious one. After all,
although this was a country which had already made an outstanding
contribution to the sport over the preceding 20 years, it had little
experience of staging major meetings, but it was about time that the Games
moved outside the cosy circle of the home countries and Canada, Australia
and New Zealand, who between them had provided the seven previous host
cities. Certainly, there was no lack of interest; on the contrary, 33 countries
entered a total of 305 men and 98 women, and most prominent among
them were three current World record-holders all making a return to the
Games.

Harry Jerome, of Canada, had gone to Perth in 1962 with a new
World record of 9.2 for 100yds to his credit. Four years later he completed
his Kingston preparations at the Canadian championships by equalling Bob
Hayes's record of 9.1. Kipchoge Keino, who had been an inexperienced
11th-placed three-miler at the 1962 Games, had been transformed during
1965-66 into the second fastest miler of all time (3:53.4) and a World
record-breaker at 3000m (7:39.5) and 5000m (13:24.2). Ron Clarke, who
had confirmed his comeback with 2nd place in the Perth three miles, had
already found a permanent place in track history with a series of astounding
World records: 12:52.4 and 12:50.4 for three miles, 13:16.6 for 5000m and

26:47.0/27:39.4 for six miles and 10,000m. As it happens, there had only been a couple of other new Commonwealth records in the three months before the 1966 Games - 2:13:45 for the marathon by the Scotsman, Alastair Wood, who had run in three past Commonwealth Games races without ever finishing; and 60.10 for the discus by a Canadian, George Puce, in California. But then the records were getting harder to beat.

Of the Commonwealth's 29 individual and relay medallists in the 1964 Olympics 18 were in Kingston. The 800m champion in Tokyo, Ann Packer, had retired, but two other British gold-medallists, Lynn Davies and Mary Rand, were competing. Welcome innovations were the 20 miles walk, decathlon and women's 440 yards, plus evening sessions to relieve many of the fears about the effect of the climate on the distance events, but there was still, inexplicably, no all-round competition for women even though the silver-medallist from the Tokyo Olympics (Rand) and the 4th-placer (Mary Peters) were on hand. A preliminary programme of 100 yards heats and the opening events of the decathlon took place on Friday 5 August, and after the first five disciplines of the all-round competition - 100m, long jump, shot, high jump and 400m - the leader was Roy Williams, of New Zealand, who was the clear favourite and had previously taken part in the 1958 long jump, placing 6th. Whatever transpired the next day, he had a great deal to live up to: he was the younger brother of Yvette Williams, Olympic champion, World record-holder and four times Empire gold-medallist.

Scheduled for Saturday 6 August were the 100 yards, six miles, steeplechase, 20 miles walk, high jump and javelin, the completion of the decathlon, and the women's shot. The six-mile race was regarded at the very least as a probable win for Ron Clarke, and by the halfway mark his World record pace (13:24.4) had disposed of everybody except the 21-year-old Kenyan champion, Naftali Temu, whose times did not remotely compare but who had raced mostly at debilitating high altitude. Clarke changed his tactics in the second half to alternate spells of fast and slow running, but nothing seemed to disturb the red-shirted Kenyan soldier, and when he took off with a 62.6 21st lap Clarke had no answer, dropping 150 yards behind. Temu's winning time was 27:14.21, the fourth fastest ever, and it occupies an historic place in the annals of the sport because it marked Kenya's first ever major championship in a distance event. We were not to know it then, although we might have had good reason to suspect so, but it was to be the first of many.

The steeplechase was no less exciting and it was equally surprising. At the bell there were still five runners in contention - Maurice Herriott, the Olympic silver-medallist, prominent amongst them - but it was the self-coached New Zealand medical student, Peter Welsh, who unexpectedly best blended speed and tactics over the last lap and won in a sensational time of 8:29.44, which was the second fastest ever recorded and a personal improvement of 12 seconds. Kerry O'Brien was 2nd for Australia just ahead of another Kenyan "learner", 20-year-old Benjamin Kogo, and Herriott finished out on his feet in 4th. Two Olympic walking champions - Norman Read from 1956 and Don Thompson from 1960 - at long last got their Commonwealth Games opportunity in the 20 miles event which began at 6 a.m. to avoid the worst of the heat and humidity. Even so, the temperature was already in the 80s when a 25-year-old Bolton print worker, Ron Wallwork, who had begun his athletics career at 14 as a shot-putter and discus-thrower, reached the finish in just under two-and-three-quarter hours and become the first Games walks champion. Three of the 12 starters formed the entire Isle of Man contingent in Kingston, and 18-year-old Phil Bannan finished in a commendable 7th place.

Harry Jerome, who had disappointed in Perth but won the bronze in the 1964 Olympic 100m, ran 9.37 in his 100 yards semi-final and then lived up to his reputation this time in the final, leading all the way and just getting home from Tom Robinson, silver-medallist for the third successive Games, 9.41 to 9.44. The next four men were separated by only 1/100th of a second and it was Ed Roberts, the Olympic 200m bronze-medallist from Trinidad, who was awarded 3rd in this classiest of sprint finals. Roy Williams duly won the decathlon to add to the family collection of gold medals, and most unusually a Games record for an individual event was broken in the course of this second day of the decathlon when Trevor Bickle, the reigning Commonwealth pole-vault champion, cleared 4.70m (15ft 5in) but finished only 8th overall. John FitzSimons threw a British record 79.78 (261ft 9in) in the first round of the javelin, and that was far too good for Nick Birks and Muhammad Nawaz, now 42, each earning their second medal, while a somewhat lacklustre high-jump competition was won by Australia's Lawrie Peckham, who later completed a bizarre double that he would probably rather forget about by placing last in the triple jump. In a quality women's shot event Val Young brought her tally of Games golds to four and Mary Peters, taking part in her third Games, was a close 2nd. In the semi-finals Dianne Burge, of Australia, ran a superlative 10.58 for 100 yards and World record-holder Judy Pollock 52.91 for 440 yards, while George Kerr was fractionally outside Peter Snell's Games record for 880 yards with 1:47.70.

A crowd of 30,000 was in attendance on Monday 8 August for finals at 880 yards, three miles, 440 yards hurdles, long jump, discus and women's 100 yards, 440 yards and high jump. The half-mile was a frenzied affair with a Trinidadian, Lennox Yearwood, tearing through the first lap in 49.7 (!) to lead by 10 yards before Wilson Kiprugut, the Olympic bronze-medallist, went ahead to take the entire bunched field (bar Yearwood) past the 660 mark. Kiprugut, Kerr and the Olympic silver-medallist, Bill Crothers, seemed to have the race between them in the finishing straight only for the unheralded second-string Australian, Noel Clough, to come from the back and win by a couple of yards in a Games record 1:46.9. It was a case of Clough slowing down the least as everyone tired after the over-eager first lap, and his time was 1.4sec faster than he had ever before achieved. Not bad for a 29-year-old previously regarded more as a low hurdler. This sort of shock happily occurs from time to time in major championships, and in proper accordance with a now established tradition Clough never ran as fast again.

Naftali Temu and Ron Clarke, the great protagonists from the six miles, lined up again at three miles, but the main rival for Clarke on this occasion was expected to be Kip Keino. At halfway the time was sub-13min pace (6:27.0) and a lap later Clarke, Keino and Scotsman Ian McCafferty were 50 yards clear. Into the last mile Clarke led by a stride or so, but the 10th lap was the slowest of the race and Keino's 56.3 last 440, even though he did not make his break until well down the back straight, was too quick for the Australian. The times were brilliant: Keino's the fourth fastest ever; Clarke's the first sub-13min not to win a race; an English record for 22-year-old Allan Rushmer in 3rd place; and a Scottish record for McCafferty, hanging on to finish 5th. The 440 hurdles, still suffering a sort of post-Potgieter syndrome, was won again by the Australian, Ken Roche.

Another batch of precocious Australians lined up for the women's 100 yards final with Dianne Burge, at 22, the senior to Joyce Bennett, still only 21 though she had won gold and silver in Perth, and 17-year-old Jennifer Lamy, and it was the compact (only 5ft1in tall) quick-striding Burge who won her country's fifth gold medal in the event and later joined the other two in qualifying for the 220 final. Judy Pollock's almost inevitable win at 440 yards was slightly slower than in her heat, probably because she already had a 10-yard lead entering the home straight, but there were British and Jamaican records for the two other medallists. The remaining women's final, the high jump, brought together the two previous champions, Michele Brown (nee Mason) and Robyn Woodhouse, and Brown achieved a feat that had so far evaded anyone else, male or female, in the history of the Games by regaining a title after an eight-year gap.

Lynn Davies was the only current male Olympic champion appearing at these Games and led the long jump from the first round. His best effort of 7.99 (26-2 3/4) came in round two and the next two places were taken by a former British international, John Morbey, now representing Bermuda, and Jamaica's Wellesley Clayton, repeating his bronze of three years earlier. Davies was not the first man to win Olympic and Commonwealth golds in that order - the Australian high jumper, John Winter, had done so in 1948-50 - and the Welshman probably took particular satisfaction from the fact that his win made up for circumstances in Perth four years earlier when he had perhaps been deprived of a medal because of the fluctuating wind conditions. The New Zealand discus-thrower, Les Mills, was competing in his third Games and also improved, from silver in 1958 and 5th in 1962, to win ahead of the Commonwealth record-holder, George Puce.

The marathon runners were up and about before dawn on Thursday 11 August because their race began at 5.30 a.m. with finals to come later in the day at 220, 440, 120 hurdles, triple jump, shot and women's 220 and javelin. Brian Kilby, the title-holder and 4th in the Tokyo Olympics, and his Coventry Godiva clubmate, Bill Adcocks, were England's formidable pair; Jim Alder, of Scotland, had been bronze-medallist at six miles; Bill Baillie, Jeff Julian and Scots-born Mike Ryan formed the seasoned NZ trio; Ron Clarke, 9th in the Tokyo Games, was going again for Australia. Clarke, as in the Olympics, set the pace and it seemed a perfectly reasonable one (around 2:20 schedule) through 10 miles, but Adcocks and Alder caught and passed him at 15 miles and by the 20-mile point (1:47:53) the Britons were over a quarter-of-a-mile ahead and Clarke was out of the race. At this stage the leaders had run admirably even-paced five-mile "splits" (26:51, 26:54, 26:48 and 27:20 for Adcocks), and it was Alder who maintained the rhythm through 25 miles (a 27:27 "split"), but his lead at the stadium entrance was only 50 yards or so and still anything could happen ... and did. Because of incompetent officiating Alder took a wrong turn and Adcocks emerged on the track first, but fortunately Alder had enough left in reserve to regain the lead and emulate fellow-Scots Duncan McLeod Wright (1930) and Joe McGhee (1954) in winning the race.

Harry Jerome and Tom Robinson had been among the starters at 220 yards, but the unexpected star of the previous Monday's unnecessarily strenuous series of three qualifying rounds had been Stanley Allotey, of Ghana, who had placed 6th in the 100 yards final and was only the 12th ranked furlong runner on pre-Games form. Allotey ran 20.9, 20.7 and 20.6, all of them Games records, and in the final he confirmed his calibre with a comfortable win in 20.65, according to the more demanding automatic timer. In the first round of the 440, also three days before, there had been an even more dominant performer as the Olympic 400m silver-medallist from Trinidad, Wendell Mottley, had set a new Commonwealth record of 45.8, and he then won his semi-final in 46.19. Two hours later in the final he went through the first 220 in 21.6 and won by a huge margin in 45.02. It was quite probably the finest one-lap race ever run because the official World record for 440 yards was a hand-timed 44.9 by Adolph Plummer, of the USA, and the best automatically-timed 400m (almost three yards shorter than 440 yards) was 45.07 by Otis Davis, again of the USA, from the 1960 Olympics. Not only that, but Mottley must rank with the Americans, Tommie Smith and Larry James, as one of the most aesthetically-pleasing of all quarter-milers. His silken-smooth raking stride was a joy to watch.

The 120 yards hurdles marked the start of an auspicious international career for the 22-year-old US-educated David Hemery as the three medallists from 1962 reached the final again and Ghulam Raziq, the defending champion, won his third successive medal. The triple jump was an all-Nigerian affair with the versatile high-jump silver-medallist, Samuel Igun, adding a gold to become the first man to win medals in these two events at the Games, and the shot had a familiar look about it with Dave

Steen, the bronze-medallist of 1962, winning from the discus leaders, Les Mills and George Puce. Anna Bocson (the former Mrs Pazera), World-record winner in 1958 and 3rd in 1962, was back again in the javelin but had to be satisfied with completing a full set of medals as 17-year-old Margaret Parker improved out of all recognition, though barely in the World's top 50 for the year. At least it showed great promise for the future, but Miss Parker never threw as far again.

Another Aussie, 17-year-old Jennifer Lamy, got the silver at 220 yards as Dianne Burge became the seventh double sprint champion in seven Games, and the remaining track action was in the heats of the men's mile, which were expected to be something of a formality with 12 to qualify and runners from Antigua, the Bahamas, India, Jamaica, Malaysia, Mauritius and Uganda all surely doomed to be out of their depth. As it happens, Robert Rwakojo encouragingly got through for Uganda in a very respectable 4:04.7, but that was in heat three and the crowd was still abuzz at the antics of the opening heat in which the three-mile champion, Kip Keino, had run a 58.9 first lap and just kept going, even though his nearest challenger was 50 yards or more behind, to break Roger Bannister's Games record with 3:57.35! Yvo Labonte, of Mauritius, came last in 4:33.27 but was by no means the slowest: a 17-year-old from Antigua was on the track for 5 minutes and 8 seconds in heat three, by which time the automatic timer had stopped. Yet the experience clearly did Fred Sowerby no harm because 12 years later he was to be a Commonwealth Games finalist at 400 metres.

The final day's competition was on Saturday 13 August with the mile and the relays as the traditional grand finales for another 30,000 crowd, and the pole vault and hammer for men and the 880, hurdles, long jump and discus for women as the supporting events. Of the seven individual titles six were won by athletes who were already gold-medallists as Trevor Bickle (pole vault), Howard Payne (hammer), Pam Kilborn (80m hurdles) and Val Young (discus) all repeated their Perth successes, and two other golds went to an Olympic champion, Mary Rand, in the long jump and to the Games three-mile winner, Kip Keino in the mile. The one remaining victory of the day was that of Canada's Abby Hoffman, who had, by contrast, finished last in the same 880 yards event four years previously.

Keino was absolutely imperious. Not only did he win in 3:55.34, but he led every step of the way through laps of 59.2, 59.5, a devastating 57.9 and an unpressed 58.7. Accustomed, as we now are, to hordes of Kenyan middle-distance and distance runners winning countless races and titles the World over, the achievements of Keino and his compatriot, Naftali Temu, may seem hardly surprising in hindsight, but it should be remembered that since Maiyoro and Chepkwony had made their dramatic debut 12 years earlier the progress of Kenyan athletics had not been as spectacular as might have been anticipated. Furthermore, although there were others, particularly in the steeplechase, who were soon to follow Keino's example, it was not until the late 1980s that a new generation of gloriously unfettered runners from the Rift Valley and the slopes of Mount Kilimanjaro began to approach Keino's level of performance in large numbers. He was a great runner who changed all our concepts of miling being an Anglo-Saxon preserve, and he remains a splendid ambassador for the sport.

The women's 880 followed the unexpected pattern of the men's race. Marise Chamberlain, now Mrs Stephen, and the silver-medallist from Perth, seemed the likely winner until the very last few strides when she wilted and Abby Hoffman, now all of 19, came through to win - but only just from the Games 440 champion, Judy Pollock, who had also placed 4th at 220. Pam Kilborn's hurdles success was narrower than had been supposed ahead of a national record by Jamaica's Carmen Smith, and both these two got further medals in a very high class 4 x 110 yards relay. The Australians won in 45.3, only one-tenth outside the World record, and Ghana then repeated that feat in the men's final - in which three of the medal-winning athletes were named Addy, Addy and Eddy! To the further confusion of the announcers and the medal-engravers there had been six separate occasions during the Games at 100 yards, 220 yards and in the relay that Gary Eddy, of Australia, had met up with either James Addy or Ebenezer Addy, of Ghana. Eddy and James Addy were both in the 100 yards final, and Eddy "won" five individual events but not the race that counted most. Those track "nuts" who revel in "name games" would surely have delighted in the fact that Eddy also ran the heats of the 4 x 440 and that the England team which eventually won the bronze medals included John Adey. The Bahamas, with Tom Robinson and 15-year-old Edwin Johnson in their quartet, had run 40.8 in the 4 x 110 heats but had been disqualified.

Two previous champions, 35-year-old Howard Payne (1962) and 39-year-old Muhammad Iqbal (1954), who had also placed 4th and 2nd respectively in 1958, renewed acquaintances yet again in the hammer final, which to their understandable annoyance was held outside the main stadium, and Payne won from an immensely promising 19-year-old Indian, Praveen Kumar, who two years later was to break Payne's own Commonwealth record. Payne's wife, Rosemary, was competing for Scotland in the discus that evening, but victory here went once more to Val Young, of New Zealand. Then a rip-roaring Games was brought to an apt climax at just before 9.20 at night with a World record 3:02.8 in the 4 x 440 yards relay by the Trinidad & Tobago team of Lennox Yearwood (47.8), Kent Bernard (45.7), Ed Roberts (44.8) and Wendell Mottley (44.5). This was still the equivalent of a couple of seconds slower than the 4 x 400 metres achieved by a US team three weeks earlier, but a marvellous performance, nevertheless, which would have been even quicker but for Yearwood replacing the injured Ed Skinner, who had run in Trinidad's Olympic bronze-medal team.

RESULTS 1966

MEN

Note: the automatic timer was frequently not in operation for some or all of the competitors.

100 YARDS (6 Aug): 1 Harry Jerome (Can) 9.41, 2 Tom Robinson (Bah) 9.44, 3 Ed Roberts (Tri) 9.52, 4 David Ejoke (Nig) 9.52, 5 Gary Eddy (Aus) 9.52, 6 Stanley Allotey (Gha) 9.53, 7 Barrie Kelly (Eng) 9.66, 8 James Addy (Gha) 9.74.

220 YARDS (11 Aug): 1 Stanley Allotey (Gha) 20.65, 2 Ed Roberts (Tri) 20.93, 3 David Ejoke (Nig) 20.95, 4 Gary Eddy (Aus) 21.05, 5 Don Domansky (Can) 21.13, 6 Gary Holdsworth (Aus) 21.40, 7 Harry Jerome (Can) 21.41, 8 Manikavasagam Jegathesan (Mal) 21.53.

440 YARDS (11 Aug): 1 Wendell Mottley (Tri) 45.08, 2 Kent Bernard (Tri) 46.06, 3 Don Domansky (Can) 46.42, 4 Daniel Rudisha (Ken) 46.45, 5 Bill Crothers (Can) 46.90, 6 Martin Winbolt Lewis (Eng) 47.02, 7 John Adey (Eng) 47.09, 8 Noel Clough (Aus) 47.53.

880 YARDS (8 Aug): 1 Noel Clough (Aus) 1:46.9, 2 Wilson Kiprugut (Ken) 1:47.2, 3 George Kerr (Jam) 1:47.2, 4 Bill Crothers (Can) 1:47.3, 5 Chris Carter (Eng) 1:48.1, 6 Ralph Doubell (Aus) 1:48.3, 7 Peter Francis (Ken) 1:48.3, 8 Lennox Yearwood (Tri) 1:57.5.

1 MILE (13 Aug): 1 Kip Keino (Ken) 3:55.34, 2 Alan Simpson (Eng) 3:57.27, 3 Ian Studd (NZ) 3:58.61, 4 Walter Wilkinson (Eng) 3:59.37, 5 Derek Graham (NI) 3:59.40, 6 Keith Wheeler (Aus) 3:59.81, 7 Ergas Leps (Can) 4:01.08, 8 Kerry O'Brien (Aus) 4:02.72, 9 Robert Rwakojo (Uga) 4:03.13, 10 Geoff Pyne (NZ) 4:03.22. Did not finish - Ralph Doubell (Aus), Graeme Grant (Sco).

3 MILES (8 Aug): 1 Kip Keino (Ken) 12:57.4, 2 Ron Clarke (Aus) 12:59.2, 3 Allan Rushmer (Eng) 13:08.6, 4 Naftali Temu (Ken) 13:10.4, 5 Ian McCafferty (Sco) 13:12.2, 6 Dick Taylor (Eng) 13:12.4, 7 Bill Wilkinson (Eng) 13:15.4, 8 Derek Graham (NI) 13:17.8, 9 Geoff Pyne (NZ) 13:18.6, 10 Ian Studd (NZ) 13:25.8, 11 Chrisantus Nyakwayo (Ken) 13:31.0, 12 Lachie Stewart (Sco) 13:40.0, 13 Benjamin Kogo (Ken) 13:42.2, 14 Bruce Tulloh (Eng) 13:46.4, 15 Pascal Mfyomi

(Tan) 13:48.2, 16 Ian Blackwood (Aus) 13:51.6, 17 Fergus Murray (Sco) 14:32.4, 18 George Kerr (Jam) 14:37.2, 19 Dilbagh Singh Kler (Mal) 14:54.8, 20 John Mowatt (Jam) 15:04.8, 21 Alifu Albert Massaquoi (SL) 15:22.0. Did not finish - Mohamed Ismail (SAr), Robert Lightburn (BH), Kerry O'Brien (Aus), Vinton Powell (Jam). Note: Bill Wilkinson was not related to Walter Wilkinson, 4th in the mile; George Kerr was not the George Kerr who ran in the 440, 880 and 4 x 440, and to add further confusion their respective initials were "E.G." and "G.E."! .

6 MILES (6 Aug): 1 Naftali Temu (Ken) 27:14.21, 2 Ron Clarke (Aus) 27:39.42, 3 Jim Alder (Sco) 28:15.4, 4 Pascal Mfyomi (Tan) 28:38.0, 5 Ron Hill (Eng) 28:42.6, 6 Dave Ellis (Can) 28:55.4, 7 Fergus Murray (Sco) 29:40.0, 8 Andy Boychuk (Can) 29:54.0, 9 Bill Baillie (NZ) 30:01.0, 10 John Mowatt (Jam) 31:13.4, 11 Harry Prowell (Guy) 31:24.0. Did not finish - Tony Cook (Aus), Robert Lightburn (BH), Glenford Robinson (Jam).

MARATHON (11 Aug): 1 Jim Alder (Sco) 2:22:07.8, 2 Bill Adcocks (Eng) 2:22:13.0, 3 Mike Ryan (NZ) 2:27:59.0, 4 Dave Ellis (Can) 2:31:46.8, 5 Jeff Julian (NZ) 2:32:45.4, 6 Ron Wallingford (Can) 2:35:13.0, 7 Chrisantus Nyakwayo (Ken) 2:44:59.4, 8 Stan Vennard (NI) 2:46:59.0, 9 Andy Boychuk (Can) 2:58:45.2, 10 Omari Abdallah (Tan) 3:08:29.6. Did not finish - Ian Blackwood (Aus), Ron Clarke (Aus), Tony Cook (Aus), Keith Graham (Jam), Brian Kilby (Eng), Wimalasena Perera (Cey), James Wahome (Ken). Note: all of the first four were British-born - Ryan in Scotland, Ellis in England.

3000 METRES STEEPLECHASE (6 Aug): 1 Peter Welsh (NZ) 8:29.44, 2 Kerry O'Brien (Aus) 8:32.58, 3 Benjamin Kogo (Ken) 8:32.81, 4 Maurice Herriott (Eng) 8:33.19, 5 Ian Blackwood (Aus) 8:41.30, 6 Ernie Pomfret (Eng) 8:41.32, 7 John Linaker (Sco) 8:41.38, 8 Naftali Chirchir (Ken) 8:47.4, 9 Lachie Stewart (Sco) 8:57.0, 10 Gerry Stevens (Eng) 9:01.2, 11 Omari Abdallah (Tan) 9:14.0, 12 Dilbagh Singh Kler (Mal) 9:53.2.

20 MILES WALK (6 Aug):1 Ron Wallwork (Eng) 2:44:42.8, 2 Ray Middleton (Eng) 2:45:19.0, 3 Norman Read (NZ) 2:46:28.2, 4 Don Thompson (Eng) 2:46:43.0, 5 Alex Oakley (Can) 2:54:25.8, 6 Felix Cappella (Can) 2:57:21.2, 7 Phil Bannan (IoM) 3:06:11.2, 8 Albert Johnson (IoM) 3:08:05.8, 9 Roy Hart (Wal) 3:15:02.6, 10 Libert Valentine (Tri) 3:22:25.4. Did not finish - Frank Clark (Aus), Richard Gawne (IoM).

120 YARDS HURDLES (11 Aug): 1 David Hemery (Eng) 14.1, 2 Mike Parker (Eng) 14.2, 3 Ghulam Raziq (Pak) 14.3, 4 Ray Harvey (Jam) 14.3, 5 Laurie Taitt

(Eng) 14.3, 6 Folu Erinle (Nig) 14.5, 7 Gurbachan Singh (Ind) 14.6, 8 David Prince (Aus) 14.6.

440 YARDS HURDLES (8 Aug): 1 Ken Roche (Aus) 50,95, 2 Kingsley Agbabokha (Nig) 51.46, 3 Peter Warden (Eng) 51.54, 4 Robin Woodland (Eng) 51.86, 5 Gary Knoke (Aus) 51.94, 6 Bill Gairdner (Can) 52.14, 7 Roger Johnson (NZ) 55.87. Note: John Sherwood (Eng) qualified but did not start.

4 x 110 YARDS RELAY (13 Aug): 1 Ghana (Ebenezer Addy, Bonner Mends, James Addy, Stanley Allotey) 39.8, 2 Jamaica (Wellesley Clayton, Pablo McNeil, Lynn Headley, Mike Fray) 40.0, 3 Australia (Gary Eddy, Allan Crawley, Gary Holdsworth, Peter Norman) 40.0, 4 Wales (Terry Davies, Lynn Davies, Keri Jones, Ron Jones) 40.2, 5 Canada (Ed Hearne, Terry Tomlinson, Don Domansky, Harry Jerome) 40.4, 6 Nigeria (Omoba Peters, Folu Erinle, Sydney Asiodu, David Ejoke) 40.4, 7 England (Dave Jones, Dave Dear, Mel Cheskin, Barrie Kelly) 40.9, 8 Trinidad & Tobago (Clifton Bertrand, Cipriani Phillip, Winston Short, Henry Noel) 41.3. Note: Allan Crawley competed in the 1962 Games for Papua-New Guinea.

4 x 440 YARDS RELAY (13 Aug): 1 Trinidad & Tobago (Lennox Yearwood, Kent Bernard, Ed Roberts, Wendell Mottley) 3:02.8, 2 Canada (Ross MacKenzie, Brian McLaren, Don Domansky, Bill Crothers) 3:04.9, 3 England (Martin Winbolt Lewis, John Adey, Peter Warden, Tim Graham) 3:06.5, 4 Jamaica (Clifton Forbes, Laurie Kahn, George Kerr, Rupert Hoilette) 3:06.8, 5 Australia (Peter Norman, Gary Knoke, Noel Clough, Ken Roche) 3:12.2, 6 Nigeria (Benedict Majekodunmi, Kingsley Agbabokha, Paulinus Nawaokoro, David Ejoke) 3:12.4, 7 Barbados (Ezra Burnham, Bertram Catwell, Charles Harewood, Keith Forde) 3:12.9, 8 Uganda (Asmani Bawala, Francis Hatega, George Odeke, Amos Omolo) 3:13.6.

HIGH JUMP (6 Aug): 1 Lawrie Peckham (Aus) 2.08, 2 Samuel Igun (Nig) 2.03, 3 Anton Norris (Bar) 2.01, 4 Crawford Fairbrother (Sco) 1.98, 5 Fela Shobande (Nig) 1.96, 6 Trevor Tennant (Jam) 1.93, 7 Bhim Singh (Ind) 1.88, 8= Ivor Bird (Ant) & Patrick Rahming (Bah) 1.83.

POLE VAULT (11 Aug): 1 Trevor Bickle (Aus) 4.80, 2 Mike Bull (NI) 4.72, 3 Gerry Moro (Can) 4.65, 4 David Stevenson (Sco) 4.65, 5 Bob Yard (Can) 4.57, 6 Trevor Burton (Eng) 4.11, 7 Norrie Foster (Sco) 4.11, 8 Augustine Soga (Gha) 3.81.

LONG JUMP (8 Aug): 1 Lynn Davies (Wal) 7.99, 2 John Morbey (Ber) 7.89, 3 Wellesley Clayton (Jam) 7.83, 4 Allan Crawley (Aus) 7.79, 5 Vic Brooks (Jam)

7.65, 6 Phil May (Aus) 7.50, 7 Dave Norris (NZ) 7.47, 8 Julius Sang (Ken) 7.41, 9 Johnson Amoah (Gha) 7.28, 10 George Ogan (Nig) 7.11, 11 Byron Lewis (Jam) 7.00, 12 Fred Alsop (Eng) 6.98, 13 Dave Gaskin (Eng) 6.91, 14 Randolph Benjamin (Ber) 6.82, 15 Alvin Young (Jam) 6.77, 16 Gerald Wisdom (Bah) 6.67, 17 Maxime Anthony (Mau) 6.61, 18 Silas Tita (PNG) 5.65.

TRIPLE JUMP (11 Aug): 1 Samuel Igun (Nig) 16.40, 2 George Ogan (Nig) 16.08, 3 Fred Alsop (Eng) 15.96, 4 Timothy Barrett (Bah) 15.73, 5 Dave Norris (NZ) 15.53, 6 Mahoney Samuels (Jam) 15.47, 7 Lennox Burgher (Jam) 15.19, 8 Vic Brooks (Jam) 15.05, 9 Trevor Thomas (Jam) 14.94, 10 Phil May (Aus) 14.92, 11 Hartley Saunders (Bah) 14.90, 12 James Ocen-Bowa (Uga) 14.89, 13 Johnson Amoah (Gha) 14.82, 14 John Okuthe (Ken) 14.70, 15 John Morbey (Ber) 14.06, 16 Maxime Anthony (Mau) 13.95, 17 Anton Norris (Bar) 13.79, 18 Lawrie Peckham (Aus) 13.13. Note: Igun's best jump was assisted by a 2.4m wind but he also had a legal clearance of 16.29.

SHOT (11 Aug): 1 Dave Steen (Can) 18.79, 2 Les Mills (NZ) 18.37, 3 George Puce (Can) 17.14, 4 Mike Lindsay (Sco) 17.03, 5 Robin Hargreaves (NZ) 16.43, 6 Robin Tait (NZ) 16.39, 7 Roy Hollingsworth (Tri) 15.22, 8 Bill Tancred (Eng) 14.93, 9 William Barrow (Ant) 14.51, 10 Zenon Andrusyshyn (Can) 14.45, 11 Ain Roost (Can) 14.18, 12 John Rolle (Bah) 13.84, 13 William Hall (Jam) 13.19. Note: Roy Hollingsworth competed for England in 1962.

DISCUS (8 Aug): 1 Les Mills (NZ) 56.19, 2 George Puce (Can) 55.93, 3 Robin Tait (NZ) 55.02, 4 Dave Steen (Can) 54.23, 5 Roy Hollingsworth (Tri) 53.92, 6 Mike Lindsay (Sco) 50.32, 7 Ain Roost (Can) 49.71, 8 Praveen Kumar (Ind) 48.97, 9 Bill Tancred (Eng) 48.87, 10 Patrick Anukwa (Nig) 47.50, 11 Philip Otieno (Ken) 45.59, 12 Muhammad Ayub (Pak) 45.44, 13 Winston Burt (Jam) 44.70, 14 Zenon Andrusyshyn (Can) 44.07, 15 Cecil Hylton (Jam) 44.04.

HAMMER (13 Aug): 1 Howard Payne (Eng) 61.98, 2 Praveen Kumar (Ind) 60.12, 3 Muhammad Iqbal (Pak) 59.56, 4 Dick Leffler (Aus) 58.04, 5 Laurie Bryce (Sco) 57.73, 6 Peter Seddon (Eng) 57.48, 7 Anthony Kipruto (Ken) 46.71.

JAVELIN (6 Aug): 1 John FitzSimons (Eng) 79.78, 2 Nick Birks (Aus) 76.15, 3 Muhammad Nawaz (Pak) 69.93, 4 Nashatar Singh (Mal) 69.34, 5 Ain Roost (Can) 66.62, 6 Dave Travis (Eng) 65.63, 7 Zenon Andrusyshyn (Can) 64.19, 8 Wilson Kiptalam (Ken) 60.68, 9 Noel Simons (Ber) 50.04, 10 Cecil Usher (BH) 47.75, 11 Hartley Saunders (Bah) 46.53, 12 Ayrton Clouden (StV) 44.91.

DECATHLON (5-6 Aug): 1 Roy Williams (NZ) 7,270 (100m 11.0, Long jump 7.24, Shot 13.61, High jump 1.85, 400m 51.2, 110m hurdles 15.0, Discus 45.24, Pole vault 3.80, Javelin 47.30, 1500m 4:55.6), 2 Clive Longe (Wal) 7,123 (11.2, 6.51, 14.86, 1.75, 51.5, 15.02, 42.02, 3.60, 55.84, 4:38.3), 3 Gerry Moro (Can) 6,983 (11.9, 6.37, 12.75, 1.78, 52.2, 15.4, 37.68, 4.60, 53.94, 4:30.6), 4 Norrie Foster (Sco) 6,728, 5 Derek Clarke (Eng) 6,691, 6 Keswick Smalling (Jam) 6,513, 7 Kiprop Koech (Ken) 6,399, 8 Trevor Bickle (Aus) 6,007, 9 Dave Gaskin (Eng) 5,828, 10 Ayrton Clouden (StV) 4,644. Did not finish - Wayne Athorne (Aus). Note: the 1964 tables on which these scores were based were updated in 1984 and the revised scores for the leading six would be as follows: Williams 7,133, Longe 6,984, Moro 6,867, Foster 6,580, Clarke 6,559, Smalling 6,400.

WOMEN

100 YARDS (8 Aug): 1 Dianne Burge (Aus) 10.6, 2 Irene Piotrowski (Can) 10.8, 3 Jill Hall (Eng) 10.8, 4 Jennifer Lamy (Aus) 10.8, 5 Joyce Bennett (Aus) 10.8, 6 Vilma Charlton (Jam) 10.9, 7 Adlin Mair (Jam) 10.9, 8 Daphne Slater (Eng) 11.1. Note: Slater nee Arden.

220 YARDS (11 Aug): 1 Dianne Burge (Aus) 23.73, 2 Jennifer Lamy (Aus) 23.86, 3 Irene Piotrowski (Can) 23.92, 4 Judy Pollock (Aus) 24.14, 5 Joyce Bennett (Aus) 24.16, 6 Una Morris (Jam) 24.40, 7 Vilma Charlton (Jam) 24.41, 8 Janet Simpson (Eng) 24.64. Note: Janet Simpson was the daughter of Violet Webb who was 3rd in the long jump in 1934.

440 YARDS (6 Aug): 1 Judy Pollock (Aus) 53.0, 2 Deirdre Watkinson (Eng) 54.1, 3 Una Morris (Jam) 54.2, 4 Rosemary Stirling (Sco) 54.4, 5 Lillian Board (Eng) 54.7, 6 Cecilia Carter (Can) 55.0, 7 Janet Maddin (Can) 55.3, 8 Gloria Dourass (Wal) 55.5.

880 YARDS (13 Aug): 1 Abby Hoffman (Can) 2:04.3, 2 Judy Pollock (Aus) 2:04.5, 3 Anne Smith (Eng) 2:05.0, 4 Rosemary Stirling (Sco) 2:05.4, 5 Pat Lowe (Eng) 2:05.8, 6 Marise Stephen (NZ) 2:05.9, 7 Pam Piercy (Eng) 2:06.3, 8 Cecilia Carter (Can) 2:13.1. Note: Stephen nee Chamberlain.

80 METRES HURDLES (13 Aug): 1 Pam Kilborn (Aus) 10.9, 2 Carmen Smith (Jam) 11.0, 3 Jenny Wingerson (Can) 11.0, 4 Cathy Chapman (Can) 11.1, 5 Pat Pryce (Eng) 11.1, 6 Ann Wilson (Eng) 11.2, 7 Brenda Matthews (NZ) 11.3, 8 Violet Odogwu (Nig) 11.5. Note: Pryce nee Nutting.

4 x 110 YARDS RELAY (13 Aug): 1 Australia (Jennifer Lamy, Pam Kilborn, Joyce Bennett, Dianne Burge) 45.3, 2 England (Maureen Tranter, Janet Simpson, Daphne Slater, Jill Hall) 45.6, 3 Jamaica (Adlin Mair, Una Morris, Vilma Charlton, Carmen Smith) 45.6, 4 Canada (Valerie Parker, Marjorie Turner, Janet Maddin, Irene Piotrowski) 45.9, 5 Wales (Liz Parsons, Gloria Dourass, Liz Gill, Thelwyn Appleby) 46.2, 6 Trinidad & Tobago (Sybil Dommartin, Sigrid Sandiford, Jocelyn Haynes, Olive Straker) 47.4, 7 Nigeria (Oyeronke Akindele, Olajumoke Bodunrin, Mairo Jinadu, Regina Okafor) 47.9, 8 Sierra Leone (Millicent Jackson, Teresa Johnson, Olive Palmer-Davis, Marie Sesay) 49.3. Note: Valerie Parker was the sister of Harry Jerome.

HIGH JUMP (8 Aug): 1 Michele Brown (Aus) 1.73, 2 Dorothy Shirley (Eng) 1.70, 3 Robyn Woodhouse (Aus) 1.70, 4 Susan Nigh (Can) 1.68, 5 Patsy Callender (Bar) 1.68, 6 Gwenda Hurst (Eng) 1.65, 7 Ann Wilson (Eng) 1.65, 8 Mary Rand (Eng) 1.62, 9 Valerie Surgeon (Jam) 1.60, 10 Lesline Cameron (Jam) 1.57, 11 Emelda Lewis (Ant) 1.47. Yvonne Sawyer (SL) failed at opening height of 1.47. Note: Brown nee Mason; Rand nee Bignal.

LONG JUMP (13 Aug): 1 Mary Rand (Eng) 6.36, 2 Sheila Parkin (Eng) 6.30, 3 Violet Odogwu (Nig) 6.15, 4 Alix Jamieson (Sco) 6.06, 5 Helen Frith (Aus) 5.97, 6 Jenny Wingerson (Can) 5.85, 7 Pam Kilborn (Aus) 5.81, 8 Cathy Chapman (Can) 5.77, 9 Ann Wilson (Eng) 5.72, 10 Gwenda Hurst (Eng) 5.62, 11 Alice Annum (Gha) 5.62, 12 Patsy Callender (Bar) 5.56, 13 Beverley Welsh (Jam) 5.46, 14 Cynthia Hyman (Jam) 5.45, 15 Ana Ramacake (Fij) 5.12, 16 Esther Maganga (Tan) 4.83, 17 Annelle Simmonds (Ant) 4.23.

SHOT (6 Aug): 1 Valerie Young (NZ) 16.50, 2 Mary Peters (NI) 16.30, 3 Nancy McCredie (Can) 15.34, 4 Jean Roberts (Aus) 14.66, 5 Diane Charteris (NZ) 14.15, 6 Brenda Bedford (Eng) 13.94, 7 Carol Martin (Can) 13.58, 8 Judith ("Jay") Dahlgren (Can) 12.88, 9 Jenny Wingerson (Can) 12.44, 10 Moira Kerr (Sco) 12.29, 11 Joan Gordon (Jam) 11.54.

DISCUS (13 Aug): 1 Valerie Young (NZ) 49.78, 2 Jean Roberts (Aus) 49.20, 3 Carol Martin (Can) 48.69, 4 Rosemary Payne (Sco) 47.68, 5 Nancy McCredie (Can) 46.00, 6 Brenda Bedford (Eng) 44.83, 7 Judith ("Jay") Dahlgren (Can) 41.66, 8 Diane Charteris (NZ) 38.46, 9 Joan Gordon (Jam) 36.62. Note: Rosemary Payne, nee Charters, was the wife of Howard Payne, the hammer winner.

JAVELIN (11 Aug): 1 Margaret Parker (Aus) 51.38, 2 Anna Bocson (Aus) 47.80, 3 Judith ("Jay") Dahlgren (Can) 47.68, 4 Jean Blake (Jam) 45.60, 5 Christa Leipert (Can) 44.45, 6 Sue Platt (Eng) 42.27, 7 Eileen Sutherland (Jam) 41.12. Note: Bocson formerly Pazera.

10.

The Stewart "clan"
raises the battle cry of Bannockburn

MEADOWBANK STADIUM, EDINBURGH, SCOTLAND
17-25 JULY 1970

THE 1968 OLYMPICS IN MEXICO CITY had been a traumatic experience. Of course, in the thin air of an altitude of 2282 metres there had been a torrent of spectacular performances in the explosive events, and Commonwealth athletes had played some part in them with World records for Ralph Doubell, of Australia, at 800m, and for David Hemery, of Great Britain, at 400m hurdles. In addition, Commonwealth records had been beaten in the men's and women's 100m, 200m and 4 x 100m and in the men's 1500m and triple jump. Many of the distance-runners had suffered terribly through the lack of oxygen, but the Commonwealth had come out of those events better than most with five medals for the Kenyans at 5000m, 10,000m and the steeplechase, including golds for Naftali Temu and Amos Biwott, and four of the leading eight places in the marathon.

As the 1970 Commonwealth Games approached World records had been broken by Australians Derek Clayton in the marathon and Kerry O'Brien in the steeplechase, and among the other significant advances were marks of 68.82 in the hammer by Howard Payne and 55.04 in the discus by his wife, Rosemary; 82.22 in the javelin by Dave Travis; and, most notably, 52.0 for 400m by Jamaican-born Londoner Marilyn Neufville, and 1.83 in the high jump by the Canadian, Debbie Brill, who had invented a new style of clearing the bar on her back in the manner of the Fosbury Flop but dubbed the "Brill Bend". A dozen of the 1966 male champions were entered again - Keino, Temu, Hemery, Lynn Davies and Payne among them

- but, oddly, the only woman returning to defend a title was Pam Kilborn, of Australia, who had just set a Commonwealth record of 13.1 for the 100m hurdles. There were 413 men and 134 women entered from 34 countries, and after 40 years there would finally be parity with the rest of the World - the 1970 Games were going metric. Even more to the athletes' liking, the track surface would be all-weather synthetic.

Not so welcome was the weather, which began windy and wet in typically Scottish midsummer fashion for a preliminary day of qualifying rounds on Friday 17 July and stayed that way much of the following week. Five men ran hand-timed 10.2s in the first or second rounds of the 100m, and there was one wind reading of + 9.8m per sec (almost 24 mph!). Saturday 18 July was the opening day of major competition with finals at 100m, 110m hurdles, high jump and hammer for men, plus the 10,000m and the 20 miles walk, and at 100m and discus for women, and it was the walker, Ron Wallwork, who was the first of the Kingston champions in action. He made a pretty good stab at it and led early on, but the Australian silver-medallist from the 1960 Olympics, Noel Freeman, was ahead at the turn and won rather easily. Howard Payne in the hammer (leading the first clean sweep of medals by one country in a Games men's throwing event), Lawrie Peckham in the high jump (with a Gambian in third place) and David Hemery at 110m hurdles all extended their reign as Commonwealth champions to eight years, and in the discus Rosemary Payne, a 37-year-old mother of twin boys aged 11, completed an unprecedented husband-and-wife double.

But it has to be said that the connoisseur's choice on this day was bound to be the 100m finals and the 10,000m. Fastest of the sprint semi-finalists were Alice Annum, breaking new ground for Ghanaian women at the age of 21, and 19-year-old Jamaican Don Quarrie, who was thought of as second-string to the Commonwealth record-holder and Olympic silver-medallist, Lennox Miller. Australia's Raelene Boyle, 4th in the Mexico 100m and still only 19, won her final from Annum, and then Quarrie led a Caribbean carve-up, winning from Miller and Trinidadian Hasley Crawford. Both events were wind-aided but not that fast, presumably because of the cool temperatures.

A huge entry of 29 lined up for the 10,000m, including 14 Africans, and most attention was focussed on Ron Clarke, the World record-holder still seeking gold in his fifth major Games appearance, and Naftali Temu, the Olympic and Commonwealth champion, but the latter was carrying an injury and never prominent once the race had begun. A group of a dozen, including Clarke, Kerry O'Brien, three Englishmen, two Kenyans and a Scot were together at halfway (14:09.2), and Clarke made the decisive break just before the end of the 18th lap, though taking Dick Taylor, of Coventry Godiva Harriers and England, and Lachie Stewart, of Shettleston Harriers and Scotland, with him. The latter's presence was a cause of immense excitement for the predominantly Scottish crowd of 30,000 and this spiralled into delirium on the last lap when Stewart responded promptly to Clarke's final effort and then went past him in the home straight to win. The second half of the race had been considerably faster (14:02.6) and Stewart was only five seconds or so outside Taylor's British record. In the 1966 Games Stewart had been 9th in the steeplechase and 12th at three miles. He was the first to admit afterwards that it was a pity that Clarke had to lose again, but there's nothing like a home win early on to bring a major Games alight.

There was a break until the following Tuesday, 21 July, and even then there was only one final, mystifyingly, at 400m hurdles for which four Africans had qualified, including the 1966 silver-medallist, Kingsley Agbabokha, but there was no David Hemery, concentrating to great effect on the high hurdles. The man who dealt best with the very strong wind was the powerfully-built Yorkshireman, John Sherwood, who had been bronze-medallist behind Hemery in the 1968 Olympics, and his win compensated for his experience at the Kingston Commonwealth Games where he had reached the final but had been unable to start because of illness. Uganda took 2nd place, though the silver-medallist, Bill Koskei, was actually a Kenyan from the same Nandi village as the bronze-medallist, and another Ugandan was 4th, both of them coached by a Briton, Malcolm Arnold. This other young man, only 20, and known as John Akii, would go on to much greater things. The pentathlon began with Mary Peters at last getting a chance to show her all-round talents in her fourth Games appearance, but the injured defending champion in the decathlon, Roy Williams, survived only three of the five first-day events.

Five finals took place on Wednesday 22 July, at 200m and discus for men and 200m, 1500m and long jump for women, with the pentathlon and decathlon also being completed. The Olympic silver-medallist and Commonwealth record-holder, Peter Norman, and the 1966 silver-medallist, Ed Roberts, were in the 200m line-up, but Quarrie became the first West Indian to complete the sprint double in a Games record 20.56 which was almost exactly on a par with Stanley Allotey's 20.65 win at the slightly longer 220 yards distance in Kingston. The under-rated Roberts was again 2nd - making five Olympic or Commonwealth medals for him so far - and Norman was 5th. Raelene Boyle maintained the perfect ladies' sequence of every Games having produced a double sprint champion, again ahead of the willowy Annum, and in the long jump Lynn Davies won his fourth major championship, though ironically benefiting from the varying wind rather than suffering from it, as he had in 1962 when he placed 4th. By further coincidence the 1962 winner, Mike Ahey, had only one decent jump this time ... and was 4th.

Five of the first six in the 1966 discus returned and George Puce, who had been born in Latvia, reversed the 1966 positions over Les Mills, who had now placed 2nd, 5th, 1st and 2nd in successive Games. Another Games veteran, Mary Peters, who had made her debut like Mills in 1958, won the pentathlon, and though the medallists represented three different countries all of them were English-born. Without Roy Williams the decathlon was still immensely exciting as Peter Gabbett, of England, who was an outstanding long jumper and sprinter, narrowly failed to make up ground in the last event, the 1500m, after a do-or-die 62sec first lap, and the winner by only 23 points out of 7,492 was the Australian, Geoff Smith, a solid and generally unspectacular all-rounder. But then that's what the decathlon - one event with 10 episodes, rather than 10 separate events - is about.

The previous Saturday Kip Keino had run another uninhibitedly fast heat, as in Kingston, but neither of his team-mates made the 1500m final and he faced three Englishmen, two Scots, two New Zealanders and two Canadians, together with an Australian and a Welshman, which suggested all sorts of possibilities for a concerted team effort to challenge the champion. Keino was having none of it, and fearsomely progressive lap times of 57.6, 57.4 and then 57.0 saw off everybody except, surprisingly, the Dutch-born Theodorus Jacobus Leonardus Quax, of New Zealand (fortunately known to all simply as "Dick"). Eventually Keino prevailed to become the first man to win successive Commonwealth titles at one mile or 1500m, but all credit to Quax for hanging on to 2nd place far ahead of a 22-year-old from Gateshead who showed his championship mettle by improving two seconds on his previous best time. More was to be heard from Brendan Foster.

Ten finals were decided the next day - Thursday 23 July - at 400m, steeplechase, pole vault and javelin for men, and at 400m, 1500m, 100m hurdles, long jump and shot for women. There was also the marathon, but still only for men: no woman had yet broken three hours for the distance and the first championship for them was not to be held for another 12 years. In the shot Mary Peters won her second gold of the Games, and though the defending champion, John FitzSimons, was beaten into 3rd place England still took all three javelin medals, led by Dave Travis, and Malawi (formerly Nyasaland) provided a pleasantly surprising 5th place by Wilfred Mwalawanda-Ngwenya. Sheila Sherwood, who had won silver medals in Kingston and Mexico, led throughout the long-jump competition and her best effort of 6.73 was a British all-comers' record and would be the second best performance in the World for the year. More importantly, perhaps, for the interests of equality in the Sherwood household she joined husband John as a Commonwealth champion, just as the Paynes had done already at these Games. In 2nd place, as in the pentathlon, was 20-year-old Ann Wilson, who was living proof - along with many others, it should be hastily added - that women athletes could be not only fleet-footed but bountifully beauteous.

The men's 400m semi-finals gave promise of a great final later in the day as Julius Sang, of Kenya, only just won the first of them from Ross Wilson, of Australia, 45.90 to 45.94, and then another Kenyan, Charles Asati, set a national record 45.59 with Fiji, Jamaica, Tanzania and Trinidad (Ed Roberts again) also getting men through. Asati, who had run in Kenya's silver-medal relay team in Mexico, produced another brilliant run in the final, winning in a time of 45.01 which set new records at Commonwealth, African, British all-comers' and Games level, though actually still intrinsically slower than Wendell Mottley's 440 yards in Kingston. The next three men all broke 46sec, including Fiji's lone athlete at the Games, Saimoni Tamani, in the bronze-medal position, and how much faster would they all have been but for being required to run semi-finals and final the same afternoon? The women's race made an even greater impression as a tall and long-legged 17-year-old Londoner, Marilyn Neufville, who had won the European indoor title for Britain four months earlier but had invoked Jamaican citizenship for the Games rather than running for England, tore round the track to win by 20 metres in 51.02, breaking the official and unofficial World records. Jamaican-born, Neufville had moved to England at the age of eight, and although she also went on to become Pan-American Games champion in 1971 and reached the Commonwealth final again in 1974 the astounding promise shown by this youngster was, unfortunately, never properly fulfilled and she did not ran as fast again as she had at Meadowbank.

The 1500m for women had been belatedly introduced to the international programme at the previous year's European Championships where a World record of 4:10.77 had been set by a Czech, Jaroslava Jehlickova, with Rita Ridley in 7th place for Great Britain. In the Edinburgh race Ridley - whose equally statuesque blonde identical twin sister, Iris, was also a fine middle-distance runner - was the winner in a dramatic finish as Sylvia Potts, of New Zealand, fell when still leading though very tired in the last few metres. The spur of now running for medals was to transform the women's 1500m event over the next two years, though, with the World record coming down to 4:01.63 by Lyudmila Bragina (USSR) and the Commonwealth record from Ridley's 1970 mark of 4:15.4 to Sheila Carey's 4:04.81, both at the Munich Olympics.

Pam Kilborn, 30, won her third consecutive hurdles gold, and her fifth gold in all, with some ease at the updated 100m distance, reversing positions with her 18-year-old team-mate and Olympic champion, Maureen Caird. Mike Bull, second-placed in the Kingston pole vault, won Northern Ireland's third gold of the Games with a British record of 5.10, and the steeplechase provided one of those complete surprises which is the essence of athletic competition. The World record-holder, Kerry O'Brien, and both the Olympic champion and the silver-medallist, Amos Biwott and Benjamin Kogo, were all in the field, but O'Brien fell full-length at the last-but-one water jump and none of the trio of Kenyans in the race could match the closing lap of Tony Manning, a postman from the outback of New South Wales. Manning won in express delivery style and never again matched his personal best of 8:26.2, but it's a frequent occurrence for athletes to produce their very best as a one-off championship performance and maybe not feel the motivation, or need it, ever to do any better again.

The marathon entry was an exceptional one. There were both the defending champion and the silver-medallist from 1966, Jim Alder and Bill Adcocks; the holder of the World's fastest time, Derek Clayton; the 1969 European champion, Ron Hill; and the Canadian, Jerome Drayton, who had won the classic annual Fukuoka race in Japan the previous December. The early pace, not surprisingly, was very quick, with Hill leading through 10 miles in 47:45 - close to 2:05 schedule, compared with Clayton's World best of 2:08:33.6 (!) - but only just ahead of Drayton and the Kenyan, Philip Ndoo. These two began to fade, but Hill went on at much the same speed through 20 miles (1:37:32) and won by over 2fi minutes from Alder with a 21-year-old, Don Faircloth, 3rd and a 38-year-old, Jack Foster, 4th. Hill's time of 2:09:28 was the second fastest ever, and among Europeans the only other man ever to have run faster than Alder and Faircloth was Bill Adcocks, 6th on this occasion. Clayton and Drayton, who had been christened Peter Buniak but changed his name because he didn't like it, both dropped out.

The fourth successive day's events on Friday 24 July were low-key, with no finals taking place, and served mainly to sort out the 800 metres runners and the 4 x 400 teams for the closing session. Ralph Doubell, the Olympic champion, qualified in the former, and the Olympic silver-medallists, Kenya, won the first relay heat and Trinidad (with Ed Roberts, naturally) the other. Set for Saturday 25 July were the finals at 800m, 5000m, triple jump and shot for men, at 800m, high jump and javelin for women, and in the three relays. To deal with the field events first, though by no means because they could be considered merely incidental, the charismatic 17-year-old Debbie Brill set a Games record 1.78 in the high jump, with Ann Wilson again in 2nd place, and another 17-year-old, Petra Rivers, already in her fourth year of throwing despite her youth, won an otherwise rather ordinary javelin event. Rivers's team-mate, Phil May, became the fourth Australian to win the men's triple jump. The first two from 1966, Dave Steen and Les Mills, and even the first two from 1962, Martyn Lucking and Mike Lindsay, all reconvened for the shot and Steen won again with a Games record 19.21. A burly 20-year-old from Lincolnshire, Geoff Capes, was a commendable 4th.

115

The women's 800 final was marred by the fall on the first lap of Sheila Carey, who had been 4th in Mexico, and it was Rosemary Stirling, a New Zealand-born member of the Wolverhampton & Bilston club but running for Scotland, who won from England's Pat Lowe with only three metres covering the first four. The favourite also came unstuck in the men's race as Ralph Doubell simply did not have the legs to match the pace of the unheralded 21-year-old Kenyan, Robert Ouko, who ran a 46.2 400 the following month, and the equally surprising pursuers were Benedict Cayenne, of Trinidad (though he had reached the Mexico Olympic final), and a Canadian, Bill Smart, who had been last but one in the 1500 the previous Wednesday, while Australia and England with five finalists between them did not get a single medal.

With Lennox Miller running second leg and Don Quarrie on anchor, the Jamaicans won the 4 x 100 in 39.46 for another fastest ever time in Britain, and the Australian women - again with a double individual champion, Raelene Boyle, on the last leg - did the same in the women's race in 44.14, though England again gave them a great contest, as they had done in every Games since the 4 x110 yards was introduced in 1954, with Madeleine Cobb (nee Weston) back in the team after 12 years. At 4 x 400 Kenya were already in front when the new 800m champion, Ouko, took over and 45.5sec later he sent Charles Asati off on a 44.6 stint which gave his team a comfortable victory over Trinidad. Asati, who had also won the 200m bronze, was running his 10th race of the Games and Ed Roberts his 12th.

This left the 5000m as the last event to be decided, and maybe stage-managed as such in the fond wish that Scotland would have some part to play. Those hopes were fulfilled beyond all expectations even though Keino, Clarke and Quax were all in the field, and the race can surely be described as one of the greatest ever displays of track distance running by British athletes. Yet another member of the dynasty established by Coventry Godiva Harriers played the major role in setting up a fast and furious tempo as the 10,000m bronze-medallist, Dick Taylor, led until two laps to go, when the quartet who took over included two Scots, Ian Stewart and Ian McCafferty, against Keino and Clarke. The last lap was covered in 55.4sec and it was Stewart amd McCafferty who led into the home straight with Keino well beaten. Stewart, who had run a 3:57.4 mile the previous month, won in a time which was a new European record and had only ever been beaten by Clarke's four-year-old World record of 13:16.6, and the 30,000 crowd, needless to say, was euphoric - no matter that the winner was a member of the famous West Midlands club, Birchfield Harriers, and his Scottish connection was through ancestry rather than birth and his accent much more Black Country than Black Watch. But then at least a dozen Edinburgh medallists, including six champions, were born in countries other than those they represented in the Games.

Lachie Stewart, whose first win of note had been in the Scottish boys' cross-country championship in 1958, was Scots through and through, not related to the Brummie Stewarts, and he finished 11th in this 5000m, his job having been done, and done well, at the start of the Games. Ian Stewart's elder brother, Peter, had narrowly missed a medal at 1500m, and there would be more to come from their sister, Mary, in the future. All in all, the Stewart "clan" served the Scottish colours bravely.

RESULTS 1970

MEN

100 METRES (18 Jul): 1 Don Quarrie (Jam) 10.24, 2 Lennox Miller (Jam) 10.32, 3 Hasley Crawford (Tri) 10.33, 4 Gary Eddy (Aus) 10.34, 5 George Daniels (Gha) 10.42, 6 Gary "Rocky" Symonds (Ber) 10.42, 7 Errol Stewart (Jam) 10.50, 8 Les Piggott (Sco) 10.55. Note: assisting wind of 3.6m.

200 METRES (22 Jul): 1 Don Quarrie (Jam) 20.56, 2 Ed Roberts (Tri) 20.63, 3 Charles Asati (Ken) 20.74, 4 Martin Reynolds (Eng) 20.83, 5 Peter Norman (Aus) 20.86, 6 George Daniels (Gha) 20.97, 7 Gary Eddy (Aus) 21.01, 8 Julius Sang (Ken) 21.09.

400 METRES (23 Jul): 1 Charles Asati (Ken) 45.01, 2 Ross Wilson (Aus) 45.61, 3 Saimoni Tamani (Fij) 45.82, 4 Claver Kamanya (Tan) 45.84, 5 Kent Bernard (Tri) 46.06, 6 Ed Roberts (Tri) 46.13, 7 Clifton Forbes (Jam) 46.19, 8 Julius Sang (Ken) 46.42.

800 METRES (25 Jul): 1 Robert Ouko (Ken) 1:46.89, 2 Benedict Cayenne (Tri) 1:47.42, 3 Bill Smart (Can) 1:47.43, 4 Chris Fisher (Aus) 1:47.78, 5 John Davies (Eng) 1:47.79, 6 Ralph Doubell (Aus) 1:47.86, 7 Martin Winbolt Lewis (Eng) 1:48.14, 8 Colin Campbell (Eng) 1:48.29.

1500 METRES (22 Jul): 1 Kip Keino (Ken) 3:36.6, 2 Dick Quax (NZ) 3:38.1, 3 Brendan Foster (Eng) 3:40.6, 4 Peter Stewart (Sco) 3:40.6, 5 John Whetton (Eng) 3:41.2, 6 Ian McCafferty (Sco) 3:42.2, 7 Phil Thomas (Wal) 3:42.6, 8 Chris Fisher (Aus) 3:43.6, 9 John Kirkbride (Eng) 3:44.2, 10 Dick Tayler (NZ) 3:45.0, 11 Bill Smart (Can) 3:48.6, 12 Ergas Leps (Can) 3:54.0.

5000 METRES (25 Jul): 1 Ian Stewart (Sco) 13:22.8, 2 Ian McCafferty (Sco) 13:23.4, 3 Kip Keino (Ken) 13:27.6, 4 Allan Rushmer (Eng) 13:29.8, 5 Ron Clarke (Aus) 13:32.4, 6 Dick Taylor (Eng) 13:33.8, 7 Dick Quax (NZ) 13:43.4, 8 John Ngeno (Ken) 13:44.6, 9 Bob Finlay (Can) 13:45.2, 10 Dick Tayler (NZ) 13:48.8, 11 Lachie Stewart (Sco) 13:51.8, 12 Derek Graham (NI) 13:54.0, 13 Bernie Plain (Wal) 14:02.0, 14 Mike Baxter (Eng) 14:03.0.

10,000 METRES (18 Jul): 1 Lachie Stewart (Sco) 28:11.8, 2 Ron Clarke (Aus)

28:13.4, 3 Dick Taylor (Eng) 28:15.4, 4 Roger Matthews (Eng) 28:21.4, 5 John Caine (Eng) 28:27.6, 6 John Ngeno (Ken) 28:31.4, 7 Philip Ndoo (Ken) 28:41.8, 8 Kerry O'Brien (Aus) 28:43.4, 9 John Stephen (Tan) 28:44.0, 10 Jerome Drayton (Can) 28:45.0, 11 Bernie Plain (Wal) 28:51.8, 12 Derek Graham (NI) 29:00.2, 13 Dick Wedlock (Sco) 29:09.8, 14 George Waluza (Mlw) 29:33.8, 15 Dave Ellis (Can) 29:37.4, 16 Alan Joslyn (Wal) 29:51.8, 17 Ghulam Razool (Pak) 30:03.0, 18 Naftali Temu (Ken) 30:04.4, 19 Fulgence Rwabu (Uga) 30:44.8, 20 Douglas Zinkala (Zam) 30:54.4, 21 Alifu Albert Massaquoi (SL) 31:06.2, 22 Dominic Chiwaya (Mlw) 31:17.8, 23 Mustapha Musa (Uga) 31:32.6, 24 Richard Mabuza (Swa) 31:33.0, 25 Robert Hackman (Gha) 31:50.4, 26 Reuben Dlamini (Swa) 32:56.8, 27 Daniel Kalusa (Zam) 33:23.6. Did not finish - Dandison Moore (SL), Donald Pierre (Gre).

MARATHON (23 Jul): 1 1 Ron Hill (Eng) 2:09:28, 2 Jim Alder (Sco) 2:12:04, 3 Don Faircloth (Eng) 2:12:19, 4 Jack Foster (NZ) 2:14:44, 5 John Stephen (Tan) 2:15:05, 6 Bill Adcocks (Eng) 2:15:10, 7 Fergus Murray (Sco) 2:15:32, 8 Don Macgregor (Sco) 2:16:53, 9 Mike Teer (NI) 2:17:24, 10 Andy Boychuk (Can) 2:18:45, 11 Mike Rowland (Wal) 2:19:08, 12 Cyril Leigh (Wal) 2:19:53, 13 Martin Cranny (NI) 2:20:23, 14 Bob Moore (Can) 2:20:47, 15 Philip Ndoo (Ken) 2:22:40, 16 Harnek Singh (Ind) 2:23:12, 17 Hedydd ("Dai") Davies (Wal) 2:23:29, 18 Jeff Julian (NZ) 2:24:03, 19 Dharamrai Birendar (Ind) 2:29:18, 20 Douglas Zinkala (Zam) 2:30:12, 21 Fulgence Rwabu (Uga) 2:34:15, 22 Kenneth Grant (Gib) 2:35:55, 23 Reuben Dlamini (Swa) 2:49:33, 24 Sergio Alacio (Gib) 2:50:39. Did not finish - Derek Clayton (Aus), Jerome Drayton (Can), Jagbir Singh (Ind), Daniel Kalusa (Zam), Richard Mabuza (Swa), Alifu Albert Massaquoi (SL), Anthony Parody (Gib), Harry Prowell (Guy).

3000 METRES STEEPLECHASE (23 Jul): 1 Tony Manning (Aus) 8:26.2, 2 Ben Jipcho (Ken) 8:29.6, 3 Amos Biwott (Ken) 8:30.8, 4 Gareth Bryan-Jones (Sco) 8:33.8, 5 Andy Holden (Eng) 8:34.6, 6 Benjamin Kogo (Ken) 8:36.2, 7 Bernard Hayward (Wal) 8:39.8, 8 Gerry Stevens (Eng) 8:39.4, 9 Grant McLaren (Can) 8:55.4. Did not finish - Kerry O'Brien (Aus).

20 MILES WALK (18 Jul): 1 Noel Freeman (Aus) 2:33:33, 2 Bob Gardiner (Aus) 2:35:55, 3 Bill Sutherland (Sco) 2:37:24, 4 Bob Dobson (Eng) 2:39:55, 5 Ron Wallwork (Eng) 2:40:10, 6 Len Duquemin (Gue) 2:42:48, 7 Shaun Lightman (Eng) 2:44:50, 8 Felix Cappella (Can) 2:45:16, 9 Alex Oakley (Can) 2:46.10, 10 John Moullin (Gue) 2:48:07, 11 Richard Rosser (Wal) 2:49:41, 12 Karl-Heinz Merschenz (Can) 2:50:32, 13 John Callow (IoM) 2:51:21, 14 Dave Smyth (NI) 2:53:49, 15 John Cannell (IoM) 2:56:19, 16 Dave Dorey (Gue) 3:03:41, 17 Nolan

Simons (Tri) 3:08:23, 18 Balakrishna Subramaniam (Sin) 3:13:22, 19 Francis Thomas (Tri) 3:14:58. Did not finish - Ian Hodgkinson (IoM). Disqualified - Bachan Singh (Ind).

110 METRES HURDLES (18 Jul): 1 David Hemery (Eng) 13.60, 2 Mal Baird (Aus) 13.86, 3 Godfrey Murray (Jam) 14.2, 4 George Neeland (Can) 14.27, 5 Brian Donnelly (Can) 14.28, 6 Rich McDonald (Can) 14.41, 7 Kwaku Ohene-Frempong (Gha) 14.77. Did not finish - Alan Pascoe (Eng). Note: assisting wind of 2.9m.

400 METRES HURDLES 21 Jul): 1 John Sherwood (Eng) 50.03, 2 Bill Koskei (Uga) 50.15, 3 Charles Yego (Ken) 50.19, 4 John Akii-Bua (Uga) 51.14, 5 Dave Scharer (Eng) 51.17, 6 Bill Gairdner (Can) 51.60, 7 Kingsley Agbabokha (Nig) 51.67, 8 Gary Knoke (Aus) 52.13.

4 x 100 METRES RELAY (25 Jul): 1 Jamaica (Errol Stewart, Lennox Miller, Carl Lawson, Don Quarrie) 39.46, 2 Ghana (Mike Ahey, James Addy, Edward Owusu, George Daniels) 39.82, 3 England (Ian Green, Martin Reynolds, Dave Dear, Brian Green) 40.05, 4 Scotland (Ian Turnbull, Les Piggott, Stuart Bell, Don Halliday) 40.09, 5 Wales (Terry Davies, Lynn Davies, John Williams, Howard Davies) 40.23, 6 Trinidad & Tobago (John Mottley, Carl Archer, Hasley Crawford, Ed Roberts) 40.37, 7 Nigeria (Timon Oyebami, Robert Ojo, Benedict Majekodunmi, Kola Abdulai) 40.98, 8 Northern Ireland (Mike Bull, Gerry Carson, John Chivers, John Kilpatrick) 41.12. Note: Ian Green and Brian Green, of England, were not related; John Mottley was the brother of 1966 440 yards champion Wendell Mottley.

4 x 400 METRES RELAY (25 Jul): 1 Kenya (Hezekiah Nyamau, Julius Sang, Robert Ouko, Charles Asati) 3:03.63, 2 Trinidad & Tobago (Melville Wong Shing, Benedict Cayenne, Kent Bernard, Ed Roberts) 3:05.49, 3 England (Martin Bilham, Len Walters, Mike Hauck, John Sherwood) 3:05.53, 4 Canada (Ian Gordon, Larry Barton, Doug Chapman, Tony Powell) 3:06.43, 5 Jamaica (Leighton Priestley, Ashman Samuels, Byron Dyce, Clifton Forbes) 3:06.44, 6 Scotland (Andy Wood, Dave Walker, Mike Maclean, Ricky Taylor) 3:09.09, 7 Nigeria (Mamman Makama, Gladstone Agbamu, Anthony Egwunyenga, Musa Dogon-Yaro) 3:09.76, 8 Malawi (Peter Ndovi, Peter Njera, Francisco Mvula, Richard Nandolo) 3:20.61.

HIGH JUMP (18 Jul): 1 Lawrie Peckham (Aus) 2.14, 2 John Hawkins (Can) 2.12, 3 Sheikh Tidiane Faye (Gam) 2.10, 4 Bhim Singh (Ind) 2.06, 5 Rick Cuttell (Can) 2.06, 6 Anthony Holbrook-Smith (Gha) 2.06, 7 Dave Wilson (Sco) 2.04, 8 Mike

Campbell (Eng) 2.01, 9 Nor Azhar Hamid (Sin) 1.98, 10 Leon Hall (Eng) 1.96, 11 Samuel Igun (Nig) 1.96, 12 Henry Jackson (Jam) 1.88.

POLE VAULT (23 Jul): 1 Mike Bull (NI) 5.10, 2 Allan Kane (Can) 4.90, 3 Bob Raftis (Can) 4.90, 4 Ray Boyd (Aus) 4.85, 5 Bruce Simpson (Can) 4.60, 6 Gordon Rule (Sco) 4,.50, 7 Stuart Tufton (Eng) 4.50, 8 David Lease (Wal) 4.50, 9 David Stevenson (Sco) 4.40, 10= Steve Chappell (Eng) & Martin Higdon (Eng) 4.30, 12 Adeola Aboyade-Cole (Nig) 3.80, 13 Patrick Oriana (Uga) 3.70.

LONG JUMP (22 Jul): 1 Lynn Davies (Wal) 8.06, 2 Phil May (Aus) 7.94, 3 Alan Lerwill (Eng) 7.94, 4 Mike Ahey (Gha) 7.78, 5 Dave Norris (NZ) 7.64, 6 Dave Walker (Sco) 7.51, 7 Geoff Hignett (Eng) 7.49, 8 Hamish Robertson (Sco) 7.37, 9 George Ogan (Nig) 7.15, 10 Gwyn Williams (Wal) 7.14, 11 Patrick Onyango (Ken) 7.10, 12 Abraham Munabi (Uga) 7.05. Note: the jumps by Davies, Lerwill, Ogan, Onyango and Munabi were wind-assisted.

TRIPLE JUMP (25 Jul): 1 Phil May (Aus) 16.72, 2 Mick McGrath (Aus) 16.41, 3 Mohinder Singh (Ind) 15.90, 4 Abraham Munabi (Uga) 15.87, 5 Johnson Amoah (Gha) 15.73, 6 Labh Singh (Ind) 15.70, 7 Samuel Igun (Nig) 15.67, 8 Patrick Onyango (Ken) 15.61, 9 Lennox Burgher (Jam) 15.23, 10 Alan Lerwill (Eng) 15.19, 11 Dave Norris (NZ) 14.46, 12 Reynold Edwards (Ant) 14.30, 13 Tony Wadhams (Eng) 13.70. Note: the jumps by Munabi and Wadhams were wind-assisted.

SHOT (25 Jul): 1 Dave Steen (Can) 19.21, 2 Jeff Teale (Eng) 18.43, 3 Les Mills (NZ) 18.40, 4 Geoff Capes (Eng) 17.06, 5 Brian Caulfield (Can) 16.83, 6 Mike Lindsay (Sco) 16.77, 7 Martyn Lucking (Eng) 16.71, 8 John Walters (Wal) 16.05, 9 Yovan Ochola (Uga) 15.36.

DISCUS (22 Jul): 1 George Puce (Can) 59.02, 2 Les Mills (NZ) 57.84, 3 Bill Tancred (Eng) 56.68, 4 Arthur McKenzie (Eng) 55.34, 5 Zigurd Strauts (Can) 55.20, 6 Robin Tait (NZ) 53.82, 7 Joe Antunovich (NZ) 53.50, 8 Mike Cushion (Eng) 51.34, 9 Mike Lindsay (Sco) 50.94, 10 Dave Steen (Can) 50.64, 11 John Walters (Wal) 48.06, 12 Yovan Ochola (Uga) 44.98, 13 Imbert Roberts (SL) 37.28.

HAMMER (18 Jul): 1 Howard Payne (Eng) 67.80, 2 Bruce Fraser (Eng) 62.90, 3 Barry Williams (Eng) 61.58, 4 Lawrie Bryce (Sco) 61.42, 5 Praveen Kumar (Ind) 60.34, 6 Warwick Nicholl (NZ) 60.02, 7 Gary Salmond (Can) 59.94, 8 Mike Cairns (Can) 59.34, 9 Tony Tenisci (Can) 57.06, 10 Niall McDonald (Sco) 55.94, 11 Yovan Ochola (Uga) 48.74. Maurice Davies (Wal) no valid throws.

JAVELIN (23 Jul): 1 David Travis (Eng) 79.50, 2 John McSorley (Eng) 76.74, 3 John FitzSimons (Eng) 73.20, 4 Sigismund Koscik (Aus) 73.12, 5 Wilfred Mwalawanda-Ngwenya (Mlw) 71.72, 6 David Birkmyre (Sco) 70.38, 7 Ken Holmes (Sco) 68.62, 8 Bill Heikkila (Can) 66.66, 9 Nigel Sherlock (Wal) 66.24, 10 Abdul Allahdad (Pak) 62.64, 11 Francois Boulle (Mau) 57.34, 12 James Wanda (Tan) 57.20, 13 Barrie Dodd (Zam) 48.38.

DECATHLON (21-22 Jul): 1 Geoff Smith (Aus) 7,492 (10.9, 6.93, 13.20, 1.70, 48.7, 15.2, 38.32, 4.20, 60.12, 4:36.0), 2 Peter Gabbett (Eng) 7,469 (10.7, 7.51, 11.86, 1.89, 48.7, 15.3, 41.70, 3.30, 55.96, 4:30.0), 3 Barry King (Eng) (11.3, 7.02, 15.63, 1.70, 51.4, 16.5, 43.60, 3.80, 65.04, 4:52.1), 4 Jim Smith (Eng) 7,033, 5 Steve Spencer (Can) 6,863, 6 Gord Stewart (Can) 6,863, 7 Roger Main (NZ) 6,548, 8 Ian Grant (Sco) 6,048, 9 David Kidner (Sco) 6,030, 10 Luc Bax (Mau) 5,250. Did not finish - Francois Boulle (Mau), Vijay Singh (Ind), Roy Williams (NZ). The points for the first eight, recalculated on the 1984 tables, would be as follows - G. Smith 7,420, Gabbett 7,400, King 7,118, J. Smith 6,903, Spencer 6,742, Stewart 6,769, Main 6,427, Grant 5,948. Spencer and Stewart had the same scores on the 1964 tables and Spencer was awarded 5th place because he had scored higher than Stewart in six of the 10 events.

WOMEN

100 METRES (18 Jul): 1 Raelene Boyle (Aus) 11.27, 2 Alice Annum (Gha) 11.33, 3 Marion Hoffman (Aus) 11.36, 4 Val Peat (Eng) 11.38, 5 Helen Golden (Sco) 11.52, 6 Anita Neil (Eng) 11.54, 7 Stephanie Berto (Can) 11.64, 8 Liz Sutherland (Sco) 11.73. Note: assisting wind of 5.3m

200 METRES (22 Jul): 1 Raelene Boyle (Aus) 22.75, 2 Alice Annum (Gha) 22.86, 3 Margaret Critchley (Eng) 23.16, 4 Helen Golden (Sco) 23.42, 5 Maureen Tranter (Eng) 23.52, 6 Jennifer Lamy (Aus) 23.62, 7 Marion Hoffman (Aus) 23.79, 8 Penny Hunt (NZ) 23.84. Note: assisting wind of 4.0m.

400 METRES (23 Jul): 1 Marilyn Neufville (Jam) 51.02, 2 Sandra Brown (Aus) 53.66, 3 Judith Ayaa (Uga) 53.77, 4 Jannette Champion (Eng) 54.27, 5 Barbara Lyall (Sco) 54.78, 6 Avril Bowring (Eng) 54.79, 7 Avril Beattie (Sco) 54.81, 8 Maeve Kyle (NI) 55.78. Note: Maeve Kyle was the oldest woman to have appeared in a Commonwealth Games final, aged 41.

800 METRES (24 Jul): 1 Rosemary Stirling (Sco) 2:06.24, Pat Lowe (Eng) 2:06.27, 3 Cheryl Peasley (Aus) 2:06.33, 4 Gloria Dourass (Wal) 2:06.64, 5 Sylvia

Potts (NZ) 2:09.76, 6 Penny Werthner (Can) 2:10.01, 7 Georgena Craig (Sco) 2:16.14, 8 Sheila Carey (Eng) 2:18.57.

1500 METRES (23 Jul): 1 Rita Ridley (Eng) 4:18.8, 2 Joan Page (Eng) 4:19.0, 3 Thelma Fynn (Can) 4:19.1, 4 Penny Werthner (Can) 4:21.0, 5 Norine Braithwaite (Eng) 4:21.3, 6 Val Robinson (NZ) 4:22.2, 7 Margaret MacSherry (Sco) 4:23.6, 8 Christine Haskett (Sco) 4:23.8, 9 Sylvia Potts (NZ) 4:25.2, 10 Anne Smith (NZ) 4:26.8. Note: Norine Braithwaite's father, Joe, was Olympic gold-medallist in trench shooting in 1968; Anne Smith had placed 3rd for England at 880 yards in the 1966 Games.

100 METRES HURDLES (23 Jul): 1 Pam Kilborn (Aus) 13.27, 2 Maureen Caird (Aus) 13.73, 3 Christine Bell (Eng) 13.82, 4 Penny McCallum (Aus) 13.82, 5 Mary Peters (NI) 13.88, 6 Sue Scott (Eng) 14.05, 7 Carmen Brown (Jam) 14.44, 8 Liz Damman (Can) 14.78. Note: Brown nee Smith.

4 x 100 METRES RELAY (25 Jul): 1 Australia (Maureen Caird, Jennifer Lamy, Marion Hoffman, Raelene Boyle) 44.14, 2 England (Anita Neil, Margaret Critchley, Madeleine Cobb, Val Peat) 44.28, 3 Canada (Joan Hendry, Joyce Sadowick, Patti Loverock, Stephanie Berto) 44.68, 4 Scotland (Pat Pennycook, Liz Sutherland, Anne Wilson, Helen Golden) 45.46, 5 Jamaica (Adlin Clarke, Yvonne Saunders, Carmen Brown, Marilyn Neufville) 45.56, 6 Wales (Michelle Smith, Pat Shiels, Ruth Martin Jones, Hilary Davies) 46.56, 7 Northern Ireland (Adrienne Lynch, Noleen McGarvey, Maeve Kyle, Linda Teskey) 46.76, 8 Nigeria (Olajumoke Bodunrin, Emilie Edet, Modupe Oshikoya, Evelyne Orhobo) 47.07. Note: Cobb nee Weston, Clarke nee Mair.

HIGH JUMP (25 Jul): 1 Debbie Brill (Can) 1.78, 2 Ann Wilson (Eng) 1.70, 3 Moira Walls (Sco) 1.70, 4 Audrey Reid (Jam) 1.67, 5 Debbie Van Kiekebelt (Can) 1.67, 6= Janet Oldall (Eng), Modupe Oshikoya (Nig) & Dorothy Shirley (Eng) 1.62, 9 Andrea Bruce (Jam) 1.62, 10 Christine Craig (Wal) 1.62. Meppi Sitali (Zam) failed at opening height (1.52).

LONG JUMP (23 Jul): 1 Sheila Sherwood (Eng) 6.73, 2 Ann Wilson (Eng) 6.50, 3 Joan Hendry (Can) 6.28, 4 Alix Stevenson (Sco) 6.23, 5 Moira Walls (Sco) 6.20, 6 Brenda Eisler (Can) 6.11, 7 Barbara-Anne Barrett (Eng) 6.11, 8 Jean ("Jinty") Jamieson (Sco) 6.02, 9 Ruth Martin-Jones (Wal) 6.00, 10 Pam Weigel (NZ) 5.72, 11 Alice Annum (Gha) 5.55, 12 Emilie Edet (Nig) 5.11, 13 Henrietta Carew (SL) 4.41. Zetha Cofie (Gha) no valid jumps. Note: Sherwood nee Parkin; Stevenson, nee Jamieson, was the wife of pole vaulter David Stevenson and she and Jean Jamieson were sisters.

SHOT (23 Jul): 1 Mary Peters (NI) 15.93, 2 Barbara Poulsen (NZ) 15.87, 3 Jean Roberts (Aus) 15.32, 4 Anna Karner (Aus) 14.52, 5 Brenda Bedford (Eng) 14.15, 6 Diane Charteris (NZ) 13.59, 7 Joan Pavelich (Can) 13.57, 8 Marleen Kurt (Can) 13.55, 9 Gay Porter (NI) 13.28, 10 Carol Martin (Can) 12.46, 11 Heather Stuart (Sco) 12.21, 12 Maureen Pearce (Wal) 11.23. Note: Joan Pavelich, 17, was the daughter of John Pavelich, 2nd in the 1954 Games shot.

DISCUS (18 Jul): 1 Rosemary Payne (Sco) 54.46, 2 Jean Roberts (Aus) 51.02, 3 Carol Martin (Can) 48.42, 4 Anna Karner (Aus) 48.16, 5 Joan Pavelich (Can) 48.12, 6 Brenda Bedford (Eng) 46.12, 7 Sally-Ann Flynn (NZ) 45.86, 8 Diane Charteris (NZ) 44.12, 9 Gay Porter (NI) 43.74, 10 Barbara James (Eng) 42.46, 11 Lillias Dykes (Sco) 42.22, 12 Marleen Kurt (Can) 40.58, 13 Jean Fielding (Eng) 40.48, 14 Wendy Blackwood (Sco) 34.80.

JAVELIN (25 Jul): 1 Petra Rivers (Aus) 52.00, 2 Anne Farquhar (Eng) 50.82, 3 Judith ("Jay") Dahlgren (Can) 49.54, 4 Angela King (Eng) 48.00, 5 Averil Williams (Wal) 47.70, 6 Carol Martin (Can) 44.86, 7 Constance Rwabiryagye (Uga) 42.02, 8 Sally-Ann Flynn (NZ) 39.94.

PENTATHLON (21-22 Jul): 1 Mary Peters (NI) 5,148 (100m hurdles 13.6, Shot 16.13, High jump 1.66, Long jump 5.73, 200m 24.3), 2 Ann Wilson (Eng) 5,037 (13.6, 11.04, 1.72, 6.55, 24.6), 3 Jenny Meldrum (Can) 4,736 (14.2, 13.11, 1.57, 5.73, 24.8), 4 Moira Walls (Sco) 4,704, 5 Sue Scott (Eng) 4,681, 6 Ruth Martin-Jones (Wal) 4,497, 7 Shirley Clelland (Eng) 4,458, 8 Yvonne Saunders (Jam) 4,441, 9 Modupe Oshikoya (Nig) 4,411, 10 Diane Jones (Can) 4,388, 11 Lindy Carruthers (Sco) 4,265, 12 Moira Niccol (Sco) 4,236, 13 June Hirst (Wal) 4,165, 14 Anita De Gregory (Bah) 3,801, 15 Genevieve Carosin (Mau) 3,403. Did not finish - Maureen Caird (Aus), Pam Kilborn (Aus), Penny McCallum (Aus). The hurdles times for Peters, Wilson, Meldrum, Walls, Clelland, Saunders, Jones, Hirst, De Gregory and Carosin were wind-assisted. Note: Meldrum nee Wingerson.

11.

Cultures in contrast, but their winning ways are the same

QUEEN ELIZABETH II STADIUM,
CHRISTCHURCH, NEW ZEALAND
25 JANUARY-2 FEBRUARY 1974

BENJAMIN WABURA JIPCHO AND Ian Reginald Thompson came from very different stock. Jipcho, born and brought up as a Sabaot tribesman on the 7,000ft-high mountain slopes of Kenya, had spent his childhood hunting antelopes with a bow and arrow and had not started school until he was 13, running barefoot the four miles each way to and from home. The birthplace of Thompson, a trainee teacher at Trinity College, in Leeds, had been industrialised Birkenhead, across the Mersey from Liverpool, and he was inspired to start running at the age of 15 after moving south to Luton, in Bedfordshire, and watching Ron Clarke break 13 minutes for three miles at the White City in 1965. In 1973 both achieved great running deeds. Ben Jipcho, still only 21 but already an Olympic and a Commonwealth silver-medallist, had twice within eight days broken the World steeplechase record on the hallowed track in Helsinki's Olympic stadium, and he had also irreverently beaten Kip Keino's Kenyan and Commonwealth mile record. Ian Thompson, hitherto the 90th ranked 5000m runner in Britain, had celebrated his 24th birthday of a few days before by making up the numbers in his Luton United Harriers' club team for the autumn-time AAA marathon championship, and though never having competed at any distance further than 10 miles he had proceeded to beat the two previous Commonwealth champions, Jim

Alder and Ron Hill, and 268 others to win the race. We were becoming accustomed to stunning revelations out of Africa - but Luton?

Jipcho's place in Kenya's team for the Xth British Commonwealth Games in New Zealand early in 1974 had long been assured, and the English selectors had no hesitation, naturally, in sending Thompson his invitation. Christchurch, a town of only 170,000 population, was apparently a popular venue for many others, too, because a record number of 15 defending champions joined Jipcho and Thompson, including the sprinters (Don Quarrie and Raelene Boyle), the Stewart "clan" (Ian and Lachie), the Sherwoods (John and Sheila), the Paynes (Howard and Rosemary) and the pentathlon and shot champions (Mary Peters ... and Mary Peters). Mary had won Britain's sole gold medal in the 1972 Munich Olympics, but the steeplechase winner there, Kip Keino, had brought his glittering career to a close and the 400m hurdles champion, John Akii-Bua, stayed away from Christchurch to tend his ill wife. In successive Olympics athletes from the Commonwealth had won 28 medals, 21 and then 15 while the East Germans had gone from four to 20, which clearly indicated some change in the balance of power of World athletics, but though the men's entries for Christchurch were down a few to 402 from 33 countries there was a record contingent of 176 women from 23 countries, including Barbados, Bermuda, Lesotho and Tonga. There had been threats of a boycott because of New Zealand's rugby-union links with South Africa, and this had thankfully been averted, but it would be a continuing issue that was not going to go away

Apart from Jipcho, whose time of 8:13.91 had given the steeplechase a serious boost in credibility, the one other 1973 World-record-breaker at the Games was going to be the extrovert Dave Bedford, who had run 27:30.8 for 10,000m but had as yet to prove his tactical acumen. Keino had also lost his Commonwealth 1500m record to Filbert Bayi (3:34.6), and rather more prosaic Commonwealth best performances had been set by the Welshman, Berwyn Price, 13.69 for 110m hurdles; the high jumpers, Barbara Lawton, of England (1.87) and John Beers, of Canada (2.21, 2.22, 2.23 and 2.24 within two months); Geoff Capes, with five shot improvements in 1972-73 and then two more on the very eve of the Games (best of 20.64); and the Stretford Athletic Club hammer-thrower, Barry Williams, with 71.26. This was now a jet-propelled age and it was all a very far cry from when the Games had last been held in New Zealand. Back in 1950 the British competitors had set off on the high seas well before Christmas, keeping fit by jogging round the swaying deck. In 1974 Geoff Capes was still at home in January lifting colossal weights in training and breaking the Commonwealth shot record for light relief in a meeting at Crystal Palace.

The weekend before the Games opened Capes beat his record again in a warm-up get-together 100 miles from Christchurch, and the next day 23,000 people turned out to watch many of the athletes have a spin round the Queen Elizabeth II Stadium track and prove its quality. England's Alan Pascoe won a fast 400m hurdles and New Zealander Rod Dixon gave the spectators a popular 3000m success, but it was the Africans who were most ominously in form: Mike Boit won an 800m from Filbert Bayi, 1:45.8 to 1:46.0, and John Kipkurgat and Ben Jipcho were first home at 1500 and 5000. Just down the road a previous generation was stirring fond memories in a veterans' meeting: Peter Snell, now 35, ran 51.5 for 400m; Albie Thomas, 38, and Dave Power, 45, also won their races; and Jack Foster, 41, set a World record for over-40s with 29:38.0 for 10,000m.

Games competition opened on Friday 25 January with two other stalwarts among the 193 athletes stretching their legs. Mary Peters, at 34, was taking part in her fifth Commonwealth Games, having finished 8th, 4th, 2nd and 1st in the shot, 1st again in the pentathlon in Edinburgh - and last in the relay as a 19-year-old in Cardiff. Howard Payne, 42, had also made his debut in 1958, placing 4th in the hammer for Northern Rhodesia, and had subsequently won the next three golds for England in that event. All five events of the pentathlon were held during the day, and it was another thrilling contest reminiscent of that Olympic win over Heide Rosendahl, of Germany, with Mary pitching her strength and technical expertise against the exuberance and raw speed of the 19-year-old Nigerian, Modupe Oshikoya, whose previous Games experience also, coincidentally, involved finishing last in the sprint relay It all came down to the closing 200m event and though Oshikoya won it by a long way in 24.15 Mary Peters kept her title by 32 points. Howard Payne's equally valiant defence was not quite so productive as he lost out to 21-year-old Ian Chipchase, from North Shields, whose admiring coach, Carlton Johnson, was in the stands to watch him. Twenty years on Johnson would still be in regular attendance at major meetings as another of his athletes won somewhat greater acclaim around the World - Jonathan Edwards.

By the very nature of the event the 10,000m was bound to be the day's dramatic climax with Dave Bedford, the World record-holder, against a trio of Kenyans and the Edinburgh heroes, Ian Stewart and Lachie Stewart. Bedford, as was his custom, set off at a gallop but at halfway (13:47) the pace was slipping and the Kenyans and David Black were still jostling at his heels and two others were closing. One of them was the New Zealander, Dick Tayler, reviving memories of the great Savidan and Matthews before the war and not to be confused with England's Dick Taylor, and when it came down to a race between him and Black over the final three laps it was the man with the greater basic speed who won. Tayler had run a 3:58.8 mile in the past, Black 4:04.4, and this time the contented coach in the stands was Arthur Lydiard, the mentor of Snell and Halberg. Just as in Edinburgh four years earlier a local man had won the 10,000m and given the Games a perfect initial impulse.

The programme for Saturday, 26 January, was made up of finals at 100, 400, 110 hurdles and the steeplechase for men and at 100, 400 and discus for women. First Raelene Boyle and then Don Quarrie retained their sprint titles, and Boyle's race in just beating the 21-year-old British record-holder, Andrea Lynch, was the rather more exciting of them. In between, another Edinburgh winner was champion again as Charles Asati, who had run in Kenya's gold-medal relay team in the Munich Olympics, won in a modest time of 46.04 from the appropriately-named Silver Ayoo, of Uganda, who had actually run a much faster 45.68 in the preceding semi-finals. Another Kenyan, Fatwell Kimaiyo, equalled Berwyn Price's Commonwealth record to win the hurdles, with Price himself in 2nd place, and a third success for Kenya came as expected in the steeplechase where Ben Jipcho won in 8:20.67, a time which only he had ever beaten, and John Davies (with a British record) for Wales and Jipcho's team-mate, Evans Mogaka, got the silver and bronze medals despite both falling on the last lap. There was nothing mysterious or complex about Jipcho's training, for it was simplicity itself - 10 miles running every day at five-minute-miling pace on rough cinder paths near his home - but at the high altitude at which he lived it was very high quality stuff indeed. A long way behind Jipcho, but noteworthy nevertheless, were twins Nathan and Howard Healey who had

128

lined up for New Zealand with personal best times just four-tenths of a second apart and halved that difference between them in finishing 10th and 11th.

Rosemary Payne, similarly, emulated husband Howard in placing 2nd in defence of her discus title. Howard had lost by 154 centimetres; Rosemary was 158 centimetres behind Jane Haist, who was winning Canada's first gold in women's throws since 1938. Howard, as previously related, had been born in South Africa and competed for two other countries in the Games, and there was another example of the Commonwealth's free-and-easy regard for national boundaries in the women's 400m final. Yvonne Saunders had been a member of the Stretford Athletic Club, in Manchester, and Britain's leading teenage high jumper in 1968, and had then run for Jamaica in the Edinburgh Commonwealth Games relay final, but by 1974 she had lived for five years in Canada, taking up 400m running there, and she won the title in 51.67 from England's Verona Bernard, who set a UK record 51.94 - impressive running for both of them, but a long way short of Marilyn Neufville's time in Edinburgh. Neufville, incidentally, reached the final again but was 6th, over three seconds slower than when she was at her best.

The first Commonwealth Games competition on a Sunday took place on 27 January with gold medals decided only in the women's shot and the decathlon, though there were plenty of heats, including the first round and semi-finals of both men's and women's 800m. Shot-putter Jane Haist added a second gold medal to her discus victory, and Mary Peters was back in 4th place, but it was the silver medal for Valerie Young, returning to competition at the age of 36 and as the mother of three children, which captured the popular attention. Mike Bull, the pole-vault champion in 1970, won the decathlon and cleared 5.00 in his speciality, though the revelation here was 22-year-old Sanitesi Latu, Tonga's only male athlete at the Games, who was still in 3rd place with two events to go. The Kenyans were breathtaking in the men's 800m semis with the gangling John Kipkurgat, no tyro at 29, running 1:44.38, which had only ever been beaten by six men, and the Olympic bronze-medallist, Mike Boit, not that much slower at 1:45.40. Though the women could not quite compare with this sense of alacrity, their 800m final was made as intriguing by the Kenyan competitors for different reasons because according to their entry forms

Sabina Chebichi, winner of the first semi-final, was only 14 and Rose Tata-Muya, who was 4th in the second semi-final, was 13!

After a rest day the enticing line-up of finals on Tuesday 29 January comprised 200, 800, 5000, 400 hurdles, high jump and long jump for men, plus the 20 miles walk, and 200, 800 and javelin for women. Again, Raelene Boyle produced the better of the performances at 200m, holding on to her title in the best possible manner with a Games record 22.50, well ahead of 21-year-old colleague Denise Robertson, whose turn would eventually come. Don Quarrie won his final by almost precisely the same margin over a somewhat lacklustre opposition. The 800s, as hoped, made up for all this, with the women first on to the track and 400m bronze-medallist Charlene Rendina, who had already beaten Dixie Willis's Games record in the semi-finals, improving further to 2:01.11, and Chebichi becoming the youngest ever medallist in 3rd place. Later in the afternoon Kipkurgat and Boit put on a magnificent display of racing with Boit in front at 200 (25.5) and Kipkurgat going ahead at 400 (51.0) and holding on all through the second lap to win in a startling 1:43.91 - the second fastest time in history to the rather surprising World record of 1:43.7 set by Marcello Fiasconaro, of Italy, the previous June - with Boit silver-medallist in 1:44.39 and New Zealand's 22-year-old John Walker improving hugely to 1:44.92 for 3rd just ahead of the Tanzanian, Filbert Bayi. It was, on the face of it, a surprise that it should have been Kipkurgat who won, and not Boit, but those who had been studying the small print of overseas athletics results before the Games would have noticed that Kipkurgat had beaten Bayi at 1500m and a week later had won the Kenyan 800m trial in 1:45.7 on a poor track.

Of the dozen finalists at 5000m five had already run at 10,000 - including Black, Bedford and Ian Stewart, the defending champion - and Jipcho had done the steeplechase. The fastest men in the field, on paper, were currently Paul Mose, of Kenya, at 13:23.2, and Brendan Foster, the 1500m bronze-medallist in Edinburgh who had won the 1973 AAA title in 13:23.8, and at 3000m the race was between Foster, Jipcho and 21-year-old Black. Over the closing 800m Jipcho followed Foster stride-for-stride and only in the last few strides did he edge ahead to win, and the times were superb: 13:14.3 to 13:14.6, new Commonwealth and UK records, and the second and third fastest ever to the World record of 13:13.0 by Emiel

Puttemans, of Belgium. The last lap was timed in 55.3, and though far outpaced Black still got his second medal of the Games. Ian Stewart was 5th and Dave Bedford over a minute behind 11th.

In the 400m hurdles the versatile Australian, Bruce Field, had broken Gert Potgieter's 12-year-old Games record with 49.49 in the semi-finals but faced something of a dilemma for the final because he had also qualified in the long jump, being held simultaneously. Having taken one token jump, Field led beyond halfway in the hurdles final until Alan Pascoe, still a relative novice after switching from 110 hurdles, came through over the last three of the 10 flights to win in 48.83, ahead of Field and Uganda's silver-medallist from 1970, Bill Koskei, now back running for his native Kenya. It was a great pity that John Akii-Bua, the Olympic champion and World record-holder at 47.82, was missing, but Pascoe took his chance and remains equally renowned for his antics afterwards when for the benefit of the cameras he unwisely attempted to clear a hurdle which was facing the wrong way and ended up flat on his back.

The walkers, so often the poor relations at major Games, set off at 5 p.m. and when they started coming back just over two-and-a-half hours later they were no doubt pleasantly surprised to find that there was still a fair-sized crowd in the stadium waiting for them. The race was a triumph for the Sheffield United Harriers' clubmates, John Warhurst and 39-year-old Roy Thorpe, who stayed together much of the way until the younger Warhurst forged on to head a British monopoly: Australia's Peter Fullager, in 3rd, was English-born and his team-mate, Ian Hodgkinson, who was 5th, had represented the Isle of Man in the 1970 Games and was actually only the second Manxman home on this occasion because Graham Young came in 4th. No fewer than seven of the 15 contestants hailed from the Isle of Man or the Channel Islands.

In the high jump Gordon Windeyer, a 19-year-old "Fosbury Flopper", beat the 1966-70 defending champion, Lawrie Peckham, a traditional straddle technician, and both of them went above the evocative 7ft (2.13) mark. In the long jump Alan Lerwill, the bronze-medallist from Edinburgh, succeeded Lynn Davies as champion. In the women's javelin Petra Rivers, the 1970 winner and the Commonwealth record-holder at 62.24, was again 1st, and the young English third-string competitor was specially commended in "Athletics Weekly" for helping point to *"a strengthening javelin future"*. She was 17-year-old Tessa Sanderson.

131

Thursday 31 January featured the marathon, together with the finals of the pole vault, discus and women's 100m hurdles and long jump. Again a considerate 5 p.m. start meant that the conditions were coolish and breezy as the largest ever Games marathon field of 33 lined up: among them, Ian Thompson, Ron Hill and Colin Kirkham for England, Jerome Drayton for Canada, Derek Clayton and John Farrington (both, incidentally, English-born) for Australia, the ageless Jack Foster for New Zealand, and a Kenyan named Kiptanui Sirma who was apparently only 15! Before 20km Thompson was already clear and although his lead at halfway over Foster was still only about 100m he drew steadily away from then on and finished in the wonderful time of 2:09:12, a new European record and inferior only to Clayton's World best. Foster set an over-40s record in 2nd place, while Hill (18th) and Clayton (a non-finisher) both suffered injuries. Young Sirma was 20th and the performances of athletes from lesser-regarded countries were excellent with Richard Mabuza, of Swaziland, becoming the first black athlete to win a Commonwealth marathon medal and Gabashane Vincent Rakabaele, of Lesotho, finishing 12th and David Cowell, of the Isle of Man, 13th.

Only six men took part in the pole vault in which Mike Bull cleared the same height as he had in winning the decathlon but had to settle for 2nd place to the Australian, Don Baird. In the discus Robin Tait was competing in his fourth Games, having placed 4th, 3rd and 6th, and this time got the gold. The women's long jump was won by the immensely talented pentathlon silver-medallist, Modupe Oshikoya, and this was, most importantly, the first title in Games history to go to a black African woman. Oshikoya was also in the 100m hurdles final and received a third medal there as the victory went to England's Judy Vernon, who could also make a unique claim so far as the Commonwealth Games were concerned which was less significant certainly than Oshikoya's but much more unlikely. Mrs Vernon, married to the British international triple jumper, John Vernon, had been born Judith Toeneboehn in St Louis, Missouri. The men's 1500m preliminaries saw Boit, Jipcho, Bayi, Foster and Walker all go through without incident and were overshadowed by Glenda Reiser's Games record 4:10.80 in the women's heats in which Mary Stewart, younger sister of Ian and Peter, set a British junior record of 4:15.25 and 14-year-old Mwinga Mwanjala-Sote, of Tanzania, improved almost 17sec to 4:19.6, just missing the final.

For the closing day, Saturday 2 February, the remaining finals were 1500, triple jump, shot and javelin for men, 1500 and high jump for women, and all the relays. In the javelin there was a startling one-off throw which effectively ended the competition early on, very much in the manner of Anna Pazera in Edinburgh 16 years earlier. Charles Clover, the 18-year-old English No2 to the defending champion, David Travis, launched a monstrous and totally unexpected second-round effort which landed at 84.92m, more than seven metres better than he had ever done before, and a new Commonwealth and UK record. No one else, Travis included, could get remotely close to that - and nor, for that matter, could Clover himself either that day or ever again. He did once exceed 80m three years later, but his meteoric career was to all intents and purposes encapsulated within a few seconds that afternoon beneath the blue skies of New Zealand. Elsewhere on the stadium infield there was yet another Commonwealth record of 20.74 by Geoff Capes in the first round to win the shot, and a surprising success for Joshua Owusu, of Ghana, in the triple jump, and a not-so-surprising one for Barbara Lawton in becoming England's first high-jump winner since Dorothy Tyler in 1950.

Australia, with Raelene Boyle winning her fifth gold medal, beat England more easily than usual in the 4 x 100 relay, and the latter only just held off Ghana, but it was a different story in the inaugural Games final at 4 x 400 for women. Sue Pettett, 18 a week earlier, and Ruth Kennedy, 17, handed Jannette Roscoe a metre lead at halfway and Verona Bernard ran a 50.4 last leg to give England a 10-metre margin over Australia at the finish. The men's relays were exciting, as always, but of no great standard, though the Australians beat the Games record at 4 x 100 and Charles Asati ran an impressive opening stage to set up Kenya's 4 x 400 win.

Glenda Reiser, who at 17 had run 4:06.71 in the Munich Olympics, led almost the whole way in the women's 1500m final to set a Games record of 4:07.78 ahead of Joan Allison (nee Page) and Thelma Wright (nee Fynn), who had also been 2nd and 3rd in Edinburgh, with Mary Stewart again improving her UK junior record in 4th place and the precocious Sabina Chebichi 5th. Reiser, like Charles Clover earlier in the javelin, had reached her peak at 18, and she did not run as fast again.

Of the 11 finalists for the men's 1500, seven had already taken part in other punishing events: Jipcho, running his fifth race of the Games, had won the 5000 and the steeplechase; Foster, Nyambui and Fitzsimons had been 2nd, 4th and 6th at 5000; Boit, Walker and Bayi had been 2nd, 3rd and 4th at 800. This might then have suggested that Rod Dixon, the Olympic 1500m bronze-medallist from Munich, would be the freshest contender of them all, but if Filbert Bayi, the Commonwealth record-holder, thought about this at all it didn't seem to make much difference to his strategy. He went off at a phenomenal pace: 54.9 at 400 and 1:52.2 at 800, which gave him a lead of 25m and put him on a schedule almost four seconds inside the World record of 3:33.1 held by Jim Ryun, of the USA. It obviously couldn't last, and as Bayi's pace slowed to 58.6 for the next 400-metre stretch so Jipcho and the New Zealanders, Dixon and Walker, began to reduce the lead, but astonishingly the featherweight Bayi held on and on as Walker came bearing down on him like some avenging Wagnerian Valkyrie with a 54.4 last lap, and at the line Bayi crossed in 3:32.16 and Walker in 3:32.52 still two metres apart. Jipcho more or less equalled Ryun's previous record (3:33.16) and Dixon was 4th in a time which only Ryun had ever beaten before. Brendan Foster, who had been the bronze-medallist in Edinburgh, ran three seconds faster for a British record of 3:37.64 and finished four places lower down the field. Bayi was the first African to have set a World record in the 79-year history of the classic "metric mile."

Eight victories and a total of 31 medals for African athletes had given these Games a brilliant aura, and for those who were counting these things only England (28) and Australia (22) had won more medals than Kenya (14), but there would be vivid sustaining memories, too, of others like the decathlete from Tonga, a walker from the Isle of Man, a Swazi marathon runner, and almost the entire Mills family. Deep down the lists of results were to be found the names of Phil Mills, 18, at 110m hurdles, Donna Mills, 17, in the high jump, and Colleen Mills, 37, at 400m. They were the son, daughter and wife of Les Mills, who had strangely been denied by the New Zealand selectors the chance to complete the household presence in Christchurch, even though he had won five medals in the shot and discus at earlier Games and was still throwing very adequately at the age of 39.

RESULTS 1974

MEN

100 METRES (26 Jan): 1 Don Quarrie (Jam) 10.38, 2 John Mwebi (Ken) 10.51, 3 Ohene Karikari (Gha) 10.51, 4 George Daniels (Gha) 10.53, 5 Greg Lewis (Aus) 10.55, 6 Kola Abdulai (Nig) 10.55, 7 Les Piggott (Sco) 10.56, 8 Graham Haskell (Aus) 10.66.

200 METRES (29 Jan): 1 Don Quarrie (Jam) 20.73, 2 George Daniels (Gha) 20.97, 3 Bevan Smith (NZ) 21.08, 4 Graham Haskell (Aus) 21.12, 5 Greg Lewis (Aus) 21.17, 6 Chris Monk (Eng) 21.26, 7 David Jenkins (Sco) 21.49, 8 John Mwebi (Ken) 21.60. Note: headwind of 0.6m.

400 METRES (26 Jan): 1 Charles Asati (Ken) 46.04, 2 Silver Ayoo (Uga) 46.07, 3 Claver Kamanya (Tan) 46.16, 4 David Jenkins (Sco) 46.46, 5 Bruce Field (Aus) 46.58, 6 Bevan Smith (NZ) 46.60, 7 Pius Olowo (Uga) 46.84, 8 Mamman Makama (Nig) 47.19.

800 METRES (29 Jan): 1 John Kipkurgat (Ken) 1:43.91, 2 Mike Boit (Ken) 1:44.39, 3 John Walker (NZ) 1:44.92, 4 Filbert Bayi (Tan) 1:45.32, 5 Andy Carter (Eng) 1:45.97, 6 Bill Hooker (Aus) 1:46.75, 7 Daniel Omwanza (Ken) 1:47.66, 8 Phil Lewis (Wal) 1:48.90.

1500 METRES (6 Feb): 1 Filbert Bayi (Tan) 3:32.16, 2 John Walker (NZ) 3:32.52, 3 Ben Jipcho (Ken) 3:33.16, 4 Graham Crouch (Aus) 3:34.22, 5 Rod Dixon (NZ) 3:33.89, 6 Mike Boit (Ken) 3:36.84, 7 Brendan Foster (Eng) 3:37.64, 8 Suleiman Nyambui (Tan) 3:39.62, 9 Dave Fitzsimons (Aus) 3:41.30, 10 John Kirkbride (Eng) 3:41.91, 11 Randal Markey (Aus) 3:44.56. Note: Tony Polhill (NZ) qualified but did not start.

5000 METRES (29 Jan): 1 Ben Jipcho (Ken) 13:14.3, 2 Brendan Foster (Eng) 13:14.6, 3 David Black (Eng) 13:23.52, 4 Suleiman Nyambui (Tan) 13:34.91, 5 Ian Stewart (Sco) 13:40.32, 6 Dave Fitzsimons (Aus) 13:42.83, 7 Joshua Kimeto (Ken) 13:46.8, 8 Gordon Minty (Wal) 13:45.48, 9 Paul Mose (Ken) 13:54.44, 10 Bryan Rose (NZ) 14:00.93, 11 Dave Bedford (Eng) 14:18.76, 12 Mustapha Musa (Uga) 14:25.39. Note: the automatic timer was not in operation for 1st, 2nd and 7th places.

10,000 METRES (25 Jan): 1 Dick Tayler (NZ) 27:46.40, 2 David Black (Eng) 27:48.49, 3 Richard Juma (Ken) 27:56.96, 4 Dave Bedford (Eng) 28:14.67, 5 Dan Shaughnessy (Can) 28:14.67, 6 Ian Stewart (Sco) 28:17.05, 7 Tony Simmons (Wal) 28:28.54, 8 Gordon Minty (Wal) 28:44.27, 9 Paul Mose (Ken) 28:52.54, 10 Lachie Stewart (Sco) 29:22.65, 11 Bernie Plain (Wal) 29:28.34, 12 Kevin Ryan (NZ) 29:49.96, 13 Philip Watson (NZ) 29:54.75, 14 David Cowell (IoM) 30:05.44, 15 Norman Morrison (Sco) 30:25.77, 16 Motseki Monethi (Les) 30:53.61, 17 Neville Dalmedo (Gib) 34:14.04, 18 Vivian Ori (PNG) 34:15.08, 19 Porohu Taia (Cki) 35:40.98. Did not finish - Patrick Kiingi (Ken).

MARATHON (31 Jan): 1 Ian Thompson (Eng) 2:09:12.0, 2 Jack Foster (NZ) 2:11:18.6, 3 Richard Mabuza (Swa) 2:12:54.4, 4 Terry Manners (NZ) 2:12:58.6, 5 John Farrington (Aus) 2:14:04.0, 6 Don Macgregor (Sco) 2:14:15.4, 7 Bernie Plain (Wal) 2:14:56.2, 8 Colin Kirkham (Eng) 2:16:06.6, 9 Malcolm Thomas (Wal) 2:16:46.8, 10 John Robinson (NZ) 2:17:05.4, 11 Brian Armstrong (Can) 2:20:52.6, 12 Gabashane Vincent Rakabaele (Les) 2:21:41.0, 13 David Cowell (IoM) 2:23:33.8, 14 Brenton Norman (Aus) 2:24:28.4, 15 Mike Teer (NI) 2:24:55.0, 16 Reuben Dlamini (Swa) 2:27:31.4, 17 Jerome Drayton (Can) 2:29:20.0, 18 Ron Hill (Eng) 2:30:24.2, 19 Frans Matsebula (Les) 2:35:05.8, 20 Kiptanui Sirma (Ken) 2:38:03.2, 21 Hassan Juma (Tan) 2:38:51.2, 22 Neville Dalmedo (Gib) 2:40:13.8, 23 Pareau Umaki (Cki) 3:04:34.2. Did not finish - Derek Clayton (Aus), James Hoeflich (WS), Patrick Kiingi (Ken), Jim McLaughlin (NI), Mustapha Musa (Uga), James Ogaro (Ken), Vivian Ori (PNG), Lachie Stewart (Sco), Amani Tapusoa (WS), Jim Wight (Sco).

3000 METRES STEEPLECHASE (26 Jan): 1 Ben Jipcho (Ken) 8:20.67, 2 John Davies (Wal) 8:24.8, 3 Evans Mogaka (Ken) 8:28.51, 4 John Bicourt (Eng) 8:29.6, 5 Euan Robertson (NZ) 8:35.2, 6 Bernie Hayward (Wal) 8:36.2, 7 Steve Hollings (Eng) 8:40.4, 8 Amos Biwott (Ken) 8:41.4, 9 Bob Hendy (Aus) 8:46.0, 10 Nathan Healey (NZ) 8:52.2, 11 Howard Healey (NZ) 8:52.4, 12 Justin Edwogu (Uga) 9:01.0, 13 Joseph Doherty (Nig) 9:23.8. Note: the automatic timer was in operation only for 1st and 3rd places. Nathan and Howard Healey were 24-year-old twins.

20 MILES WALK (29 Jan): 1 John Warhurst (Eng) 2:35:23.0, 2 Roy Thorpe (Eng) 2:39:02.2, 3 Peter Fullager (Aus) 2:42:08.2, 4 Graham Young (IoM) 2:42:55.2, 5 Ian Hodgkinson (Aus) 2:44:55.4, 6 Les Stevenson (NZ) 2:46:56.2, 7 Ross Haywood (Aus) 2:50:56.0, 8 Allan Callow (IoM) 2:53:12.2, 9 Len Duquemin (Gue) 2:53:37.4, 10 John Moullin (Gue) 2:57:27.2, 11 Robin Waterman (Gue) 3:00:14.2, 12 Derek Harrison (IoM) 3:00:32.4. Did not finish - Elisha Kasuka

(Ken), Carl Lawton (Eng), Kevin Taylor (NZ). Note: Ian Hodgkinson had competed for the Isle of Man in the 1970 Games.

110 METRES HURDLES (26 Jan): 1 Fatwell Kimaiyo (Ken) 13.69, 2 Berwyn Price (Wal) 13.84, 3 Max Binnington (Aus) 13.88, 4 Warren Parr (Aus) 14.04, 5 Charles Kirkpatrick (NI) 14.25, 6 Adeola Aboyade-Cole (Nig) 14.39, 7 Godwin Obasogie (Nig) 14.39, 8 Vince Plant (Aus) 14.89.

400 METRES HURDLES (29 Jan): 1 Alan Pascoe (Eng) 48.83, 2 Bruce Field (Aus) 49.32, 3 Bill Koskei (Ken) 49.34, 4 Fatwell Kimaiyo (Ken) 49.63, 5 Cosmas Silei (Ken) 50.02, 6 Bill Hartley (Eng) 50.20, 7 Gary Knoke (Aus) 50.23, 8 Colin O'Neill (Wal) 50.58. Note: Bill Koskei had competed for Uganda in the 1970 Games.

4 x 100 METRES (2 Feb): 1 Australia (Greg Lewis, Lawrie D'Arcy, Andrew Ratcliffe, Graham Haskell) 39.31, 2 Ghana (Albert Lomotey, Ohene Karikari, Kofi Okyir, George Daniels) 39.61, 3 Nigeria (Timon Oyebami, Benedict Majekodunmi, Kola Abdulai, James Olakunle) 39.70, 4 Jamaica (Richard Hardware, Alfred Daley, Lennox Miller, Don Quarrie) 39.77, 5 Scotland (Les Piggott, Don Halliday, Gus McKenzie, David Jenkins) 39.80. 6 England (Brian Green, Chris Monk, Ian Matthews, Derek Cole) 39.97, 7 New Zealand (Grant Anderson, Trevor Cochrane, Bevan Smith, Kerry Hill) 40.41, 8 Kenya (Paul Njoroge, Tochi Mochache, Charles Asati, John Mwebi) 40.50.

4 x 400 METRES RELAY (2 Feb): 1 Kenya (Charles Asati, Francis Musyoki, Bill Koskei, Julius Sang) 3:04.43, 2 England (John Wilson, Andy Carter, Bill Hartley, Alan Pascoe) 3:06.66, 3 Uganda (Pius Olowo, William Dralu, Samuel Kakonge, Silver Ayoo) 3:07.45, 4 Australia (Bruce Field, Gary Knoke, Max Binnington, Bill Hooker) 3:07.51, 5 New Zealand (Phil Kear, Richard Endean, Trevor Cochrane, Bevan Smith) 3:08.01, 6 Wales (Colin O'Neill, Wyn Leyshon, Phil Lewis, Mike Delancy) 3:08.61, 7 Nigeria (Musa Dogon-Yaro, Bruce Ijirigho, Chris Owoeye, Mamman Makama) 3:08.81, 8 Fiji (Samuela Bulai, Seru Gukilau, Aca Simolo, Richard Kermode) 3:23.35.

HIGH JUMP (29 Jan): 1 Gordon Windeyer (Aus) 2.16, 2 Lawrie Peckham (Aus) 2.14, 3 Claude Ferragne (Can) 2.12, 4 John Beers (Can) 2.10, 5 John Hawkins (Can) 2.10, 6 Nor Azhar Hamid (Sin) 2.08, 7 Sheikh Tidiane Faye (Gam) 2.05, 8 Sumuni Lanyumi (Tan) 1.95, 9 Clark Godwin (Ber) 1.95.

POLE VAULT (31 Jan): 1 Don Baird (Aus) 5.05, 2 Mike Bull (NI) 5.00, 3 Brian

Hooper (Eng) 5.00, 4 Ray Boyd (Aus) 4.80, 5 Peter Tracy (NZ) 4.60. David Lease (Wal) failed at opening height (4.40). 6 competed.

LONG JUMP (29 Jan): 1 Alan Lerwill (Eng) 7.94, 2 Chris Commons (Aus) 7.92, 3 Joshua Owusu (Gha) 7.75, 4 Kingsley Adams (Gha) 7.68, 5 Bruce Field (Aus) 7.63, 6 John Okobo (Nig) 7.58, 7 Fidelis Ndyabagye (Uga) 7.50, 8 Murray Tolbert (Aus) 7.42, 9 John Delamere (NZ) 7.31, 10 Kerry Hill (NZ) 7.18, 11 Willie Kirkpatrick (NI) 6.90. Tony Moore (Fij) no valid jumps.

TRIPLE JUMP (2 Feb): 1 Joshua Owusu (Gha) 16.50, 2 Mohinder Singh (Ind) 16.44, 3 Moise Pomaney (Gha) 16.23, 4 Johnson Amoah (Gha) 15.63, 5 Phil May (Aus) 15.63, 6 Dave Norris (NZ) 15.41, 7 Don Commons (Aus) 15.35, 8 Johnson Mogusu (Ken) 15.29, 9 Gerry Swan (Ber) 15.19, 10 Alan Lerwill (Eng) 15.08, 11 Willie Clark (Sco) 14.86, 12 Michael Sharpe (Ber) 14.86. Note: Don Commons was the brother of Chris Commons.

SHOT (2 Feb): 1 Geoff Capes (Eng) 20.74, 2 Mike Winch (Eng) 19.36, 3 Bruce Pirnie (Can) 18.68, 4 Bill Tancred (Eng) 18.13, 5 Robin Tait (NZ) 17.71, 6 Ray Rigby (Aus) 16.98, 7 Tony Satchwell (Jer) 16.29, 8 Sitiveni Rabuka (Fij) 14.14.

DISCUS (31 Jan): 1 Robin Tait (NZ) 63.08, 2 Bill Tancred (Eng) 59.48, 3 John Hillier (Eng) 57.22, 4 Ain Roost (Can) 56.70, 5 Geoff Capes (Eng) 51.84, 6 Samuel Onyac (Uga) 49.68, 7 Tony Satchwell (Jer) 48.74, 8 Thomas Gibure (Tan) 44.40, 9 Walter Otim-Okello (Uga) 42.16, 10 Sitiveni Rabuka (Fij) 34.98.

HAMMER (25 Jan): 1 Ian Chipchase (Eng) 69.56, 2 Howard Payne (Eng) 68.02, 3 Peter Farmer (Aus) 67.48, 4 Barry Williams (Eng) 66.82, 5 Murray Cheater (NZ) 65.82, 6 Chris Black (Sco) 64.40, 7 Warwick Nicholl (NZ) 63.72, 8 Lawrie Bryce (Sco) 59.52, 9 Sitiveni Rabuka (Fij) 32.66.

JAVELIN (2 Feb): 1 Charles Clover (Eng) 84.92, 2 David Travis (Eng) 79.92, 3 John Mayaka (Ken) 77.56, 4 Rick Dowswell (Can) 73.88, 5 Brian Roberts (Eng) 73.54, 6 Anthony Oyakhire (Nig) 72.42, 7 Rob Lethbridge (Aus) 66.22. 7 competed.

DECATHLON (26-27 Jan): 1 Mike Bull (NI) 7,417 (11.16, 7.01, 13.65, 1.88, 49.8, 15.30, 38.86, 5.00, 43.54, 4:46.9), 2 Barry King (Eng) 7,277 (11.58, 6.78, 15.28, 1.88, 50.8, 16.73, 45.02, 3.80, 59.02, 4:37.7), 3 Rob Lethbridge (Aus) (11.28, 7.18, 11.28, 1.91, 48.6, 15.85, 36.28, 3.40, 69.22, 4:30.4), 4 David Kidner (Sco) 7,188, 5 Sanitesi Latu (Ton) 7,140, 6 Mene Mene (NZ) 6,993, 7

Roger Main (NZ) 6,799, 8 Terry Beaton (Aus) 6,780, 9 Geoff Wood (NZ) 6,622, 10 Saulekalcka Tunidau (Fij) 5,471, 11 Sitiveni Rabuka (Fij) 5,332 Did not finish - Ray Knox (NI), Stewart McCallum (Sco). Note: Mene Mene's full name was Iafeta Sua'mene.

WOMEN

100 METRES (26 Jan): 1 Raelene Boyle (Aus) 11.27, 2 Andrea Lynch (Eng) 11.31, 3 Denise Robertson (Aus) 11.50, 4 Alice Annum (Gha) 11.52, 5 Wendy Brown (NZ) 11.59, 6 Marjorie Bailey (Can) 11.66, 7 Rosie Allwood (Jam) 11.73, 8 Jennifer Lamy (Aus) 11.83.

200 METRES (29 Jan): 1 Raelene Boyle (Aus) 22.50, 2 Denise Robertson (Aus) 22.73, 3 Alice Annum (Gha) 22.90, 4 Marjorie Bailey (Can) 23.13, 5 Ruth Williams (Jam) 23.39, 6 Wendy Brown (NZ) 23.44, 7 Robyn Boak (Aus) 23.45, 8 Patti Loverock (Can) 23.76.

400 METRES (26 Jan): 1 Yvonne Saunders (Can) 51.67, 2 Verona Bernard (Eng) 51.94 , 3 Charlene Rendina (Aus) 52.08, 4 Jannette Roscoe (Eng) 53.18, 5 Judy Canty (Aus) 53.50, 6 Marilyn Neufville (Jam) 54.04, 7 Penny Hunt (NZ) 54.30, 8 Beth Nail (Aus) 54.54. Note: Roscoe nee Champion.

800 METRES (29 Jan): 1 Charlene Rendina (Aus) 2:01.11, 2 Sue Haden (NZ) 2:02.04, 3 Sabina Chebichi (Ken) 2:02.61, 4 Joan Allison (Eng) 2:03.10, 5 Lorraine Moller (NZ) 2:03.63, 6 Maureen Crowley (Can) 2:05.26, 7 Shirley Somervell (NZ) 2:05.83, 8 Rose Tata-Muya (Ken) 2:13.26. Note: Allison nee Page.

1500 METRES (2 Feb): 1 Glenda Reiser (Can) 4:07.78, 2 Joan Allison (Eng) 4:10.66, 3 Thelma Wright (Can) 4:12.26, 4 Mary Stewart (Sco) 4:14.73, 5 Sabina Chebichi (Ken) 4:18.56, 6 Anne Garrett (NZ) 4:21.05, 7 Jenny Orr (Aus) 4:22.54, 8 Sylvia Potts (NZ) 4:23.12, 9 Elizabeth Chelimo (Ken) 4:26.8, 10 Sue Haden (NZ) 4:27.8, 11 Sheila Carey (Eng) 4:29.6. Did not finish - Norine Braithwaite (Eng). Note: Wright nee Fynn; Mary Stewart was the sister of Ian Stewart, 1st (1970) and 5th (1974) at 5000, and 6th at 10,000 (1974), and Peter Stewart, 4th at 1500 (1970).

100 METRES HURDLES (31 Jan): 1 Judy Vernon (Eng) 13.45, 2 Gaye Dell (Aus) 13.54, 3 Modupe Oshikoya (Nig) 13.69, 4 Jenny Jones (Aus) 13.83, 5 Michelle Miles (NZ) 13.89, 6 Sally Moir (Aus) 13.93, 7 Brenda Matthews (NZ) 13.95, 8 Liz Damman (Can) 13.97.

4 x 100 METRES RELAY (2 Feb): 1 Australia (Jennifer Lamy, Denise Robertson, Robyn Boak, Raelene Boyle) 43.51, 2 England (Sonia Lannaman, Barbara Martin, Judy Vernon, Andrea Lynch) 44.30, 3 Ghana (Rose Assiedua, Josephine Ocran, Hannah Afriyie, Alice Annum) 44.35, 4 Canada (Lyn Kellond, Liz Damman, Patti Loverock, Marjorie Bailey) 44.51, 5 New Zealand (Kim Robertson, Brenda Matthews, Gail Wooten, Wendy Brown) 44.68, 6 Nigeria (Uti Ufon-Uko, Beatrice Ewuzie, Ashanti Obi, Modupe Oshikoya) 45.22, 7 Scotland (Chris Salmond, Ruth Watt, Alison McRitchie, Helen Golden) 46.22, 8 Tanzania (Rose Mfunya, Amira Mohamed, Philomena Chezi, Nzaeli Kyomo) 46.43.

4 x 400 METRES RELAY (2 Feb): 1 England (Sue Pettett, Ruth Kennedy, Jannette Roscoe, Verona Bernard) 3:29.23, 2 Australia (Margaret Ramsay, Judy Canty, Terri-Anne Wangman, Charlene Rendina) 3:30.72, 3 Canada (Margaret MacGowan, Maureen Crowley, Brenda Walsh, Yvonne Saunders) 3:33.92, 4 Scotland (Margaret Coomber, Evelyn McMeekin, Rosemary Wright, Helen Golden) 3:35.21, 5 New Zealand (Colleen Mills, Sue Gukilau, Lorraine Tong, Penny Hunt) 3:37.53, 6 Nigeria (Rosaline Joshua, Ngozi Nwosu, Sola Adeduro, Florence Mbakwe) 3:40.83, 7 Ghana (Helen Opoku, Mercy Adomah, Rose Assiedua, Alice Annum) 3:43.78, 8 Kenya (Elizabeth Cheptum, Sabina Chebichi, Rose Tata-Muya, Elizabeth Chelimo) 3:51.91. Note: Coomber nee MacSherry, Wright nee Stirling. Colleen Mills was the wife of Les Mills, winner of five shot and discus medals 1958-70.

HIGH JUMP (2 Feb): 1 Barbara Lawton (Eng) 1.84, 2 Louise Hanna (Can) 1.82, 3 Brigitte Bittner (Can) 1.80, 4 Ruth Watt (Sco) 1.78, 5 Val Harrison (Eng) 1.76, 6 Debbie McCawley (Aus) 1.73, 7 Ann Wilson (Eng) 1.73, 8 Mary Peters (NI) 1.70, 9 Gladys Ng Mei Chai (Mal) 1.70, 10 Bernardine Lewis (Gre) 1.70, 11 Jenny Symon (Aus) 1.65, 12 Donna Mills (NZ) 1.60, 13 Sue Scott (Aus) 1.60, 14 Susan Burnside (NZ) 1.55. Note: Donna Mills was the daughter of Les and Colleen Mills.

LONG JUMP (31 Jan): 1 Modupe Oshikoya (Nig) 6.46, 2 Brenda Eisler (Can) 6.38, 3 Ruth Martin-Jones (Wal) 6.38, 4 Myra Nimmo (Sco) 6.34, 5 Lyn Tillett (Aus) 6.30, 6 Erica Nixon (Aus) 6.25, 7 Sheila Sherwood (Eng) 6.21, 8 Maureen Chitty (Eng) 6.20, 9 Pam Hendren (NZ) 6.11, 10 Sue New (Aus) 5.59, 11 Susan Burnside (NZ) 5.58, 12 Ann Wilson (Eng) 5.51. Note: Hendren nee Weigel.

SHOT (27 Jan): 1 Jane Haist (Can) 16.12, 2 Valerie Young (NZ) 15.29, 3 Jean Roberts (Aus) 15.24, 4 Mary Peters (NI) 14.88, 5 Barbara Poulsen (NZ) 14.60, 6 Brenda Bedford (Eng) 14.48, 7 Rosemary Payne (Sco) 14.19, 8 Diane Jones (Can)

14.15, 9 Evelyn Okeke (Nig) 13.81, 10 Gael Mulhall (Aus) 13.57, 11 Carol Martin (Can) 13.40.

DISCUS (26 Jan): 1 Jane Haist (Can) 55.52, 2 Rosemary Payne (Sco) 53.94, 3 Carol Martin (Can) 53.16, 4 Jean Roberts (Aus) 53.12, 5 Dorothy Swinyard (Eng) 51.30, 6 Meg Ritchie (Sco) 51.02, 7 Sally-Ann Mene (NZ) 48.80, 8 Sue Culley (Aus) 48.04, 9 Gael Mulhall (Aus) 46.12, 10 Rose Hart (Gha) 4132, 11 Mereoni Vibose (Fij) 40.66, 12 Losaline Faka'ata (Ton) 34.24. Note: Mene, nee Flynn, was the wife of Mene Mene, 6th in the decathlon.

JAVELIN (29 Jan): 1 Petra Rivers (Aus) 55.48, 2 Jenny Symon (Aus) 52.14, 3 Sharon Corbett (Eng) 50.26, 4 Pru French (Eng) 50.00, 5 Tessa Sanderson (Eng) 48.54, 6 Sandra McGookin (NZ) 47.84, 7 Mereoni Vibose (Fij) 45.84, 8 Susan James (Wal) 43.24, 9 Margaret Philpott (Aus) 42.70, 10 Joan Amsi (Tan) 42.12, 11 Sally Mene (NZ) 40.44, 12 Doristine Okuofu (Nig) 36.80.

PENTATHLON (25 Jan): 1 Mary Peters (NI) 4,455 (13.94, 15.05, 1.74, 5.81, 25.00), 2 Modupe Oshikoya (Nig) 4,423 (13.72, 10.44, 1.74, 6.50, 24.15), 3 Ann Wilson (Eng) 4,236 (13.98, 11.25, 1.74, 6.01, 25.37), 4 Erica Nixon (Aus) 4,206, 5 Barbara Poulsen (NZ) 4,158, 6 Diane Jones (Can) 4,072, 7 Sue Mapstone (Eng) 4,060, 8 Sue Scott (Aus) 4,058, 9 Janet Honour (Eng) 4,043, 10 Sue New (Aus) 3,881, 11 Susan Burnside (NZ) 3,726, 12 Miriama Tuisorisori (Fij) 3,572. Did not finish - Myra Nimmo (Sco), Elenoa Phillips (Fij). Note: Honour nee Oldall.

12.

Is he Gidemas? Is he Gidamis?
Whoever he is, he's won

THE 1976 OLYMPICS HAD BEEN a chastening experience for Commonwealth athletes. Only seven of them won medals, compared to East Germany's 27. Only three men in the field events placed in the first eight. Only four women placed in the first eight in any individual events. Admittedly, the absence of the Africans, pulled out late in the day by their governments because of New Zealand's rugby-union tour of South Africa, cost the likes of Boit, Bayi and Akii-Bua dear, but it still appeared as if the old Empire was sliding down the athletics league.

In the early summer of 1978, though, it was a Kenyan runner whose performances caused the biggest stir. Henry Rono was a 26-year-old from the Rift Valley who in 1976 had been recommended to John Chaplin, the coach at Washington State University, in the USA, by Kip Keino and had promptly begun winning races for Chaplin at cross-country and on the boards indoors before running 13:22.1 for 5000m and 27:37.1 for 10,000m during the 1977 outdoor track season. Even so, he had then astonished everyone in a triangular inter-university match on 8 April 1978 at the famed Berkeley track in California by reducing Dick Quax's World record for 5000m to 13:08.4. In the next couple of months he broke three further World records by decisive margins: more than eight seconds off Ben Jipcho's World steeplechase record with 8:05.4, again in a relatively minor collegiate meet; exactly eight seconds off the 10,000 metres record (held by another Kenyan, Samson Kimobwa, also now at the same university) with 27:22.47; and then four seconds better than Brendan Foster's 3000m record with 7:32.1. Rono, Kimobwa and Quax were all duly entered for the Commonwealth Games, for which Canada became the first country to play host on three occasions. Don Quarrie returned to defend his sprint titles, and among the recent Commonwealth record-breakers present were Greg Joy, of Canada (2.31 indoors in the high jump); 20-year-old Daley Thompson (8,238pts in the decathlon); and Tessa Sanderson (a javelin throw of 67.20).

There were 39 countries and a total of 545 athletes (369 men, 176 women) entered for the Edmonton athletics events. The one disappointing absence was that of Nigeria, withdrawing because of the rugby-union links between New Zealand and South Africa, and that deprived the Games of some fine 400m runners coached by the 1968 Olympic champion and World record-holder, Lee Evans, as well as the sublimely talented all-rounder, Modupe Oshikoya. Also missing were the leading British middle-distance men, Steve Ovett and Sebastian Coe, preferring to concentrate on the European Championships later in August, and John Walker, who was recovering from two leg operations.

The athletics events began in the new 42,000-capacity £21-million Commonwealth Stadium for the first time on a Sunday, 6 August, with the 10,000m and hammer finals and the women's pentathlon. Brendan Foster, a medal-winner at 1500 and 5000 in the two previous Commonwealth Games, had broken Dave Bedford's European record at 10,000m with 27:30.3 in the AAA Championships and faced, among others, Kimobwa and Quax, but Rono had preferred to run the steeplechase heats the same day. With the temperature approaching 30degC the pace was not over-quick and at halfway (14:08.8) the leading group of seven contained all three Englishmen and two Kenyans - though not Kimobwa, who was way below his 1977 form. Musyoki tried to break away without success and the decisive move came in characteristically courageous manner from Foster with still 1400m left, and he won unchallenged. The hammer title went to Peter Farmer, of Australia, who had been 3rd in 1974, and the best performance of the day by World standards (or, rather, series of performances) came from Diane Konihowski, of Canada, who as Miss

Jones had placed 10th and 6th in the pentathlon at the two previous Games and 6th again at the 1976 Olympics. This time she produced a fine new Commonwealth record of 4,768pts, which included a World-class high jump of 1.88, a 6.41 long jump, and 2:12.1 for the 800m which had replaced the 200 as the closing event.

The finals on Monday 7 August were at 100, 400, steeplechase, 110 hurdles and women's 100, 400, 3000 and discus, and the English women had a field day ... on the track. Sonia Lannaman won the 100 from Raelene Boyle, beaten for the first time in seven Commonwealth Games finals, and Donna Hartley was 10m clear at 400, as Verona Elder (nee Bernard) again finished 2nd. Then the 26-year-old twins, Paula Fudge and Ann Ford (nee Yeoman), made the debut of the women's 3000 in the Commonwealth Games an historic one by finishing 1st and 3rd. The only women's victory of the day which was denied to England also set a precedent because it was achieved in the discus by a Rumanian! She was Carmen Ionesco, who had placed 7th for Rumania as a 21-year-old in the 1972 Munich Olympics.

In the men's 100 Don Quarrie, bidding for his third successive win, faced the Olympic champion, Hasley Crawford, and the new British record-holder at 10.15, Allan Wells, and was still behind them both with only 20m of the race left, but he came with a rush to win in 10.03, aided by a stiff following wind. The margin was only 4/100ths-of-a-second ahead of Wells - who was thus the first medallist from the home countries at 100 yards or metres since Cyril Holmes in 1938 and was making a belated breakthrough into World-class at the age of 26. The finalists at 400m included Fred Sowerby, of Antigua, who had been the slowest miler in the heats at the 1966 Games, but there was not to be a rags-to-riches story here even though the winning time of the Australian, Rick Mitchell, who had been 6th in the Montreal Olympics, was the slowest in the Games for 16 years. At 110 hurdles the first four from Christchurch qualified again and were all together on the run-in from the 10th and last barriers, but it was Berwyn Price, of Wales, who dipped the most efficiently as only 5/100ths split the quartet and the defending champion, Fatwell Kimaiyo, was the one who missed a medal.

Henry Rono was, of course, clear favourite for the steeplechase with almost 18secs to spare over the next man in the pre-Games ranking-lists - and that was another Kenyan, James Munyala. Surviving from the 1974 final were the silver-medallist, John Davies, of Wales, and the New Zealanders, Euan Robertson and Howard Healey, but none of them could offer any sort of challenge to the World record-holder. Rono won by the greatest margin since George Bailey back in 1930 and his Kenyan team-mates took both the other medals. This meant that Kenya had now won eight of the 12 steeplechase medals at the Commonwealth Games from 1966 onwards and it marked the first occasion that three men from the same country other than England or Australia had placed 1-2-3 in any event. Kenyans had also won gold and silver at the steeplechase in the last two Olympics that they had contested.

Wind-assisted or not, the opening decathlon efforts of 10.50 for 100m and 8.11 for the long jump by Daley Thompson were tremendous and at the end of the first day he led by a massive 541pts from Australia's Peter Hadfield, with the defending champion, Mike Bull, almost 1,200pts behind in 10th place. The next day, Tuesday 8 August, Daley couldn't quite keep that momentum going and but for a 4.80 pole vault and a brave 4:25.8 in the ultimate exhausting 1500 he was always a shade or so off his best. Even so he ran up a score of 8,467pts, which beat the Games record by almost 1,000 and his own Commonwealth record. It was also third best on the all-time rankings to the 8,618 World-record score by Bruce Jenner, of the USA, at the 1976 Olympics and to the European record of 8,498 being achieved almost simultaneously to the Edmonton competition by Guido Kratschmer, of Germany. Hadfield's commendable silver-medal score of 7,623 left him around 10 per cent down on Daley.

The other finals of the day were in the road walk, now at 30 kilometres and therefore a bit shorter than the former distance of 20 miles, and in the women's shot. The walkers were sent off at 3 p.m., which was not at all sensible in the 26degC heat, and the early leaders paid the price, though the Australian, Willi Sawall, had admittedly thrown caution to the winds and gone striding past 10km on an ambitious schedule three minutes inside his Commonwealth record. Before 20km England's Olly Flynn, very tall for a walker at 6ft 4in (1.93), had overtaken the leader and he went on to win by almost a minute, ruefully describing himself afterwards in comparison with his Eastern European rivals in international competition as "the best amateur in the World". The women's shot was won by Gael Mulhall, of Australia, who was to cross paths on frequent further occasions with the 20-year-old bronze-medallist making her Games debut for England, Judy Oakes.

After a day's break competition resumed on Thursday 10 August with finals at 200, 800, 5000, 400 hurdles, high jump and long jump for men and 200, 800 and javelin for women, and no wonder there was a crowd of 35,000 in the stadium with such an exciting programme in prospect. Sadly, Don Quarrie suffered leg problems in his 200 semi-final and was just edged out of a chance of going for his sixth sprint gold. This left Allan Wells, James Gilkes (Guyana) and 18-year-old Paul Narracott (Australia) as the only ones repeating from the 100 final and they all improved: Wells, leading by several metres into the straight, just held off Gilkes, 20.12 to 20.18 wind-aided, and Narracott was 4th. It was the first Games gold for a Scot, man or woman, at any distance shorter than 5000 metres since the expatriate F.A.R. Hunter had won the 440 hurdles in 1934, and apart from Wells himself three days earlier it was the first Scots medal of any kind in the sprints since Ian Young's bronze, again in 1934. In the women's 200 Denise Boyd (nee Robertson), who had been 2nd in 1974, won from the 100m champion, Sonia Lannaman. In stark contrast to Scotland's experience in men's events this was Australia's 15th gold medal in 20 women's sprint finals.

The 800m was lacking Steve Ovett, Sebastian Coe and John Walker, and when the African champion, James Maina, was disqualified in the semi-finals two days earlier it seemed as if the final would be a low-key affair. In truth it was, but at least it gave the opportunity for victory to the prolific Mike Boit, whose first title this was at the age of 29. Neither was the women's 800 particularly fast, but it was a third win for the Peckham family as Judy (nee Canty), who had been 5th in the 1974 400 and had also won a silver at 4 x 400, followed the example of husband Lawrie, twice the high-jump champion. Mrs Peckham's team-mate, Charlene Rendina, deserved all credit despite coming last in defence of her title. She was making a comeback after giving birth and was still breast-feeding her year-old daughter.

Even a decade after Dick Fosbury had invented his revolutionary method of high-jumping on his back, the elegant straddle style was still thankfully in use and Claude Ferragne, the bronze-medallist four years earlier, employed it to gain what was surprisingly Canada's first win in the event, and a 20-year-old Scot, Brian Burgess, tied for 3rd place to avert a Canadian clean sweep of medals. The long jump went to Jamaican-born Roy Mitchell, of England, with Australia's Chris Commons 2nd, as in 1974, and both of them short of Daley Thompson's decathlon leap (though it was achieved with a stronger wind). Anna Pazera's Games record (and former World record) was finally surpassed by Tessa Sanderson, also like Mitchell born in Jamaica, and in so doing she restored respectability to what had become a rather second-rate event over the years. In 6th place with 49.16 was 17-year-old Fatima Whitbread, which compared very favourably with the 44.30 throw which had earned 5th position for her mother, Margaret Callender, back in the 1958 Games.

All three medallists from the 10,000 lined up again at 5000, but they made no greater impression on Henry Rono than had his steeplechase opponents. Mike McLeod, the doughty 10,000 bronze-medallist from the Elswick (pronounce it "Elz-ick") Harriers club in the North-East, was still with Rono just after 3000m, though that was as near as anyone got. Rono led by half the length of the straight at the bell and won easing off with the under-rated Musyoki getting his second silver and Foster his fourth medal. At 400 hurdles John Akii-Bua, disappointingly, had not put in an appearance, while Alan Pascoe, the title-holder, and Bill Koskei, twice a medallist, had qualified again but neither of them were in their form of old. The gold went instead to Daniel Kimaiyo in 49.48, which was precisely the same time with which he had beaten Akii-Bua the previous month for the African title, though he had run 49.20 in the Edmonton semi-finals. Kimaiyo, so far as was known, was no relation to the 1974 champion at 110 hurdles, Fatwell Kimaiyo.

The only track final on Friday August 11 was for the women's 100 hurdles, but it was by no means a downbeat day. The pole vault, discus and women's high jump and long jump were also decided. There were heats for the men's 1500, and above all else there was the marathon. Among the 34 runners who set out along the roads in reasonably cool conditions were the bronze-medallist and 4th-placer from 1974, Richard Mabuza and Terry Manners, and the enigmatic Jerome Drayton, whose previous record in the Games amounted to a non-finish and a 17th but who had to some extent redeemed himself with 6th place in the Montreal Olympics. At 20km Drayton led a group of five, including Kevin Ryan, of New Zealand, and

Shivnath Singh, of India, who had both run sub-2:12 earlier in the year, and the pace was pointing towards a winning time of around 2:15. At 30km and 35km the leader was the Scots-born Canadian, Paul Bannon, with Drayton only 100m or so behind at the latter checkpoint, and soon afterwards Drayton went ahead.

But closing fast was an African - not Mabuza, who was back in 7th place, nor the Kenyans, who were well out of it, but a Tanzanian named Shahanga who did not figure at all in the ranking-lists. He had been 75secs down at 30km, 40secs down at 35km, and was now at 40km only 13 secs behind. In the last 2,195 metres of the classic race distance he took three-quarters of a minute out of Drayton and finished at a sprint, looking remarkably fresh. Whether his name was Gidamis or Gidemas Shahanga, and whether he was 21 years old or only 19, or just maybe no more than 17, was still not apparent after the post-race grilling by a bewildered press. What did emerge is that he had run another marathon only 15 days before at the African Games in Algiers, finishing in 7th place almost 11 minutes behind Richard Mabuza. What a glorious happening it was, though, that a completely unheralded young man from a family of 14 living in a small mountainside town in the Serengeti National Park area of a country whose formal title was Jamhuri ya Mwungano wa Tanzania should become so unexpected a Commonwealth Games champion.

The women's 100 hurdles final was totally dominated by the English trio and Lorna Boothe, with a wind-aided 12.98, became the third Jamaican-born member of the England team at these Games to win a gold medal. Shirley Strong, only just 19, and Sharon Colyear, both from Stretford A.C., took 2nd and 3rd places. The women's high jump went to an 18-year-old Australian, Katrina Gibbs, beating Debbie Brill, the champion of eight years previously and the Commonwealth record-holder who at the advanced age of 24 was six years older than any of the others in the top half-dozen. Sue Reeve, of Birchfield Harriers, won the long jump eight years after placing 5th in the pentathlon. Both men's field events went to Canada: Bruce Simpson beat the title-holder, Don Baird, in the pole vault, and Borys Chambul won a dull discus final enlivened only by Brad Cooper becoming the second man from the Bahamas ever to win a Games medal.

The 1500 heats were also missing Sebastian Coe and Steve Ovett but were still of supreme quality. Filbert Bayi, the 1974 World record-breaking winner, went through with Rod Dixon and David Moorcroft, among others, but two future World record-holders could only manage 9th and 10th places. Steve Cram, the 17-year-old English schools' champion, had been sent to Edmonton simply for the experience after running a 3:57.4 mile, and judging by his exploits in later years he learned a lot; Steve Jones, of Wales, had already run the 5000 final earlier in the Games and would eventually find his forte as the World's fastest marathon-runner.

The concluding day was Saturday 12 August with the 1500 for men and women, plus the men's triple jump, shot and javelin, and all four relays. The weather was typically English - cool and lots of rain - and that no doubt played a part in what turned out to be a highly profitable day for the England team. Naturally, the men's 1500 was regarded as the major event by many among the 43,000 spectators, and who could argue with that, in view of a legacy of winners such as Lovelock, Bannister, Elliott, Snell, Keino and Bayi? Of the 12 men in the line-up four were Africans (Bayi, for Tanzania, and three from Kenya); one each was from Canada and New Zealand; and the remaining six were from the home countries. As in Christchurch Bayi led from the gun, though the relatively easier pace (very swift, even so) meant that there were still six men in with a chance at 1200m, and it was David Moorcroft, for England, who prevailed in a desperately close finish over Bayi and the Scotsmen, John Robson and Frank Clement, all separated by merely 18/100ths of a second. Moorcroft thus became the first Englishman since Roger Bannister to win the mile or 1500 at the Games; Bayi became only the third man, after Jerry Cornes in 1930-34 and Kip Keino in 1966-70, to win two medals at either of the distances; and Robson became the first Scottish medallist at either the mile or 1500m.

The women's 1500 was also won by England, creating another bizarre "record" for the Games. Mary Stewart's victory meant that she emulated brother Ian as a Commonwealth champion, but Ian had represented Scotland while Mary, who had also run for Scotland in 1974 and finished 4th, this time opted for England. Scotland again took 4th place through Chris McMeekin, whose twin sister, Evelyn, had finished 6th in the 800 two days earlier. Geoff Capes won the shot again for England, though well short of his 1974 record, and there was a fourth individual English success of the day for Keith Connor, only 20 and born in the West

149

Indies island of Anguilla, who broke the British record in the triple jump with 16.76 and then achieved further massive leaps of 17.21 and 17.17 with the wind only just over the 2m per sec legal limit. The javelin went to the 21-year-old Canadian, Phil Olsen, who had been promising much by breaking junior records since he was 16.

Canada and Ghana had won the previous day's heats for the men's 4 x 100 relay, and as Jamaica were without the injured Don Quarrie it seemed that the race would be between these two and Trinidad & Tobago, but Scotland had the 200 champion, Allan Wells. He ran a powerful second leg down the back straight and not only did the Scots win narrowly from Trinidad and Jamaica but they broke the British record with 39.24. The only previous Scottish relay medals had been bronze back in 1934, though they had been a very respectable 4th in 1970 and 5th in 1974. England's women, with 18-year-old Kathy Smallwood running second and 100m champion Sonia Lannaman on anchor, won their 4 x 100 event much more easily, with five metres or so to spare. At 4 x 400 there was yet another England win - their sixth of the day - with Ruth Kennedy and Verona Elder adding to their gold medals of four years earlier. In the men's race it seemed that there was even a seventh title to celebrate when Richard Ashton, who had finished 6th in the individual event, ran a startling last leg to bring England past Jamaica and then Kenya right on the line, but the English team was disqualified for apparently impeding the Kenyans during the third leg and an impassioned appeal by the team management against what may have been a harsh decision was turned down.

Though athletes from the home countries had previously faced the situation of Commonwealth Games and European Championships coming close together - it had happened in 1954, 1958 and 1966 - circumstances were rather different in 1978. Far greater competitive demands were now being made year-round, and for some a choice had to be made. Steve Ovett won the 1500 at the European Championships in Prague in almost precisely the same time as Moorcroft had achieved in Edmonton, and Moorcroft was 3rd. Ovett and Sebastian Coe were 2nd and 3rd at 800, but it took a once-in-a-lifetime 1:43.84 by the East German, Olaf Beyer, to do it, and as we all now know the East Germans developed a rather more advanced programme of scientific and medical support for their athletes than anyone else during the 1970s and 1980s. Of the other Edmonton champions Wells was subsequently 6th in Prague, Foster 4th, Mitchell 7th, Connor 6th, Thompson 2nd, Sonia Lannaman 8th, Donna Hartley 6th, Paula Fudge 8th and Tessa Sanderson 2nd.- and in some cases this was due, of course, to the competition simply being stronger. For example, Foster ran over 40sec faster in Prague at 10,000m but still didn't get a medal; Marita Koch, of East Germany, broke the World record in the women's 400m with 48.94, almost three seconds faster than Hartley had run in Edmonton; and Paula Fudge set a Commonwealth record time for 3000m in the European final which was 25sec quicker than she had done in Edmonton - and was still 15sec behind the Soviet winner.

Then there were, of course, the unsung heroes and heroines of Edmonton who did not figure at all among the medallists, nor even among the finalists, and none surely more courageous and enterprising than the team of 10 from the West African republic of The Gambia. Even by the widely-recognised standards of deprivation suffered throughout the continent in everyday living, let alone in pursuing a sporting ambition, the Gambians were at a marked disadvantage: the country had no track, and apparently not even an area of grass large enough to lay down a track, and there had been no domestic competitions of any kind for three years prior to 1978. Yet in their Edmonton heats Bakary Banana Jarjue ran 10.91 for 100m, Ousmane N'Dure 22.01 for 200m, Bambo Fatty 50.98 for 400m, and Georgiana Freeman 24.52 in the women's 200m. Giving opportunity to such raw and untried talent remains as much an achievement for the Commonwealth Games movement as the handing-out of honours to the elite. Maybe more so.

RESULTS 1978

MEN

100 METRES (7 Aug): 1 Don Quarrie (Jam) 10.03, 2 Allan Wells (Sco) 10.07, 3 Hasley Crawford (Tri) 10.09, 4 James Gilkes (Guy) 10.15, 5 Mike McFarlane (Eng) 10.29, 6 Paul Narracott (Aus) 10.31, 7 Chris Brathwaite (Tri) 10.32, 8 Ernie Obeng (Gha) 10.34. Note: assisting wind of 7.5m.

200 METRES (19 Aug): 1 Allan Wells (Sco) 20.12, 2 James Gilkes (Guy) 20.18, 3 Colin Bradford (Jam) 20.43, 4 Paul Narracott (Aus) 20.74, 5 Floyd Brown (Jam) 20.79, 6 Rick Hopkins (Aus) 20.88, 7 Trevor Hoyte (Eng) 20.90, 8 Calvin Dill (Ber) 21.07. Note: assisting wind of 4.3m.

400 METRES (7 Aug): 1 Rick Mitchell (Aus) 46.34, 2 Joe Coombs (Tri) 46.54, 3 Glenn Bogue (Can) 46.63, 4 Mike Solomon (Tri) 46.97, 5 Glen Cohen (Eng) 46.99, 6 Richard Ashton (Eng) 47.32, 7 Fred Sowerby (Ant) 47.51, 8 Bryan Saunders (Can) 48.01.

800 METRES (10 Aug): 1 Mike Boit (Ken) 1:46.39, 2 Seymour Newman (Jam) 1:47.30, 3 Peter Lemashon (Ken) 1:47.57, 4 Chum Darvall (Aus) 1:47.74, 5 Garry Cook (Eng) 1:48.06, 6 Halidu Zinenta (Gha) 1:48.15, 7 John Higham (Aus) 1:48.90, 8 Glen Grant (Wal) 1:49.3.

1500 METRES (12 Aug): 1 David Moorcroft (Eng) 3:35.48, 2 Filbert Bayi (Tan) 3:35.59, 3 John Robson (Sco) 3:35.60, 4 Frank Clement (Sco) 3:35.66, 5 Wilson Waigwa (Ken) 3:37.49, 6 Glen Grant (Wal) 3:38.05, 7 Richard Tuwei (Ken) 3:40.51, 8 Rod Dixon (NZ) 3:41.34, 9 Jim McGuinness (NI) 3:42.59, 10 Tim Hutchings (Eng) 3:43.05, 11 Paul Craig (Can) 3:43.42, 12 Kipsubai Koskei (Ken) 3:45.45.

5000 METRES (10 Aug): 1 Henry Rono (Ken) 13:23.04, 2 Mike Musyoki (Ken) 13:29.92, 3 Brendan Foster (Eng) 13:31.35, 4 Mike McLeod (Eng) 13:33.20, 5 Suleiman Nyambui (Tan) 13:34.1, 6 Nat Muir (Sco) 13:34.94, 7 Tony Simmons (Wal) 13:39.81, 8 Rod Dixon (NZ) 13:43.69, 9 Allister Hutton (Sco) 13:50.06, 10 Kipsubai Koskei (Ken) 13:52.54, 11 Steve Jones (Wal) 13:54.6, 12 Nick Rose (Eng) 13:55.18, 13 Lawrie Spence (Sco) 14:28.10, Did not finish - Alan Thurlow (NZ). Dave Fitzsimons (Aus) qualified but did not start.

10,000 METRES (6 Aug): 1 Brendan Foster (Eng) 28:13.65, 2 Mike Musyoki (Ken) 28:19.14, 3 Mike McLeod (Eng) 28:34.30, 4 David Black (Eng) 28:37.90, 5 Suleiman Nyambui (Tan) 28:56.7, 6 Tony Simmons (Wal) 20:01.2, 7 Joel Cheruiyot (Ken) 29:20.15, 8 Allister Hutton (Sco) 29:30.68, 9 Dick Quax (NZ) 29:58.00, 10 Alan Thurlow (NZ) 30:05.24, 11 Samson Kimobwa (Ken) 30:13.40, 12 Shivnath Singh (Ind) 30:26.67, 13 Peter Butler (Can) 31:17.18, 14 Aurelio Falero (Gib) 31:31.39, 15 Ngwila Musonda (Zam) 31:59.5, 16 Gabashane Vincent Rakabaele (Les) 32:08.43, 17 Patrick Chiwala (Zam) 32:14.9, 18 Nicholas Akers (Cay) 33:29.01, 19 Motlalepula Thabana (Les) 35:32.24, 20 Henry Baptiste (StL) 35:57.36.

MARATHON (11 Aug): 1 Gidamis Shahanga (Tan) 2:15:39.8, 2 Jerome Drayton (Can) 2:16:13.5, 3 Paul Bannon (Can) 2:16:51.6, 4 Kevin Ryan (NZ) 2:17:15.3, 5 Greg Hannon (NI) 2:17:25.0, 6 Paul Ballinger (NZ) 2:17:45.9, 7 Richard Mabuza (Swa) 2:19:48.6, 8 Mike Critchley (Wal) 2:19:50.9, 9 Trevor Wright (Eng) 2:20:14.6, 10 Stan Curran (Eng) 2:21:17.6, 11 Brian Maxwell (Can) 2:21:46.3, 12 Jeff Norman (Eng) 2:22:22.7, 13 Terry Manners (NZ) 2:22:59.7, 14 Emmanuel Ndiemandoi (Tan) 2:24:54.2, 15 Dave Chettle (Aus) 2:25:14.5, 16 Steve Kelly (IoM) 2:27:35.3, 17 Jim Butterfield (Ber) 2:30:16.7, 18 Jim Dingwall (Sco) 2:32:53.8, 19 David Newton (IoM) 2:33:05.1, 20 Thomas Ruto (Ken) 2:36:43.8, 21 Gary Wilkinson (Ber) 2:37:30.3, 22 Patrick Chiwala (Zam) 2:37:59.7, 23 Hector Romero (Gib) 2:42:24.8, 24 Ray Swan (Ber) 2:42:34.3, 25 Mike Rowland (Wal) 2:48:10.0, 26 Kenneth Hlasa (Les) 2:52:34.8, 27 Francis Mohlomanyane (Les) 2:52:57.8, 28 Baba Ibrahim Suma-Keita (SL) 2:56:07.1, 29 James Bernard (StV) 3:03:04.6, 30 Henry Baptiste (StL) 3:11:08.1. Did not finish - Richard Juma (Ken), John Kirimiti (Ken), Jim McLaughlin (NI), Shivnath Singh (Ind). Note: Trevor Wright was the husband of Rosemary Wright (nee Stirling), winner of the 800 metres in 1970.

3000 METRES STEEPLECHASE (7 Aug): 1 Henry Rono (Ken) 8:26.54, 2 James Munyala (Ken) 8:32.21, 3 Kiprotich Rono (Ken) 8:34.07, 4 Euan Robertson (NZ) 8:41.32, 5 Howard Healey (NZ) 8:43.75, 6 Dennis Coates (Eng) 8:47.35, 7 Tony Staynings (Eng) 8:48.87, 8 Ian Gilmour (Sco) 8:49.68, 9 John Wild (Eng) 8:57.94, 10 John Davies (Wal) 9:02.0, 11 Rob Evans (Can) 9:06.43, 12 Joe Sax (Can) 9:15.27. Note: Henry and Kip Rono were not related.

30 KILOMETRES WALK (8 Aug): 1 Olly Flynn (Eng) 2:22:03.7, 2 Willi Sawall (Aus) 2:22:58.6, 3 Tim Erickson (Aus) 2:26:34.0, 4 Brian Adams (Eng) 2:29:41.5, 6 Amos Seddon (Eng) 2:29:57.5, 7 Helmut Boeck (Can) 2:31:20.9, 8 Graham Young (IoM) 2:33:14.9, 9 Marcel Jobin (Can) 2:35:01.3, 10 Elisha Kasuka (Ken)

2:43:25.2, 11 Rashid Chege (Ken) 2:45:12.5, 12 Vellasamy Subramaniam (Mal) 2:56:07.1. Did not finish - Allan Callow (IoM), Robby Lambie (IoM), David Munyao (Ken), Mike Parker (NZ).

110 METRES HURDLES (7 Aug): 1 Berwyn Price (Wal) 13.70, 2 Max Binnington (Aus) 13.73, 3 Warren Parr (Aus) 13.73, 4 Fatwell Kimaiyo (Ken) 13.75, 5 Philip Sang (Ken) 13.97, 6 Phil Mills (NZ) 14.09, 7 Ross Pownall (NZ) 14.18, 8 Don Wright (Aus) 14.31. Note: assisting wind of 6.15m. Phil Mills was the son of Les and Colleen Mills, and was the fourth member of the family to take part in a Commonwealth Games final.

400 METRES HURDLES (10 Aug): 1 Daniel Kimaiyo (Ken) 49.48, 2 Garry Brown (Aus) 50.04, 3 Alan Pascoe (Eng) 50.09, 4 Peter Kipchumba (Ken) 50.50, 5 Bill Koskei (Ken) 50.69, 6 Clive Barriffe (Jam) 51.50, 7 Gary Oakes (Eng) 51.60, 8 Phil Mills (NZ) 52.01. Note: this was the 12th appearance in a final by a member of the Mills family, covering six different events - shot, discus, 110 hurdles, 400 hurdles and women's 4 x 400 and high jump!

4 X 100 METRES RELAY (12 Aug): 1 Scotland (David Jenkins, Allan Wells, Cameron Sharp, Drew McMaster) 39.24, 2 Trinidad & Tobago (Eldwin Noel, Hasley Crawford, Chris Brathwaite, Ephraim Serrette) 39.29, 3 Jamaica (Errol Quarrie, Colin Bradford, Oliver Heywood, Floyd Brown) 39.33, 4 Canada (Desai Williams, Marvin Nash, Hugh Fraser, Cole Doty) 39.60, 5 Ghana (Ernie Obeng, Albert Lomotey, George Enchill, Ohene Karikari) 39.73, 6 England (Brian Green, Tim Bonsor, Les Hoyte, Trevor Hoyte) 40.05, 7 Australia (Don Wright, Paul Narracott, Max Binnington, Rick Hopkins) 40.24, 8 Bermuda (Kimberley Wade, Dennis Trott, Calvin Dill, Gregory Simons) 40.33. Note: Errol Quarrie was the brother of Don Quarrie; Les and Trevor Hoyte, of England, were brothers.

4 x 400 METRES RELAY (12 Aug): 1 Kenya (Washington Njiri, Daniel Kimaiyo, Bill Koskei, Joel Ngetich) 3:03.54, 2 Jamaica (Clive Barriffe, Bert Cameron, Colin Bradford, Floyd Brown) 3:04.00, 3 Australia (John Higham, Chum Darvall, Garry Brown, Rick Mitchell) 3:04.23, 4 Canada (Frank Van Doorn, Darce Bowen, Brian Saunders, Glenn Bogue) 3:05.94, 5 Trinidad & Tobago (Mike Paul, Mike Solomon, Ray Astor, Joe Coombs) 3:06.7, 6 Scotland (Roger Jenkins, Peter Hoffman, Paul Forbes, David Jenkins) 3:07.73, 7 Antigua & Barbuda (Elroy Turner, Cuthbert Jacobs, Lester Flax, Fred Sowerby) 3:10.45. England (Terry Whitehead, Alan Pascoe, Glen Cohen, Richard Ashton) finished 1st in 3:03.53 but were disqualified. Note: Roger and David Jenkins were brothers.

HIGH JUMP (10 Aug): 1 Claude Ferragne (Can) 2.20, 2 Greg Joy (Can) 2.18, 3= Dean Bauck (Can) & Brian Burgess (Sco) 2.15, 5 Gordon Windeyer (Aus) 2.15, 6 Mark Naylor (Eng) 2.10, 7 Baljit Singh (Mal) 2.05, 8 Winston Strachan (Bah) 2.00, 9 Bernard Rault (Mau) 2.00. Masud Twawakali (Tan) failed at opening height (2.00).

POLE VAULT (11 Aug): 1 Bruce Simpson (Can) 5.10, 2 Don Baird (Aus) 5.10, 3 Brian Hooper (Eng) 5.00, 4 Jeff Gutteridge (Eng) 5.00, 5 Harold Heer (Can) 4.80, 6 Glenn Colivas (Can) 4.80. Mike Bull (NI) & Allan Williams (Eng) failed at opening height (4.80).

LONG JUMP (10 Aug): 1 Roy Mitchell (Eng) 8.06, 2 Chris Commons (Aus) 8.04, 3 Suresh Babu (Ind) 7.94, 4 Dennis Trott (Ber) 7.89, 5 Rick Rock (Can) 7.85, 6 Emmanuel Mifetu (Gha) 7.82, 7 Bogger Mushanga (Zam) 7.68, 8 Ken Lorraway (Aus) 7.57, 9 Willie Kirkpatrick (NI) 7.53, 10 Jim McAndrew (Can) 7.48, 11 Ravi Kumar (Ind) 7.41. Note: the jumps by all competitors except Trott and Ravi Kumar were wind-assisted.

TRIPLE JUMP (12 Aug): 1 Keith Connor (Eng) 17.21, 2 Ian Campbell (Aus) 16.93, 3 Aston Moore (Eng) 16.69, 4 Ken Lorraway (Aus) 16.27, 5 Mike Nipinak (Can) 16.24, 6 Phil Wood (NZ) 16.05, 7 Steve Hanna (Bah) 15.97, 8 David Johnson (Eng) 15.84, 9 John Phillips (Wal) 15.59, 10 Dave Watt (Can) 15.29, 11 Gideon Cheruiyot (Ken) 15.28, 12 Gerry Swan (Ber) 15.06, 13 Maxwell Peters (Ant) 15.06. Note: the jumps of Connor, Campbell and Peters were wind-assisted.

SHOT (12 Aug): 1 Geoff Capes (Eng) 19.77, 2 Bruno Pauletto (Can) 19.33, 3 Bishop Dolegiewicz (Can) 18.45, 4 Mike Mercer (Can) 17.83, 5 Mike Winch (Eng) 16.93, 6 Bob Dale (Eng) 16.89, 7 Bahadur Singh (Ind) 16.57, 8 Jugraj Singh (Ind) 16.50, 9 Gurdeep Singh (Ind) 15.74, 10 Wayne Martin (Aus) 15.54, 11 Keith Falle (Jer) 15.32, 12 Brad Cooper (Bah) 14.92, 13 Michael Obangi (Ken) 13.68. Note: Bishop Dolegiewicz's proper first name was Zbigniew.

DISCUS (11 Aug): 1 Borys Chambul (Can) 59.70, 2 Brad Cooper (Bah) 57.30, 3 Rob Gray (Can) 55.48, 4 Robin Tait (NZ) 55.22, 5 Wayne Martin (Aus) 54.98, 6 Peter Tancred (Eng) 54.78, 7 John Hillier (Eng) 52.26, 8 Dick Priman (Aus) 50.42, 9 Mike Winch (Eng) 50.22, 10 Praveen Kumar (Ind) 49.42, 11 John Ruto (Ken) 43.14. Michael Obangi (Ken) no valid throw. Note: Peter Tancred was the brother of Bill Tancred, who had placed 9th, 3rd and 2nd in the discus in the three previous Games.

HAMMER (6 Aug): 1 Peter Farmer (Aus) 71.10, 2 Scott Neilson (Can) 69.92, 3 Chris Black (Sco) 68.14, 4 Paul Dickenson (Eng) 66.42, 5 Jim Whitehead (Eng) 65.48, 6 Ian Chipchase (Eng) 64.80, 7 Martin Girvan (NI) 60.86, 8 Gus Puopolo (Aus) 59.74, 9 Absolon Simiti (Ken) 43.38. Harold Willers (Can) no valid throws.

JAVELIN (12 Aug): 1 Phil Olsen (Can) 84.00, 2 Mike O'Rourke (NZ) 83.18, 3 Peter Yates (Eng) 78.58, 4 Brian Roberts (Eng) 75.10, 5 David Ottley (Eng) 74.28, 6 Luc Laperriere (Can) 73.44, 7 Manfred Rohkamper (Aus) 71.74, 8 John Mayaka (Ken) 70.00, 9 Robert Moulder (Ber) 69.64, 10 John Corazza (Can) 69.14, 11 Zakayo Malekwa (Tan) 64.12, 12 A. Taylor (TCI) 43.96.

DECATHLON (7-8 Aug): 1 Daley Thompson (Eng) 8,467 (10.50, 8.11, 14.43, 2.07, 47.85, 14.92, 41.68, 4.80, 56.60, 4:25.8), 2 Peter Hadfield (Aus) 7,623 (10.98, 7.28, 13.48, 1.92, 49.24, 15.59, 46.52, 4.00, 60.80, 4:54.5), 3 Alan Drayton (Eng) 7,484 (11.03, 7.15, 11.85, 1.95, 50.17, 14.86, 40.60, 4.40, 57.22, 4:54.1), 4 Graeme "Buster" Watson (Eng) 7,261, 5 Pan Zeniou (Cyp) 7,201, 6 Rob Town (Can) 7,138, 7 Robert Sadler (NZ) 7,117, 8 Charles Kokoyo (Ken) 6,775, 9 Mike Bull (NI) 6,610, 10 Tony Verhoeven (Can) 6,453, 11 Zenon Smiechowski (Can) 5,807, 12 Dunstan Campbell (Gre) 5,515. Did not finish - Craig Considine (Aus). Note: the 100m and long jump were wind-assisted.

WOMEN

100 METRES (7 Aug): 1 Sonia Lannaman (Eng) 11.27, 2 Raelene Boyle (Aus) 11.35, 3 Denise Boyd (Aus) 11.37, 4 Hannah Afriyie (Gha) 11.38, 5 Bev Goddard (Eng) 11.40, 6 Patti Loverock (Can) 11.40, 7 Lelieth Hodges (Jam) 11.47, 8 Wendy Clarke (Eng) 11.48. Note: assisting wind of 2.8m. Denise Boyd (nee Robertson) was the wife of Ray Boyd, 4th in the 1974 pole vault.

200 METRES (10 Aug): 1 Denise Boyd (Aus) 22.82, 2 Sonia Lannaman (Eng) 22.89, 3 Colleen Beazley (Aus) 22.93, 4 Bev Goddard (Eng) 22.95, 5 Kathy Smallwood (Eng) 22.96, 6 Helen Golden (Sco) 23.28, 7 Patti Loverock (Can) 23.47, 8 Linda McCurry (NI) 23.71. Note: assisting wind of 5m.

400 METRES (7 Aug): 1 Donna Hartley (Eng) 51.69, 2 Verona Elder (Eng) 52.94, 3 Beth Nail (Aus) 53.06, 4 Joslyn Hoyte (Eng) 53.22, 5 June Griffith (Guy) 53.25, 6 Karen Williams (Sco) 53.66, 7 Helen Blake (Jam) 54.15, 8 Maxine Corcoran (Aus) 54.46. Note: Donna Hartley was the wife of Bill Hartley, 6th at 400 hurdles and 2nd at 4 x 400 in the 1974 Games; Elder nee Barnard.

800 METRES (10 Aug): 1 Judy Peckham (Aus) 2:02.82, 2 Tekla Chemabwai (Ken) 2:02.87, 3 Jane Colebrook (Eng) 2:03.10, 4 Liz Barnes (Eng) 2:03.41, 5 Francine Gendron (Can) 2:04.02, 6 Evelyn McMeekin (Sco) 2.04.10, 7 Anne Mackie-Morelli (Can) 2:04.16, 8 Charlene Rendina (Aus) 2:04.82. Note: Judy Peckham (nee Canty) was the wife of Lawrie Peckham, high-jump champion in 1966-70 and 2nd in 1974, and the daughter of Judy Canty, 2nd in the long jump in 1950.

1500 METRES (12 Aug): 1 Mary Stewart (Eng) 4:06.34, 2 Chris Benning (Eng) 4:07.53, 3 Penny Werthner (Can) 4:08.14, 4 Chris McMeekin (Sco) 4:12.43, 5 Hilary Hollick (Wal) 4:12.72, 6 Alison Wright (NZ) 4:12.93, 7 Francine Gendron (Can) 4:16.88, 8 Angela Cook (Aus) 4:17.30, 9 Wayva Kiteti (Ken) 4:18.72, 10 Ann Kiprop (Ken) 4:23.17, 11 Chris Boxer (Eng) 4:26.14, 12 Margaret Coomber (Sco) 4:26.28. Note: Mary Stewart was 4th for Scotland in the 1974 Games; Evelyn and Chris McMeekin were 21-year-old twins.

3000 METRES (7 Aug): 1 Paula Fudge (Eng) 9:12.95, 2 Heather Thomson (NZ) 9:20.69, 3 Ann Ford (Eng) 9:24.05, 4 Shauna Miller (Can) 9:30.75, 5 Nancy Rooks (Can) 9:34.14, 6 Angela Cook (Aus) 9:43.56, 7 Mwinga Mwanjala-Sote (Tan) 9:49.98, 8 Rose Thomson (Ken) 10:00.46, 9 Debbie Scott (Can) 10:02.59, 10 Wayva Kiteti (Ken) 10:12.56, 11 Dianah Chepyator (Ken) 10:18.49, 12 Modesta Masaka (Tan) 10:45.79, 13 Kandasamy Jayamani (Sin) 11:13.01, 14 Beatrice Delancy (TCI) 11:20.87. Did not finish - Theodora Corea (StV), Penny Yule (Eng). Note: Paula Fudge and Ann Ford (nee Yeoman) were 26-year-old twins; Rose Thomson and Dianah Chepyator were sisters.

100 METRES HURDLES (11 Aug): 1 Lorna Boothe (Eng) 12.98, 2 Shirley Strong (Eng) 13.08, 3 Sharon Colyear (Eng) 13.17, 4 Elaine Davidson (Sco) 13.76, 5 Gail Wooten (NZ) 13.77, 6 Sharon Lane (Can) 13.88, 7 Diane Konihowski (Can) 14.11, 8 June Caddle (Bar) 14.13. Note: assisting wind of 3.6m. Konihowski nee Jones.

4 x 100 METRES RELAY (12 Aug): 1 England (Bev Goddard, Kathy Smallwood, Sharon Colycar, Sonia Lannaman) 43.70, 2 Canada (Angela Bailey, Patti Loverock, Margaret Howe, Marjorie Bailey) 44.26, 3 Australia (Roxanne Gelle, Denise Boyd, Colleen Beazley, Lyn Jacenko) 44.78, 4 New Zealand (Wendy Brown, Penny Hunt, Gail Wooten, Kim Robertson) 45.06, 5 Jamaica (Normalee Murray, Dorothy Scott, Maureen Gottshalk, Carmetta Drummond) 45.75, 6 Trinidad & Tobago (Marilyn Bradley, Joanne Gardner, Janice Bernard, Ester Hope) 45.80, 7 Scotland (Elaine Davidson, Margot Wells, Helen Golden, Karen Williams) 45.91. 7 teams

competed. Note: Angela Bailey and Marjorie Bailey, of Canada, were not related; Jacenko nee Tillett; Margot Wells was the wife of Allan Wells, 2nd at 100, 1st at 200 and 4 x 100.

4 x 400 METRES RELAY (12 Aug): 1 England (Ruth Kennedy, Joslyn Hoyte, Verona Elder, Donna Hartley) 3:27.19, 2 Australia (Judy Peckham, Denise Boyd, Maxine Corcoran, Beth Nail) 3:28.65, 3 Canada (Margaret Stride, Debbie Campbell, Anne Mackie-Morelli, Rachelle Campbell) 3:35.83, 4 Scotland (Ann Harley, Evelyn McMeekin, Helen Golden, Karen Williams) 3:36.52, 5 Ghana (Helen Opoku, Grace Bakari, Georgina Aidoo, Hannah Afriyie) 3:37.12, 6 Jamaica (Debbie Byfield-White, Maureen Gottshalk, Normalee Murray, Helen Blake) 3:37.92. 6 teams competed.

HIGH JUMP (11 Aug): 1 Katrina Gibbs (Aus) 1.93, 2 Debbie Brill (Can) 1.90, 3 Julie White (Can) 1.83, 4 Gillian Hitchen (Eng) 1.80, 5 Barbara Simmonds (Eng) 1.78, 6 Maggie Woods (Can) 1.78, 7 Val Rutter (Eng) 1.75, 8 Wendy Phillips (NI) 1.70, 9 Adventina Matakwaya-Matungwa (Tan) 1.60. Note: Rutter nee Harrison.

LONG JUMP (11 Aug): 1 Sue Reeve (Eng) 6.59, 2 Erica Hooker (Aus) 6.58, 3 June Griffith (Guy) 6.52, 4 Sue Hearnshaw (Eng) 6.40, 5 Shonel Ferguson (Bah) 6.24, 6 Jeanette Yawson (Gha) 6.19, 7 Ruth Howell (Wal) 6.17, 8 Lyn Jacenko (Aus) 6.14, 90 Jill Ross (Can) 6.07, 10 Diane Konihowski (Can) 6.05, 11 Noeline Hodgins (NZ) 5.86, 12 Esther Otieno (Ken) 5.84. Note: the jumps by Ferguson, Yawson and Ross were wind-assisted. Reeve nee Scott; Hooker nee Nixon; Howell nee Martin-Jones.

SHOT (8 Aug): 1 Gael Mulhall (Aus) 17.31, 2 Carmen Ionesco (Can) 16.45, 3 Judy Oakes (Eng) 16.14, 4 Angela Littlewood (Eng) 15.71, 5 Bev Francis (Aus) 15.66, 6 Venissa Head (Wal) 15.52, 7 Luigina Torso (Aus) 15.09, 8 Meg Ritchie (Sco) 14.99, 9 Lucette Moreau (Can) 14.92, 10 Herina Obuya-Malit (Ken) 12.04, 11 Branwen Smith (Ber) 11.80.

DISCUS (7 Aug): 1 Carmen Ionesco (Can) 62.16, 2 Gael Mulhall (Aus) 57.60, 3 Lucette Moreau (Can) 56.64, 4 Meg Ritchie (Sco) 55.66, 5 Janet Thompson (Eng) 53.70, 6 Lesley Mallin (Eng) 50.56, 7 Luigina Torso (Aus) 47.10, 8 Venissa Head (Wal) 45.72, 9 Beryl Bethel (Bah) 43.50, 10 Lilian Cherotich (Ken) 40.72.

JAVELIN (10 Aug): 1 Tessa Sanderson (Eng) 61.34, 2 Alison Hayward (Can) 54.52, 3 Laurie Kern (Can) 53.60, 4 Eunice Nekesa (Ken) 51.46, 5 Margaret Philpott (Aus) 50.08, 6 Fatima Whitbread (Eng) 49.16, 7 Shara Spragg (Eng)

49.02, 8 Diane Williams (Sco) 46.02, 9 Bev Francis (Aus) 45.52, 10 Jackie Zaslona (Wal) 41.08, 11 Sonia Smith (Ber) 39.34, 12 Elizabeth Twyford (StL) 29.62. Jeanette Kieboom (Aus) no valid throws.

PENTATHLON (6 Aug): 1 Diane Konihowski (Can) 4,768 (13.85, 14.87, 1.88, 6.41, 2:12.1), 2 Sue Mapstone (Eng) 4,222 (14.17, 11.32, 1.75, 6.06, 2:19.3), 3 Yvette Wray (Eng) 4,211 (14.16, 12.15, 1.64, 6.04, 2:15.6), 4 Jill Ross (Can) 4,205, 5 Karen Page (NZ) 4,099, 6 Ruth Howell (Wal) 4,022, 7 Barbara Beable (NZ) 3,989, 8 Julie White (Can) 3,940, 9 Wendy Phillips (NI) 3,594, 10 Jennifer Swanston (Bar) 3,517. Did not finish - Glynis Saunders (Aus). Note: Beable nee Poulsen.

13.

Is it Wells? Is it McFarlane?
Yes and no, it's both of them

QUEEN ELIZABETH II STADIUM, BRISBANE, AUSTRALIA,
3-9 OCTOBER 1982

THE 1982 GAMES WERE SCHEDULED very early in the Australian summer, and for better or worse they began in Brisbane only three weeks after a large number of the athletes from Britain had been taking part in the European Championships. Steve Cram (1500), Keith Connor (triple jump) and Daley Thompson (decathlon) had won titles in Athens, and although he had been beaten into 3rd place there the performance of the year had previously been achieved at 5000m by the reigning Commonwealth 1500m champion, David Moorcroft, when he reduced Henry Rono's World record by almost six seconds to a tantalising 13:00.41 at the renowned Bislett Games in Oslo in early July.

Thompson, with a score of 8,743pts in Athens, and Rob de Castella, of Australia, who had run a 2:08:18 marathon in Japan the previous December, were current World record-holders among the 507 athletes from 40 countries entered in Brisbane. Commonwealth record-holders on hand included Bert Cameron, of Jamaica, who had run a 44.58 400 the previous year; Milt Ottey, of Canada, who had raised the high-jump mark to 2.32; Brad Cooper, of the Bahamas, who had thrown the discus 66.72; sprinters Angella Taylor, of Canada (11.03) and Kathy Smallwood, of England (22.13 and 50.46); Gael Mulhall, of Australia, up to 18.85 in the shot; Meg Ritchie, of Scotland, 67.48 in the discus; and Judy Livermore, of England, with 6,259 in the heptathlon (which had replaced the pentathlon).

The athletics events began on Sunday 3 October with the 10,000 final, as usual, and the hammer. There were 25,000 spectators, but the Queen Elizabeth II Stadium remained less than half-full. Despite still holding the World record and leading the current Commonwealth rankings, Henry Rono wasn't selected for Kenya, which left England's Julian Goater as the fastest man at the start of the 10,000 but the Games marathon winner from 1978, Gidamis Shahanga, as the most intriguing participant, having now become a student in the USA and run a 27:38.1 10,000 in California in April. Shahanga and his Tanzanian team-mate, Barie, led at halfway in a modest 14:16.0, and Goater quite rightly did his best to burn them off with a three-lap acceleration later on, but they caught him again and shared the race between them on the last lap, with Shahanga winning as a useful warm-up for his defence of the marathon title five days later. The other gold medal of the day was also won by a US-based student, 21-year-old Bob Weir, and he set a British hammer-throw record of 75.08 in the process. Newly-eligible Hans-Martin Lotz, 4th for Australia, had contested the 1962 and 1966 European Championships for West Germany.

The crowd was 30,000 for the finals of the 100, 400, steeplechase, 110 hurdles and women's 100, 400, 3000 and discus, and completion of the heptathlon, which were the features of the second day, Monday 4 October. The finalists for the men's 100 did not include the man who had held the title for 12 years, Don Quarrie, but did include the man who had run him closer than anyone, Allan Wells, the 1978 silver-medallist at 100 and champion at 200 - Wells had run the fastest semi-final time of 10.20, but Quarrie was last-but-one in the other semi-final in 10.43. The times in the final, helped by a 5.9m tailwind, were sensational: Wells winning in 10.02 from a 20-year-old Canadian, Ben Johnson, 10.05, and less than two-tenths of a second covering all the finishers on the nine-lane track. The women's 100 was not at all overshadowed with Angella Taylor, of Canada (like Johnson born in Jamaica), legally improving her Commonwealth record in the final to 11.00 - and very much needing to run that fast to keep at bay Merlene Ottey, already at 22 the Olympic 200m bronze-medallist from 1980.

Since winning the 1978 Commonwealth title at 400m Rick Mitchell had taken the silver medal at the 1980 Olympics, albeit boycotted by the

161

USA, and now faced Bert Cameron, who was one of only nine athletes in a Jamaican team of derisory proportions. Neither of them was in his best sub-45 form, though it was still Cameron who won comfortably, and the windy conditions certainly affected the times. So Raelene Boyle's success in the women's final in 51.26 was all the more creditable for that. Having won six gold medals in the Games of 1970 and 1974 but just a single silver in 1978, she had switched to the 400, as sprinters often do, and her victory over Michelle Scutt, of Wales, who had the fastest pre-Games time of 50.63, was no great surprise. Scutt had the consolation of winning what was only the second medal ever by a Welsh woman.

The steeplechase provided a third successive Games victory by a Kenyan, and the pattern of the race was one which was to be repeated at the various distances in which the Kenyans were involved over the years to come. Richard Tuwei, who had placed 7th at 1500 in the 1978 Games and had run that distance in 3:40.12 in July, was the fastest of the Kenyan trio in the rankings and appeared to be their likely winner, and yet he was the one who did all the pacemaking. Then, after England's Graeme Fell had taken the lead on the last lap it was the Kenyan third string, Julius Korir, who came past him to win and improve his previous best time by over seven seconds. Korir's coach was Kip Keino and it seems feasible that the Kenyan team management had decided beforehand that he was their best chance and instructed the others, including namesake Amos Korir, accordingly to run in support. In the women's 3000m Wendy Smith, of England, had set a Commonwealth record 8:46.01 in the same Oslo meeting at which David Moorcroft had broken the World 5000m record, and her main opposition came from two New Zealanders who had earlier in their careers not quite reached the top rank: at the 1974 Games Anne Audain (then Garrett) had placed 6th at 1500 and Lorraine Moller 5th at 800, and it was Audain's basic speed which took her to victory in Brisbane, breaking Smith's record with 8:45.53.

Daley Thompson led the decathlon by 464pts after the first five events, while Glynis Nunn, of Australia, who had failed to finish the 1978 event because of injury, won a close heptathlon contest by 68pts from Judy Livermore. In the women's discus Meg Ritchie won Scotland's second gold in the event after Rosemary Payne in 1970, with the title-holder, Carmen Ionesco, out of the medals. In the 110 hurdles Berwyn Price was only fractionally slower than when he had won four years earlier, 13.73 as against 13.70, but this time he was 6th as Guyana-born Mark McKoy, of Canada, improved wondrously from a previous wind-assisted best of 13.67 to a legal new Commonwealth record of 13.37, ahead of the former holder, England's Mark Holtom, who himself ran 13.43. Australia's Max Binnington, running in his third successive Games final, was also quicker than ever before but 5th this time.

On the third day, Tuesday 5 October, only two events came to a conclusion - the decathlon and the women's shot - and presumably most of the 10,000 spectators present came for Daley Thompson's sake. He did not disappoint, though there was no question in the blustery conditions over the two days of him threatening his World record. His winning margin was 406pts - equivalent to, say, around nine seconds at 400m or about 27 metres in the javelin - over Dave Steen, of Canada, who was the nephew of the 1966-70 shot-putt champion. In the women's shot Judy Oakes, who had been 3rd in 1978 and was coached by Mike Winch (who had placed 2nd and 5th in the shot in previous Games and would be 2nd again in Brisbane), broke the British record with 17.92 and beat the title-holder, Gael Mulhall. Without Coe, the World record-holder, or Ovett, the Olympic champion, who had both declined selection, England's presence in the 800-metre preliminaries was further depleted when Garry Cook, fastest in the field on paper, fell and failed to qualify. All three Kenyans got through.

The fourth day's finals on Thursday 7 October were at 200, 800, 5000, 400 hurdles, high jump and long jump for men, and 200, 800, 400 hurdles and javelin for women, with the 30km road walk also taking place, which was as captivating a programme of events as anyone could wish for, and 58,000 people turned up to enjoy it. Nothing - other than Aussie wins, of course - satisfied them more than a remarkable men's 200 in which, despite the closest of scrutinies of the photo-finish print by the judges, Scotsman Allan Wells and Englishman Mike McFarlane could not be separated in a time of 20.43. The automatic pictures taken by the photo-finish camera show an image of each athlete at the moment he or she crosses the line, with the time to one-hundredth of a second recorded continuously on the frame; so any margin of difference, however minimal, can be detected, and in this instance there simply wasn't any. A dead-heat in the

163

age of electronic timing is not unique - it had already happened only three days before for 5th place in the women's 100m and occurred again for 3rd place in the women's 100m hurdles at the 1984 Olympics - but remains rare. Incidentally, largely unnoticed behind Wells and McFarlane was Cameron Sharp, 3rd again as he had been at 100, and back in 8th place for England the versatile Luke Graeme Lynton George Watson, familiarly known as "Buster", who was completing an unusual combination, having been 4th in the 1978 decathlon.

The first four from the women's 100 were also in the 200 final, and four of the first five from 1978 had qualified again - Boyd (the title-holder), Pekin (nee Beazley), Callender (nee Goddard) and Smallwood. With the wind just over the limit Ottey won from the ninth and outside lane in 22.19, ahead of Smallwood, and the 100m champion, Taylor. Boyd was 4th and it was the first time Australia had not won the event since 1962 and the first time they had not had a medallist since 1934. To counter that, Australian men won their country's first titles at 800m and 400m hurdles since 1966: Peter Bourke, whose Austrian-born coach, Franz Stampfl, had been Roger Bannister's mentor, managed the rare feat of running a faster second lap to win the 800 from James Maina; and Brisbane schoolteacher Garry Brown, who had been 2nd in 1978 and whose coach, Gary Knoke, had run in four Commonwealth Games finals but never won a medal, became the hurdles champion, with Mike Whittingham, whose father had been one of Sydney Wooderson's prewar World-record pacemakers, best of the British in 4th place, and the year's fastest man at 49.17, Jamaica's Karl Smith, a very distant last.

The World record-holder, David Moorcroft, must have considered Peter Koech, of Kenya, as his main rival for the 5000m title. Koech had only finished 15th in the 10,000 four days before, but he had run 13:09.50 for 5000m during the summer and had given Moorcroft a great race over two miles at Crystal Palace six weeks before the Games opened. Koech led at 3000, but at no more than 13:45 pace, and Moorcroft ran the last 800 in 1:58.5 and only his team-mate, Nick Rose, was able to offer any sort of challenge. Cyprus, competing in the Games for only the second time, took 5th place here to follow 6th in the 800 earlier, both by athletes whose mother-tongue was Greek, and then to further exemplify the Commonwealth's cultural diversity two of the medals in the road walk were won by French-speaking Canadians as the first seven men broke the Games record and Steve Barry took the gold for Wales in a British record 2hrs 10mins 16secs.

There was another Welsh victory in the women's 800, though as her name would suggest Kirsty McDermott's allegiance was based on a residential qualification as she was of English parentage and born in Scotland. No matter, because the Commonwealth Games rules are free and easy about that sort of thing, and anyway McDermott's Welsh roots were deep enough - she had won titles at all ages in the Welsh schools' championships. There was no appearance here by the young African prodigies of eight years earlier, though Rose Tata-Muya did run in the 400 and 400 hurdles heats and the relay at these Games and would figure again in a career of astonishing longevity lasting almost a quarter-of-a-century. The 400m hurdles for women, still to be introduced at Olympic level, was held for the first time and Debbie Flintoff rewarded the enterprise of the organisers and the support of the Australian crowd with a new Commonwealth record of 55.89. Flintoff had originally been a pentathlete, and the bronze medal went to Yvette Wray, who had won another bronze in the Games pentathlon in 1978. Last was Sandra Farmer, of Jamaica, who later married American hurdler Dave Patrick and won Olympic and World Championships silver medals for the USA.

In the men's high jump the Jamaican-born Canadian holder of the Commonwealth record, Milt Ottey, duly won - but only just from 20-year-old Steve Wray, of the Bahamas, whose previous best was 2.23 from 1981 and who improved that three times and even attempted a World record 2.36 along with Ottey! The Bahamas also got silver in the men's long jump, though Steve Hanna was a long way behind the Games record of 8.13 for the Australian favourite, Gary Honey, and there was another home success in the women's javelin with Sue Howland beating the Games record held by the absent defending champion, Tessa Sanderson. The winner in 1970 and 1974, Petra Rivers, placed 2nd ahead of England's Fatima Whitbread.

On to the fifth day of competition - Friday 8 October - and the marathon, together with finals in the pole vault, discus and women's 100 hurdles, high jump and long jump. The activities started with the men's 1500 heats, in which Steve Cram, John Walker and Mike Boit all predictably qualified, and Brian Yon predictably didn't. In fact, Yon was considerably slower than anyone else in finishing last in heat three in 4:24.05, but then he came from the World's most celebrated remote island, St Helena, more than a thousand miles from the African coast, and any training run of 10 miles or so would have taken him the full length of his homeland. His time was a national record of which he has cause to feel proud.

On the strength of his World best performance in winning the previous year's classic annual Fukuoka race in Japan, Rob de Castella was clear favourite for the marathon title, but among the 13 Africans in the field of 35 was Gidamis Shahanga, the unexpected winner four years earlier and now the new 10,000m champion. Starting at 6 a.m. Shahanga and his team-mate, Juma Ikangaa, who had won the African title in August but only ranked 20th fastest in the field, went off down the road at World-record schedule and maintained almost exactly even pace through the first 20km ("splits" of 30:11 and 30:22). The next 10km stretch was much the same (30:37) and Ikangaa led Shahanga by only 30 metres or so, with de Castella keeping the leaders' margin to about a minute as the New Zealander, Kevin Ryan, who had been 4th in 1978, and the Scots pair, John Graham and Graham Laing, followed. Just after 37km de Castella caught first Shahanga and then Ikangaa, but the latter responded magnificently and regained the lead twice more before de Castella finally got away in the last 2km of the race. The winning time on a hilly course round the streets of Brisbane and then along the river bank was 2:09:18, just a minute short of the World record, and the race was made all the more dramatic for the striking physical contrast between the burly de Castella, whose rolling gait was considerably more effective than it was aesthetically pleasing, and the slight, spindly, short-striding Ikangaa, whose improvement was even greater than Shahanga's four years earlier, from a previous best of 2:21:05 to 2:09:30! In the same circumstances as Shahanga, who finished 6th, there was mystery surrounding Ikangaa's age, and he was believed at the time to have been only 18, though subsequent research has revealed conflicting but more likely birthdates of 19 July 1957 or 1960.

It was a day of remarkable success for the group of 700 North Atlantic islands known as the Bahamas. Brad Cooper, the 1978 silver-medallist, won the discus and Shonel Ferguson the women's long jump. This meant that so far in the Games the Bahamas team of six had between them won two golds, two silvers and a bronze - a fair haul for a country whose population was 10,000 less than that of either Bolton, Walsall or Kingston-upon-Hull! In the discus the 42-year-old New Zealander, Robin Tait, was 8th, competing in a record sixth Commonwealth Games and having previously been 4th, 3rd, 6th, 1st and 4th again, while at the other end of the age range the long-jump bronze medal went to the 18-year-old English schools' champion, Bev Kinch. The women's high-jump winner was Debbie Brill, whose literal up-and-down career had included a previous win at the 1970 Games and 24 Commonwealth records, and the pole vault provided yet another example of man-and-wife success in the Games as Ray Boyd, husband of the 1978 200m champion, won gold in his third Games appearance. The remaining final of the day was the women's 100 hurdles with the first two from 1978, Lorna Boothe and Shirley Strong, facing the first two from the 1982 pentathlon, Glynis Nunn and Judy Livermore. Boothe had won by a tenth-of-a-second in Edmonton, but Strong was the stronger this time by a slightly wider margin, and the pentathletes, competent hurdlers even so, were run out of it.

The closing session on Saturday 9 October again brought in a capacity crowd of 58,000 for the men's and women's 1500s, the four relays, and on the infield the men's triple jump, shot and javelin. At 1500 Steve Cram, now at 21 the new European champion of a month's standing, faced those seasoned campaigners, John George Walker and Michael Kipsubut Boit - Walker, 30, the Olympic champion of 1976 and the first man to break 3:50 for the mile but never a Commonwealth winner, and Boit, 33, Commonwealth gold and Olympic bronze at 800 but not a medallist at 1500. The race, though, was not wildly exciting as Boit led through 800 in outside 2:05 until Cram turned on a last lap estimated at under 51sec to win with Walker, who had followed Cram for as long as he could, passing Boit for 2nd place

Canada, England and New Zealand each won field-event gold medals. Keith Connor, the defending champion, who had raised his Commonwealth triple-jump record to 17.57 as a student in the USA earlier in the year, produced two enormous leaps of 17.81 and 17.72 which had only ever been exceeded by the World record of 17.89 set at high altitude by Joao Carlos de Oliveira, of Brazil. Both of Connor's performances were wind-assisted and could not therefore be recognised for record purposes,

167

but that detracted little from their merits. Connor's team-mate, Aston Moore, repeated his 3rd place of 1978 and 19-year-old Norbert Elliott was 6th but suffered the unenviable distinction of being the only member of the Bahamas team not to win a medal. Bruno Pauletto, Italian by birth, won the shot and 3rd place went to another Canadian, Luby Chambul, the younger brother of the 1978 discus winner. In the javelin Mike O'Rourke, 2nd in 1978, improved the one vital place with a Games record 89.48, but the defending champion, Phil Olsen, and the bronze-medallist from 1978, Peter Yates, were both out of the medals and the 3rd place this time went to Zakayo Malekwa, of Tanzania, who had finished far behind them in Edmonton.

Another athlete who was an "also-ran" in 1978 did even better in Brisbane. England's Christina Boxer improved from 11th place to 1st and with some ease, too, after Lorraine Moller, of New Zealand, had led the first lap. Moller, already bronze-medallist at 3000, showed a commendable turn of speed to finish 3rd, considering that she had already embarked on a marathon career which would prove extremely successful and which had brought her the World's seventh fastest ever time in 1981. In the last two places, but certainly not outclassed, were 13-year-old Justina Chepchirchir, of Kenya, and 17-year-old Yvonne Murray, of Scotland, who had both also performed with distinction in the 3000 five days before.

The Nigerians had sent only six men to Brisbane and the best that any of their sprinters could do in the individual events was a 5th place in a 200m semi-final. Yet four of them compensated for their lack of blazing speed by impeccable baton-changing to bring out the true essence of the 4 x 100m relay and win in a Games record 39.15. Canada, with three sprint finalists and the high hurdles gold-medallist, came 2nd, and Scotland were 3rd, though they fielded the double sprint champion, the double sprint bronze-medallist and another 100m finalist. The English women, including three of the team which had won in Edmonton and placed 3rd in the 1980 Olympics, also demonstrated the advantages of technical expertise with a Games record exactly four seconds slower than the Nigerian men, and the Australians were for once well out of it in 4th place. England won the men's 4 x 400 with as lead-off man Steve Scutt, whose wife had finished 2nd in the individual 400, and Mrs Scutt was in action again for Wales in the women's 4 x 400, but neither her team nor England's (who dropped the baton) won medals and Scotland did instead to everyone's surprise behind Canada and Australia. Canada's Angella Taylor started the last leg five metres in front of the great Raelene Boyle and lost all of it except a vital five inches or so to win by 2/100ths of a second. Victory for Australia would have been a perfect end for these Brisbane Games, but it could not possibly have been a better race with which to finish.

RESULTS 1982

MEN

100 METRES (4 Oct): 1 Allan Wells (Sco) 10.02, 2 Ben Johnson (Can) 10.05, 3 Cameron Sharp (Sco) 10.07, 4 Paul Narracott (Aus) 10.09, 5 Mike McFarlane (Eng) 10.11, 6 Tony Sharpe (Can) 10.11, 7 Drew McMaster (Sco) 10.16, 8 Desai Williams (Can) 10.17, 9 Gerard Keating (Aus) 10.18. Note: assisting wind of 5.9m.

200 METRES (7 Oct): 1= Mike McFarlane (Eng) & Allan Wells (Sco) 20.43, 3 Cameron Sharp (Sco) 20.55, 4 Paul Narracott (Aus) 20.65, 5 Bruce Frayne (Aus) 20.72, 6 Tony Sharpe (Can) 20.77, 7 Donovan Reid (Eng) 20.87, 8 Graeme ("Buster") Watson (Eng) 20.88, 9 Desai Williams (Can) 21.04.

400 METRES (4 Oct): 1 Bert Cameron (Jam) 45.89, 2 Rick Mitchell (Aus) 46.61, 3 Gary Minihan (Aus) 46.68, 4 Mike Okot (Uga) 46.81, 5 Todd Bennett (Eng) 47.06, 6 Phil Brown (Eng) 47.11, 7 Tim Bethune (Can) 47.34, 8 Greg Parker (Aus) 47.57, 9 James Atuti (Ken) 48.01.

800 METRES (7 Oct): 1 Peter Bourke (Aus) 1:45.18, 2 James Maina (Ken) 1:45.45, 3 Chris McGeorge (Eng) 1:45.60, 4 John Walker (NZ) 1:46.23, 5 Brett Crew (Aus) 1:46.82, 6 Spyros Spyrou (Cyp) 1:47.64, 7 Juma Ndiwa (Ken) 1:47.74, 8 Paul Forbes (Sco) 1:49.05, 9 Sammy Koskei (Ken) 1:52.43.

1500 METRES (9 Oct): 1 Steve Cram (Eng) 3:42.37, 2 John Walker (NZ) 3:43.11, 3 Mike Boit (Ken) 3:43.33, 4 Graham Williamson (Sco) 3:43.84, 5 Mike Hillardt (Aus) 3:44.03, 6 Colin Reitz (Eng) 3:44.35, 7 Mike Gilchrist (NZ) 3:44.50, 8 Tony Rogers (NZ) 3:45.11, 9 Wilson Waigwa (Ken) 3:46.18, 10 Pat Scammell (Aus) 3:46.62.

5000 METRES (7 Oct): 1 David Moorcroft (Eng) 13:33.00, 2 Nick Rose (Eng) 13:35.97, 3 Peter Koech (Ken) 13:36.95, 4 Zacharia Barie (Tan) 13:39.03, 5 Philippos Philippiou (Cyp) 13:39.13, 6 Nat Muir (Sco) 13:40.84, 7 John Andrews (Aus) 13:42.62, 8 Peter Renner (NZ) 13:45.00, 9 Neil Lowsley (NZ) 13:45.70, 10 Raj Kumar (Ind) 13:46.40, 11 Roger Hackney (Wal) 13:51.20, 12 Zephaniah Ncube (Zim) 13:51.90, 13 Wilson Waigwa (Ken) 14:05.02, 14 Tim Hutchings (Eng) 14:11.59, 15 Martin Umar Mukhtar (Nig) 14:43.73, 16 Bineshwar Prasad (Fij) 16:40.49.

10,000 METRES (3 Oct): 1 Gidamis Shahanga (Tan) 28:10.15, 2 Zacharia Barie (Tan) 28:10.55, 3 Julian Goater (Eng) 28:16.11, 4 Charlie Spedding (Eng) 28:24.94, 5 Allister Hutton (Sco) 28:28.62, 6 Dennis Fowles (Wal) 28:33.89, 7 Zephaniah Ncube (Zim) 28:38.85, 8 Lawrie Whitty (Aus) 28:43.93, 9 Mike McLeod (Eng) 28:46.97, 10 Marios Kassianidis (Cyp) 28:57.94, 11 Steve Jones (Wal) 29:13.68, 12 Peter Butler (Can) 29:16.89, 13 Esau Zwane (Swa) 30:02.74, 14 Nada Meta (Tan) 30·03.84, 15 Peter Koech (Ken) 30:06.0, 16 Erastus Kemei (Ken) 30:36.00, 17 Nicholas Akers (Cay) 35:21.79, 18 David Bonn (Cay) 41:21.49. Note: the following athletes were misdirected by officials and stopped one lap short - Shiri Chand (Fij) 30:57.42, Tau John Tokwepota (PNG) 31:14.88, Abel Smith Manumanua (PNG) 32:05.96, Mackay Talasasa (Sol) 34:30.44.

3000 METRES STEEPLECHASE (4 Oct): 1 Julius Korir (Ken) 8:23.94, 2 Graeme Fell (Eng) 8:26.64, 3 Greg Duhaime (Can) 8:29.14, 4 Roger Hackney (Wal) 8:32.84, 5 Peter Renner (NZ) 8:34.32, 6 Philippos Philippiou (Cyp) 8:35.23, 7 Amos Korir (Ken) 8:38.48, 8 Colin Reitz (Eng) 8:41.94, 9 Peter Larkins (Aus) 8:42.68, 10 Richard Tuwei (Ken) 8:45.98, 11 Neil Lowsley (NZ) 8:47.23, 12 Paul Davies-Hale (Eng) 8:50.73. Fell was the husband of Debbie Campbell, 3rd in the 4 x 400 in 1978.

MARATHON (8 Oct): 1 Rob de Castella (Aus) 2:09:18, 2 Juma Ikangaa (Tan) 2:09:30, 3 Mike Gratton (Eng) 2:12:06, 4 John Graham (Sco) 2:13:04, 5 Kevin Ryan (NZ) 2:13:42, 6 Gidamis Shahanga (Tan) 2:14:25, 7 Graham Laing (Sco) 2:14:54, 8 Ian Ray (Eng) 2:15:11, 9 Mike Dyon (Can) 2:15:22, 10 Rob Wallace (Aus) 2:15:24, 11 Ray Smedley (Eng) 2:15:50; 12 Sam Hlawe (Swa) 2:16:32, 13 Dennis Fowles (Wal) 2:16:49, 14 Greg Hannon (NI) 2:17:32, 15 Peter Butler (Can) 2:18:17, 16 Sipho Gamedze (Swa) 2:18:44, 17 Emmanuel Ndimandoi (Tan) 2:19:16, 18 Marios Kassianidis (Cyp) 2:19:51, 19 Sammy Mogere (Ken) 2:21:44, 20 Wilson Theleso (Bot) 2:23:10, 21 Esau Zwane (Swa) 2:26:38, 22 Musaope Phiri (Zim) 2:28:27, 23 James Maweu (Ken) 2:29:15, 24 Esau Magwaza (Zim) 2:30:05, 25 Matthews Kambale (Mlw) 2:33:34, 26 Mackay Talasasa (Sol) 2:36:16, 27 Motsemme Kgaotsang (Bot) 2:37:39, 28 Abel Smith Manumanua (PNG) 2:42:07, 29 Nicholas Akers (Cay) 3:02:33. Did not finish - Don Greig (NZ), Wayne Madden (Fij), Gary Palmer (NZ), Shiri Chand (Fij), Tau John Tokwepota (PNG), Lawrie Whitty (Aus).

30 KILOMETRES WALK (7 Oct): 1 Steve Barry (Wal) 2:10:16, 2 Marcel Jobin (Can) 2:12:24, 3 Guillaume Leblanc (Can) 2:14:56, 4 Willi Sawall (Aus) 2:15:23, 5 Francois Lapointe (Can) 2:17:02, 6 Tim Erickson (Aus) 2:19:45, 7 Roger Mills (Eng) 2:21:54, 8 Murray Lambden (IoM) 2:22:12, 9 Andrew Jachno (Aus) 2:24:15, 10

Rob Elliott (Gue) 2:24:28, 11 Mike Parker (NZ) 2:26:07, 12 Graham Young (IoM) 2:27:04, 13 Paul Blagg (Eng) 2:30:42, 14 Mutal Kiplangat (Ken) 2:34:51, 15 Kevin Taylor (NZ) 2:37:37, 16 Elisha Kasuka (Ken) 2:39:32, 17 John Mutinda (Ken) 2:50:54. Did not finish - Chand Ram (Ind). Disqualified - Robby Lambie (IoM).

110 METRES HURDLES (4 Oct): 1 Mark McKoy (Can) 13.37, 2 Mark Holtom (Eng) 13.43, 3 Don Wright (Aus) 13.58, 4 Wilbert Greaves (Eng) 13.66, 5 Max Binnington (Aus) 13.72, 6 Berwyn Price (Wal) 13.73, 7 Philip Sang (Ken) 14.08, 8 Karl Smith (Jam) 14.11, 9 Warren Parr (Aus) 14.15.

400 METRES HURDLES (7 Oct): 1 Garry Brown (Aus) 49.27, 2 Peter Rwamuhanda (Uga) 49.95, 3 Greg Rolle (Bah) 50.50, 4 Mike Whittingham (Eng) 51.04, 5 Lloyd Guss (Can) 51.23, 6 Stan Devine (Sco) 51.68, 7 Eric Spence (Can) 51.84, 8 Gary Oakes (Eng) 51.96, 9 Karl Smith (Jam) 53.52.

4 x 100 METRES RELAY (9 Oct): 1 Nigeria (Lawrence Adegbeingbe, Iziak Adeyanju, Samson Olajidie Oyeledun, Ikpoto Eseme) 39.15, 2 Canada (Ben Johnson, Tony Sharpe, Desai Williams, Mark McKoy) 39.30, 3 Scotland (Gus McCuaig, Allan Wells, Cameron Sharp, Drew McMaster) 39.30, 4 Australia (Paul Narracott, Gerard Keating, Bruce Frayne, Peter Gandy) 39.39, 5 England (Harry King, Donovan Reid, Mike McFarlane, Jim Evans) 39.67, 6 Ghana (Ernie Obeng, William Hammond, Samuel Aidoo, Awudu Nuhu) 40.52, 7 Kenya (Alfred Nyambane, Peter Wekesa, John Anzrah, James Maina) 40.94, 8 Zimbabwe (Charles Gumbura, Gian-Franco Poggioli, Zena Murambakuyawa, Christopher Madzokere) 41.75, 9 Western Samoa (William Fong, Siolei Saufoi, Rolagi Faa Mausili, Joe Leota) 41.91.

4 x 400 METRES RELAY (9 Oct): 1 England (Steve Scutt, Garry Cook, Todd Bennett, Phil Brown) 3:05.45, 2 Australia (Gary Minihan, John Fleming, Greg Parker, Rick Mitchell) 3:05.82, 3 Kenya (Elisha Bitok, Juma Ndiwa, John Anzrah, James Maina) 3:06.33, 4 Canada (Doug Hinds, Ian Newhouse, Lloyd Guss, Tim Bethune) 3:07.04, 5 Barbados (Hamil Grimes, David Carter, Gordon Hinds, Richard Louis) 3:12.44, 6 Zambia (Charles Lupiya, David Lyamba Nyambe, Dick Kunda, David Lishebo) 3:13.85, 7 Ghana (John Akuttey, William Hammond, Awudu Nuhu, Edward Pappoe) 3:14.31, 8 Zimbabwe (Glen Taute, Mark Fanucci, Glen de Souza, Njere Shumba) 3:15.18, 9 Botswana (Pius Kganneyang, Temba Mpophu, Shepero Mogapi, Joseph Ramotshabi) 3:18.70.

HIGH JUMP (7 Oct): 1 Milt Ottey (Can) 2.31, 2 Steve Wray (Bah) 2.31, 3 Nick Saunders (Ber) 2.19, 4 David Abrahams (Eng) 2.19, 5= Greg Joy (Can) & Alain

Metellus (Can) 2.16, 7 Geoff Parsons (Sco) 2.16, 8 Roger Te Puni (NZ) 2.13, 9 David Anderson (Aus) 2.13, 10 Angus Waddell (Aus) 2.10, 11 Terry Lomax (NZ) 2.10, 12 Clifford Lisette (Mau) 2.05, 13 Trevor Llewellyn (Wal) 2.05, 14 Edouard Robsen (Van) 1.95.

POLE VAULT (8 Oct): 1 Ray Boyd (Aus) 5.20, 2 Jeff Gutteridge (Eng) 5.20, 3 Graham Eggleton (Sco) 5.20, 4 Bruce Simpson (Can) 5.10, 5 Keith Stock (Eng) 4.85, 6 Andy Stewart (Aus) 4.85, 7 Kieran McKee (NZ) 4.70. Dave Steen (Can) failed at opening height (4.70).

LONG JUMP (7 Oct): 1 Gary Honey (Aus) 8.13, 2 Steve Hanna (Bah) 7.79, 3 Steve Walsh (NZ) 7.75, 4 John Herbert (Eng) 7.54, 5 Steve Knott (Aus) 7.53, 6 Moses Kiayi (Ken) 7.48, 7 Delroy Poyser (Jam) 7.24, 8 Stalia Issah (Gha) 7.03, 9 Norbert Elliott (Bah) 6.47. Note: the jumps by Hanna, Poyser and Issah were wind-assisted.

TRIPLE JUMP (9 Oct): 1 Keith Connor (Eng) 17.81, 2 Ken Lorraway (Aus) 17.54, 3 Aston Moore (Eng) 16.76, 4 Steve Hanna (Bah) 16.56, 5 John Herbert (Eng) 16.48, 6 Norbert Elliott (Bah) 16.36, 7 Marios Hadjiandreou (Cyp) 16.31, 8 Moses Kiayi (Ken) 14.91. Note: all jumps were wind-assisted.

SHOT (9 Oct|): 1 Bruno Pauletto (Can) 19.55, 2 Mike Winch (Eng) 18.25, 3 Luby Chambul (Can) 17.46, 4 Richard Slaney (Eng) 17.35, 5 Simon Rodhouse (Eng) 17.18, 6 Matt Barber (Aus) 15.33, 7 Stephen Chikomo (Zim) 13.72, 8 Christopher Pullen (Zim) 13.45.

DISCUS (8 Oct): 1 Brad Cooper (Bah) 64.04, 2 Rob Gray (Can) 60.66, 3 Bishop Dolegiewicz (Can) 60.34, 4 Richard Slaney (Eng) 60.14, 5 Bob Weir (Eng) 59.26, 6 Peter Tancred (Eng) 58.82, 7 Dick Priman (Aus) 54.30, 8 Robin Tait (NZ) 54.22, 9 Christopher Pullen (Zim) 51.60, 10 Stephen Chikomo (Zim) 41.50. Mark Robinson (NZ) no valid throws.

HAMMER (3 Oct): 1 Bob Weir (Eng) 75.08, 2 Martin Girvan (NI) 73.62, 3 Chris Black (Sco) 69.84, 4 Hans-Martin Lotz (Aus) 68.82, 5 Paul Dickenson (Eng) 67.96, 6 Harold Willers (Can) 65.06, 7 Phil Spivey (Aus) 63.62, 8 Gus Puopolo (Aus) 59.74, 9 Michael Lambourn (Zim) 50.66, 10 Cornelius Kemboi (Ken) 43.64.

JAVELIN (9 Oct): 1 Mike O'Rourke (NZ) 89.48, 2 Laslo Babits (Can) 84.88, 3 Zakayo Malekwa (Tan) 80.22, 4 Phil Olsen (Can) 77.96, 5 William Sang (Ken) 77.64, 6 Peter Yates (Eng) 77.40, 7 David Ottley (Eng) 75.00, 8 David Hookway (NZ) 69.72, 9 George Odera (Ken) 65.56, 10 Cornelius Kemboi (Ken) 62.88, 11

Ritchie Okesene (WS) 55.96, 12 Jioji Nadavo (Fij) 53.06. Justin Arop (Uga) no valid throws.

DECATHLON (4-5 Oct): 1 Daley Thompson (Eng) 8,410 (10.66, 7.71, 15.17, 2.04, 47.59, 15.00, 44.58, 4.90, 62.98, 4:43.48), 2 Dave Steen (Can) 8,004 (11.39, 7.30, 13.36, 1.98, 48.71, 15.52, 42.96, 4.80, 67.20, 4:24.21), 3 Fidelis Obikwu (Eng) 7,726 (11.50, 7.05, 14.62, 2.07, 50.17, 16.46, 42.32, 4.60, 58.92, 4:30.44), 4 Peter Hadfield (Aus) 7,511, 5 Peter Dyer (NZ) 7,316, 6 Charles Kokoyo (Ken) 7,118, 7 Greg Haydenluck (Can) 6,766, 8 Colin Boreham (NI) 6,727, 9 Pan Zeniou (Cyp) 6,273, 10 Cornelius Kemboi (Ken) 6,176, 11 Samuela Tabua (Fij) 5,819. Did not finish - Sanitesi Latu (Ton), Brad McStravick (Sco), James Middleton (Aus), Chris Nunn (Aus).

WOMEN

100 METRES (4 Oct): 1 Angella Taylor (Can) 11.00, 2 Merlene Ottey (Jam) 11.03, 3 Colleen Pekin (Aus) 11.24, 4 Angela Bailey (Can) 11.30, 5= Wendy Hoyte (Eng) & Rufina Uba (Nig) 11.31, 7 Heather Oakes (Eng) 11.39, 8 Helen Davey (Aus) 11.44, 9 Sonia Lannaman (Eng) 11.48. Note: Pekin nee Beazley, Hoyte nee Clarke. Heather Oakes was the wife of Gary Oakes, 400m hurdles finalist in 1978 and 1982.

200 METRES (7 Oct): 1 Merlene Ottey (Jam) 22.19, 2 Kathy Smallwood (Eng) 22.21, 3 Angella Taylor (Can) 22.48, 4 Denise Boyd (Aus) 22.72, 5 Colleen Pekin (Aus) 22.89, 6 Bev Callender (Eng) 22.92, 7 Grace Jackson (Jam) 23.25, 8 Angela Bailey (Can) 23.42, 9 Helen Barnett (Eng) 23.57. Note: assisting wind of 2.5m Note: Denise Boyd was the wife of Ray Boyd, winner of the pole vault; Callender nee Goddard.

400 METRES (4 Oct): 1 Raelene Boyle (Aus) 51.26, 2 Michelle Scutt (Wal) 51.97, 3 Joslyn Hoyte-Smith (Eng) 52.53, 4 Gladys Taylor (Eng) 52.56, 5 Kim Robertson (NZ) 53.02, 6 Molly Killingbeck (Can) 53.10, 7 Charmaine Crooks (Can) 53.16, 8 June Griffith (Guy) 53.67, 9 Linsey Macdonald (Sco) 53.87. Note: Hoyte-Smith nee Hoyte.

800 METRES (7 Oct): 1 Kirsty McDermott (Wal) 2:01.31, 2 Anne Clarkson (Sco) 2:01.52, 3 Heather Barralet (Aus) 2:01.70, 4 Terri-Ann Cater (Aus) 2:01.91, 5 Shireen Hassan (Eng) 2:02.21, 6 Lorraine Baker (Eng) 2:03.17, 7 Chrissie Hughes (NZ) 2:04.87, 8 Francine Gendron (Can) 2:06.21, 9 Evelyn Adiru (Uga) 2:06.23. Note: Cater nee Wangman.

1500 METRES (9 Oct): 1 Chris Boxer (Eng) 4:08.28, 2 Gillian Dainty (Eng) 4:10.80, 3 Lorraine Moller (NZ) 4:12.67, 4 Dianne Rodger (NZ) 4:13.10, 5 Geri Fitch (Can) 4:13.40, 6 Kim Lock (Wal) 4:14.02, 7 Kath Pilling (Eng) 4:14.86, 8 Hilary Hollick (Wal) 4:15.69, 9 Justina Chepchirchir (Ken) 4:15.86, 10 Yvonne Murray (Sco) 4:16.59.

3000 METRES (4 Oct): 1 Anne Audain (NZ) 8:45.53, 2 Wendy Smith (Eng) 8:48.47, 3 Lorraine Moller (NZ) 8:55.76, 4 Dianne Rodger (NZ) 9:06.05, 5 Bev Bush (Can) 9:12.02, 6 Geri Fitch (Can) 9:12.78, 7 Debbie Peel (Eng) 9:15.37, 8 Justina Chepchirchir (Ken) 9:15.40, 9 Hilary Hollick (Wal) 9:18.33, 10 Yvonne Murray (Sco) 9:21.45, 11 Linah Cheruiyot (Ken) 9:26.58, 12 Debbie Scott (Can) 9:32.20, 13 Kim Lock (Wal) 9:36.00, 14 Megan Sloane (Aus) 9:36.56, 15 Yuko Gordon (HK) 10:24.50. Did not finish - Mary Chepkemboi (Ken), Ruth Smeeth (Eng).

100 METRES HURDLES (9 Oct): 1 Shirley Strong (Eng) 12.78, 2 Lorna Boothe (Eng) 12.90, 3 Sue Kameli (Can) 13.10, 4 Karen Nelson (Can) 13.10, 5 Judy Livermore (Eng) 13.25, 6 Glynis Nunn (Aus) 13.31, 7 Sylvia Forgrave (Can) 13.38, 8 Maria Usifo (Nig) 13.39, 9 Elaine McMaster (Sco) 13.57. Note: assisting wind of 4.5m. Nunn, nee Saunders, was the wife of Chris Nunn, who competed in the decathlon; McMaster, nee Davidson, was the wife of Drew McMaster, 1st at 4 x 100 in 1978 and 3rd in 1982.

400 METRES HURDLES (7 Oct): 1 Debbie Flintoff (Aus) 55.89, 2 Ruth Kyalisima (Uga) 57.10, 3 Yvette Wray (Eng) 57.17, 4 Sue Morley (Eng) 57.57, 5 Lyn Foreman (Aus) 57.62, 6 Andrea Page (Can) 57.70, 7 Margaret Southerden (Sco) 58.36, 8 Gwen Hall (Can) 58.49, 9 Sandra Farmer (Jam) 59.07.

4 x 100 METRES RELAY (9 Oct): 1 England (Wendy Hoyte, Kathy Smallwood, Bev Callender, Sonia Lannaman) 43.15, 2 Canada (Angela Bailey, Marita Payne, Angella Taylor, Molly Killingbeck) 43.66, 3 Jamaica (Lelieth Hodges, Merlene Ottey, Cathy Rattray, Grace Jackson) 43.69, 4 Australia (Jenny Flaherty, Denise Boyd, Colleen Pekin, Helen Davey) 43.84, 5 Nigeria (Elizabeth Mokogwu, Maria Usifo, Tutu Ogunde, Rufina Uba) 44.60, 6 Trinidad & Tobago (Janice Bernard, Gillian Forde, Maxine McMillan, Angela Williams) 44.74, 7 Ghana (Grace Armah, Mercy Addy, Georgina Aidoo, Mary Mensah-Afriyie) 45.93, 8 Kenya (Geraldine Shitandayi, Ruth Waithera, Joyce Odhiambo, Alice Adala) 46.13, 9 Gambia (Georgiana Freeman, Amie N'Dow, Jabou Jawo, Frances Jatta) 47.51.

4 x 400 METRES RELAY (9 Oct): 1 Canada (Charmaine Crooks, Jill Richardson, Molly Killingbeck, Angella Taylor) 3:27.70, 2 Australia (Leanne Evans, Denise

Boyd, Debbie Flintoff, Raelene Boyle) 3:27.72, 3 Scotland (Sandra Whittaker, Ann Clarkson, Angela Bridgeman, Linsey Macdonald) 3:32.92, 4 England (Yvette Wray, Gladys Taylor, Kathy Smallwood, Joslyn Hoyte-Smith) 3:35.35, 5 Wales (Carmen Smart, Kirsty McDermott, Diane Fryar, Michelle Scutt) 3:35.76, 6 New Zealand (Terry Genge, Chrissie Hughes, Janine Robson, Kim Robertson) 3:40.63, 7 Kenya (Ruth Atuti, Alice Adala, Rose Tata-Muya, Ruth Waithera) 3:40.77. 7 teams competed.

HIGH JUMP (8 Oct): 1 Debbie Brill (Can) 1.88, 2 Chris Stanton (Aus) 1.88, 3 Barbara Simmonds (Eng) 1.83, 4 Brigitte Reid (Can) 1.83, 5 Vanessa Browne (Aus) 1.83, 6 Diana Elliott (Eng) 1.80, 7 Ann-Marie Cording (Eng) 1.80, 8 Katrina Gibbs (Aus) 1.80, 9 Sharon McPeake (NI) 1.74, 10= Ursula Fay (NI) & Julie White (Can) 1.74, 12 Sharon Coetzee (Zim) 1.65, 13 Sarah Owen (Wal) 1.65. Note: Reid nee Bittner.

LONG JUMP (8 Oct): 1 Shonel Ferguson (Bah) 6.91, 2 Robyn Strong (Aus) 6.88, 3 Bev Kinch (Eng) 6.78, 4 Linda Garden (Aus) 6.53, 5 Sue Hearnshaw (Eng) 6.50, 6 Maroula Lambrou (Cyp) 6.38, 7 Glynis Nunn (Aus) 6.38, 8 Pam Hendren (NZ) 6.33, 9 Noeline Hodgins (NZ) 6.27, 10 Gillian Regan (Wal) 6.16. Note: all jumps except those of Lambrou and Regan were wind-assisted.

SHOT (5 Oct): 1 Judy Oakes (Eng) 17.92, 2 Gael Mulhall (Aus) 17.68, 3 Rose Hauch (Can) 16.71, 4 Bev Francis (Aus) 16.40, 5 Angela Littlewood (Eng) 15.97, 6 Carmen Ionesco (Can) 15.80, 7 Meg Ritchie (Sco) 15.63, 8 Mariette van Heerden (Zim) 14.15, 9 Glenda Hughes (NZ) 14.13, 10 Elizabeth Olaba (Ken) 12.84, 11 Herina Obuya-Malit (Ken) 12.59, 12 Marie-Lourdes Ally Samba (Mau) 11.37.

DISCUS (4 Oct): 1 Meg Ritchie (Sco) 62.98, 2 Gael Mulhall (Aus) 58.64, 3 Lynda Whiteley (Eng) 54.78, 4 Carmen Ionesco (Can) 54.52, 5 Mariette van Heerden (Zim) 53.42, 6 Venissa Head (Wal) 50.64, 7 Lesley Bryant (Eng) 50.22, 8 Janette Picton (Eng) 47.80, 9 Mereoni Vibose (Fij) 41.36, 10 Helen Alyek (Uga) 40.16,. 11 Herina Obuya-Malit (Ken) 37.88, 12 Christine Bechard (Mau) 37.74.

JAVELIN (7 Oct): 1 Sue Howland (Aus) 64.86, 2 Petra Rivers (Aus) 62.28, 3 Fatima Whitbread (Eng) 58.86, 4 Pam Matthews (Aus) 55.16, 5 Monique Lapres (Can) 52.30, 6 Celine Chartrand (Can) 50.14, 7 Sharon Gibson (Eng) 49.56, 8 Mereoni Vibose (Fij) 47.30, 9 Elizabeth Olaba (Ken) 40.96, 10 Christine Bechard (Mau) 31.68. Margaret Sakala (Zim) no valid throws.

1966. Deprived of a medal as much by a swirling wind as by the opposition at the 1962 Commonwealth Games, Lynn Davies won the long jump for Wales in 1966 and again in 1970. His even greater achievement was to become Olympic champion on a rainswept day in Tokyo in 1964, but he then suffered the unenviable experience of standing forlornly by at the 1968 Olympics as the prodigious American, Bob Beamon, broke the World record by an unprecedented margin and effectively ended the competition in the very first round.

1966. Winner of the shot putt in Kingston was Dave Steen, of Canada, who had also been the bronze-medallist in 1962 and would be champion again in 1970. His nephew, also named Dave Steen, would be silver-medallist behind Daley Thompson in the 1982 and 1986 decathlons and would also beat Thompson by 22 points for the Olympic bronze in 1988.

1970. Sylvia Potts, of New Zealand, falls in the last few metres of the 1500 metres final and the English pair, Rita Ridley (472) and Joan Page (469) come by her to take 1st and 2nd places ahead of Thelma Fynn, of Canada. Page and Fynn were also the silver and bronze medallists four years later. Mrs Potts eventually clambered to her feet and finished 9th, still in a personal best time, and at the 1990 Games her son, Richard, ran in the 5000 metres heats.

1966. Early morning in Kingston, Jamaica, and the stadium is deserted, but the marathon winner - Jim Alder, of Scotland - appears not to notice. His expression, though, is as much one of relief as excitement because he had been misdirected by officials as he entered the arena and had lost his lead to England's Bill Adcocks. Fortunately, he had enough in reserve to overtake Adcocks and claim his rightful victory. Coincidentally, the Games marathon had also been won by Scots on the two previous occasions it had been held in the Americas: by Duncan McLeod Wright in 1930 and Joe McGhee in 1954, both in Canada. At the 1994 Games, again in Canada, the bronze medallist was Mark Hudspith, of England, who was coached by Alder.

1970. Marilyn Neufville sets a new World record of 51.02 to win the 400 metres for Jamaica. It was one second faster than she had ever run before and represented an amazing breakthrough for a 17-year-old, but she sadly never fulfilled that immense promise, though she ran again in the 1974 final. Born in Jamaica she had been brought up in London and opted to compete for her native island, rather than for England, in Edinburgh.

1974. Dave Bedford, in the manner of Ron Clarke, was a spectacular record-breaker who was never quite the same runner in a major championships when others were at his elbows and heels. As World record-holder Bedford was favoured to win the 10,000 metres in Christchurch, but he ended up out of the medals and the gold went instead to a local hero, Dick Tayler, who like so many champions before him had played only a minor role in his previous Games appearance - 10th in the Edinburgh 5,000 metres. In this photo the eventual silver and bronze medallists, England's Dave Black and Kenya's Richard Juma, lead Tayler and the bearded Bedford.

1974. The first black African woman to win a Commonwealth gold medal was the exuberantly versatile Modupe Oshikoya, of Nigeria, in the long jump in Christchurch. The same afternoon she took the bronze medal at 100 metres hurdles, and six days earlier she had finished only 32 points behind the Olympic champion, Mary Peters, in an intensely exciting pentathlon competition. Regrettably, but perhaps almost inevitably considering the social barriers she faced, Oshikoya's athletics career never really blossomed after this and her great potential remained largely untapped.

1978. (above) Closely watched by a line of track officials, England finish 1-2-3 in the women's 100 metres hurdles as Lorna Boothe (far left) wins from Shirley Strong (far right) and Sharon Colyear (second from right), who were both members of the Stretford club in Manchester. Boothe's time was a wind-assisted Games record of 12.98.
1982 (below) Strong and Boothe attack the barriers in their 1982 re-match, with Strong this time taking the gold medal and bearing Boothe's Game record with a wind-assisted time of 12.78.

1978. (above) Less than two tenths of a second separated the first four runners at the end of a thrilling 1500 metres final. It was David Moorcroft (161) who triumphed for England ahead of the Tanzanian defending champion Filbert Bayi, with Scotsmen John Robson (far left) and Frank Clement (far right) third and fourth.

1982 (right) Moorcroft leads team-mate Nick Rose en route to victory at the following Games, thgis time at 5000 metres. Rose took the silver and Zacharia Barie of Tanzania (left) finished fourth.

1986. Marathon winners celebrate an Australian double. The men started half-an-hour before the women and the eventual margin between Rob de Castella and Lisa Martin had stretched to 45 minutes and 52 seconds by the time the latter crossed the finishing line. De Castella had also won four years previously, but it was the debut for women, and the pair of them made for a graphic contrast in styles: he broad-chested and powerful, lumbering along with much more grit than grace; she trim and precise, striding out purposefully with make-up unblemished.

1986. Is it a pole-vaulter coming to ground? Or maybe an energetic cheerleader? It's actually Simon Baker, the winner of that most sedate of events, the 30 kilometres walk, revelling in uninhibited joy after completing the course. Maintaining the strict tempo of always having one or other foot in contact with the ground, as required by the vigilant judges, places enormous demands on the technique and concentration of race walkers pounding the roads for more than two hours. So it's hardly surprising that Baker kicked up his heels after it was all over.

1990. The enthralling finish of an eventful 5000 metres. Kenya's John Ngugi still leads into the home straight, but from what had seemed a hopeless situation on the last lap Andrew Lloyd, of Australia (0050), and Ian Hamer, of Wales (1119), are closing fast, with New Zealand's Kerry Rodger and another Kenyan, Moses Tanui, not far behind. The English-born Lloyd passed Ngugi in the last few strides to win the gold by less than one-tenth of a second and Hamer took the bronze.

1990. Linford Christie wins the 100 metres for England in a
wind-assisted time of 9.93. Bruny Surin of Canada (right) placed
third and Abullahi Tetengi of Nigeria (left) was sixth. Christie,
born in Jamaica, had not begun his international career until the
age of 26, four years earlier, and had finished second to the subsequently disgraced Ben Johnson at the 1986 Commonwealth
Games in Edinburgh. Christie won again in Victoria in 1994 and
his even greater achievements were to take the gold medals at the
Olympic Games of 1992 and the World Championships of 1993.
The pressing commercial demands of international athletics
meant that after the 100 metres in Victoria he flew back to
Europe to race in a Grand Prix meeting and therefore missed the
4 x 100 metres relay, in which a depleted England team could
only place third.

1990. A double success for England and for Sale Harriers. Diane Edwards (right) narrowly wins the 800 metres from her team-mate and club-mate, Ann Williams, after leading the race from start to finish. Sharon Stewart and Wendy Old, of Australia, finished
third and fourth ahead of another English runner, Lorraine Baker, and another
Australian, Gail Luke, with Nicky Knapp, of Canada, seventh. Edwards (later Mrs
Modahl) travelled again to the 1994 Games in Victoria, but suffered the traumatic experience of being sent home before her race because of an apparent positive drugs test. She
steadfastly protested her innocence through the courts of law, was eventually given per-
mission to run again, and at the 1998 Games in Kuala Lumpur placed a valiant third to
Maria Mutola, of Mozambique, in a time which was considerably faster than she had
achieved eight years earlier.

1994. Denise Lewis, of England, leads Jane Flemming, of Australia, in the 800 metres, which was the last of the seven events in the two-day heptathlon. Lewis had thrown the javelin five metres further than ever before to take a surprising lead in the competition and needed to finish within 5.5 seconds of Flemming at 800 metres to win the gold. Flemming ran 2:13.07 and Lewis stayed just close enough to her, with a personal best of 2:17.60 to succeed by a margin of eight points.

1994. Cathy Freeman, of Australia, salutes the cheering spectators after her 400 metres victory in a time of 50.38, which beat the Games record set 24 years earlier in Edinburgh by Marilyn Neufville. Freeman had made history at the age of 16 at the 1990 Games when she had been a member of the winning 4 x 100 metres relay and was thus the first aborigine athlete to win a gold medal for Australia. She went on to even greater success at 400 metres in the World Championships and Olympic Games.

1998. Thabiso Moqhali, from the southern African country of Lesotho, wins the marathon in Kuala Lumpur's city centre. He had competed insignificantly at the Games of 1990 and 1994, but his victory brought Lesotho their first ever Games medal, and maybe good advice helped. Moqhali's team manager had previously run in the Commonwealth Games marathon.

HEPTATHLON (3-4 Oct): 1 Glynis Nunn (Aus) 6,282 (100m hurdles 13.33, Shot 13.32, High jump 1.77, 200m 24.12, Long jump 6.51, Javelin 35.30, 800m 2:12.17), 2 Judy Livermore (Eng) 6,214 (13.22, 13.32, 1.80, 25.01, 6.10, 38.76, 2:12.11), 3 Jill Ross (Can) 5,981 (13.93,`11.37, 1.74, 24.76, 6.08, 39.94, 2:11.99), 4 Kathy Warren (Eng) 5,692 , 5 Terry Genge (NZ) 5,679, 6 Julie White (Can) 5,575, 7 Jocelyn Millar (Aus) 5,505, 8 Connie Polman (Can) 5,333, 9 Karen Forbes (NZ) 5,288, 10 Sarah Owen (Wal) 5,227, 11 Frida Kiptala (Ken) 5,032, 12 Elizabeth Olaba (Ken) 4,664. Did not finish - Katie Harders (Aus).

14.

Despite all the absent friends,
Liz is the toast of the town

MEADOWBANK STADIUM, EDINBURGH, SCOTLAND
26 JULY-2 AUGUST 1986

THE BRITISH GOVERNMENT'S REFUSAL to take sanctions against South Africa and so bring pressure to bear on the country's policy of apartheid cost the Commonwealth Games the presence of 32 countries. Of course, boycotts of major sporting occasions had become commonplace in the 1980s - the Americans had pulled out of the Moscow Olympics because of Soviet involvement in Afghanistan, and the Soviets had retaliated by not going to the Los Angeles Games and persuading many of their Eastern Bloc cohorts to do the same. What these gestures had in common was that they did not seem to achieve anything, other than giving their political manipulators a cheap and easy option to be seen to be making some sort of "grand" gesture. It has to be said, though, that Commonwealth countries had dedicated themselves since the late 1970s to economic and sporting action against apartheid, and the fact that the Commonwealth Games of 1986 were to be held in Britain provided an irresistible opportunity to demonstrate against what would be seen as old colonial values. If the absence of those 32 member nations, almost all from the African and Asian continents and the Caribbean, was to play any part in the eventual dismantling of apartheid, then the prospect of a devalued Games in Edinburgh would be a small price to pay.

Considering the lack of any West Indian or Nigerian sprinters, hurdlers and jumpers and Kenyan and Tanzanian middle-distance and distance runners, and taking into account the generally dismal weather, the athletics competition was far better than anyone had any right to hope for. Performances such as 10.07 for 100m, 1:43.22 for 800m, 2:10:15 for men and 2:26:07 for women in the marathon, 8,663 in the decathlon, 54.94 in the women's 400m hurdles and 69.80 in the women's javelin are World-class in any setting, and that's what we got, rather to our surprise, from some of Edinburgh's champions. In what was essentially a three-way match between Britain, Australasia and Canada, there was rarely any sense of apologetic dejection. It was actually rather a good Games, even if the repercussions of the boycott left us wondering whether it would ever survive to a further celebration four years on.

There were 244 men and 171 women entered from 16 countries, and all but 19 men and five women represented one or other of the British teams, or Australia, New Zealand or Canada. There was a puny but welcome presence from Botswana, Lesotho and Malawi, and there were lone athletes from Gibraltar, Hong Kong and the Cook Islands. From its population of 140,000 or so spread across 83 islands in the South Pacific Ocean the republic of Vanuatu rallied to the flag and sent a contingent of four.

Ten o'clock on a grey and gloomy Saturday morning with a raw wind gusting in off the Firth of Forth is not everybody's idea of the perfect place to begin a restful and relaxing weekend, but it seemed to suit Judy Simpson very well. As Judy Livermore she had taken part in an enthralling contest with the Olympic champion-to-be, Glynis Nunn, in the Brisbane heptathlon, eventually losing by 68pts, and here she was in Edinburgh as Mrs Simpson, married to a pole-vaulting clubmate at Birchfield Harriers, with her eyes very firmly on the crown, and another Australian, Jane Flemming, as her rival. At least Simpson had the wind at her back when she ran 13.11 for 100m hurdles to begin her 1986 challenge in front of a few hundred hardy spectators. Saturday 26 July was the opening day of the Games, and they <u>had</u> opened, and Simpson and Flemming were certainly determined to make a go of it. The contrast in physiques between the long-legged Jamaican-born 27-year-old from Birmingham, with her shoulder-length jet tresses held back by a beaded headband, and the blonde bronzed 21-year-old looking every inch a Bondi Beach surf maiden lightened up the entire day, and by the end of it Simpson led Flemming, as she needed to if she was to win, by 141pts after four events.

The 10,000m was the first final to patently suffer from the boycott. Only 12 runners started - the smallest entry since 1934 for the event or its predecessor at six miles - and there were no Africans. Yet it still produced the second fastest winning time in Games history, inferior only to 1974, as Jon Solly repeated his AAA championships victory over Steve Binns, a fellow-member of the renowned Yorkshire road-running club, Bingley Harriers, by no more than three or four metres. Naturally, we were to muse afterwards, as we would in similar vein time and time again over the next few days, as to what would have happened if Paul Kipkoech, Some Muge or Mike Musyoki, all of whom had achieved faster times earlier in the year, would have been running for Kenya, but no disrepect is intended to Solly or Binns. They could only beat whoever was there. By contrast the hammer was unaffected by absenteeism and was won by another Northern-based athlete, David Smith, from the City of Hull, with Ulsterman Martin Girvan having to settle for a second successive silver.

Sunday 27 July featured finals at 100 and 400 for men and women, 110 hurdles, steeplechase and women's 3000 and discus, but again it was an all-rounder who set the tone for the day. An all-rounder? The all-rounder, more like. Having won the European title and two Commonwealth and two Olympic titles already, Daley Thompson could have been forgiven for treating this competition with some disdain, but true to form he rapped out his fastest ever decathlon 100 in 10.37 at an hour on a Sunday morning when most citizens of Edinburgh were at best thinking of getting out of bed to go for a newspaper. Thompson "won" all the other day's four events to lead overnight by 472pts, and his performances at 100, long jump and 400 would have all got him in the first six in the individual events. Nothing much had changed since Brisbane: his halfway lead then had been 464 and his chief rival, though he would probably feel flattered to be called such, was again Dave Steen, of Canada.

Ben Johnson, 2nd to Allan Wells in 1982, was a much better sprinter now - if that is the best way, with the advantage of hindsight, to describe his improvement - and he won the 100 in the fastest ever legal Games time of 10.07, while the silver went to Linford Christie, who at the age of 26 had finally been persuaded by his coach at Thames Valley Harriers, Ron Roddan, to take training seriously and had begun what would prove to be the most illustrious of careers by winning the European indoor 200 title the previous February. There was an English victory over Canada in the women's 100, and an impressive one, as Heather Oakes, 7th in 1982, and Paula Dunn both beat the defending champion, Jamaican-born Angella Issajenko (nee Taylor).

For the 400 finals there were regrets at the absence of the likes of Innocent Egbunike, of Nigeria, and Grace Jackson, of Jamaica, but it's a matter of conjecture as to what difference this made to the shareout of medals or the entertainment for an encouraging near-capacity attendance of 23,000. Roger Black, 20, had won the European junior title the previous year in his first season of serious training and he beat one of the World's best quarter-milers - Australia's Darren Clark, 4th in the 1984 Olympics ahead of Egbunike - by over 4/10ths of a second to become the first English champion in this Games event since Bill Roberts almost half-a-century before. Debbie Flintoff, the inaugural 400 hurdles champion in Brisbane who was already the fastest Commonwealth runner of the year on the flat at 50.78, won the women's 400 from Trinidad-born Jillian Richardson, of Canada, and England's Kathy Cook (nee Smallwood) added yet another medal to a collection which would reach record-breaking proportions before she retired.

In defence of his 110 hurdles title Canada's Mark McKoy faced a pair of 19-year-old prodigies, Jon Ridgeon for England and Colin Jackson for Wales. Ridgeon had beaten Jackson in the previous year's European Junior Championships, and then at the World Junior Championships in Athens a week before the Edinburgh Games opened Jackson had won from Ridgeon in 13.44. With a strong following wind, which is not always to the liking of high hurdlers, McKoy came home in 13.31 by a clear metre from Jackson, with the Australian, Don Wright, getting his second bronze in his third successive final. The steeplechase lacked the title-holder, Julius Korir, who had since become Olympic champion, and four other Kenyans who ran faster than 8:16 for the event during the year, but it didn't go short of drama as Graeme Fell, who had been 2nd to Korir in 1982 as a member of England's team but had taken up Canadian qualifications this time, narrowly won the race and Wales got another silver through Roger Hackney.

The women's 3000 was without Zola Budd, the South African-born British record-holder who had been controversially and probably unconstitutionally ruled out of the Games because of disputes over her "Englishness", but it was an excellent race nonetheless, with six of the nine contestants having previously been in a Games final. Lynn Williams, the Olympic bronze-medallist whose husband, Paul, had finished 6th at 10,000 the previous evening, won it from her Canadian team-mate, Debbie Bowker (nee Scott), who had placed only 12th in Brisbane, but even greater excitement was generated by Yvonne Murray, whose home was in Musselburgh just down the road from the stadium. She led from 1600m to within 50m of the finish and was rewarded with bronze. A moderate though closely-fought women's discus competition provided Gael Martin (nee Mulhall), of Australia, with her second gold medal and fifth medal in all in the Games since 1978, and Venissa Head won a third silver of the day for Wales.

Amid all this Judy Simpson and Jane Flemming continued their enthralling heptathlon duel throughout the afternoon. Flemming narrowed the lead from the overnight 141pts to 103 after the long jump and then went ahead in the javelin by 23pts. As they lined up for the seventh and final event, the 800m, at 4 p.m. they would have known that the difference between them amounted to only 1.6secs on the scoring tables, and Simpson gave it everything to overcome the disadvantage. At the finish she was just under two seconds faster than Flemming and she had won the title by a scant four points - 6,282 to 6,278.

Monday 28 July saw the completion of the decathlon, and finals at 400 hurdles for men and women and in the 10,000 and shot for women. It rained again, but at least the wind had dropped, which suited the women in the 10,000 who were going to make history, whatever happened, because the Commonwealth Games organisers had pre-empted both the Olympics and the European Championships in staging the race for the first time. At halfway the two contesting the lead were Anne Audain, of New Zealand, who had won the 3000 in Brisbane, and 22-year-old Liz Lynch, the UK champion - and, much more meaningfully for most of the crowd, a member of Dundee Hawkhill Harriers. Both of them were running much faster than ever before, and Lynch was looking so much the more at ease that it was little surprise, but wildly exciting for the spectators, when she sped away with two laps to go and won in a time which beat the existing Commonwealth record by over 35 seconds. The bronze medal went to

Angela Tooby, for Wales, whose identical twin sister, Susan, came in 6th, and their career best performances were to make them the most successful women twins in athletics history, according to their points scores on the tables devised by the International Amateur Athletic Federation to enable comparisons to be made between different events. Liz Lynch, interestingly, was not an exceptional athlete in her teens: in 1978, at 14, she was the 16th fastest junior 1500 runner in Scotland, and in 1980 she was the 52nd ranked under-17 in Britain at 3000m (49 places behind Yvonne Murray). Then in 1983 she had gone off to the University of Alabama on an athletics scholarship and transformed herself by dint of steely determination and sheer hard training into a World-class distance-runner. Much more was to come from the future Mrs McColgan.

In the shot Gael Martin completed a throws' double ahead of Judy Oakes, but not without considerable comment afterwards. In 1981 Martin had been suspended after failing a drugs test, as had 65 other athletes during the period 1974-85 (among whom Maroula Lambrou, of Cyprus, who, having, refused to take a test in 1982, the year she was 6th in the Games long jump, was the only other prominent Commonwealth athlete). Martin was unabashed and won in Edinburgh with a Games record; Judy Oakes, who had finished 3rd when Martin had won in 1978 and then beaten her in 1982, was furious and when interviewed by "Athletics Weekly" retorted that "any athlete found to be guilty on drug-test evidence should not be allowed to compete again - ever." There was another completed double, but not a contentious one, when Debbie Flintoff won the 400 hurdles by an even bigger margin than four years before to add to her earlier 400 flat gold. In the men's 800 semi-finals Steve Cram and Peter Elliott were impressive winners for England, while Tom McKean and Paul Forbes qualified for Scotland, and they were joined by Sebastian Coe, but he was clearly out-of-sorts in struggling home 3rd.

In the men's 400 hurdles the notable absentee was Henry Amike, of Nigeria, but that does not detract from a first ever track win at the Games for Northern Ireland as Phil Beattie improved his best time by a large margin to 49.60. A large margin was also the identifying feature of Daley Thompson's relentless passage of right to the decathlon title, winning for the third successive Games and also "winning" eight of the 10 individual events en route. Dave Steen, of Canada, was again 2nd, and among the other noteworthy finishers in this punishing competition were 20-year-old Michael Smith, of Canada, in 7th position and in last but not least place Alfred Oddie, of Blackburn Harriers, setting an Isle of Man record.

The reduced programme of events was thin enough to condense into four days or so, but the organisers - presumably, as much as anything else, to keep faith with the ticket-buying public - adhered to the original schedule, and there was a rather frustrating two-day break before athletics resumed. Of course, it's easy to complain about this if you're an athletics fanatic and forget that there are all sorts of other sports going on in the Games, and that there are lots of people who like to slip away to some cycling or swimming, or even sightseeing round Edinburgh Castle and Arthur's Seat, as an alternative pleasure. In any case, the 48-hour wait was worth it.

The finals on Thursday 31 July were at 200, 800, 5000, high jump and long jump for men, and at 200, 800 and javelin for women. Sebastian Coe withdrew from the 800 final with a throat infection, but even the World record-holder himself at his best would have been very hard put to win his first Commonwealth gold. Peter Elliott flew through the first lap in 51sec, with the lolloping Australian, Pat Scammell, next and Cram about five metres behind, but into the final curve Cram swept into the lead and covered the last 200 in around 25sec to win in 1:43.22, which remained a time which only Cram himself beat anywhere in the World during 1986, and which was 7/10ths better than John Kipkurgat's outstanding Games record of 1974. In a marvellous career which had already brought him World records at 1500m and the mile and gold medals at World, European and Commonwealth level, this was one of the very finest races which Cram ever ran. The hugely talented but untried gawky Geordie lad who had been just another non-qualifier in the heats eight years earlier had become a masterful and majestic God of the Stadium, and Tom McKean's otherwise excellent Scottish record 1:44.80 in 2nd place seemed positively but undeservedly subservient.

Vanuatu's allegiance was rewarded with a very commendable second national record at the Games by Jerry Jeremiah , who on the eve of his 23rd birthday added a 21.87 at 200m to his earlier clocking of 10.66 for 100m, but the only outsider in an England-v-Australia-v-Canada match which constituted the 200 final was Simon Baird, Northern Ireland's first male sprint finalist at any Commonwealth Games. The Canadian, Atlee Mahorn, who was also a 45.62 man at 400, and Todd Bennett, who was really a 400 runner with a best of 45.35, outlasted Ben Johnson in the straight and it was Canada's first Games win at 200, though Percy Williams back in 1930, Harry Jerome in 1966, and then Johnson in Edinburgh had won at 100 yards or 100 metres. With the Jamaicans, Merlene Ottey and Grace Jackson, excluded by boycott and engaged instead in the Grand Prix series, the women's 200 was a gift for multiple-medallists Angella Issajenko and Kathy Cook, and again it was Canada's first Games win in the longer sprint.

Kirsty Wade (nee McDermott) ended the Welsh silver streak with her second win at 800, and though she did not need to remotely approach her Commonwealth record of 1:57.42 she still ran the fastest winning time in Games history. Completing British occupation of the victory dais were 20-year-old Diane Edwards, from Sale Harriers, in Manchester, and the Olympic 5th-placer, Lorraine Baker, from another famous old club, Coventry Godiva. The women's javelin brought together every champion since 1970 - Petra Rivers (1970-74), Tessa Sanderson (1978) and Sue Howland (1982) - and in their 32nd meeting since 1977 Tessa won from her English team-mate, Fatima Whitbread. Tessa thus took a 21-11 lead in the series, and was also Olympic champion and now twice Commonwealth champion, but the show was not yet over by any means.

After his success at 5000m Steve Ovett was still not the first athlete to become Olympic, European and Commonwealth champion - Lynn Davies had done so 20 years earlier - but it was a telling tribute to Ovett's great range of talents that he had won his golds at 800, 1500 and 5000 metres. Ovett's abilities extended from 400m, at which he had won his first junior title, up to the half-marathon, and in any discussion as to who has been Britain's greatest all-round runner only the names of Sydney Wooderson (49.3 for 440 yards in 1938 through to the National 10-mile cross-country title a decade later) and Sebastian Coe (a 46.87 400 and the Yorkshire 5000 title in successive years) can be considered alongside, though claims may undoubtedly be made for Derek Johnson and Steve Cram. As in the 10,000m race English athletes were all over the 5000, though Canada's Paul Williams was still on the heels of Ovett, Jack Buckner and Tim Hutchings at the bell. Both Buckner and Hutchings had graduated to 5000 from 1500 but were no match for Ovett's kick finish, and much

185

further back was John Walker, the silver-medallist at 1500 from 1974 and 1982, who was finding the transition to the longer distance not anywhere near as natural as he might have supposed.

The Jamaican-born Milt Ottey kept his high-jump title, but the gangling Anglo-Scot, Geoff Parsons, who at 6ft 8in (2.03) was tall even for this event, equalled his British record of 2.28 in second place with 20-year-old Dalton Grant back in 7th. Gary Honey was also successful in defence of his long-jump title and his best legal effort of 8.08 was an exceptional one without the opposition being capable of pressing him hard. The road walk out to Prestonpans and back was won by Australia's Simon Baker in a Games record time, but the event must have been losing its appeal to the Manxmen and the Channel Islanders because after all their past endeavours, and even with the event on their doorsteps, only one of them turned out and he was last man home.

Friday 1 August was marathon day, and at long last it was to involve both men and women - the latter group starting half-an-hour later. Not only was Rob de Castella back to defend his title, having also become the inaugural World champion in 1983, and Charlie Spedding, the Olympic bronze-medallist, leading the British challenge, but there were actually six Africans among the 21 male starters. None of them, admittedly, was in the class of the sadly missed Tanzanians, Ikangaa and Shahanga - the best of them being Sam Hlawe, of Swaziland, who had finished 45th in Los Angeles almost 11 minutes behind Spedding - but any race would surely be enlivened by the presence of a runner from Botswana named Bigboy Josie Matlapeng. De Castella led from the start at a metronomic pace through successive five-mile stretches of 24:44, 24:43 and 24:10, and by then his only company was the Scotsman, John Graham, who had been the 4th placer in Brisbane, and he'd had to work very hard to catch the leader. Over the next five miles (run in 24:54) de Castella drew three-quarters of a minute clear and short of a calamitous collapse wasn't going to lose after that He did indeed win by almost a minute from a Blackpool-born Canadian, Dave Edge, with another Australian, Steve Moneghetti, getting the bronze medal on his marathon debut, and Graham again in 4th place. Bigboy Matlapeng came in 14th. Charlie Spedding, suffering one of those unaccountably bad days that marathon-runners have nightmares about, dropped out.

If anything, the women's winner was even more impressive. Not only did Lisa Martin finish almost two minutes ahead of the second runner, but she broke the Commonwealth record in what was virtually a solo time-trial and became the fifth fastest woman marathon runner ever with 2:26:07. Married at the time to the American, Kenny Martin, who had won the 1984 US marathon title in 2:11:24, Mrs Martin had been 7th in the Los Angeles Olympic marathon and she came from an interesting athletic background. At 19 she was a competent but by no means international-class 400m hurdler. She then graduated to the marathon almost unnoticed, and without having achieved anything of great note at any intermediary distance, while a student at the University of Oregon, winning a race in the USA in December 1983 with the 15th best time in the World for the year. In Edinburgh she led almost from the start and maintained a fast even tempo all the way (separate halves of 1:12:27 and 1:13:40). It was a dazzling performance, and yet the others weren't overawed: Lorraine Moller, who had run in Games finals at 800, 1500 and 3000 since 1974, was 2nd and Odette Lapierre, of Canada, 3rd in their personal best times, and there was even a national record for Vanessa Tilbury, of Botswana, who was last but one of the 11 finishers.

The finals taking place back in the stadium while all this was happening on the roads outside were at pole vault and discus for men and 100 hurdles, high jump and long jump for women. Andy Ashurst gained England's first pole-vault win since 1958 ahead of Canada's Jamaican-born Bob Ferguson, though even the winning height at a Games record of 5.30 would barely scrape into the top 170 in the World for the year, and a modest discus competition of much the same calibre was notable only for a promising 3rd place by the 18-year-old Australian, Werner Reiterer. Chris Stanton, who had been 2nd to Debbie Brill in 1982, won the high jump, and Brill - who had become champion at 17 when the Games had last been in Edinburgh 16 years before - was a commendable 5th. Back in 10th place was another Canadian, Linda Cameron, who was Jamaican-born and the wife of the 1982 400 champion, Bert Cameron, one of the stars barred from these Games by the boycott. The long jump was won, against expectations, with only one valid jump by England's third-string, Joyce Oladapo.

The only track final was at 100 hurdles and the winning time was unspectacular, but as the victor was one Sally Gunnell the event now assumes considerably more importance in historical terms than it did when it took place. Gunnell's first title success had been in the English schools' junior long jump in 1980 at the age of 13 and she had then set age-group heptathlon records and a British junior 100 hurdles record in 1984. It would not be until 1988 that she would turn her serious attentions to 400 hurdles, and that's a story which must await a further chapter, but this Commonwealth Games gold established her as the leading Briton in what was then her major event and unquestionably marks a significant turning-point in her athletic development, guided then as it would always be by Bruce Longden, one of the most perceptive of coaches.

The closing events on Saturday 2 August were the 1500 for men and women, the four relays and the men's triple jump, shot and javelin, and the weather was still cold and wet. Steve Cram was overwhelming favourite for the 1500, and the other nine finalists behaved as if that was enough to decide the outcome already - except for Cram's team-mate, John Gladwin, who made a break with still over a lap to go after a desperately slow first half-mile. He wasn't going to hold off Cram, who can be excused for winning the easiest way he knew how (even if his time did turn out to be by eight seconds the slowest in Games history), but Gladwin's enterprise earned him a silver medal for his pains. Cram's was the first Games middle-distance double since Herb Elliott in 1958 and Peter Snell in 1962 and the only occasion other than Kip Keino in 1966-70 that a title at 1500 or a mile had been retained. Smart company, indeed. There was another double in the women's 1500 in which Kirsty Wade, the 800 champion, and Lynn Williams, the 3000 champion, met. The pace was again not fast early on, and a final lap of just over 60sec gave Wade the title and the first 800-1500 double achieved by a woman at the Games.

English athletes won all three field events, and though none of the performances were World-shattering they showed promise for the future. John Herbert and Mike Makin were 1-2 in the triple jump; 21-year-old Billy Cole was the gold-medallist in the shot; and Olympic silver-medallist David Ottley won the javelin on his third Games appearance, with 21-year-old Mick Hill throwing a personal best 78.56 for 2nd place and 18-year-old Gavin Lovegrove, of New Zealand, 3rd. The Canadians - or, rather, Ben Johnson - overtook England, without the injured Linford Christie, on the anchor leg to win the 4 x 100, but the English women beat Canada. The same two countries then exchanged 4 x 400 victories, with England's men and Canada's women (all of the latter born in the West Indies) both winning with some ease. Kathy Cook held off Debbie Flintoff for 2nd place on the last leg and so obtained her seventh Games medal.

Maybe 10 or a dozen of the 38 gold medals awarded in Edinburgh were better merited by absent contenders, but it had been a good Games. despite everything. Even so, there was still a nagging thought in my mind as I trudged across the forecourt of Princes Street station to catch the train back to Warrington. Would there ever, I wondered dolefully, be another Commonwealth Games? Events were soon to temporarily suppress such doubts, because the British team travelled on to an immensely successful European Championships in Stuttgart at the end of August. There were wins for Christie, Black,. Coe, Cram, Buckner, Thompson, the 4 x 400 team and Whitbread (including a World record in qualifying), and it can now be seen that the foundations for what was to become known as the Golden Decade of British athletics were laid in what had seemed to be the inauspicious surroundings of a flawed Commonwealth Games.

RESULTS 1986

MEN

100 METRES (27 Jul): 1 Ben Johnson (Can) 10.07, 2 Linford Christie (Eng) 10.28, 3 Mike McFarlane (Eng) 10.35, 4 Desai Williams (Can) 10.36, 5 Elliot Bunney (Sco) 10.37, 6 Clarence Callender (Eng) 10.42, 7 Gerard Keating (Aus) 10.55, 8 Jamie Henderson (Sco) 10.68.

200 METRES (31 Jul): 1 Atlee Mahorn (Can) 20.31, 2 Todd Bennett (Eng) 20.54, 3 Ben Johnson (Can) 20.64, 4 Robert Stone (Aus) 20.94, 5 Simon Baird (NI) 20.96, 6 Mike Dwyer (Can) 20.98, 7 John Dinan (Aus) 21.07, 8 John Regis (Eng) 21.08. Note: assisting wind of 2.15m.

400 METRES (27 Jul): 1 Roger Black (Eng) 45.57, 2 Darren Clark (Aus) 45.98, 3 Phil Brown (Eng) 46.80, 4 Kriss Akabusi (Eng) 46.83, 5 Brian Whittle (Sco) 47.10, 6 David Johnston (Aus) 47.24, 7 Bruce Frayne (Aus) 47.29, 8 Andre Smith (Can) 47.97.

800 METRES (31 Jul): 1 Steve Cram (Eng) 1:43.22, 2 Tom McKean (Sco) 1:44.80, 3 Peter Elliott (Eng) 1:45.42, 4 Pat Scammell (Aus) 1:45.86, 5 Malcolm Edwards (Wal) 1:47.27, 6 Simon Hoogewerf (Can) 1:49.04, 7 Paul Forbes (Sco) 1:51.29. Sebastian Coe (Eng) qualified but did not start.

1500 METRES (2 Aug): 1 Steve Cram (Eng) 3:50.87, 2 John Gladwin (Eng) 3:52.17, 3 Dave Campbell (Can) 3:54.06, 4 Rob Harrison (Eng) 3:54.44, 5 Peter Bourke (Aus) 3:54.48, 6 Pat Scammell (Aus) 3:55.28, 7 Steve Martin (NI) 3:55.42, 8 Mike Hillardt (Aus) 3:56.90, 9 Neil Horsfield (Wal) 3:57.08, 10 John Robson (Sco) 3:57.20. Note: Harrison was the brother of Val Rutter, 5th in the women's high jump in 1974 and 7th in 1978.

5000 METRES (31 Jul): 1 Steve Ovett (Eng) 13:24.11, 2 Jack Buckner (Eng) 13:25.87, 3 Tim Hutchings (Eng) 13:26.84, 4 Paul Williams (Can) 13:28.51, 5 John Walker (NZ) 13:35.34, 6 Dave Burridge (NZ) 13:36.79, 7 Terry Greene (NI) 13:39.11, 8 Nat Muir (Sco) 13:40.92, 9 Paul McCloy (Can) 13:42.57, 10 Rob Lonergan (Can) 13:47.44, 11 Kerry Rodger (NZ) 13:52.04, 12 Peter McColgan (NI) 13:58.75, 13 George Mambosasa (Mlw) 14:18.33, 14 Thabiso Moqhali (Les) 14:48.91, 15 Jamie Marsh (Gue) 15:26.22, 16 Paul Sheard (Gue) 15:52.32.

10,000 METRES (26 Jul): 1 Jon Solly (Eng) 27:57.42, 2 Steve Binns (Eng) 27:58.01, 3 Steve Jones (Wal) 28:02.48, 4 Paul McCloy (Can) 28:29.11, 5 Steve Moneghetti (Aus) 28:29.20, 6 Paul Williams (Can) 28:41.79, 7 Terry Greene (NI) 28:47.18, 8 Peter Butler (Can) 28:50.81, 9 John Bowden (NZ) 29:25.65, 10 Mike McLeod (Eng) 29:57.23, 11 Allister Hutton (Sco) 30:16.50, 12 Jamie Marsh (Gue) 33:27.28.

3000 METRES STEEPLECHASE (27 Aug): 1 Graeme Fell (Can) 8:24.49, 2 Roger Hackney (Wal) 8:25.15, 3 Colin Reitz (Eng) 8:26.14, 4 Peter Renner (NZ) 8:27.12, 5 Nick Peach (Eng) 8:37.64, 6 Mike Gilchrist (NZ) 8:43.96, 7 Peter McColgan (NI) 8:45.51, 8 Eddie Wedderburn (Eng) 8:46.42, 9 Philippe Laheurte (Can) 8:52.53, 10 Tom Hanlon (Sco) 8:53.56, 11 Colin Hume (Sco) 9:05.40, 12 Richard Charleston (Sco) 9:21.73, 13 Bob Rice (Can) 9:25.84. Note: Fell was 2nd for England in 1982.

MARATHON (1 Aug): 1 Rob de Castella (Aus) 2:10:15, 2 Dave Edge (Can) 2:11:08, 3 Steve Moneghetti (Aus) 2:11:18, 4 John Graham (Sco) 2:12:10, 5 Art Boileau (Can) 2:12:58, 6 Phil O'Brien (Eng) 2:14:54, 7 Ieuan Ellis (Wal) 2:15:12, 8 Kevin Forster (Eng) 2:16:36, 9 Martin Deane (NI) 2:16:49, 10 Fraser Clyne (Sco) 2:17:30, 11 Peter Butler (Can) 2:18:52, 12 Sam Hlawe (Swa) 2:20:06, 13 John Campbell (NZ) 2:21:25, 14 Bigboy Josie Matlapeng (Bot) 2:24:05, 15 Grenville Wood (Aus) 2:26:48, 16 Kenneth Hlasa (Les) 2:29:47, 17 George Mosweu (Bot) 2:33:23, 18 Johnson Mbangiwa (Bot) 2:36:13, 19 Brian Holden (Gue) 2:39:12, 20 Toka Maama (Les) 2:45:13. Did not finish - Charlie Spedding (Eng).

30 KILOMETRES WALK (31 Jul): 1 Simon Baker (Aus) 2:07:47, 2 Guillaume Leblanc (Can) 2:08:38, 3 Ian McCombie (Eng) 2:10:36, 4 Chris Maddocks (Eng) 2:12:42, 5 Willi Sawall (Aus) 2:14;29, 6 Murray Day (NZ) 2:15:11, 7 Martin Rush (Eng) 2:16:01, 8 Steve Johnson (Wal) 2:21;05, 9 Graham Seatter (NZ) 2:22:48, 10 Steve Partington (IoM) 2:23:02. Disqualified - Francois Lapointe (Can).

110 METRES HURDLES (27 Jul): 1 Mark McKoy (Can) 13.31, 2 Colin Jackson (Wal) 13.42, 3 Don Wright (Aus) 13.64, 4 Nigel Walker (Wal) 13.69, 5 Jon Ridgeon (Eng) 13.76, 6 Wilbert Greaves (Eng) 13.76, 7 David Nelson (Eng) 13.97, 8 Jeff Glass (Can) 14.39. Note: assisting wind of 4.46m.

400 METRES HURDLES (28 Jul): 1 Phil Beattie (NI) 49.60, 2 Max Robertson (Eng) 49.77, 3 John Graham (Can) 50.25, 4 Lloyd Guss (Can) 50.56, 5 Mark Holtom (Eng) 50.58, 6 Gary Oakes (Eng) 50.82, 7 Pierre Leveille (Can) 51.54, 8 Ken Gordon (Aus) 51.59.

4 x 100 METRES RELAY (2 Aug): 1 Canada (Mark McKoy, Atlee Mahorn, Desai Williams, Ben Johnson) 39.15, 2 England (Lincoln Asquith, Daley Thompson, Mike McFarlane, Clarence Callender) 39.19, 3 Scotland (Jamie Henderson, George McCallum, Cameron Sharp, Elliot Bunney) 40.41, 4 Fiji (Maloni Bole, Joe Rodan, Albert Miller, Samuela Yavala) 43.11. Disqualified - Australia (Robert Stone, John Dinan, Gary Honey, Gerard Keating). 5 teams competed.

4 x 400 METRES RELAY (2 Auig): 1 England (Kriss Akabusi, Roger Black, Todd Bennett, Phil Brown) 3:07.19, 2 Australia (Bruce Frayne, Miles Murphy, David Johnston, Darren Clark) 3:07.81, 3 Canada (Anton Skerritt, Andre Smith, John Graham, Atlee Mahorn) 3:08.69, 4 Scotland (Martin Johnston, Tom McKean, Paul Forbes, Brian Whittle) 3:18.03. Disqualified - Botswana (Sunday Maweni, Joseph Ramotshabi, Zachariah Machangani, Mbiganyi Thee). 5 teams competed.

HIGH JUMP (31 Jul): 1 Milt Ottey (Can) 2.30, 2 Geoff Parsons (Sco) 2.28, 3= Alain Metellus (Can) & Henderson Pierre (Eng) 2.14, 5 Floyd Manderson (NI) 2.14, 6 Natty Crooks (Can) 2.10, 7 Dalton Grant (Eng) 2.10, 8 Fayyaz Ahmed (Eng) 2.08, 9 John Atkinson (Aus) 2.05. Edouard Robsen (Van) failed at opening height (2.00). Note: Crooks was the brother of Charmaine Crooks, 7th in the 400 and 1st at 4 x 400 in 1982.

POLE VAULT (1 Aug): 1 Andy Ashurst (Eng) 5.30, 2 Bob Ferguson (Can) 5.20, 3 Neil Honey (Aus) 5.20, 4 Dave Steen (Can) 5.10, 5 Brian Hooper (Eng) 5.00, 6 Daley Thompson (Eng) 4.90, 7 Simon Arkell (Aus) 4.75, 8 Brad McStravick (Sco) 4.45. Steve Wilson (Aus) failed at opening height (4.90). Note: Neil Honey was the brother of Gary Honey, 1st in the long jump in 1982 and 1986.

LONG JUMP (31 Jul): 1 Gary Honey (Aus) 8.08, 2 Fred Salle (Eng) 7.83, 3 Kyle McDuffie (Can) 7.79, 4 John King (Eng) 7.70, 5 Derrick Brown (Eng) 7.65, 6 Edrick Floreal (Can) 7.50, 7 David Culbert (Aus) 7.41, 8 Ken McKay (Sco) 7.39, 9 Nelson Chan Ka-Chiu (HK) 6.83, 10 Simon Shirley (Aus) 6.81, 11 William Akanaoa (Cki) 6.01. Note: the jumps by McDuffie, King, Brown and McKay were wind-assisted.

TRIPLE JUMP (2 Aug): 1 John Herbert (Eng) 17.27, 2 Mike Makin (Eng) 16.87, 3 Peter Beames (Aus) 16.42, 4 Gary Honey (Aus) 16.16, 5 Aston Moore (Eng) 16.07, 6 George Wright (Can) 15.86, 7 Craig Duncan (Sco) 15.68, 8 Edrick Floreal (Can) 15.58, 9 David Wood (Wal) 15.28.

SHOT (2 Aug): 1 Billy Cole (Eng) 18.16, 2 Joe Quigley (Aus) 17.97, 3 Stuart Gyngell (Aus) 17.70, 4 Graham Savory (Eng) 17.31, 5 Rob Venier (Can) 17.26, 6

John Minns (Aus) 16.99, 7 Luby Chambul (Can) 16.86, 8 Shaun Pickering (Wal) 16.79, 9 Eric Irvine (Sco) 16.73, 10 Andy Vince (Eng) 16.68, 11 John Reynolds (NI) 15.92, 12 Tony Satchwell (Jer) 15.47.

DISCUS (1 Aug): 1 Ray Lazdins (Can) 58.86, 2 Paul Nandapi (Aus) 57.74, 3 Werner Reiterer (Aus) 57.34, 4 Paul Mardle (Eng) 56.90, 5 Graham Savory (Eng) 56.42, 6 Richard Slaney (Eng) 56.00, 7 Vlad Slavnic (Aus) 54,48, 8 George Patience (Sco) 52.54, 9 Shaun Pickering (Wal) 51.30, 10 John Reynolds (NI) 45.34.

HAMMER (26 Jul): 1 David Smith (Eng) 74.06, 2 Martin Girvan (NI) 70.48, 3 Phil Spivey (Aus) 70.30, 4 Michael Jones (Eng) 70.10, 5 Joe Quigley (Aus) 69.30, 6 Matt Mileham (Eng) 67.96, 7 Hans-Martin Lotz (Aus) 66.14, 8 Chris Black (Sco) 63.88, 9 Shaun Pickering (Wal) 62.64.

JAVELIN (2 Aug): 1 David Ottley (Eng) 80.62, 2 Mick Hill (Eng) 78.56, 3 Gavin Lovegrove (NZ) 76.22, 4 Daryl Brand (Eng) 72.70, 5 Mike Mahlovich (Can) 71.42, 6 Peter Massfeller (Can) 70.86, 7 Colin Mackenzie (Wal) 70.82, 8 Murray Keen (Aus) 68.14, 9 John Stapylton-Smith (NZ) 65.76, 10 Tim Newenham (Wal) 65.48, 11 Mike Brennan (Can) 64.68, 12 Stewart Maxwell (Sco) 62.34.

DECATHLON (27-28 Jul): 1 Daley Thompson (Eng) 8,663 (10.37, 7.70, 15.01, 2.08, 47.30, 14.22, 43.72, 5.10, 60.82, 4:39.63), 2 Dave Steen (Can) 8,173 (11.14, 7.40, 13.22, 2.02, 48.45, 14.91, 43.62, 5.00, 60.18, 4:22.65), 3 Simon Poelman (NZ) 8,015 (10.80, 7.02, 14.32, 2.05, 51.07, 14.51, 44.40, 4.80, 56.68, 4:32.87), 4 Brad McStravick (Sco) 7,563, 5 Stuart Andrews (Aus) 7,512, 6 Gordon Orlikow (Can) 7,4242, 7 Michael Smith (Can) 7,363, 8 Simon Shirley (Aus) 7,290, 9 Greg Richards (Eng) 7,278, 10 Albert Miller (Fij) 7,158, 11 Alfred Oddie (IoM) 6,058. Did not finish - Peter Fossey (Aus), Eugene Gilkes (Eng).

WOMEN

100 METRES (27 Jul): 1 Heather Oakes (Eng) 11.20, 2 Paula Dunn (Eng) 11.21, 3 Angella Issajenko (Can) 11.21, 4 Angela Bailey (Can) 11.35, 5 Sandra Whittaker (Sco) 11.59, 6 Kaye Jeffrey (Sco) 11.59, 7 Pippa Windle (Eng) 11.68, 8 Sallyanne Short (Wal) 11.74. Note: Issajenko nee Taylor.

200 METRES (31 Jul): 1 Angella Issajenko (Can) 22.91, 2 Kathy Cook (Eng) 23.18, 3 Sandra Whittaker (Sco) 23.46, 4 Simmone Jacobs (Eng) 23.48, 5 Maree Chapman (Aus) 23.64, 6 Esmie Lawrence (Can) 23.87, 7 Sian Morris (Wal) 23.97.

Did not finish - Jennifer Stoute (Eng). Note: Kathy Cook (nee Smallwood) was the wife of Garry Cook, 1st at 4 x 400 in 1982.

400 METRES (27 Jul): 1 Debbie Flintoff (Aus) 51.29, 2 Jillian Richardson (Can) 51.62, 3 Kathy Cook (Eng) 51.88, 4 Marita Payne (Can) 52.00, 5 Charmaine Crooks (Can) 52.02, 6 Maree Chapman (Aus) 52.08, 7 Sharon Stewart (Aus) 53.53, 8 Angela Piggford (Eng) 53.67.

800 METRES (31 Jul): 1 Kirsty Wade (Wal) 2:00.94, 2 Diane Edwards (Eng) 2:01.12, 3 Lorraine Baker (Eng) 2:01.79, 4 Anne Purvis (Sco) 2:02.17, 5 Camille Cato (Can) 2:03.26, 6 Renee Belanger (Can) 2:03.85, 7 Brit McRoberts (Can) 2:05.10, 8 Julie Schwass (Aus) 2:05.14. Note: Wade nee McDermott, Purvis nee Clarkson.

1500 METRES (2 Aug): 1 Kirsty Wade (Wal) 4:10.91, 2 Debbie Bowker (Can) 4:11.94, 3 Lynn Williams (Can) 4:12.66, 4 Chris Boxer (Eng) 4:12.84, 5 Yvonne Murray (Sco) 4:14.36, 6 Chrissie Pfitzinger (NZ) 4:16.81, 7 Penny Just (Aus) 4:17.13, 8 Lynne MacDougall (Sco) 4:17.25, 9 Anne Hare (NZ) 4:17.56, 10 Suzanne Morley (Eng) 4:26.96. Note: Bowker nee Scott, Pfitzinger nee Hughes. Lynn Williams was the wife of Paul Williams, 4th at 5000 and 6th at 10,000 in 1986.

3000 METRES (27 Jul): 1 Lynn Williams (Can) 8:54.29, 2 Debbie Bowker (Can) 8:54.83, 3 Yvonne Murray (Sco) 8:55.32, 4 Chris Benning (Eng) 9:03.45, 5 Lorraine Moller (NZ) 9:03.89, 6 Chrissie Pfitzinger (NZ) 9:09.35, 7 Jane Shields (Eng) 9:13.65, 8 Wendy Sly (Eng) 9:14.04, 9 Marcella Robertson (Sco) 9:51.33. Note: Sly nee Smith.

10,000 METRES (28 Jul): 1 Liz Lynch (Sco) 31:41.42, 2 Anne Audain (NZ) 31:53.31, 3 Angela Tooby (Wal) 32:25.38, 4 Nancy Rooks (Can) 32:30.71, 5 Sue Lee (Can) 32:30.75, 6 Susan Tooby (Wal) 32:56.78, 7 Marina Samy (Eng) 33:10.94, 8 Carole Rouillard (Can) 33:22.31, 9 Andrea Everett (Sco) 33:56.43, 10 Christine Price (Sco) 33:59.90, 11 Debbie Peel (Eng) 36:03.79. Did not finish - Jill Clarke (Eng), Debbie Elsmore (NZ), Chris McMiken (NZ). Note: Angela and Susan Tooby were 25-year-old twin sisters.

MARATHON (1 Aug): 1 Lisa Martin (Aus) 2:26:07, 2 Lorraine Moller (NZ) 2:28:17, 3 Odette Lapierre (Can) 2:31:48, 4 Lizanne Bussieres (Can) 2:35:18, 5 Lorna Irving (Sco) 2:36:34, 6 Angie Pain (Eng) 2:37:57, 7 Glynis Penny (Eng) 2:38:47, 8 Moira O'Neill (NI) 2:42:29, 9 Mary O'Connor (NZ) 2:46:48, 10

Vanessa Tilbury (Bot) 2:47:24, 11 Maureen Oddie (IoM) 2:59:05. Did not finish - Julia Gates (Eng). Note: Maureen Oddie was the sister of Alfred Oddie, 11th in the decathlon.

100 METRES HURDLES (1 Aug): 1 Sally Gunnell (Eng) 13.29, 2 Wendy Jeal (Eng) 13.41, 3 Glynis Nunn (Aus) 13.44, 4 Julie Rocheleau (Can) 13.46, 5 Lesley-Ann Skeete (Eng) 13.66, 6 Jane Flemming (Aus) 13,.69, 7 Kay Morley (Wal) 13.83. Did not finish - Judith Rodgers (NI). Note: Kay Morley was the sister of Sue Morley, 4th in the 400m hurdles in 1982.

400 METRES HURDLES (28 Jul): 1 Debbie Flintoff-King (Aus) 54.94, 2 Donalda Duprey (Can) 56.55, 3 Jenny Laurendet (Aus) 56.57, 4 Gwen Wall (Can) 57.49, 5 Yvette Wray (Eng) 57.59, 6 Aileen Mills (Eng) 58.01, 7 Elaine McLaughlin (NI) 58.28, 8 Alyson Evans (Wal) 58.31. Note: Flintoff-King nee Flintoff, Laurendet nee Low.

4 x 100 METRES RELAY (2 Aug): 1 England (Paula Dunn, Kathy Cook, Joan Baptiste, Heather Oakes) 43.39, 2 Canada (Angela Bailey, Esmie Lawrence, Angela Phipps, Angella Issajenko) 43.83, 3 Wales (Helen Miles, Sian Morris, Sallyanne Short, Carmen Smart) 45.37, 4 Scotland (Ann Girvan, Kaye Jeffrey, Angela Bridgeman, Sandra Whittaker) 45.84. Did not finish - Australia (Kerry Johnson, Robyn Lorraway, Nicole Boegman, Jane Flemming). 5 teams competed. Note: Robyn Lorraway, nee Strong, was the wife of Ken Lorraway, 4th in the triple jump in 1978 and 2nd in 1982.

4 x 400 METRES RELAY (2 Aug): 1 Canada (Charmaine Crooks, Marita Payne, Molly Killingbeck, Jillian Richardson) 3:28.92, 2 England (Jane Parry, Linda Keough, Angela Piggford, Kathy Cook) 3:32.82, 3 Australia (Maree Chapman, Sharon Stewart, Julie Schwass, Debbie Flintoff) 3:32.86, 4 Scotland (Sandra Whittaker, Anne Purvis, Dawn Kitchen, Fiona Hargreaves) 3:42.86. 4 teams competed.

HIGH JUMP (1 Aug): 1 Chris Stanton (Aus) 1.92, 2 Sharon McPeake (NI) 1.90, 3 Janet Boyle (NI) 1.90, 4 Diana Davies (Eng) 1.90, 5 Debbie Brill (Can) 1.88, 6 Trudy Painter (NZ) 1.86, 7 Jayne Barnetson (Sco) 1.83, 8 Jennifer Little (Eng) 1.83, 9 Vanessa Browne (Aus) 1.83, 10 Linda Cameron (Can) 1.80, 11= Louise Manning (Eng) & Jenny Talbot (Aus) 1.75. Alison Armstrong (Can) failed at opening height (1.75). Note: Davies nee Elliott.

LONG JUMP (1 Aug): 1 Joyce Oladapo (Eng) 6.43, 2 Mary Berkeley (Eng) 6.40, 3 Robyn Lorraway (Aus) 6.35, 4 Kim Hagger (Eng) 6.34, 5 Sharon Clarke (Can)

6.20, 6 Jayne Mitchell (NZ) 6.19, 7 Tracey Smith (Can) 6.13, 8 Nicole Boegman (Aus) 6.06, 9 Gillian Regan (Wal) 6.05, 10 Megan McLean (Aus) 5.86, 11 Linda Spenst (Can) 5.80, 12 Lorraine Campbell (Sco) 5.65.

SHOT (28 Jul): 1 Gael Martin (Aus) 19.00, 2 Judy Oakes (Eng) 18.75, 3 Myrtle Augee (Eng) 17.52, 4 Melody Torcolacci (Can) 16.76, 5 Yvonne Hanson-Nortey (Eng) 16.52, 6 Astra Etienne (Aus) 16.33, 7 Rose Hauch (Can) 15.29, 8 Jackie McKernan (NI) 11.77. Note: Martin nee Mulhall.

DISCUS (27 Jul): 1 Gael Martin (Aus) 56.42, 2 Venissa Head (Wal) 56.20, 3 Karen Pugh (Eng) 54.72, 4 Julia Avis (Eng) 52.48, 5 Gale Zaphiropoulos (Can) 52.28, 6 Kathy Farr (Eng) 51.08, 7 Michelle Brotherton (Can) 49.84, 8 Astra Etienne (Aus) 49.80, 9 Jackie McKernan (NI) 49.08, 10 Melody Torcolacci (Can) 47.56, 11 Morag Bremner (Sco) 47.06.

JAVELIN (31 Jul): 1 Tessa Sanderson (Eng) 69.80, 2 Fatima Whitbread (Eng) 68.54, 3 Sue Howland (Aus) 64.74, 4 Jeanette Kieboom (Aus) 56.18, 5 Celine Chartrand (Can) 55.80, 6 Karen Hough (Wal) 53.32, 7 Anna Lockton (Eng) 52.90, 8 Faye Roblin (Can) 50.92, 9 Kristy Evans (Can) 49.50, 10 Shona Urquhart (Sco) 48.04, 11 Petra Rivers (Aus) 47.32, 12 Lyn Osmers (NZ) 38.70.

HEPTATHLON (26-27 Jul): 1 Judy Simpson (Eng) 6,282 (13.11, 1.85, 14.36, 24.99, 6.21, 36.52, 2:13.72), 2 Jane Flemming (Aus) 6,278 (13.32, 1.79, 12.70, 24.17, 6.33, 43.12, 2:15.63), 3 Kim Hagger (Eng) 5,823 (13.45, 1.79, 12.20, 25.02, 6.30, 35.72, 2:28.49), 4 Joanne Mulliner (Eng) 5,659, 5 Linda Spenst (Can) 5,634, 6 Terry Genge (NZ) 5,632, 7 Lyn Osmers (NZ) 5,511, 8 Val Walsh (Sco) 5,420. Did not finish - Alison Armstrong (Can), Sharon Jaklofsky-Smith (Aus), Jocelyn Millar-Cubit (Aus). Note: Simpson nee Livermore.

15.

Sammy sees off Seb to get his one and only "big hooray"

MOUNT SMART STADIUM, AUCKLAND, NEW ZEALAND
27 JANUARY-3 FEBRUARY 1990

THE LIST OF COMPETITORS MADE rewarding reading. The first name in the first heat of the first round of the first event on the opening day of the XIVth Commonwealth Games in Auckland was that of Fabian Muyaba, of Zimbabwe. He was, it must be said, no sprinter of any great renown, and it was inconceivable that he would present the slightest cause for concern to Linford Christie, four lanes away from him. In any case, with seven runners on the starting line, and the first five home qualifying for the next round, this would not in normal circumstances be a race to stir the passions, but it was the simple fact that Muyaba was there at all which gladdened the heart. The Africans and the West Indians had returned, and the likes of Muyaba, just 19, were the living proof of the renaissance of the Commonwealth Games. As it happens, he acquitted himself admirably, going on to reach the semi-finals and run his best-ever time of 10.46.

The entries for the Games broke all records - 672 athletes, including 242 women, from 47 countries. Equally as welcome as the major athletics powers such as Jamaica and Trinidad, Kenya and Nigeria - all of them lifting the ban that had blighted Edinburgh - was the smallest Commonwealth "country". Among the newcomers was Norfolk Island, an external territory of Australia located over a thousand kilometres north of Auckland in the South Pacific Ocean, with a population of 1,912 mostly descended from the "Bounty" mutineers.

197

Commonwealth athletes had enjoyed their customary mixed fortunes at the Seoul Olympics two years earlier, with the men winning 43 top-eight places in the running events, one in the walks, two in the decathlon and only two in the eight field events, and the women striking a more even balance with 18 in running finals and six in the field. Among the men were four Olympic champions, all of them from Kenya, but not for the last time the Kenyan authorities were in dispute with some of their US-based athletes, and though the champions at 5000m (John Ngugi) and the steeplechase (Julius Kariuki) were selected for Auckland those at 800m (Paul Ereng) and 1500m (Peter Rono) were not, and nor were the 1987 World title-winners at 800m (Billy Konchellah) and 10,000m (Paul Kipkoech). There was, briefly, a fifth gold-medallist from the Commonwealth in Seoul, but Canada's Ben Johnson had been stripped ignominiously of his 100m title within days after testing positive for banned drugs.

The venue for the athletics was the refurbished 38,000-capacity Mount Smart Stadium, where a new nine-lane Rekotan all-weather surface had been laid down and officially named "The John Walker Track". Another of New Zealand's sporting heroes, Peter Snell, was the last runner in the relay to bring the Queen's message to the opening ceremony, which commemorated the 150th anniversary of the signing of the Treaty of Waitangi, by which the British Lieutenant-Governor had established sovereignty over North Island and at the same time claimed South Island by right of discovery. The first day of athletics competition at these Commonwealth Games on Saturday 27 January brought together a fascinating match at 10,000m. For England there was Eamonn Martin, who at 31 had run in World Championships and Olympic Games, had broken the British record on his debut at the distance, and was able to afford to bring his family and his training-partner out to Auckland with him two months before the Games. For Kenya there was 17-year-old Joseph Kibor, who we were reliably informed had sold the family goats to raise the bus-fare for the first of Kenya's Games trial races which he had won as a complete unknown. The pace for the opening half of the Auckland race, made by the Australians, was inconclusive (14:09 at 5000) and when the most experienced of the Kenyans, Moses Tanui, moved ahead only Martin, barefoot Kibor, England's Gary Staines and Canada's Paul Williams sustained the chase, and though all but Kibor were still together at the bell Martin's last half-lap in 25.8 carried him to a comfortable win. Kibor ran the fastest time ever for a 17-year-old in 5th place, and rather more than 10 minutes, and seven or so laps, behind were a sheep-shearer and a tax officer from the Falkland Islands whose training for Auckland had consisted of apprehensive runs round a military airfield with a careful eye open for the take-offs and landings.

Hammer-throwing standards took a small turn for the better when Sean Carlin, of Australia, went ahead of the defending champion, David Smith, in the last round with a Games record 75.86 which would rank 46th in the World for the year. In the heptathlon Judy Simpson and Jane Flemming renewed their rivalry after their desperately close contest in Edinburgh, but even though she was only a last-minute addition to the Australian team on this occasion Flemming built up an impervious 220-point lead in the first four events, thanks to such fine performances as 13.21 for the 100 hurdles and a slightly wind-aided 23.62 at 200, and went on to set personal bests in the three remaining events the next day and win by a vast margin with Simpson 3rd.

Following a now familiar pattern the programme for the second day - Sunday 28 January - featured the 100 and 400 finals, the steeplechase and 110 hurdles for men, and the 3000 and discus for women. Three from England, three from Nigeria, and one each from Australia, Canada and Trinidad lined up for the men's 100 with Christie, the Olympic silver-medallist, having already broken the Games record at 10.02 in the semi-finals. With an aiding wind Christie went even faster, only 1/100th outside the World record revised to 9.92 in Carl Lewis's favour after the discrediting of Ben Johnson, and in 2nd place was Nigeria's Davidson Ezinwa, aged just 18, whose twin brother, Osmond, also made the final. The women's 100 was not quite of the same calibre and Merlene Ottey, who had been 2nd in the 1982 Games, won her 13th championship medal quite comfortably.

The 400s were both of very high quality, and if it was the women's that more firmly captured the attention it was because the winner was much the lesser known of the two. Fatima Yusuf, another Nigerian 18-year-old, improved her pre-Games best of 51.99 to 51.69 in the previous day's first heat, only for her even younger team-mate, Charity Opara, who was 17, to break the African record with 51.12 in the second heat. But it was Yusuf from lane three who won the final with a time of 51.08 which was only fractionally outside Marilyn Neufville's 20-year-old Games record. Darren Clark, having twice been 4th in the Olympics, and also the silver-medallist in Edinburgh in 1986, was at his best in the men's 400, setting a Games record of 44.60 (a time which only five other men in the World were to beat in 1990), and the two Kenyans behind him were both under 45sec.

Kenya entered only two men for the steeplechase but that was enough for 1-2 as the Olympic champion and 1989 World Cup winner, Julius Kariuki, won from Joshua Kipkemboi, who was actually the national title-holder. Their backgrounds made for an interesting contrast - Kariuki apparently having abandoned a career in the Kenyan Army to become a biochemistry student in the USA, and Kipkemboi still a serving Army corporal. The other men's final of the day was at 110 hurdles and Colin Jackson, who had been 2nd as a 19-year-old in Edinburgh, had shown scintillating form in his heat, equalling his own Commonwealth and European record of 13.11. In the final he was even better - 13.08 - and all credit to Tony Jarrett for running 13.34 behind him and leading home three other Britons to a singular Games achievement. Even in the prewar Games, when there were far fewer competitors, and in 1986, when the boycott had kept so many away, the home countries had never before filled the first five places in any event.

Like Darren Clark and Colin Jackson, Yvonne Murray had come close to winning in Edinburgh in 1986, placing 3rd at 3000 to two Canadians, and she lined up for that event again with the defending 10,000 champion, Liz McColgan, as one of her team-mates. Between them they dominated the race, with McColgan leading until the last two laps, and then Murray making her break, but - as had happened in Edinburgh - Scotland had to give best to Canada as Angela Chalmers, whose fastest 1989 time had been eight seconds slower than Murray's, made a timely improvement to beat Murray, with McColgan and a third Scotswoman, Karen Hutcheson, following in. The women's discus, as usual, was way off World class, but there was an encouraging victory by Lisa-Marie Vizaniari, an 18-year-old kick-boxing exponent from New South Wales who later in the year came 2nd in the World Junior Championships.

Though there were only three finals taking place, the programme for Monday 29 January still provided seven-and-a-half hours of continuous action, starting with the decathlon 110 hurdles at 12.30 p.m. The overnight leader after the previous day's five events was Canada's Michael Smith, the 7th placer in Edinburgh and still only 22, and he began this second session of activities with his fastest ever hurdles of 14.34. Another personal best in the discus gave him an unassailable lead, barring accidents, and his eventual total of 8,525pts would have gone a long way towards satisfying even the now retired Daley Thompson himself. England's Eugene Gilkes, who had lost his 400m points score in Edinburgh because of running out of his lane, traced his footsteps rather more carefully this time and finished 3rd overall.

The 400 hurdles finals provided second gold medals at the Games, though in different events to those in Edinburgh, for two athletes who were to become ikons of British athletics in the 1990s. Just after 5.50.p.m. Sally Jane Janet Gunnell, from Chigwell, in Essex, won her first title in the event, beating the 1986 champion, Debbie Flintoff-King, and having won the 100 hurdles herself at those Edinburgh Games. Spot on 20 minutes later, give or take a few seconds, Kriss Kezie Uche Chukwu Duru Akabusi, North London-born of Nigerian parents and an Army warrant officer who had been in England's winning 4 x 400 team in 1986, won his final. Both Gunnell and Akabusi had made the courageous decision to switch events after coming close to World class in their earlier disciplines, and though neither of them even set Games records in Auckland theirs were, in many ways, the most significant victories of the meeting. Also in the women's final was Rose Tata-Muya, of Kenya, who had made her Games debut as a 13-year-old back in 1974, while the bronze-medallist again in the men's race, after Nigeria's Henry Amike was disqualified for trailing his leg round two hurdles, was Canada's John Graham, who had competed in both Summer and Winter Olympics in 1988 as a hurdler and a bobsledder.

As a not very serious aside, it could now be said that Akabusi might lay claim to having the longest name in Commonwealth Games history. He was perfectly happy, though, for the announcers to restrict themselves to plain "Kriss Akabusi", and so this probably meant that a Ceylonese high jumper from 1958 named Nagalingam Ethirveerasingham should still be regarded as the "record-holder" in this category. A sprinter from Madagascar called Jean-Louis Ravelomanantsoa, who had reached the Olympic 100m final in 1968, is usually quoted as the best known tongue twister in World athletics, but his was not even the longest name in his land.

Madagascar's hammer champion was Andriantsifenta Andriamahasolo. The strongest women's candidate in this category is the surprise 4th-placed athlete from India in the 1984 Olympic 400 hurdles final, whose name was Pillavullakandi Thekeparampil Usha. Considerately, she was content to be known simply as "P.T."

Judy Oakes got another surprise in the women's shot, but it wasn't the re-emergence of her least favourite opponent, Gael Martin; rather, it was the win by her team-mate and perennial No 2, Myrtle Augee, who threw her personal best of 18.48 Among the vast array of qualifying heats three Kenyans, Seb Coe and Tom McKean reached the 800 final and three other Kenyans plus England's Jack Buckner and Mark Rowland got through at 5000. The second round of the men's 200, even allowing for a bit of a helping wind, was startlingly fast with the slowest of four races being won by England's Ade Mafe in 20.58.

The next two days were devoted exclusively to the marathon runners with the races held separately - Tuesday 30 January for men and Wednesday 31 January for women. They fully deserved their showcase, but they got it at the expense of a grandstand finish, because both races were concluded outside the main stadium. One could not but wonder whether the picturesque course, which started under the harbour bridge and wended its way along Auckland's Waterfront Drive before shuttling back and forth on a bizarre circuit to finish near St Helen's Bay, was designed more with the idea of showing off the city's tourist attractions than with providing a stimulating challenge for the competitors.

Allowing for the financial incentives which the big-city invitation marathons were now beginning to offer, the entry for the men's race was remarkably strong. Rob de Castella was back to seek a third successive win and with him was the 1986 bronze-medallist, Steve Moneghetti; Juma Ikangaa, who had run such a memorable race against de Castella in 1982, returned; and of the 15 Africans among the 28 starters the most notable of all was Kenya's World champion and Olympic silver-medallist, Douglas Wakiihuri. Ikangaa led a large group early on, but at 20km Wakiihuri had only Moneghetti and the second and third of the Tanzanians, Ibrahim Hussein and Simon Robert Naali, with him, and by 30km (after successive 10km stretches of 30:58, 30:37 and 30:40 on the predominantly flat harbour-side roads) Hussein had been dropped. It was only in the last kilometre that Wakiihuri drew away and the margin among the first three was by far the smallest yet in 14 Games marathons - 11 seconds, compared with 63 in Edinburgh. Wakiihuri, now 26, had gone to live in Japan at 18 because he believed that was where he would get the best marathon-running advice and guidance. He had learned the language, and after his first coach, Kiyoshi Nakamura, was accidentally drowned in 1984 he had linked up with Shinetsi Murao and had won the 1987 World title as a virtual unknown. Neither Ikangaa nor de Castella were ever in contention for medals after the first 20km. Bigboy Josie Matlapeng, of Botswana, finished in the same position, 14th, as in Edinburgh but was almost four minutes faster.

The next day it was the turn of the women, with the defending champion, Lisa Martin, an overwhelming favourite. Now divorced from Kenny Martin and due to marry the Kenyan distance-runner, Yobes Ondieki, immediately after the Games, she set off in precisely the same manner as in Edinburgh and simply ran away from the field from the start, and her eventual winning margin was more than eight minutes. It was an astonishing exhibition conducted in solitary splendour, and with her tightly-bunched hair, immaculate makeup, gleaming ear-rings, pearl necklace and neat green-and-white leotard she looked as unruffled as if she was scampering round the corner to a housewives' aerobics class rather than accomplishing a World-class marathon time of 2:25:28. It was the 18th fastest ever by a woman and would have got her 18th place in the men's race ahead of Australia's third man home. A long way behind her were runners from Cyprus, Bermuda and Zimbabwe who all still broke their national records.

Action in the stadium resumed on Thursday 1 February with the finals at 200 and 800, the men's 5000, high jump and long jump, and the women's javelin. Linford Christie was not selected at 200, which was not so surprising because although he had finished 4th in that event in the Seoul Olympics he regarded it very much as a second choice, and England still had all of their three runners through to the final. John Regis was the most experienced of them and he ran his fastest ever time of 20.16, but his team-mate, Marcus Adam, beat him with 20.10 in a race which was marginally wind-aided, and Ade Mafe completed the first clean sweep of medals for one country in a men's sprint event. The first three in the women's 100 ran again at 200 and the order was the same and the margins were not much different with Merlene Ottey winning her third Games gold medal.

The Kenyan trio in the men's 800 faced five runners from the home countries and it was a fairly typical barging-and-boring type of championship final with the first lap an indifferent 52.5 and everyone looking for the perfect tactical position from which to strike. In the end it was the Kenyans who proved much the strongest, and almost as if it was pre-ordained it was the least regarded of them, 31-year-old Sammy Tirop, who won. Tirop, whose previous best time of 1:47.05 had dated from 1986, improved out of all recognition to 1:44.3 in the Kenyan trials, and in a Games preview written for the British magazine, "Athletics Today", the Kenyan journalist, Charles Ouko, had delightfully summed up Tirop's chances by saying that "in view of his age Auckland could be his first and last chance for a big hooray." Tirop returned to Kenya apparently satisfied to be a Commonwealth champion and never figured again in international competition. The better known Nixon Kiprotich was 2nd to Tirop and was also to get the Olympic silver two years later. Best of the rest, most surprisingly, was the English No3, Matthew Yates, while Seb Coe - who had preferred the European Championships in 1978 and 1982 and was ill in 1986 - still didn't get a Commonwealth medal, finishing an uninspired 6th.

England fared much better in the women's race - or, rather, Sale Harriers did. Diane Edwards led all the way with laps of fractionally under and fractionally over the minute and won in a Games record 2:00.25 from her clubmate and training partner, Ann Williams, both of the personable pair being coached by Norman Poole at Wythenshawe Park, in Manchester. Edwards had been running 800s for more than a decade, patiently working her way through the national rankings from 11th place as a junior in 1980 and then winning the silver medal in Edinburgh and reaching the Olympic final in 1988, while Williams had been the English schools' 400 champion in 1982 and then moved up in distance, recognising her limitations in basic speed. It was the first 1-2 in nine Commonwealth Games finals for women at 880 or 800 since Gladys Lunn and Ida Jones, also of England, in 1934.

Kenya's formidable trio at 5000 were John Ngugi (the Olympic champion), Yobes Ondieki (the 4th fastest man ever at the distance) and Moses Tanui (already the silver-medallist at 10,000 in Auckland). Eamonn Martin had qualified but decided not to start, which seemed to leave Jack Buckner, the European champion and Commonwealth silver-medallist from 1986, and Mark Rowland, Olympic steeplechase bronze-medallist in

1988, as the most likely challengers to the Kenyans. To describe the race as bizarre would be a gross understatement: within the first four laps Ngugi, Buckner and Ondicki were all brought down in two separate falls, and yet Ngugi picked up the pace from 2:42 for the first kilometre to 2:36 for the second, led by 10m or so at halfway, and then ran right away from everybody in the familiar loping style of his which had already brought him four World cross-country titles to establish a seemingly impregnable lead of 40m at the bell. Yet the race was stolen from him in the very last few strides as two complete outsiders - Andrew Lloyd, of Australia, and Ian Hamer, of Wales - burst away from a group of half-a-dozen in the closing 200m in pursuit of the minor medals and Lloyd suddenly found to his amazement that he could catch the leader. He won by less than a metre, and it might well be that Ngugi misjudged it, believing the race was his and unaware that Lloyd was approaching fast.

Lloyd was English-born and had overcome grievous personal misfortune. His first wife had been killed in a car crash five years earlier in which he had suffered severe injuries, and he had then undergone a series of operations over the next three years. He was now married to Carolyn Schuwalow, who had placed 5th in the 3000 four days before. If anything, the breakthrough by Hamer - to whom Lloyd gave full credit for taking the initiative in their last-lap duel and, in effect, pacing him to gold - was even more remarkable. Regarded as a 1500m runner, his only noteworthy success at 5000 had been to win a Wednesday night race at his local Cwmbran track the previous September in his fastest time of 13:45.3. In Auckland he improved by almost 20sec for the first medal for Wales in a Commonwealth three miles or 5000m.

The men's high jump was a marvellous contest between Nick Saunders, of Bermuda, and Dalton Grant, of England, who had been the only two Commonwealth male athletes to place in the first eight in any of the field events at the 1988 Olympics. Saunders and Grant were uncannily closely matched, sharing the Commonwealth records at 2.35 indoors and 2.34 out (the latter first set by Saunders in finishing 5th in Seoul), and they were both astute tacticians. Saunders passed at 2.26 and 2.32 and then after one failure at 2.34 elected to take his next two attempts at 2.36, as he was perfectly entitled to do. Grant cleared 2.34 at the second attempt to equal his British record and take the lead, but at 2.36 Saunders went over at his second attempt for a new Commonwealth record and Grant, having failed twice, then elected to go for broke at 2.38. He knocked the bar down with the one attempt available to him, which left Saunders as the winner, understandably failing three times at 2.40 after such a nerve-racking ordeal. Neither Saunders, at 1.88, nor Grant, at 1.86, were particularly tall for the event and their ability to leap far above their own stature compares with any high jumper except the remarkable American, Franklin Jacobs, who was only 1.73 (5-8) and yet cleared 2.32 (7-7⁄) indoors in 1978!

The African champion from Nigeria, Yusuf Ali, who led the Commonwealth rankings by a wide margin, had the long jump won from the second round onwards, clearing a massive 8.39 with the help of a strong tailwind, and a spirited silver medal for Australia was won by David Culbert and not the champion of 1982-86, Gary Honey, who was well out of it. The New Zealanders, not expected to figure at all, did rather well with both Jonathan Moyle and Willie Hinchcliff (nephew of his country's Prime Minister who was in the grandstand to watch the event) clearing 7.97. Unremarked in minor places were Bruny Surin and Glenroy Gilbert, who would go on to win World and Olympic gold medals in Canada's 4 x 100 relay team, and 16-year-old Kareem Streete-Thompson, of the Cayman Islands, who emigrated to the USA soon after and within four years was the eighth best long jumper of all-time. The withdrawal through injury of the former World record-holder, Fatima Whitbread, still left two former champions in the women's javelin and Tessa Sanderson won her third Commonwealth title in 12 years ahead of Sue Howland, the 1982 winner reinstated after a drug-taking suspension.

The penultimate day, Friday 2 February, began with the men's 30km walk, held in residential Devonport, a 10-minute ferry ride across the harbour from the city, and starting at 7 a.m., to be followed by the newly-introduced 10km race for women at 10.45 a.m. The first four finishers from 1986 were among the small but select field of 13 who started in the men's event, but the defending champion, Simon Baker, who had been 6th in the Olympic 50km, had a rare off day and his fellow-Australian, Andrew Jachno, was the pacemaker until the Canadian, Guillaume Leblanc, came through in the last 5km to cross the line just over a minute ahead. It completed a logical progression for him, because he had been bronze-medallist in 1982 and silver-medallist in 1986. Leblanc was born in Sept-

Iles, Quebec, and as his name implies his first language was French. The women's race was won, as universally forecast, by Australia's Kerry Saxby, who had set 21 World records, with the most recent of them a fortnight before the Games opened, and she finished exactly two minutes ahead of New Zealand's Anne Judkins.

By that stage of the morning there was plenty of vociferous support for the contestants from the customers in the harbour-front pubs where pints of the wholesome local DB bitter were being sunk with gusto. And why not? After all, Dominion Breweries of Auckland, Mangatainoka and Timaru were official sponsors of the Games along with Air New Zealand, NEC, ASB Bank, Nikon, BP, Seiko, Telecom, Kodak, Toyota, Lotto TM, Television New Zealand and Unisys, with another 125 companies in support, ranging from Graham Crosbie Motorcycles to Tip Top Ice Cream Ltd. At NZ$80 million, the Commonwealth Games had become a corporate-driven public relations affair, far beyond the pockets of the dozen public-spirited chaps who'd had a whip-round to pay for a few extra phones and a couple of new-fangled telex machines at those humble Auckland Games of 40 years earlier.

The afternoon's main events were the finals for the men's pole vault and discus and the women's high jump and long jump, occupying the time from 2 p.m. onwards until the women's 10,000 began at 7.10. Since winning the 10,000 in Edinburgh Liz McColgan (nee Lynch) had finished 5th in the 1987 World Championships and 2nd at the 1988 Olympics. She held the Commonwealth record with the third fastest ever time of 31:06.99, and though her racing in 1989 had not been up to her usual standards since finishing 2nd in the World Indoor Championships 3000 at the start of the year, she had demonstrated her readiness for her first 10,000 since Seoul by getting the bronze medal in the Auckland 3000. Again she faced Anne Audain, with whom she had fought out the 1986 race, and again the New Zealander led early on but at a moderate pace. Two-thirds of the way through the race England's Jill Hunter, who had won the Women's AAA title in her only other attempt at the distance five months earlier, increased the pace, but McColgan went ahead with 1200m remaining and won convincingly, having run the second half almost a minute faster than the first half.

Australia's Simon Arkell improved from 7th place in 1986 to win the pole vault, and like the 5000 champion, Andrew Lloyd, he had been born

207

in England. The 1982 and 1986 champions, Brad Cooper and Ray Lazdins, were both in the men's discus, but neither was any match for the 21-year-old US-based Nigerian, Adewale Olukoju, who became the first black athlete from Africa to win a Commonwealth Games gold in the throws. Though also not of World-class standard the women's high jump was the most exciting contest of the day, if only for the fact that the leading six competitors all cleared the same height and New Zealanders took 1st, 3rd and 4th= positions. Tania Murray, a 19-year-old from Dunedin, became the host country's first winner of the Games after a protracted series of jump-offs with Janet Boyle, of Northern Ireland. "The crowd just lifted me every time I cleared the bar," enthused the new champion afterwards. "The crowd cheered every time I missed, but they were just great," graciously commented the silver-medallist (who had also been the bronze-medallist in Edinburgh). Jane Flemming, already the heptathlon champion, won the long jump with England's 20-year-old Fiona May 3rd.

Sally Gunnell, having won the 400 hurdles, was back on the track to defend her 100 hurdles title, but Kay Morley beat her by the best part of three metres with a Welsh record 12.91. Coached by Malcolm Arnold, whose better known protégé, Colin Jackson, had won the men's high hurdles, Morley was born in Yorkshire, qualifying for Wales by residence, and her sister, Sue, had been 4th for England in the 1982 400 hurdles. Two other gold-medallists - heptathletes Glynis Nunn-Cearns (1982) and Jane Flemming (1990) - also finished behind Morley. The day's 1500 heats saw Peter Elliott and Tony Morrell through for England, together with three Kenyans and John Walker, making his final appearance at the age of 38, but Seb Coe was a non-starter again with swollen glands.

The closing programme on Saturday 3 February contained, by convention, the men's and women's 1500s, the men's triple jump, shot putt and javelin, and the four relays, but there was nothing run-of-the-mill about the competitions. Peter Elliott, the amiably forthright Yorkshireman who was single-handedly taking up the middle-distance mantle of Coe, Cram and Ovett, had run superbly in pre-Games meetings and carried that form through to the 1500 final. William Tanui (Olympic 800 champion two years later) was apparently the elected Kenyan pacemaker, leading through the 800 in just under 1:56 and still in front approaching the bell, but when Elliott began his surge for home he proved irresistible, bounding through the last lap in 53sec with his legs stretching out relentlessly and his arms pumping in their characteristic low-slung raking manner, to win in 3:33.39, still short of Filbert Bayi's 1974 Games record and yet a performance of absolute majesty. A New Zealander was 3rd, but it was Peter O'Donoghue and not the sentimental favourite, John Walker. Spurned by the Gods on this swansong day, Walker was brought down on the second lap by the Australian, Pat Scammell, who had developed an unenviable reputation over the years for getting in people's way. Elliott, typically open-hearted, persuaded Walker to accompany him on his lap of honour.

Chris Cahill, who as Chris Boxer had finished 11th in 1978, 1st in 1982 and 4th in 1986, led into the home straight after a slow start to the women's 1500 but was passed by the 3000 winner, Angela Chalmers. Born in Manitoba, of Sioux Indian descent, and married to an American and living in Arizona, Chalmers had been 14th and last in the Seoul Olympic 3000 and blossomed in Auckland with two splendid performances. Rangey and powerful, she presented an exhilarating sight on the track, and her emergence into World-class after five years of modestly successful international competition was one of the compelling features of the Auckland athletics. Her Sioux name was "Dusmanwe", which translates literally as "Walk Fast Woman".

In Edinburgh England's men had won all three field events on the last day, and they duly took gold again in the shot and javelin, with 22-year-old Simon Williams, like so many other Auckland competitors a student in the USA, in the former event, and a youthful Steve Backley, still nine days short of his 21st birthday, in the latter - and winning the first gold and, for that matter the first medal, of what was to accumulate into a stockpile of trophies as the 1990s rolled on. Another future World star, with a shade more experience than Backley but also with his best years well ahead of him, ought really to have completed the treble in the triple jump, and after four rounds 23-year-old Jonathan Edwards was, indeed, leading, but no one - least of all, Edwards himself - could have expected a Cypriot, Marios Hadjiandreou, to achieve a lifetime best of 16.95 in the fifth round, and Edwards's final effort of 17m-plus in response was a marginal foul. "I was beaten," said Edwards ruefully afterwards, "by somebody I'd never heard of." Only the most studious of statistical experts would have recalled that Hadjiandreou had been 7th in the 1982 Games.

England won the men's 4 x 100 in a Games record 38.67, with Linford Christie on the anchor leg, and the women's 4 x 400 in some comfort from Australia, though there were only four teams entered in this event. In the women's 4 x 100 16-year-old Cathy Freeman became Australia's first gold-medallist of aboriginal origin, and it was a victory which must have particularly warmed the heart of the Australian headquarters manageress. She was 58-year-old Marjorie Nelson M.B.E., who had won a shoal of Olympic and Commonwealth medals in her time. The men's 4 x 400 was devalued by the disqualification of Australia, England and Trinidad & Tobago in the second heat because their last-leg runners were standing on the wrong takeover line, and this left Kenya as easy winners of the final, with a makeshift Scottish team consisting of 1500m runner David Strang, 800m finalists Tom McKean and Brian Whittle, and 400m hurdler Mark Davidson as the most unlikely of silver medallists.

At a vibrant closing ceremony Dame Kiri Te Kanawa heart-rendingly sang "Now Is The Hour", and there was a palpable feeling of nostalgic regret that the Auckland Games were now all over bar the shouting of the exuberant Maori dancers and the carefree cavorting athletes. The Sunday morning after the Games, savouring a glass or two of chilled New Zealand Chardonnay in a harbourside bistro, was a time for mellow reflection for those of us about to embark on the long flight home. In the most convivial of company, the events of the preceding week or so were bound to take on an enhanced glow, but the facts spoke for themselves. It had been a marvellous Games held in a city of which the most obvious charm was that it seemed 10 or 15 years behind the frenzied times and whose citizens had been so fulsome in their welcome. "Honour of Commonwealth", for sure, and "Glory of Sport", too, and someone murmured at one stage as the afternoon slipped pleasantly by that Malaysia had decided to apply to stage the Games of 1998. Now, that did sound interesting.

Wistful memories of John Walker, the Tarzan of the Track

Back in 1988 Peter Matthews, the editor of the international athletics annual published by the Association of Track & Field Statisticians, which is regarded as the "Wisden" of the sport, asked me to record my impressions of 1500-metre running during the 1980s, and as these remain as vivid now as they were then I see no reason to revise my original thoughts, even if they seem more than a degree or two over the top in retrospect. Of course, Coe, Cram and Ovett - who between them shared 11 gold medals and 17 World records at various distances - were the three men who dominated middle-distance running in that decade, but even then as I penned my notes both the 1500m record and the World title were already held by Africans.

Though Cram and Ovett were still around, and Elliott was the genuine World-class article, it still felt as if the end of an era was approaching. The Commonwealth Games in the very first month of the next decade appropriately marked one of its final flings, and as is so often the way in sport, as in life, it turned out to be a complete anti-climax. Coe fell ill and Walker fell over, and with respect to the sublime talents of Coe it was Walker for whom we felt the deeper pangs of sympathy. This was a man who had realised his greatest achievements long before the 1980s: breaking the World record but coming second in the 1500 at the 1974 Commonwealth Games; running the first sub-3:50 mile in 1975; setting a phenomenal 2000m World record and then winning the Olympic 1500 in 1976. Yet he soldiered on right through the 1980s, "majestic and fearsome as an All-Black flanker driving for the tryline" (as I enthused in my purple prose for the ATFS annual), racing here, there and everywhere at home in the early months of the year and then in Europe and at the major championships through each long, hot summer. He lost as often as he won, but he never gave less than his all. Another analogy I once used, and I still rather like it, is of Walker like Lex Barker playing Tarzan in one of those fondly-remembered Hollywood movies, hair streaming in the wind as he swung effortlessly through the jungle, and everything always turning out alright in the end, regardless of what perils lay in wait. In the most memorable decade in the history of athletics, John Walker still stood out as one of the most charismatic of competitors, winning or losing.

RESULTS 1990

MEN

100 METRES (28 Jan): 1 Linford Christie (Eng) 9.93, 2 Davidson Ezinwa (Nig) 10.05, 3 Bruny Surin (Can) 10.12, 4 Marcus Adam (Eng) 10.14, 5 Tim Jackson (Aus) 10.17, 6 Abdullahi Tetengi (Nig) 10.20, 7 John Regis (Eng) 10.22, 8= Neil De Silva (Tri) & Osmond Ezinwa (Nig) 10.35. Assisting wind of 3.9m. Note: Davidson and Osmond Ezinwa were 18-year-old twins.

200 METRES (1 Feb): 1 Marcus Adam (Eng) 20.10, 2 John Regis (Eng) 20.16, 3 Ade Mafe (Eng) 20.26, 4 Neil De Silva (Tri) 20.40, 5 Davidson Ezinwa (Nig) 20.44, 6 Cyprian Enweani (Can) 20.54, 7 Paul Greene (Aus) 20.58, 8 Kennedy Ondiek (Ken) 20.60, 9 Abdullahi Tetengi (Nig) 20.96. Assisting wind of 2.4m. Note: Paul Greene was the grandson of Paul Magee, 6th in the 400 hurdles in 1938.

400 METRES (28 Jan): 1 Darren Clark (Aus) 44.60, 2 Samson Kitur (Ken) 44.88, 3 Simeon Kipkemboi (Ken) 44.93, 4 Robert Stone (Aus) 45.25, 5 Devon Morris (Jam) 45.68, 6 Mark Garner (Aus) 46.10, 7 Grant Gilbert (NZ) 46.18, 8 Stephen Mwanzia (Ken) 46.35, 9 Todd Bennett (Eng) 46.64.

800 METRES (1 Feb): 1 Sammy Tirop (Ken) 1:45.98, 2 Nixon Kiprotich (Ken) 1:46.00, 3 Matthew Yates (Eng) 1:46.62, 4 Brian Whittle (Sco) 1:46.85, 5 Ikem Billy (Eng) 1:47.16, 6 Sebastian Coe (Eng) 1:47.24, 7 Tom McKean (Sco) 1:47.27, 8 Simon Doyle (Aus) 1:48.06, 9 Robert Kibet (Ken) 1:48.57.

1500 METRES (3 Feb): 1 Peter Elliott (Eng) 3:33.39, 2 Wilfred Kirochi (Ken) 3:34.41, 3 Peter O'Donoghue (NZ) 3:35.14, 4 Simon Doyle (Aus) 3:35.70, 5 Tony Morrell (Eng) 3:35.87, 6 William Tanui (Ken) 3:37.77, 7 Joseph Chesire (Ken) 3:40.58, 8 Mbiganyi Thee (Bot) 3:44.34, 9 Ian Hamer (Wal) 3:46.23, 10 Dave Campbell (Can) 3:50.07, 11 Pat Scammell (Aus) 3:50.47, 12 John Walker (NZ) 3:53.77.

5000 METRES (1 Feb): 1 Andrew Lloyd (Aus) 13:24.86, 2 John Ngugi (Ken) 13:24.94, 3 Ian Hamer (Wal) 13:25.63, 4 Kerry Rodger (NZ) 13:26.79, 5 Moses Tanui (Ken) 13:28.31, 6 Paul Williams (Can) 13:33.68, 7 Mark Rowland (Eng) 13:35.69, 8 Pat Carroll (Aus) 13:48.16, 9 Yobes Ondieki (Ken) 13:58.75, 10 Paul McCloy (Can) 14:00.26, 11 Charles Mulinga (Zam) 14:03.59, 12 Jack Buckner

(Eng) 14:10.59, 13 Malcolm Norwood (Aus) 14:19.33, 14 Roger Hackney (Wal) 14:27.06. Eamonn Martin (Eng) qualified but did not start. Note: William Tanui (6th at 1500) and Moses Tanui were not related.

10,000 METRES (27 Jan): 1 Eamonn Martin (Eng) 28:08.57, 2 Moses Tanui (Ken) 28:11.56, 3 Paul Williams (Can) 28:12.71, 4 Gary Staines (Eng) 28:13.62, 5 Joseph Kibor (Ken) 28:27.56, 6 Peter Brett (Aus) 28:37.16, 7 Kerry Rodger (NZ) 28:46.55, 8 Paul McCloy (Can) 29:02.21, 9 Carey Nelson (Can) 29:02.29, 10 Sammy Kibiwott Bitok (Ken) 29:25.46, 11 Isaac Simelane (Swa) 29:28.59, 12 Tim Hutchings (Eng) 29:34.12, 13 Malcolm Norwood (Aus) 30:06.70, 14 Mark Furlan (NZ) 30:39.90, 15 John Mwathiwa (Mlw) 30:52.26, 16 Clive Hamilton (Jam) 31:13.91, 17 Moneri Lebesa (Les) 31:45.94, 18 Derrick Adamson (Jam) 31:59.11, 19 Aaron Dupnai (PNG) 32:33.25, 20 William Goss (Fal) 39:51.71, 21 Peter Biggs (Fal) 40:26.14. Did not finish - Troy Chinhoyi (Zim), Zachariah Ditetso (Bot).

3000 METRES STEEPLECHASE (28 Jan): 1 Julius Kariuki (Ken) 8:20.64, 2 Joshua Kipkemboi (Ken) 8:24.26, 3 Colin Walker (Eng) 8:26.50, 4 Graeme Fell (Can) 8:27.64, 5 Shaun Creighton (Aus) 8:33.59, 6 Eddie Wedderburn (Eng) 8:34.66, 7 Roger Hackney (Wal) 8:36.62, 8 Peter Renner (NZ) 8:38.61, 9 Greg Cameron (NZ) 8:42.08, 10 Alain Boucher (Can) 8:42.97, 11 Sean Wade (NZ) 8:45.16, 12 Tom Hanlon (Sco) 8:45.76, 13 Mick Hawkins (Eng) 8:48.93.

MARATHON (30 Jan): 1 Douglas Wakiihuri (Ken) 2:10:27, 2 Steve Moneghetti (Aus) 2:10:34, 3 Simon Robert Naali (Tan) 2:10:38, 4 Steve Jones (Wal) 2:12:44, 5 Ibrahim Hussein (Tan) 2:13:20, 6 Daniel Nzioka (Ken) 2:13:17, 7 Rex Wilson (NZ) 2:13:48, 8 Geoff Wightman (Eng) 2:14:16, 9 Steve Brace (Wal) 2:16:16, 10 Thabiso Moqhali (Les) 2:17:33, 11 Juma Ikangaa (Tan) 2:18:47, 12 Ernest Tjela (Les) 2:18:48, 13 Rob de Castella (Aus) 2:18:50, 14 Bigboy Josie Matlapeng (Bot) 2:20:18, 15 Motsemme Kgaotsang (Bot) 2:20:41, 16 John Mwathiwa (Mlw) 2:23:31, 17 Paul Herlihy (NZ) 2:24:52, 18 Nicholas Nyengerai (Zim) 2:26:20, 19 Brad Camp (Aus) 2:27:05, 20 David Mponye (Les) 2:27:26, 21 Vusie Thomas Dlamini (Swa) 2:27:55, 22 Gord Christie (Can) 2:32:19, 23 Sebio Sikanyika (Zam) 2:33:23. Did not finish - John Campbell (NZ), Tony Milovsorov (Eng), Alfredo Shahanga (Tan), Carl Thackery (Eng), Bill Tweed (Jer). Note: Alfredo Shahanga was the brother of Gidamis Shahanga, 1st (1978) and 6th (1982) in the marathon, 1st (1982) at 10,000.

30 KILOMETRES WALK (2 Feb): 1 Guillaume Leblanc (Can) 2:08:28, 2 Andrew Jachno (Aus) 2:09:29, 3 Ian McCombie (Eng) 2:09:20, 4 Francois Lapointe (Can) 2:12:41, 5 Mark Easton (Eng) 2:14:52, 6 Chris Maddocks (Eng) 2:15:07, 7= Simon

213

Baker (Aus) & Paul Copeland (Aus) 2:19:55, 9 Steve Partington (IoM) 2:20:11, 10 Shane Donnelly (NZ) 2:24:01, 11 Martin Archambault (Can) 2:29:22, 12 Sean Sullivan (NZ) 2:35:40. Did not finish - Moetu Tangitamaiti (Cki).

110 METRES HURDLES (28 Jan): 1 Colin Jackson (Wal) 13.08, 2 Tony Jarrett (Eng) 13.34, 3 David Nelson (Eng) 13.54, 4 Hughie Teape (Eng) 13.58, 5 Nigel Walker (Wal) 13.78, 6 Kyle Vander-Kuyp (Aus) 14.07, 7 Akwasi Abrefa (Gha) 14.12, 8 Grant McNeil (NZ) 14.20, 9 Tim Soper (NZ) 14.28.

400 METRES HURDLES (29 Jan): 1 Kriss Akabusi (Eng) 48.89, 2 Gideon Yego (Ken) 49.25, 3 John Graham (Can) 50.24, 4 Leigh Miller (Aus) 50.25, 5 Samuel Matete (Zam) 50.34, 6 Joseph Maritim (Ken) 50.54, 7 Barnabas Kinyor (Ken) 50.73, 8 Lawrence Lynch (Eng) 51.51. Disqualified - Henry Amike (Nig), originally 3rd in 49.26.

4 x 100 METRES RELAY (3 Feb): 1 England (Clarence Callender, John Regis, Marcus Adam, Linford Christie) 38.67, 2 Nigeria (Victor Nwankwo, Davidson Ezinwa, Osmond Ezinwa, Abdullahi Tetengi) 38.85, 3 Jamaica (Wayne Watson, John Mair, Clive Wright, Ray Stewart) 39.11, 4 Australia (Shane Naylor, Paul Greene, Steve McBain, Fred Martin) 39.25, 5 Canada (Everton Anderson, Mike Dwyer, Cyprian Enweani, Peter Ogilvie) 39.43, 6 Scotland (Elliot Bunney, Dave Clark, Jamie Henderson, Mark Davidson) 39.61, 7 Papua New Guinea (Ezekiel Wartovo, John Hou, Emmanuel Mack, Takale Tuna) 40.94, 8 Gambia (Abdurahman Jallow, Lamin Marikong, Abdoulieh Janneh, Clifford Adams) 41.65, 9 New Zealand (Murray Gutry, Gary Henley-Smith, Grant Gilbert, Dale McClunie) 44.34.

4 x 400 METRES RELAY (3 Feb): 1 Kenya (Samson Kitur, Stephen Mwanzia, David Kitur, Simeon Kipkemboi) 3:02.48, 2 Scotland (Mark Davidson, Tom McKean, David Strang, Brian Whittle) 3:04.68, 3 Jamaica (Clive Wright, Devon Morris, Trevor Graham, Howard Burnett) 3:04.96, 4 New Zealand (Darren Dale, Andrew Collins, Anthony Green, Dale McClunie) 3:06.23, 5 Canada (Mike McLean, Steve O'Brien, Paul Osland, Anton Skerritt) 3:06.73, 6 Pakistan (Bashir Ahmad, Muhammad Fayyaz, Behre Karam, Muhammad Sadaqat) 3:11.90, 7 Seychelles (Giovanni Fanny, Percy Larame, Philip Sinon, Joseph Adam) 3:18.22. Because of disqualifications in the heats only 7 teams competed in the final. Note: Samson and David Kitur were brothers.

HIGH JUMP (1 Feb): 1 Nick Saunders (Ber) 2.36, 2 Dalton Grant (Eng) 2.34, 3= Milt Ottey (Can) & Geoff Parsons (Sco) 2.23, 5= David Anderson (Aus) &

Alain Metellus (Can) 2.23, 7 John Holman (Eng) 2.20, 8 Roger Te Puni (NZ) 2.20, 9- Steve Chapman (Eng), Ian Garrett (Aus) & Marc Howard (Aus) 2.15, 12 Alex Zaliauskas (Can) 2.15, 13 Raul Griffith (Guy) 2.05, 14 Jeff Brown (NZ) 2.00, 15 Steve Ritchie (Sco) 2.00, 16 Roger Brehaut (Gue) 1.95.

POLE VAULT (2 Feb): 1 Simon Arkell (Aus) 5.35, 2 Ian Tullett (Eng) 5.25, 3 Simon Poelman (NZ) 5.20, 4 Neil Honey (Aus) 5.20, 5 Paul Just (Can) 5.10, 6 Adam Steinhardt (Aus) 5.10, 7= Bob Ferguson (Can) & Paul Gibbons (NZ) 5.10, 9 Doug Wood (Can) 5.00, 10 Matt Belsham (Eng) 5.00, 11 Derek McKee (NZ) 4.80. Andy Ashurst (Eng) failed at opening height (5.00).

LONG JUMP (1 Feb): 1 Yusuf Alli (Nig) 8.39, 2 David Culbert (Aus) 8.20, 3 Festus Igbinoghene (Nig) 8.18, 4 Stewart Faulkner (Eng) 7.97, 5 Jonathan Moyle (NZ) 7.97, 6 Willie Hinchcliff (NZ) 7.97, 7 Bruny Surin (Can) 7.85, 8 Glenroy Gilbert (Can) 7.80, 9 John King (Eng) 7.62, 10 Gary Honey (Aus) 7.54, 11 Kareem Streete-Thompson (Cay) 7.53. Barrington Williams (Eng) no valid jumps. All jumps were wind-assisted.

TRIPLE JUMP (3 Feb): 1 Marios Hadjiandreou (Cyp) 16.95, 2 Jonathan Edwards (Eng) 16.93, 3 Edrick Floreal (Can) 16.89, 4 John Herbert (Eng) 16.65, 5 Festus Igbinoghene (Nig) 16.65, 6 Andrew Murphy (Aus) 16.57, 7 Vernon Samuels (Eng) 16.45, 8 Paul Nioze (Sey) 16.25, 9 Matt Sweeney (Aus) 15.99, 10 Mohamed Zaki Sadri (Mal) 15.78, 11 Brian Wellman (Ber) 15.65. George Wright (Can) no valid jumps. The jumps by Igbinoghene, Sweeney and Zaki Sadri were wind-assisted.

SHOT (3 Feb): 1 Simon Williams (Eng) 18.54, 2 Adewale Olukoju (Nig) 18.48, 3 Paul Edwards (Wal) 18.17, 4 Werner Reiterer (Aus) 17.78, 5 John Minns (Aus) 17.49, 6 Abi Ekoku (Eng) 17.45, 7 Lorne Hilton (Can) 17.06, 8 Steve Whyte (Sco) 17.00, 9 Matt Simson (Eng) 16,89, 10 Rob Venier (Can) 16.87, 11 Courtney Ireland (NZ) 16.74, 12 Michalis Louca (Cyp) 16.25.

DISCUS (2 Feb): 1 Adewale Olukoju (Nig) 62.62, 2 Werner Reiterer (Aus) 61.56, 3 Paul Nandapi (Aus) 59.94, 4 Brad Cooper (Bah) 58.98, 5 Paul Mardle (Eng) 58.76, 6 Ray Lazdins (Can) 57.84, 7 Graham Savory (Eng) 57.44, 8 Darrin Morris (Sco) 56.10, 9 Rob McManus (Can) 53.66, 10 Mark Robinson (NZ) 53.64. Abi Ekoku (Eng) no valid throws.

HAMMER (27 Jan): 1 Sean Carlin (Aus) 75.66, 2 David Smith (Eng) 73.52, 3 Angus Cooper (NZ) 71.26, 4 Phil Spivey (Aus) 70.74, 5 Phil Jensen (NZ) 68.96, 6 Paul Head (Eng) 68.14, 7 Peter Baxevanis (Aus) 68.06, 8 Shane Peacock (Eng)

66.74, 9 Ian Maplethorpe (Can) 60.62, 10 Steve Whyte (Sco) 60.48, 11 Darren McFee (Can) 57.76.

JAVELIN (3 Feb): 1 Steve Backley (Eng) 86.02, 2 Mick Hill (Eng) 83.32, 3 Gavin Lovegrove (NZ) 81.66, 4 Nigel Bevan (Wal) 79.70, 5 Mike O'Rourke (NZ) 79.00, 6 Mark Roberson (Eng) 75.38, 7 John Stapylton-Smith (NZ) 72.80, 8 Justin Arop (Uga) 70.74, 9 Steve Feraday (Can) 68.20, 10 Mike Mahlovich (Can) 64.74, 11 Murray Keen (Aus) 65.64, 12 Christakis Telonis (Cyp) 62.36, 13 Jeffrey Danbe (Bot) 49.78.

DECATHLON (28-29 Jan): 1 Michael Smith (Can) 8,525 (10.85, 7.52w, 14.62, 2.05, 47.77, 14.34, 47.56, 4.70, 64.18, 4:24.06), 2 Simon Poelman (NZ) 8,207 (10.97, 7.62w, 15.64, 2.05, 51.13, 14.45, 44.72, 4.60, 57.36, 4:26.59), 3 Eugene Gilkes (Eng) 7,705 (11.01, 7.08, 14.19, 1.87, 47.64, 14.92w, 44.98, 4.20, 46.46, 4:17.96), 4 Alex Kruger (Eng) 7,663, 5 Chris Bradshaw (Aus) 7,402, 6 Richard Hesketh (Can) 7,274, 7 Garth Peet (Can) 7,245, 8 Duncan Mathieson (Sco) 7,149, 9 Stuart Andrews (Aus) 7,134, 10 Peter Henry (NZ) 7,071, 11 Terry Lomax (NZ) 6,995, 12 Ferdinand Nongkas (PNG) 5,869, 13 Homelo Vi (Ton) 5,858. Did not finish - Mark Bishop (Eng), Dean Smith (Aus).

WOMEN

100 METRES (28 Jan): 1 Merlene Ottey (Jam) 11.02, 2 Kerry Johnson (Aus) 11.17, 3 Pauline Davis (Bah) 11.20, 4 Stephanie Douglas (Eng) 11.39, 5 Sallyanne Short (Wal) 11.41, 6 Briar Toop (NZ) 11.46, 7 Simmone Jacobs (Eng) 11.53, 8 Paula Dunn (Eng) 11.55, 9 Oliver Acii (Uga) 11.65.

200 METRES (1 Feb): 1 Merlene Ottey (Jam) 22.76, 2 Kerry Johnson (Aus) 22.88, 3 Pauline Davis (Bah) 23.15, 4 Jennifer Stoute (Eng) 23.16, 5 Paula Dunn (Eng) 23.33, 6 Sallyanne Short (Wal) 23.35, 7 Kathy Sambell (Aus) 23.56, 8 Linda Keough (Eng) 23.66, 9 Oliver Acii (Uga) 24.14.

400 METRES (28 Jan): 1 Fatima Yusuf (Nig) 51.08, 2 Linda Keough (Eng) 51.63, 3 Charity Opara (Nig) 52.01, 4 Maree Holland (Aus) 52.68, 5 Jennifer Stoute (Eng) 53.44, 6 Angela Piggford (Eng) 53.45, 7 Gail Harris (Can) 54.24, 8 Cheryl Allen (Can) 54.36, 9 Mercy Addy (Gha) 57.01. Note: Holland nee Chapman.

800 METRES (1 Feb): 1 Diane Edwards (Eng) 2:00.25, 2 Ann Williams (Eng) 2:00.40, 3 Sharon Stewart (Aus) 2:00.87, 4 Wendy Old (Aus) 2:01.70, 5 Lorraine Baker (Eng) 2:01.77, 6 Gail Luke (Aus) 2:02.71, 7 Nicky Knapp (Can) 2:03.79, 8

Brit Lind-Petersen (Can) 2:07.40, 9 Toni Hodgkinson (NZ) 2:09.11. Note: Lind-Petersen nee McRoberts.

1500 METRES (3 Feb): 1 Angela Chalmers (Can) 4:08.41, 2 Chris Cahill (Eng) 4:08.75, 3 Bev Nicholson (Eng) 4:09.00, 4 Yvonne Murray (Sco) 4:09.54, 5 Lynne MacIntyre (Sco) 4:09.75, 6 Debbie Bowker (Can) 4:11.20, 7 Michelle Baumgartner (Aus) 4:12.74, 8 Shireen Bailey (Eng) 4:13.31, 9 Sarah Collins (Aus) 4:13.52, 10 Karen Hutcheson (Sco) 4:13.77, 11 Chrissie Pfitzinger (NZ) 4:17.36, 12 Robyn Meagher (Can) 4:28.51. Note: Cahill nee Boxer, MacIntyre nee MacDougall, Bailey nee Hassan.

3000 METRES (28 Jan): 1 Angela Chalmers (Can) 8:38.38, 2 Yvonne Murray (Sco) 8:39.46, 3 Liz McColgan (Sco) 8:47.66, 4 Karen Hutcheson (Sco) 8:48.72, 5 Carolyn Schuwalow (Aus) 8:53.89, 6 Ruth Partridge (Eng) 8:59.77, 7 Leah Pells (Can) 9:02.29, 8 Jenny Lund (Aus) 9:03.43, 9 Lizanne Bussieres (Can) 9:04.59, 10 Anne Hare (NZ) 9:15.49, 11 Alison Wyeth (Eng) 9:23.12, 12 Sonia Barry (NZ) 9:25.91, 13 Brenda Walker (IoM) 9:36.90, 14 Annie Kagona (Mlw) 9:51.41, 15 Khanyisile Lukhele (Swa) 10:15.63. Did not finish - Nicky Morris (Eng), Chrissie Pfitzinger (NZ). Note: McColgan nee Lynch, Partridge nee Smeeth.

10,000 METRES (2 Feb): 1 Liz McColgan (Sco) 32:23.56, 2 Jill Hunter (Eng) 32:33.21, 3 Barbara Moore (NZ) 32:44.73, 4 Carole Rouillard (Can) 32:49.36, 5 Jane Ngotho (Ken) 32:54.20, 6 Sue Hobson (Aus) 32:54.92, 7 Jenny Lund (Aus) 32:58.68, 8 Jane Shields (Eng) 32:59.42, 9 Lizanne Bussieres (Can) 33:16.65, 10 Sue Lee (Can) 33:22.63, 11 Anne Audain (NZ) 33:40.13, 12 Karen McLeod (Sco) 34:24.71, 13 Anne Hannam (NZ) 34:42.62. Did not finish - Wendy Sly (Eng), Susan Tooby (Wal).

MARATHON (31 Jan): 1 Lisa Martin (Aus) 2:25:28, 2 Tani Ruckle (Aus) 2:33.15, 3 Angie Pain (Eng) 2:36:35, 4 Sally Ellis (Eng) 2:37:46, 5 Debbie Noy (Eng) 2:39:01, 6 Andri Avraam (Cyp) 2:39:19, 7 Helen Moros (NZ) 2:39:36, 8 Odette Lapierre (Can) 2:41:36, 9 Sheila Catford (Sco) 2:43:38, 10 Sandra Mewett (Ber) 2:46:21, 11 Lynn Harding (Sco) 2:47:24, 12 Moira O'Neill (NI) 2:48:52, 13 Liesl Hunter (Zim) 2:52:52; 14 Maryse Justin-Pyndiah (Mau) 2:55:50. Did not finish - Margaret Buist (NZ).

10 KILOMETRES WALK (2 Feb): 1 Kerry Saxby (Aus) 45:03, 2 Anne Judkins (NZ) 47:03, 3 Lisa Langford (Eng) 47:23, 4 Lorraine Jachno (Aus) 47:35, 5 Janice McCaffrey (Can) 48:26, 6 Bev Hayman (Aus) 48:50, 7 Helen Elleker (Eng) 49:51, 8 Alison Baker (Can) 50:54. Did not finish - Ann Peel (Can), Betty Sworowski

(Eng). Disqualified - Jane Jackson (NZ). Note: Lorraine Jachno was the wife of Andrew Jachno, 9th (1982) and 2nd (1990) in the 30km walk.

100 METRES HURDLES (2 Feb): 1 Kay Morley (Wal) 12.91, 2 Sally Gunnell (Eng) 13.12, 3 Lesley-Ann Skeete (Eng) 13.31, 4 Jane Flemming (Aus) 13.37, 5 Glynis Nunn-Cearns (Aus) 13.47, 6 Jenny Laurendet (Aus) 13.52, 7 Judith Robinson (NI) 13.55, 8 Helen Pirovano (NZ) 13.61. Disqualified - Louise Fraser (Eng). Note: Nunn-Cearns formerly Nunn, Laurendet nee Low, Robinson nee Rodgers.

400 METRES HURDLES (29 Jan): 1 Sally Gunnell (Eng) 55.38, 2 Debbie Flintoff-King (Aus) 56.00, 3 Jenny Laurendet (Aus) 56.74, 4 Wendy Cearns (Eng) 57.53, 5 Elaine McLaughlin (NI) 57.54, 6 Lorraine Hanson (Eng) 57.58, 7 Rosey Edeh (Can) 57.86, 8 Donalda Duprey (Can) 58.31, 9 Rose Tata-Muya (Ken) 59.93.

4 x 100 METRES RELAY (3 Feb): 1 Australia (Cathy Freeman, Monique Dunstan, Kathy Sambell, Kerry Johnson) 43.87, 2 England (Stephanie Douglas, Jennifer Stoute, Simmone Jacobs, Paula Dunn) 44.15, 3 Nigeria (Beatrice Utondu, Fatima Yusuf, Charity Opara, Chioma Ajunwa) 44.67, 4 New Zealand (Helen Pirovano, Michelle Seymour, Jayne Moffitt, Bev Peterson) 44.77. Canada (France Gareau, Nadine Halliday, Katie Anderson, Stacy Bowen) disqualified. 5 teams competed.

4 x 400 METRES RELAY (3 Feb): 1 England (Angela Piggford, Jennifer Stoute, Sally Gunnell, Linda Keough) 3:28.08, 2 Australia (Maree Holland, Sharon Stewart, Sue Andrews, Debbie Flintoff-King) 3:30.74, 3 Canada (Rosey Edeh, France Gareau, Cheryl Allen, Gail Harris) 3:33.26, 4 New Zealand (Jill Cockram, Jayne Moffitt, Carlene Dillmore, Toni Hodgkinson) 3:39.64. 4 teams competed.

HIGH JUMP (2 Feb): 1 Tania Murray (NZ) 1.88, 2 Janet Boyle (NI) 1.88, 3 Tracy Phillips (NZ) 1.88, 4= Vanessa Ward (Aus) & Trudy Woodhead (NZ) 1.88, 6 Jenny Talbot (Aus) 1.88, 7 Deann Bopf (Aus) 1.85, 8 Leslie Estwick (Can) 1.85, 9= Jeannie Cockcroft (Can) & Diana Davies (Eng) 1.80, 11= Linda Cameron (Can) & Nkechi Madubuko (Nig) 1.80, 13 Sharon Hutchings (NI) 1.80, 14 Michelle Wheeler (Eng) 1.75, 15 Jo Jennings (Eng) 1.70. Dionne Gardner (Nor) failed at opening height (1.65). Note: Ward nee Browne, Woodhead nee Painter; Hutchings, nee McPeake, was the wife of Tim Hutchings, 14th (1982) and 3rd (1986) at 5000, 12th (1990) at 10,000.

218

LONG JUMP (2 Feb): 1 Jane Flemming (Aus) 6.78, 2 Beatrice Utondu (Nig) 6.65, 3 Fiona May (Eng) 6.55, 4 Chioma Ajunwa (Nig) 6.48, 5 Jayne Moffitt (NZ) 6.46, 6 Shonel Ferguson (Bah) 6.41, 7 Mary Berkeley (Eng) 6.33, 8 Sandra Priestley (Aus) 6.32, 9 Kim Hagger (Eng) 6.27, 10 Sharon Jaklofsky-Smith (Aus) 6.25, 11 Lisa Ball (NZ) 6.21, 12 Euphemia Huggins (Tri) 6.19, 13 Donna Smellie (Can) 5.73. The jumps by Utondu, Ferguson, Berkeley, Jaklofsky-Smith and Ball were wind-assisted. Note: Moffitt nee Mitchell.

SHOT (29 Jan): 1 Myrtle Augee (Eng) 18.48, 2 Judy Oakes (Eng) 18.43, 3 Yvonne Hanson-Nortey (Eng) 16.00, 4 Melody Torcolacci (Can) 15.49, 5 Nicole Carkeek (Aus) 15.13, 6 Christine King (NZ) 14.40, 7 Janice Maxwell (NZ) 14.09. 7 competed.

DISCUS (28 Jan): 1 Lisa-Marie Vizaniari (Aus) 56.38, 2 Jackie McKernan (NI) 54.86, 3 Astra Vitols (Aus) 53.84, 4 Liz Ryan (NZ) 53.70, 5 Janette Picton (Eng) 53.14, 6 Jane Aucott (Eng) 52.20, 7 Vanessa French (Aus) 51.20, 8 Sharon Andrews (Eng) 51.18, 9 Michelle Brotherton (Can) 49.64, 10 Siololovau Ikavuka (Ton) 48.62. Note: Vitols nee Etienne. After retiring from discus-throwing Janette Picton took up distance-running and was 24th in the 1996 London Marathon in 2:51:26!

JAVELIN (1 Feb): 1 Tessa Sanderson (Eng) 65.72, 2 Sue Howland (Aus) 61.18, 3 Kate Farrow (Aus) 58.98, 4 Sharon Gibson (Eng) 57.26, 5 Nicky Emblem (Sco) 56.96, 6 Caroline White (Wal) 55.18, 7 Kaye Nordstrom (NZ) 53.52, 8 Kirsten Smith (NZ) 52.34, 9 Cheryl Coker (Can) 50.10, 10 Matilda Kisava (Tan) 49.20, 11 Iammo Gapi Launa (PNG) 49.08, 12 Schola Mujjawamaria (Uga) 46.48, 13 Valerie Tulloch (Can) 45.76, 14 Lorri LaRowe (Can) 45.16.

HEPTATHLON (27-28 Jan): 1 Jane Flemming (Aus) 6,695 (13.21, 1.82, 13.76, 23.62w, 6.57, 49.28, 2:12.53), 2 Sharon Jaklofsky-Smith (Aus) 6,115 (13.54, 1.76, 13.16, 24.58w, 6.42w, 39.94, 2:19.34), 3 Judy Simpson (Eng) 6,085 (13.39, 1.73, 14.89, 25.29, 6.03w, 39.42, 2:14.59), 4 Joanne Mulliner (Eng) 5,913, 5 Joanne Henry (NZ) 5,764, 6 Jocelyn Millar-Cubit (Aus) 5,762, 7 Catherine Bond (Can) 5,760, 8 Donna Smellie (Can) 5,584, 9 Cassandra Kelly (NZ) 5,244, 10 Lyn Osmers (NZ) 5,222, 11 Iammo Gapi Launa (PNG) 4,833, 12 Marie-Lourdes Appadoo (Mau) 4,740. Did not finish - Kim Hagger (Eng), Shona Urquhart (Sco). Note: Appadoo nee Ally Samba.

16.

Sepeng's medal is the 52nd
and the colour bar is broken

CENTENNIAL STADIUM, VICTORIA B.C., CANADA
22-28 AUGUST 1994

THE 1994 GRAND PRIX SERIES had begun on 15 May with $2.2 million of prize-money as the major earning opportunity of the year for the World's foremost athletes. Leading up to the finals in Paris on 10 September, there were to be 15 meetings in Brazil, the USA, Italy, France, Switzerland, England, Sweden, Norway, Monaco, Germany and Belgium, plus nine Grand Prix II meetings and nine major international invitation meetings. World Championships were being staged during the year at cross-country (Budapest in March), road relays (Greece in April), in junior events (Portugal in July) and at the half-marathon (Norway in September). The USA met Africa in a match at Durham, North Carolina, in early July. The Goodwill Games were in St Petersburg, in Russia, later the same month. The European Cup final was in Birmingham in June, leading on to the World Cup final - involving teams representing Africa, the Americas, Asia, Europe, Germany, Great Britain, Oceania and the USA - in London in September. Oh, and of course there were the European Championships in Helsinki on 7-14 August.

    The wonder of it all is that in spite of this fraught itinerary there were still plenty of athletes willing and able to go to Victoria, British Columbia, for the Commonwealth Games, starting on 22 August. Linford Christie and Colin Jackson, who had both won European titles in Helsinki, were among those to defy jet-lag and fly on to Canada direct from the Grand Prix meeting in Brussels on 19 August. Zambia's ex-World champion at 400 hurdles, Samuel Matete, cut things even finer by winning a Grand Prix race in Cologne on 21 August, resolving financial differences with his national federation, and still managing to turn up in Victoria in time for his qualifying heat three days later. Remarkably, and gratifyingly, 53 of the 70 eligible countries sent teams totalling 478 men and 244 women. Newly-integrated South Africa was warmly welcomed back after a 36-year absence; but India, the most populous country of all with 57 per cent of the Commonwealth's 1,500 million people, failed to put in an appearance, even though they had originally entered 17 athletes.

The World Championships, first held in 1983, were now taking place every two years and eight Commonwealth competitors had won titles in 1993. Linford Christie, Frankie Fredericks, Colin Jackson and Sally Gunnell were in Victoria, but the other four weren't. The Kenyan administrators were again in dispute with some of their overseas-based champions and Paul Ruto (800), Ismael Kirui (5000) and Moses Kiptanui (steeplechase) were not selected. Jamaica's Merlene Ottey preferred to run in Gothenburg and Copenhagen, rather than defend her Commonwealth sprint titles. Christie, Gunnell, Kenya's William Tanui (800) and Matthew Birir (steeplechase), and Canada's Mark McKoy (110 hurdles) had won Olympic titles in Barcelona in 1992, but Tanui and Birir had also fallen foul of officialdom and McKoy had taken up Austrian citizenship.

Victoria, scenically situated in Vancouver Island, off the West coast of mainland British Columbia, was a marvellously hospitable and congenial venue with a population of only 283,000, of whom 13,000 had volunteered their services to help with the Games. Stately buildings presided over the Inner Harbour waterfront and the city streets were broad and the traffic unhurried, though the athletics stadium on the University of Victoria campus in the suburban Gordon Head area had a distinctly makeshift look to it. The spectator capacity had been increased to 35,000 with the installation of temporary seating, but there was a disconcertingly spartan precariousness about the main stand which made its predecessors at Meadowbank and Mount Smart seem positively lavish by comparison. In the event, nothing of consequence went awry and the meeting was conducted to everyone's general satisfaction, though it was not as well attended as could have been expected.

221

There was only one final, the hammer, on Monday 22 August and it produced mixed fortunes for the Carlin family from Australia. Sean, the defending champion, won again, but younger brother Paul failed to register a valid throw and so was not placed at all. The first and second rounds of the men's 100 served to reduce the number of participants from 61 to 16, and the qualities of the track were proven in the process as Christie ran 10.02 and Fredericks 10.04. The next day they were quicker in the semi-finals as Christie won the first of them in 9.98 and Fredericks the second in a wind-aided 10.01. Then the 34-year-old Christie continued his imperious form in the final, winning with a time of 9.91, which only the Americans, Leroy Burrell and Carl Lewis, had ever beaten in acceptable circumstances, while 2nd place went most surprisingly to the US-based Horace Dove-Edwin, from Sierra Leone, who improved from a pre-Games best of 10.25 to 10.02. Unfortunately, it was far too good to be true and subsequent drug-testing revealed his use of the anabolic steroid, stanozolol, as a result of which he was banned from competition. There was particular cause for grievance on the part of Damien Marsh, from Goondoowindi, Queensland, who had equalled his national record of 10.19 in the same semi-final as Dove-Edwin but had been eliminated in 5th place.

The other finals on Tuesday 23 August were at 100 for women, 400 for men and women, the men's steeplechase and 110 hurdles, the women's 3000 and discus, and completion of the heptathlon. In the women's 100 Mary Onyali, of Nigeria, became the first African woman champion in the sprints with some ease in 11.06 after an 11.03 semi-final which was to rank 7th fastest in the World for the year, and the heptathlon was a rather more competitive affair. Jane Flemming, the silver-medallist in 1986 and champion in 1990, had led overnight by 47pts from the Canadian, Catherine Bond-Mills, and the contest seemed to be strictly between the two of them. Instead, England's Denise Lewis began the second day by narrowing the margin with a 6.44 long jump, and she then launched a colossal javelin throw of 53.68, which improved her best by over five metres and took her into the lead. She managed to stay within the necessary five seconds of Flemming in the closing 800 and won by eight points. In 1986 Flemming had lost by half that margin to Judy Simpson, also of Birchfield Harriers and England.

Charles Gitonga, of Kenya, was a surprise winner of the 400 from the outside lane, ahead of the flamboyant US-educated Du'aine Ladejo, of England, and though he finished in last place 22-year-old Bobang Phiri made his mark as the first black South African to take part in a Commonwealth Games final. The women's 400 also made history, and on two counts, because Cathy Freeman became the first aboriginal Australian woman to win an individual Games title, and both she and the other medallists, defending chamopion Fatima Yusuf (Nigeria) and World Championships bronze-medallist Sandie Richards (Jamaica), at last broke Marilyn Neufville's Games record from 1970. Colin Jackson precisely repeated his performance of Auckland, equalling his Games record of 13.08 to win the high hurdles, and all of the first four were from the home countries with another aboriginal Australian, Kyle Vander-Kuyp, next to finish, as he had been in 1990.

The steeplechase final provided the first real test for the Kenyan "B" team selections made by Kip Keino, and any illusions that the opposition may have harboured about having an easy ride were promptly dispelled. Johnstone Kipkoech and Gideon Chirchir, only ranked eighth and ninth at home, ran away from everybody else and were both six seconds or so inside the Games record, though there was some consolation for the former champion, Graeme Fell, in getting a bronze medal in his fourth Games appearance at the age of 35. Kipkocch's selection was particularly inspired because he had not figured at all in the Kenyan championships and his previous best time dated from 1991, but he certainly did not lack for experience: he had run his first steeplechase race 11 years before at the age of 14! Two of the Kenyan teenagers in the women's 3000 started off at a breakneck speed, but the defending champion, Angela Chalmers, reeled them in before halfway and went on in solitary splendour to a scintillating victory in what turned out to be the 3rd fastest performance in the World during 1994. Both Chalmers and her runner-up, Robyn Meagher (pronounced "Marr"), lived in Victoria and they were ecstatically acclaimed by the crowd.

The women's discus was won by the largest margin ever of more than six metres, and not surprisingly so because Daniela Costian was by far the most able practitioner of the event yet to have taken part in the Games. As a Rumanian she had been a 60m-plus thrower since the age of 18 in 1983, but had been suspended for a drugs violation after placing 7th in the 1986

European Championships. In 1988 she had thrown 73.84, within a metre of the existing World record, but had defected soon after and had then been granted Australian citizenship in 1990. Curiously, she was not the first Rumanian-born women's discus champion at the Commonwealth Games, having been preceded by Canada's Carmen Ionesco in 1978, and the Australian team's coach for the throwing events in Victoria was also a Rumanian, Ion Zamfirache, who had ranked 12th best discus-thrower in the World in 1985 with 67.30.

Wednesday 24 August featured just three finals - men's 5000, women's 10,000 and shot - but activities still got under way at 9 a.m. to complete the decathlon. Peter Winter, of Australia, had led overnight and despite the early hour produced an excellent hurdles time of 14.47, but defending champion Michael Smith went ahead with a much superior discus throw and eventually retained his title with 252pts to spare. Former champions were also dominant in the women's shot, though the 1990 winner, Myrtle Augee, was beaten by her team-mate, Judy Oakes, whose win was her second in five Games appearances, and 3rd place went to the discus gold-medallist in Auckland, Lisa-Marie Vizaniari.

Yvonne Murray, of Scotland, had passed up a chance to run in the 3000 so that she could concentrate her attentions on an event, the 10,000 metres, which she had only attempted once before - and that had been nine years earlier. It might have seemed foolhardy to take on Elana Meyer, of South Africa, who was the Olympic silver-medallist at the distance and twice African champion, and who would be spurred on by the incentive of becoming South Africa's first Commonwealth champion since 1958, but it made for a riveting race. Meyer, with her pecking stride and eccentric manner of bobbing her head up and down as if in dire straits but still apparently smiling beatifically, picked up the pace in the last 10 laps and was shadowed all the way by Murray, much the taller and more composed, and when it came to the last lap Murray sprinted away quite easily. Her time was not exceptional, ranking 18th in the World for the year, and Meyer ran over a minute faster in London 17 days later, but it was a highly impressive performance by Murray and meant that Scotland had won the women's 10,000 title on each of the three occasions it had been contested. Liz McColgan, now concentrating on the marathon, was an absentee, recovering from injury.

The Kenyan plan at 5000 metres, for which they had selected none of their 10 fastest men of the year, was presumably to set it up for the 18-year-old World junior cross-country champion, Philip Mosima, but it proved to be over-ambitious. The three Kenyans shared the pace until the last kilometre, though by then it had slipped to a 13:34 schedule, and in a hectic last-lap sprint Rob Denmark was the quickest of a trio of Englishmen and the African challenge came for once from Zimbabwe, with Philemon Hanneck 2nd.

Thursday 25 August was given over to the two walking events round a 2.5km circuit of Beacon Hill Park, close to the city centre. The men's 30km race began at 7 a.m. with Tim Berrett, the English-born Canadian who had placed 7th in the previous year's World Championships 50km, as the local favourite and the 36-year-old Australian Institute of Sport staff coach, Simon Baker, attempting to regain the title he had won in 1986. Berrett and the New Zealander, Scott Nelson, led until the last three laps when the Welsh-born hairdresser, Nick A'Hern, and not Baker, came through to take 1st place for Australia. The women's race was won again by Kerry Saxby (now Saxby-Junna), who like Simon Baker was employed at the Australian Institute of Sport where in her role of tour-guide she presumably maintained a more sedate pace than when she was racing.

Ten finals were held on Friday 26 August: the 200s, 800s and 400 hurdles for men and women, the men's high jump, long jump and discus and the women's javelin. With Christie having already returned to Europe to resume Grand Prix racing, only Frankie Fredericks of the 100 finalists was involved at 200 and he won in a time of 19.97, which was to be faster than anyone except Michael Johnson in a non-altitude race during 1994. The women's 200 intriguingly brought together the champions at 100 and 400, and the wonderfully lissome Freeman became Australia's seventh winner of the title - but the first since 1978 - with a national record of 22.25. Only Gwen Torrence, Irina Privalova and Merlene Ottey ran faster in 1994, and it was obviously a bit of a shame that Ottey (who had recorded 22.51 in Gothenburg two nights earlier) wasn't there, but it was Freeman's sixth race in four days and she may well have still had something in hand.

At 800 there were again leading Kenyans absent, but there was no doubting the talent of Patrick Konchellah - younger brother of the twice World champion, Billy Konchellah - who had run 1:44.24 in Germany the previous month and won the Brussels Grand Prix race on the eve of the Games. The other Kenyan finalist, Sammy Serem, led the first lap (no surprise to anyone!) and South Africa's Hezekiel Sepeng was in front along the final back straight, but Konchellah came through for Kenya's fifth Commonwealth gold at the distance. Sepeng, who had placed 5th in the 1993 World Championships at the age of 19, became the first black South African medallist in the Commonwealth Games, and Savieri Ngidhi won Zimbabwe's second medal in three days. At the previous year's World Championships seven of the eight finalists at 800 had been from the Commonwealth, but only Sepeng and the enigmatic Scot, Tom McKean, were also in the Victoria final. McKean, 2nd in 1986, was 7th in 1990 and 8th this time. All the drama and sensation of the women's 800 had been played out before the race was even run, with the defending champion, Diane Modahl (nee Edwards), sent home from Victoria following results of a drug test earlier in the summer, and so whatever followed was bound to be an anti-climax. The winning time was the slowest since 1978, but it provided Inez Turner, a college student in the USA, with Jamaica's first Commonwealth win at any distance further than 400 metres.

Sally Gunnell had won the 100 hurdles in Edinburgh and the 400 hurdles in Auckland. Since then she had become the pre-eminent exponent of this relatively new event for women, and by the time the Games in Victoria came round she was World and Olympic champion and World record-holder. She won, and she broke the Games record, but she stuttered a bit and the margin over Deon Hemmings, of Jamaica, was no more than three metres or so. The men's event was taken, as expected, by Samuel Matete, and it was the first success for Zambia in the Games since it was established as a republic in 1964, though Edna Maskell had won the 80m hurdles for Northern Rhodesia in 1954. Either England or Australia had provided the women's javelin champion at every Games from 1958 onwards, and as there was no Tessa Sanderson or Fatima Whitbread on this occasion it was the turn of Australia and Louise McPaul in a fairly nondescript event. The men's long-jump title was retained for Nigeria by Obinna Eregbu, the African Games winner in 1993 and a student at Central Arizona University, in the USA, but it was also a somewhat disappointing competition after Eregbu had cleared 8.22 in the qualifying round two days earlier.

The men's high jump, by contrast, was equally as exciting as the Auckland battle of wits and wills between Nick Saunders and Dalton Grant. The protagonists in Victoria were Tim Forsyth, a 20-year-old 6ft 6in tall (1.98) Australian who had won Olympic bronze in Barcelona, and Steve Smith, a 21-year-old Liverpudlian who had been World junior champion in 1992 and World senior bronze-medallist within a year. Both failed three times at 2.34 and once more at their extra jump at the same height; both cleared 2.32 and then failed again at 2.34; and eventually Forsyth cleared 2.32 and Smith didn't. The bronze in a high-calibre competition went to Geoff Parsons, competing in his fourth Games for Scotland and winning his third medal with a personal best 2.31. The discus was another close affair as Austrian-born Werner Reiterer, of Australia, threw 62.76 in the third round and Nigeria's defending champion, Adewale Olukoju, responded with identical throws of 62.46 in rounds five and six. Olukoju had won from Reiterer in 1990, and 3rd place went to England's Bob Weir, returning to the Games after a 12-year absence, having won the hammer in Brisbane in 1982.

The finals for Saturday 27 August were the 10,000 and pole vault for men and 100 hurdles, high jump and long jump for women, but the day began with the women's marathon at 7 a.m. This was held on a predominantly flat course winding through the main streets of the city, and with only 16 runners starting - and none of them in the forefront of World class - it did not offer much prospect of being a spectacle. In fact, it was an excellent race with the French-Canadians, Carole Rouillard and Lizanne Bussieres, taking the first two places. For both of them it was their third Games: Rouillard, only 5ft 1in tall (1.53), had been 8th and 4th at 10,000 in Edinburgh and Auckland; Bussieres, a doctor of medicine, had been 4th in the Edinburgh marathon and 9th at 3000 and 10,000 in Auckland. The oldest woman competitor at the Games also scored a personal triumph - Pauline Vea, 38, from the Friendly Islands of Tonga, improved her previous best from 3hrs 19mins to 2:56:59.

The 10,000 began in startling fashion with Daniel Komen, the lanky 18-year-old Kenyan who had won the World junior titles at 5000 and 10,000 the previous month, tearing off round the first lap in under 58sec and leading after a kilometre (26min pace!) by the length of the straight. Presumably, it was all part of the Kenyan Grand Design because when

Komen began to tire his team-mate, Lameck Aguta, took up the running and went on to win rather easily. Apart from Komen's impetuosity the race was undistinguished: Aguta's winning time was only the 118th fastest in the World in 1994, and even at this mediocre level no runners from the home countries were within half-a-minute of him. There were medals for Zimbabwe (again) and Zambia, and the defending champion, Eamonn Martin, was a distant 6th, one place ahead of Ramachandran Murusamy, who gave the hosts for 1998, Malaysia, some cause for modest celebration by breaking the national record. Komen eventually came in 9th, but the experience was to stand him in good stead

For once the men's pole vault had a genuine World-class performer in the person of Okkie Brits, the 21-year-old 6ft 6in (1.98) tall South African who had taken the Commonwealth record up to 5.85, but the competition was a let-down in the full meaning of the word. Brits came in at 5.50 and missed on all of his three attempts and so was never actually in direct confrontation with the unexpected 20-year-old winner from Wales, Neil Winter, who was the only one to clear 5.40 and who then failed at 5.55. The women's high jump was much more interesting with Alison Inverarity, the svelte daughter of a legendary Australian Test cricketer, winning from South Africa's Charmaine Weavers after both had cleared 1.94. There was another Australian gold in the women's long jump as Nicole Boegman, whose previous Games appearance was in 8th place in 1986, won from England's Nigerian-born Yinka Idowu, a massively talented athlete who never was to realise her potential because of the demands of medical studies. There was a first ever win for Jamaica in the 100 hurdles through Michelle Freeman, ahead of the entrancing English duo, Jackie Agyepong and Samantha Farquharson, who had both - for reasons best known to themselves - had their thighs tattooed specially for the occasion. Best not to dwell on that too long.

The athletics events closed on Sunday 28 August with nine finals: 1500, triple jump, shot and javelin for men; 1500 for women; and the four relays; and to start the proceedings at 7 a.m. the men's marathon. Among the 30 starters in that opening event were 16 Africans, but there was no doubt that Australia's Steve Moneghetti, 3rd in 1986 and 2nd in 1990, was the favourite. He fulfilled expectations with a performance of devastating mastery on an overcast and occasionally wet morning - gradually increasing his pace from 16:27 for the opening 5km to 14:58 for the stretch between 35km and 40km and finishing more than three minutes ahead of his team-mate, Sean Quilty, who had the satisfaction of improving his personal best and completing the first 1-2 by the same country in a Commonwealth Games men's marathon. It was a good day, too, for the stragglers because national records were set by runners from Antigua, St Vincent and the Falkland Islands.

Jonathan Edwards had safely qualified for the triple jump final the previous day, but the man who so surprisingly beat him four years earlier, Marios Hadjiandreou, had fallen well short at 15.89. Edwards, being the pragmatist that he is, no doubt did not take it for granted that the gold was now his, and yet it must have still been a bit of a shock when his fellow-countryman, Julian Golley, opened with a personal best 17.03 and Bermuda's Brian Wellman cleared 17.00. Edwards eventually reached 17.00 in the fifth round to get the silver ahead of Wellman on the strength of their third best jumps. The triple jump seems to favour smaller countries, and Dominica's Jerome Romain was 4th at 16.61 (though he had cleared a wind-assisted 17.05 in qualifying) and Vissen Moonegan set a national record of 16.35 for Mauritius in reaching the final. Two personal bests earned Matt Simson, of England, the shot title, and the javelin was entirely an exercise in déjà vu because the first four - Backley, Hill, Lovegrove and Bevan - had also been the first four in Auckland.

Canada's formidable quartet of Donovan Bailey, Carlton Chambers, Glenroy Gilbert and Bruny Surin won the 4 x 100, which was some consolation for Bailey, already an immensely promising 10.03 man at 100, who had controversially been left out of the individual event. Nigeria's women also broke the Games record at 4 x 100 in becoming the first country other than Australia or England to win a women's sprint relay, except for Canada's success in the anomalous 660 yards event of 1934. England won both 4 x 400 relays but only as a result of Australia's Cathy Freeman getting disqualified for obstructing the Nigerian runner, Fatima Yusuf.

The 1500 finals were interesting, but no more than that. Reuben Chesang, Kenya's 7th fastest man of the year, justified Kip Keino's faith in him by becoming only the second Kenyan (after Keino) to win the event. Kelly Holmes, who had been an English schools' champion as a teenager but had then been lost to the sport until the Army revived her career, won the women's race in slowish time but stylish manner.

On the day that the Commonwealth Games came to a close a Grand Prix II meeting was taking place at Rieti, in Italy, where the winners included Roger Black at 400, Kenya's Benson Koech (800) and Atoi Boru (1500), and Colin Jackson at 110 hurdles, while Linford Christie was 2nd at 100. At the Grand Prix meeting in Berlin two days later on 30 August, the two Britons were joined by eight other new Commonwealth champions - Donovan Bailey, Patrick Konchellah, Samuel Matete, Tim Forsyth, Steve Backley, Angela Chalmers, Nicole Boegman and Daniela Costian. In a diminishing World how much longer could the Commonwealth Games maintain an honourable place?

Postscript: Despite the drugs a spirit of innocence still survives

There had been the occasional drugs-related issues in the past at the Commonwealth Games, but 1994 was, sadly, the year that the sordid business caught up with them. Diane Modahl and her shot-putter team-mate, Paul Edwards, were both sent home after the results were announced of earlier drug tests. Horace Dove-Edwin was disqualified for the use of steroids, and the Jamaican hurdler, Robert Foster, was also struck from the results for the lesser offence of using a banned ephedrine stimulant. In total, 10 current or former Games medallists had now received some form of ban over the years as a result of drugs-testing, and whether or not this was an indication that abuse was widespread was really no more than a matter of guesswork. Mrs Modahl fought her four-year ban vigorously and was reinstated in 1996 when her test was declared to have been unreliable. Edwards was eventually banned for life.

Of course, these matters grabbed the headlines, but the most striking memory of those Victoria Games for me is very different. One day Kip Keino came up to the BBC radio commentary position high in the grandstand to be interviewed, and it was fascinating to listen to the great man talking about Kenyan athletics and about the orphanage which he had set up and which he managed. Afterwards, in casual conversation I asked him whether by any chance he knew what had become of Nyandika Maiyoro, that revelationary barefooted runner I had first seen at the AAA

Championships 40 years before, and to my astonishment and delight Kip replied with a broad smile, "He is here!" It transpired that Kip had invited three of the pioneering Kenyan team of 1954 - Maiyoro, quarter-miler Charles Musembi and half-miler Kiptalam Keter - to return to Canada as special guests, together with Archie Evans, the former colonial commissioner who had managed the first Kenyan athletes to go abroad and who deserves credit as one of the architects of the country's athletics success.

A couple of days later, just as I was leaving the stadium after the competition had finished, I met a group of Kenyan officials and asked whether Nyandika Maiyoro was with them. "Why, this is he!" responded one of the group, pointing to the balding portly chap by his side. It was a nostalgic meeting as I told Nyandika Maiyoro how deep an impression he had made on me as a youth all those years ago, and he - clearly amazed and obviously pleased that anyone should remember him after all this time - excitedly drew his colleagues around him to relate the tale of this bizarre encounter with a strange and voluble Englishman.

RESULTS 1994

MEN

100 METRES (23 Aug): 1 Linford Christie (Eng) 9.91, 2 Michael Green (Jam) 10.05, 3 Frankie Fredericks (Nam) 10.06, 4 Ato Boldon (Tri) 10.07, 5 Glenroy Gilbert (Can) 10.11, 6 Olapade Adeniken (Nig) 10.11, 7 Gus Nketia (NZ) 10.42. Horace Dove-Edwin (SL), originally 2nd in 10.02, disqualified after a positive drugs test. Note: Nketia ran in the 1990 Games for Ghana.

200 METRES (26 Aug): 1 Frankie Fredericks (Nam) 19.97, 2 John Regis (Eng) 20.25, 3 Daniel Effiong (Nig) 20.40, 4 Damien Marsh (Aus) 20.54, 5 Terry Williams (Eng) 20.62, 6 Oluyemi Kayode (Nig) 20.64, 7 Steve Brimacombe (Aus) 20.67, 8 Troy Douglas (Ber) 20.71.

400 METRES (23 Aug): 1 Charles Gitonga (Ken) 45.00, 2 Du'aine Ladejo (Eng) 45.11, 3 Sunday Bada (Nig) 45.45, 4 Paul Greene (Aus) 45.50, 6 Patrick Delice (Tri) 45.89, 7 Eswort Coombes (StV) 45.96, 8 Bobang Phiri (SA) 46.35.

800 METRES (26 Aug): 1 Patrick Konchellah (Ken) 1:45.18, 2 Hezekiel Sepeng (SA) 1:45.76, 3 Savieri Ngidhi (Zim) 1:46.06, 4 Craig Winrow (Eng) 1:46.91, 5 Brendan Hanigan (Aus) 1:47.24, 6 Sammy Serem (Ken) 1:47.30, 7 Martin Steele (Eng) 1:48.04, 8 Tom McKean (Sco) 1:50.81.

1500 METRES (28 Aug): 1 Reuben Chesang (Ken) 3:36.70, 2 Kevin Sullivan (Can) 3:36.78, 3 John Mayock (Eng) 3:37.22, 4 Whaddon Nieuwoudt (SA) 3:37.96, 5 Julius Kipkoech (Ken) 3:38.10, 6 Brian Treacy (NI) 3:38.93, 7 Steve Green (Jam) 3:39;19, 8 Kevin McKay (Eng) 3:39.72, 9 Julius Achon (Uga) 3:40.10, 10 Graham Hood (Can) 3:41.23, 11 Gareth Brown (Sco) 3:42.66, 12 David Strang (Sco) 3:48.70.

5000 METRES (24 Aug): 1 Rob Denmark (Eng) 13:23.00, 2 Philemon Hanneck (Zim) 13:23.20, 3 John Nuttall (Eng) 13:23.54, 4 Jon Brown (Eng) 13:23.96, 5 Philip Mosima (Ken) 13:24.07, 6 Jonathan Wyatt (NZ) 13:35.46, 7 Paul Kipsambu (Ken) 13:39.53, 8 Justin Hobbs (Wal) 13:45.53, 9 Laban Chege (Ken) 13:47.34, 10 Jeff Schiebler (Can) 13:50.26, 11 Jason Bunston (Can) 13:50.65, 12 Sipho Dlamini (Swa) 13:56.62, 13 Christian Weber (Can) 13:57.41, 14 Tendai Chimusasa (Zim) 13:59.36, 15 Dermot Donnelly (NI) 14:00.00.

10,000 METRES (27 Aug): 1 Lameck Aguta (Ken) 28:38.22, 2 Tendai Chimusasa (Zim) 28:47.72, 3 Fackson Nkandu (Zam) 28:51.72, 4 Martin Jones (Eng) 29:08.53, 5 Paul Fonseca (Can) 29:14.85, 6 Eamonn Martin (Eng) 29.15.81, 7 Ramachandran Murusamy (Mal) 29:30.19, 8 Paul Patrick (Aus) 29:35.95, 9 Daniel Komen (Ken) 29:37.91, 10 Chris Robison (Sco) 29:50.23, 11 Paul Clode (NZ) 29:50.93, 12 Paul McCloy (Can) 30:09.91, 13 Zachariah Ditetso (Bot) 30:14.87, 14 Isaac Simelane (Swa) 30:28.42, 15 Pamenos Ballantyne (StV) 31:06.70. Did not finish - Robbie Johnston (NZ), Thabiso Moqhali (Les), John Sherban (Sco).

MARATHON (28 Aug): 1 Steve Moneghetti (Aus) 2:11:49, 2 Sean Quilty (Aus) 2:14:57, 3 Mark Hudspith (Eng) 2:15:11, 4 Dale Rixon (Wal) 2:16:15, 5 Pat Carroll (Aus) 2:16:27, 6 Nicholas Kioko (Ken) 2:16:37, 7 Carey Nelson (Can) 2:16:52, 8 Colin Moore (Eng) 2:18:07, 9 Brian Deacon (Can) 2:18:46, 10 Zachariah Nyambaso (Ken) 2:18:51, 11 Elphas Sabelo Ginindza (Swa) 2:19:33, 12 Mothusi Tsiana (Bot) 2:20:00, 13 John Mwathiwa (Mlw) 2:20:11, 14 Ronald Mujuni (Uga) 2:20:37, 15 Owen Machelm (SA) 2:20:39, 16 Fritz Awdseb (Nam) 2:21:27, 17 Smartex Tambala (Mlw) 2:22:00, 18 Moses Matabane (Les) 2:22:03, 19 Thabiso Ralekhetla (Les) 2:22:04, 20 Benedict Ako (Tan) 2:22:12, 21 Paul Rotich (Ken) 2:23:20, 22 Cephas Matafi (Zim) 2:24:13, 23 Cordoy Simon (Ant) 2:31:49, 24 Dane Samuel (StV) 2:33:01, 25 Poulo Makhoahle (Les) 2:33:44, 26 Brett Forgesson (Ber) 2:34:23, 27 James Gombedza (Zim) 2:43:01, 28 Hugh Marsden (Fal) 2:43:31. Did not finish - Dave Buzza (Eng), Peter Maher (Can).

3000 METRES STEEPLECHASE (23 Aug): 1 Johnstone Kipkoech (Ken) 8:14.72, 2 Gideon Chirchir (Ken) 8:15.25, 3 Graeme Fell (Can) 8:23.28, 4 Chris Walker (Eng) 8:27.78, 5 Tom Buckner (Eng) 8:29.84, 6 Joel Bourgeois (Can) 8:31.19, 7 Justin Chaston (Wal) 8:32.20, 8 Paul Chemase (Ken) 8:35.31, 9 Godfrey Siamusiye (Zam) 8:41.83, 10 Spencer Duval (Eng) 8:49.08, 11 Shaun Creighton (Aus) 8:54.27, 12 Zeba Crook (Can) 8:57.24, 13 Terrance Armstrong (Ber) 9:06.99. Note: Tom Buckner was the brother of Jack Buckner, 2nd at 5000 in 1986 and 12th in 1990.

30 KILOMETRES WALK (25 Aug): 1 Nick A'Hern (Aus) 2:07:53, 2 Tim Berrett (Can) 2:08:22, 3 Scott Nelson (NZ) 2:09:10, 4 Darrell Stone (Eng) 2:11:30, 5 Martin St Pierre (Can) 2:11:51, 6 Simon Baker (Aus) 2:14:02, 7 Steve Partington (IoM) 2:14:15, 8 Craig Barrett (NZ) 2:14:19, 9 Chris Britz (SA) 2:14:28, 10 Justus Kavulanya (Ken) 2:14:37, 11 Stephen Akoi (Ken) 2:14:37, 12 Chris Maddocks (Eng) 2:18:14, 13 Mark Easton (Eng) 2:20:10, 14 Steve Taylor (IoM) 2:21:34. Did not finish - Martin Bell (Sco).

110 METRES HURDLES (23 Aug): 1 Colin Jackson (Wal) 13.08, 2 Tony Jarrett (Eng) 13.22, 3 Paul Gray (Wal) 13.54, 4 Andy Tulloch (Eng) 13.69, 5 Kyle Vander-Kuyp (Aus) 13.75, 6 Ken Campbell (Sco) 13.86, 7 Tim Kroeker (Can) 13.93. Robert Foster (Jam), originally 6th in 13.78, disqualified after a positive drugs test.

400 METRES HURDLES (26 Aug): 1 Samuel Matete (Zam) 48.67, 2 Gideon Biwott (Ken) 49.43, 3 Barnabas Kinyor (Ken) 49.50, 4 Gary Cadogan (Eng) 49.71, 5 Rohan Robinson (Aus) 49.76, 6 Ken Harnden (Zim) 50.02, 7 Peter Crampton (Eng) 50.37, 8 Ian Weakley (Jam) 51.25.

4 x 100 METRES RELAY (28 Aug): 1 Canada (Donovan Bailey, Carlton Chambers, Glenroy Gilbert, Bruny Surin) 38.39, 2 Australia (Shane Naylor, Tim Jackson, Paul Henderson, Damien Marsh) 38.88, 3 England (Jason John, Toby Box, Philip Goedluck, Terry Williams) 39.39, 4 Jamaica (Garth Robinson, Warren Johnson, John Mair, Leon Gordon) 39.44, 5 Scotland (Elliot Bunney, Ian Mackie, Jamie Henderson, Dougie Walker) 39.56, 6 Ghana (Christian Nsiah, Eric Nkansah-Appiah, Salaam Gariba, Nelson Boateng) 39.76, 7 Gambia (Abdurahman Jallow, Samuel Johnson, Ebrima Bojang, Abdoulieh Janneh) 41.54, 8 Botswana (Jwagamana Karesaza, Justice Dipeba, Kenneth Moima, Moatshe Molebatsi) 41.55. Note: Mark Smith ran the leadoff leg for England and Duncan Mathieson the leadoff leg for Scotland in the heats. Sierra Leone had originally qualified for the final (Denton Guy-Williams, Joslyn Thomas, Sanusi Turay, Horace Dove-Edwin) but were disqualified after the positive result of Dove-Edwin's drugs test and were replaced by Gambia.

4 x 400 METRES RELAY (28 Aug): 1 England (David McKenzie, Peter Crampton, Adrian Patrick, Du'aine Ladejo) 3:02.14, 2 Jamaica (Orville Taylor, Dennis Blake, Linval Laird, Garth Robinson) 3:02.32, 3 Trinidad & Tobago (Patrick Delice, Neil De Silva, Hayden Stephen, Ian Morris) 3:02.78, 4 Nigeria (Omokoro Alohan, Olapade Adeniken, Emmanuel Okoli, Sunday Bada) 3:03.06, 5 Australia (Simon Hollingsworth, Michael Joubert, Brett Callaghan, Paul Greene) 3:03.46, 6 South Africa (Herman de Jager, Arnaud Malherbe, Riaan Dempers, Bobang Phiri) 3:03.87, 7 Wales (Peter Maitland, Jamie Baulch, Paul Gray, Iwan Thomas) 3:07.80. Kenya (Abednigo Matilu, Gideon Biwott, Julius Chepkwony, Charles Gitonga) disqualified.

HIGH JUMP (26 Aug): 1 Tim Forsyth (Aus) 2.32, 2 Steve Smith (Eng) 2.32, 3 Geoff Parsons (Sco) 2.31, 4 Cory Siermachesky (Can) 2.28, 5 Dalton Grant (Eng) 2.28, 6 Lochsley Thomson (Aus) 2.28, 7= Richard Duncan (Can) & Brendan

Reilly (Eng) 2.25, 9 Ian Thompson (Bah) 2.25, 10 Loo Kum Zee (Mal) 2.15, 11 Marcus George (StL) 2.15, 12 Khemraj Naiko (Mau) 2.10.

POLE VAULT (27 Aug): 1 Neil Winter (Wal) 5.40, 2 Curtis Heywood (Can) 5.30, 3 James Miller (Aus) 5.30, 4 Fotis Stephani (Cyp) 5.30, 5 Mike Edwards (Eng) 5.20, 6 Andy Ashurst (Eng) 5.20, 7 Greg Halliday (Aus) 5.20, 8 Nick Buckfield (Eng) 5.20, 9 Jeff Miller (Can) 5.20, 10 Owen Clements (Can) 5.00, 11 Demingo Kapal (Bru) 4.20. Failed at opening heights - Riaan Botha (SA) 5.20, Okkie Brits (SA) 5.50, Adam Steinhardt (Aus) 5.00.

LONG JUMP (26 Aug): 1 Obinna Eregbu (Nig) 8.05, 2 David Culbert (Aus) 8.00, 3 Ian James (Can) 7.93, 4 Ayodele Aladefa (Nig) 7.93, 5 Fred Salle (Eng) 7.88, 6 Jai Taurima (Aus) 7.87, 7 Jerome Romain (Dom) 7.69, 8 Craig Hepburn (Bah) 7.65, 9 Benjamin Koech (Ken) 7.62, 10 Brian Thomas (Can) 7.59, 11 Ron Chambers (Jam) 7.53, 12 Andrew Owusu (Gha) 7.36. Note: the jumps by Ergebu, James and Romain were wind-assisted.

TRIPLE JUMP (28 Aug): 1 Julian Golley (Eng) 17.03, 2 Jonathan Edwards (Eng) 17.00, 3 Brian Wellman (Ber) 17.00, 4 Jerome Romain (Dom) 16.61, 5 Edrick Floreal (Can) 16.61, 6 Francis Agyepong (Eng) 16.33, 7 Ndabazihle Mdhlongwa (Zim) 16.02, 8 James Sabulei (Ken) 15.99, 9 Jacob Katonon (Ken) 15.96, 10 Andrew Murphy (Aus) 15.83, 11 Wikus Olivier (SA) 15.73, 12 Vissen Moonegan (Mau) 15.46.

SHOT (28 Aug): 1 Matt Simson (Eng) 19.49, 2 Courtney Ireland (NZ) 19.38, 3 Chima Ugwu (Nig) 19.26, 4 Carel le Roux (SA) 18.50, 5 Scott Cappos (Can) 18.35, 6 Burger Lambrechts (SA) 18.15, 7 Nigel Spratley (Eng) 17.96, 8 John Minns (Aus) 17.96, 9 Elias Louca (Cyp) 17.67, 10 Michalis Louca (Cyp) 17.41, 11 Peter Dajia (Can) 16.26, 12 Steve Whyte (Sco) 16.17, 13 Felix Hyde (Gha) 15.82, 14 Lee Wiltshire (Wal) 15.22. Note: Elias and Michalis Louca were brothers.

DISCUS (26 Aug): 1 Werner Reiterer (Aus) 62.76, 2 Adewale Olukoju (Nig) 62.46, 3 Bob Weir (Eng) 60.86, 4 Martin Swart (SA) 56.42, 5 Frits Potgieter (SA) 56.10, 6 Glen Smith (Eng) 55.84, 7 Ray Lazdins (Can) 55.60, 8 Darrin Morris (Sco) 54.98, 9 Brad Cooper (Bah) 54.22, 10 Kevin Brown (Eng) 54.06, 11 Richard Misterowicz (Can) 52.28, 12 Alex Stanat (Can) 51.90, 13 Muhammad Javed (Pak) 50.30.

HAMMER (22 Aug): 1 Sean Carlin (Aus) 73.48, 2 Paul Head (Eng) 70.18, 3 Peter Vivian (Eng) 69.80, 4 Michael Jones (Eng) 68.42, 5 Angus Cooper (NZ) 67,92, 6 Boris Stoikos (Can) 65.84, 7 John Stoikos (Can) 64.82, 8 Demetri Dionisopoulos

(Aus) 63.52, 9 Steve Whyte (Sco) 63.36, 10 Ian Maplethorpe (Can) 62.76, 11 Russell Devine (Sco) 61.9. Paul Carlin (Aus) no valid throws. Note: Sean and Paul Carlin were brothers, Boris and John Stoikos were brothers.

JAVELIN (28 Aug): 1 Steve Backley (Eng) 82.74, 2 Mick Hill (Eng) 81.84, 3 Gavin Lovegrove (NZ) 80.42, 4 Nigel Bevan (Wal) 80.38, 5 Louis Fouche (SA) 77.00, 6 Andrew Currey (Aus) 74.88, 7 Mark Roberson (Eng) 73.78, 8 Philip Spies (SA) 72.70, 9 Larry Steinke (Can) 68.14, 10 Graham Morfitt (Can) 66.96, 11 Louis Brault (Can) 66.76.

DECATHLON (23-24 Aug): 1 Michael Smith (Can) 8,326 (11.00, 6.94, 16.22, 1.98, 48.85, 14.82, 48.62, 5.10, 67.98, 4:47.38), 2 Peter Winter (Aus) 8,074 (10.79, 7.65, 13.68, 1.95, 47.95, 14.47, 41.08, 4.90, 60.40, 4:54.94) 3 Simon Shirley (Eng) 7,980 (10.89, 7.11, 14.16, 2.04, 48.90, 14.87, 38.38, 4.60, 63.80, 4:32.34), 4 Dean Smith (Aus) 7,926, 5 Doug Pirini (NZ) 7,840, 6 Rafer Joseph (Eng) 7,663, 7 Alex Kruger (Eng) 7,640, 8 Jamie Quarry (Sco) 7,610, 9 Brendan Tennant (Aus) 7,549, 10 Georgios Andreou (Cyp) 7,080, 11 Richard Hesketh (Can) 6,999, 12 Victor Houston (Bar) 6,898, 13 Greg Turner (Can) 6,360, 14 Sekona Vi (Ton) 6,266. Did not finish - Simon Poelman (NZ), Joel Wade (Blz). Note: Simon Shirley was 8th in 1986 for Australia.

WOMEN

100 METRES (23 Aug): 1 Mary Onyali (Nig) 11.06, 2 Christy Opara-Thompson (Nig) 11.22, 3 Paula Thomas (Eng) 11.23, 4 Melinda Gainsford (Aus) 11.31, 5 Dahlia Duhaney (Jam) 11.34, 6 Hermin Joseph (Dom) 11.36, 7 Mary Tombiri (Nig) 11.38, 8 Stephanie Douglas (Eng) 11.48. Note: Thomas nee Dunn.

200 METRES (26 Aug): 1 Cathy Freeman (Aus) 22.25, 2 Mary Onyali (Nig) 22.35, 3 Melinda Gainsford (Aus) 22.86, 4 Paula Thomas (Eng) 22.69, 5 Pauline Davis (Bah) 22.77, 6 Dahlia Duhaney (Jam) 22.85, 7 Merlene Frazer (Jam) 23.18, 8 Geraldine McLeod (Eng) 23.52.

400 METRES (23 Aug): 1 Cathy Freeman (Aus) 50.38, 2 Fatima Yusuf (Nig) 50.53, 3 Sandie Richards (Jam) 50.59, 4 Phyllis Smith (Eng) 51.46, 5 Renee Poetschka (Aus) 51.51, 6 Melanie Neef (Sco) 52.09, 7 Bisi Afolabi (Nig) 52.21, 8 Kylie Hanigan (Aus) 52.55.

800 METRES (26 Aug): 1 Inez Turner (Jam) 2:01.74, 2 Charmaine Crooks (Can) 2:02.35, 3 Gladys Wamuyu (Ken) 2:03.12, 4 Cathy Dawson (Wal) 2:03.17, 5

Selina Kosgei (Ken) 2:03.78, 6 Lisa Lightfoot (Aus) 2:03.82, 7 Melanie Collins (Aus) 2:04.09, 8 Sandra Dawson (Aus) 2:04.41.

1500 METRES (28 Aug): 1 Kelly Holmes (Eng) 4:08.86, 2 Paula Schnurr (Can) 4:09.65, 3 Gwen Griffiths (SA) 4:10.16, 4 Leah Pells (Can) 4:10.82, 5 Margaret Leaney (Aus) 4:11.48, 6 Jackline Maranga (Ken) 4:12.84, 7 Robyn Meagher (Can) 4:13.91, 8 Julia Sakara (Zim) 4:18.11, 9 Lynn Gibson (Eng) 4:18.36, 10 Palaniappan Jayanthi (Mal) 4:24.31, 11 Sheila Seebaluck (Mau) 4:26.45, 12 Chan Man Yee (HK) 4:26.95, 13 Jennifer Fisher (Ber) 4:26.96, 14 Rosemary Turare (PNG) 4:37.17. Did not finish - Gifty Abankwa (Gha).

3000 METRES (23 Aug): 1 Angela Chalmers (Can) 8:32.17, 2 Robyn Meagher (Can) 8:45.59, 3 Alison Wyeth (Eng) 8:47.98, 4 Sonia McGeorge (Eng) 8:54.91, 5 Susie Power (Aus) 8:59.23, 6 Rose Cheruiyot (Ken) 9:00.89, 7 Leah Pells (Can) 9:03.66, 8 Laura Adam (Sco) 9:06.63, 9 Gwen Griffiths (SA) 9:15.47, 10 Eunice Sagero (Ken) 9:18.15, 11 Jackline Okemwa (Ken) 9:28.24, 12 Chan Man Yee (HK) 9:37.10, 13 Elizabeth Mongudhi (Nam) 9:38.95, 14 Hawa Hussein (Tan) 9:42.80, 15 Rosemary Turare (PNG) 10:18.11, 18 Motena Moshao (Les) 10:29.50

10,000 METRES (24 Aug): 1 Yvonne Murray (Sco) 31:56.97, 2 Elana Meyer (SA) 32:06.02, 3 Jane Omoro (Ken) 32:13.01, 4 Suzanne Rigg (Eng) 33:01.40, 5 Vikki McPherson (Sco) 33:02.74, 6 Ulla Marquette (Can) 33:16.29, 7 Michelle Dillon (Aus) 33:19.01, 8 Anne Hare (NZ) 33:19.66, 9 Lioudmila Alexeeff (Can) 33:33.59, 10 Angie Hulley (Eng) 33:45.04, 11 Krishna Stanton (Aus) 33:50.14, 12 Palaniappan Jayanthi (Mal) 34:23.71, 13 Zahara Hyde (Eng) 34:43.24, 14 Jebiwott Keitany (Ken) 35:10.51. Did not finish - Carole Montgomery (Can). Note: Hulley nee Pain.

MARATHON (27 Aug): 1 Carole Rouillard (Can) 2:30:41, 2 Lizanne Bussieres (Can) 2:31:07, 3 Yvonne Danson (Eng) 2:32:24, 4 Karen Macleod (Sco) 2:33:16, 5 Nyla Carroll (NZ) 2:34:03, 6 Angelina Kanana (Ken) 2:35:02, 7 Hayley Nash (Wal) 2:35:39, 8 Sally Ellis (Eng) 2:37:14, 9 Carol Galea (Mlt) 2:39:40, 10 Kerryn McCann (Aus) 2:40:10, 11 Danuta Bartoszek (Can) 2:40:44, 12 Lynn Harding (Sco) 2:40:57, 13 Sally Eastall (Eng) 2:41:32, 14 Pauline Vea (Ton) 2:56:59, 15 Tani Ruckle (Aus) 3:06:27. Did not finish - Sue Hobson (Aus).

10 KILOMETRES WALK (25 Aug): 1 Kerry Saxby-Junna (Aus) 44:25, 2 Anne Manning (Aus) 44:37; 3, Janice McCaffrey (Can) 44:54, 4 Holly Gerke (Can) 45:43, 5 Vicky Lupton (Eng) 45:58, 6 Lisa Langford (Eng) 46:01, 7 Verity Snook (Sco) 46:06, 8 Jane Saville (Aus) 47:14, 9 Carolyn Partington (IoM) 47:21, 10

237

Grace Karimi (Ken) 48:20, 11 Karen Smith (Eng) 48:45, 12 Alison Baker (Can) 51:28. Did not finish - Agnetha Chelimo (Ken). Disqualified - Linn Murphy (NZ). Note: Carolyn Prtington was the wife of Steve Partington, 7th in the 30km walk.

100 METRES HURDLES (27 Aug): 1 Michelle Freeman (Jam) 13.12, 2 Jackie Agyepong (Eng) 13.14, 3 Samantha Farquharson (Eng) 13.38, 4 Dionne Rose (Jam) 13.42, 5 Donalda Duprey (Can) 13.75, 6 Lesley Tashlin (Can) 13.85, 7 Jane Flemming (Aus) 13.98. Did not finish - Clova Court (Eng).

400 METRES HURDLES (26 Aug): 1 Sally Gunnell (Eng) 54.51, 2 Deon Hemmings (Jam) 55.11, 3 Debbie Ann Parris (Jam) 55.25, 4 Donalda Duprey (Can) 55.39, 5 Gowry Retchakan (Eng) 56.69, 6 Jackie Parker (Eng) 56.72, 7 Karlene Haughton (Jam) 57.00, 8 Maria Usifo (Nig) 59.20.

4 x 100 METRES RELAY (28 Aug): 1 Nigeria (Faith Idehen, Mary Tombiri, Christy Opara-Thompson, Mary Onyali) 42.99, 2 Australia (Monique Miers, Cathy Freeman, Melinda Gainsford, Kathy Sambell) 43.43, 3 England (Stephanie Douglas, Geraldine McLeod, Simmone Jacobs, Paula Thomas) 43.46, 4 Jamaica (Michelle Freeman, Dionne Rose, Merlene Frazer, Dahlia Duhaney) 43.51, 5 Bahamas (Eldece Clarke, Debbie Ferguson, Dedra Davis, Pauline Davis) 44.89, 6 Canada (Tanja Reid, France Gareau, Karen Clarke, Simone Tomlinson) 45.15, 7 Ghana (Doris Manu, Naomi Mills, Agnes Yaa Nuamah, Mercy Addy) 45.72. 7 teams competed. Note: Miers nee Dunstan.

4 x 400 METRES RELAY (28 Aug): 1 England (Phyllis Smith, Tracy Goddard, Linda Keough, Sally Gunnell) 3:27.06, 2 Jamaica (Revoli Campbell, Deon Hemmings, Inez Turner, Sandie Richards) 3:27.63, 3 Canada (Alana Yawichuk, Stacy Bowen, Donalda Duprey, Charmaine Crooks) 3:32.52, 4 Ghana (Helena Wrappah, Agnes Yaa Nuamah, Gifty Abankwa, Mercy Addy) 3:47.49. Australia (Lee Naylor, Kylie Hanigan, Renee Poetschka, Cathy Freeman), originally 1st in 3:26.84, and Nigeria (Bisi Afolabi, Emily Odoemenam, Lade Akinremi, Fatima Yusuf), originally 5th in 3:34.67, disqualified. 6 teams competed. Note: Lee Naylor is the sister of Shane Naylor, 2nd at 4 x100.

HIGH JUMP (27 Aug): 1 Alison Inverarity (Aus) 1.94, 2 Charmaine Weavers (SA) 1.94, 3 Debbie Marti (Eng) 1.91, 4 Tania Dixon (NZ) 1.91, 5= Lea Haggett (Eng) & Andrea Hughes (Aus) 1.88, 7 Julia Bennett (Eng) 1.85, 8 Sara McGladdery (Can) 1.85, 9= Desire du Plessis (SA) & Tracy Phillips (NZ) 1.80, 11 Leslie Estwick (Can) 1.80, 12 Corinna Wolf (Can) 1.75. Note: Dixon nee Murray.

LONG JUMP (27 Aug): 1 Nicole Boegman (Aus) 6.82, 2 Yinka Idowu (En 6.73, 3 Christy Opara-Thompson (Nig) 6.72, 4 Jackie Edwards (Bah) 6.68, 5 Joanne Henry (NZ) 6.65, 6 Chantal Brunner (NZ) 6.63, 7 Dionne Rose (Jam) 6.47, 8 Denise Lewis (Eng) 6.32, 9= Leslie Estwick (Can) & Jane Flemming (Aus) 6.21, 11 Pauline Davis (Bah) 5.98, 12 Ruth Irving (Sco) 5.90. The jumps by Boegman, Opara-Thompson, Edwards, Rose, Lewis, Estwick and Flemming were wind-assisted.

SHOT (24 Aug): 1 Judy Oakes (Eng) 18.16, 2 Myrtle Augee (Eng) 17.64, 3 Lisa-Marie Vizaniari (Aus) 16,61, 4 Georgette Reed (Can) 16.45, 5 Christine King (NZ) 16.27, 6 Maggie Lynes (Eng) 16.23, 7 Alison Grey (Sco) 15.25, 8 Shannon Kekula-Kristiansen (Can) 14.98, 9 Beatrice Faumuina (NZ) 14.80, 10 Samantha Cox (Aus) 14.52, 11 Erin Breaugh (Can) 14.25, 12 Iammo Gapi Launa (PNG) 12.71, 13 Tea Ai Seng (Bru) 12.61.

DISCUS (23 Aug): 1 Daniela Costian (Aus) 63.72, 2 Beatrice Faumuina (NZ) 57.12, 3 Lizette Etsebeth (SA) 55.74, 4 Sharon Andrews (Eng) 55.34, 5 Jackie McKernan (NI) 54.86, 6 Lisa-Marie Vizaniari (Aus) 53.88, 7 Debbie Callaway (Eng) 53.16, 8 Theresa Brick (Can) 52.12, 9 Alison Lever (Aus) 51.66, 10 Lorraine Shaw (Eng) 50.50. Alison Grey (Sco) and Tea Ai Seng (Bru) no valid throws.

JAVELIN (26 Aug): 1 Louise McPaul (Aus) 63.76, 2 Kirsten Hellier (NZ) 60.40, 3 Sharon Gibson (Eng) 58.20, 4 Joanne Stone (Aus) 57.60, 5 Valerie Tulloch (Can) 57.26, 6 Kate Farrow (Aus) 56.98, 7 Laverne Eve (Bah) 55.54, 8 Kaye Nordstrom (NZ) 54.90, 9 Isabelle Surprenant (Can) 52.32, 10 Iammo Gapi Launa (PNG) 49.20, 11 Stephanie Proctor (Can) 49.18, 12 Karen Costello (Sco) 48.58.

HEPTATHLON (22-23 Aug): 1 Denise Lewis (Eng) 6,325 (13.66, 1.74, 13.22, 25.11, 6.44, 53.68, 2:17.60), 2 Jane Flemming (Aus) 6,317 (13.32, 1.77, 14.10, 24.06, 6.29, 39.76, 2:13.07), 3 Catherine Bond-Mills (Can) 6,193 (13.79, 1.86, 13.57, 24.64, 6.22, 37.62, 2:14.04), 4 Joanne Henry (NZ) 6,121, 5 Jenny Kelly (Eng) 5,658, 6 Nancy Fletcher (Guy) 5,611, 7 Kim Vanderhock (Can) 5,467, 8 Caroline Kola (Ken) 5,407, 9 Emma Lindsay (Sco) 5,353, 10 Kendall Matheson (Can) 4,539. Did not finish - Lillyanne Beining (PNG), Clova Court (Eng), Lisa Gibbs (Wal). Note: Bond-Mill nee Bond.

17.

£330 million buys a resplendent Olympic dress rehearsal

BUKIT JALIL NATIONAL STADIUM,
KUALA LUMPUR, MALAYSIA
16-21 SEPTEMBER 1998

IF THERE IS A PHRASE IN THE MALAY language which means "half-measures" it doesn't seem to be used very often. Kuala Lumpur had won the Commonwealth Games Federation's vote over Adelaide in 1992 for the right to stage the Games six years later, and the Malaysian authorities promptly set about a programme of massive spending on new sports facilities, development and training. They engaged the services of more than 70 foreign coaches in various sports, of which the great majority were from China or the former Soviet Union, and the National Sports Complex on the outskirts of the sprawling city was the jewel in the crown, incorporating on one site the most up-to-date venues for athletics, swimming, gymnastics, squash and hockey. The main stadium alone had a capacity of 100,000. The total spend was in the order of 2,000 million Ringits (£330 million) and not much secret was made about the fact that the long-term ambition was to stage an Olympic Games, maybe even as early as the year 2008.

Taking place at the end of another hectic summer of athletics, the 1998 Commonwealth Games were bound to be bereft of some of the leading athletes. As usual, there was a host of Kenyan absentees, including four sub-1:44 800m runners and five sub-8:10 steeplechasers, and the IAAF did not help matters by sanctioning the World Cup in Johannesburg the previous weekend and a lucrative meeting in Tokyo which was a direct clash

240

of dates. Frankie Fredericks, the Commonwealth champion at 200, valiantly took part in all three, but Colin Jackson controversially withdrew late in the day from the Welsh team to save his energies for Tokyo. There were 822 athletes (528 men, 294 women) entered from 57 countries, including Cameroon and Mozambique, as both had become newly-elected members of the Commonwealth, which meant that former World champion Maria Mutola would be taking part. The current World champions in attendance were Ato Boldon (after some doubts), Daniel Komen, Marius Corbett and Beatrice Faumuina.

The opening day of athletics competition was Wednesday 16 September, featuring finals of the men's 10,000 and a new event still to receive World or Olympic recognition, the women's hammer. Debbie Sosimenko, the Commonwealth record-holder from Australia in the latter event, became the first champion of 1998 after an excellent competition in which three others were over 60 metres and the next three - including Caroline Fournier, of Mauritius - over 59 metres. The 10,000 was without nine of the 10 fastest Commonwealth runners of the year, including World Championships silver-medallist Paul Tergat, and even more worryingly there were only 12 runners at the start, which represented the smallest entry at six miles or 10,000 metres since 1934. Even so, there was an impressive win in very hot and humid conditions by Kenya's 20-year-old national champion, Simon Maina, who strode unflurried round the track to win by the best part of a lap from his team-mate, William Kalya. Due to some team-management oversight, these were the only two Kenyans taking part, and with all due regard to the hard-earned bronze for the 1994 marathon champion, Steve Moneghetti, any of at least a dozen or so Kenyans would probably have beaten him on the day.

The first event on Thursday 17 September was the 20 kilometres walk, beginning at 7 a.m. and covering the best part of eight laps of a 2619-metre circuit on roads around the up-market suburb of Lake Titiwangsa. For the first time in the Games the race-walkers were contesting the orthodox international distances of 20km and 50km, rather than the compromise 30km event held on previous occasions, and Australia's Nick A'Hern, a hairdresser by profession, made a stylish transition by winning his second successive gold, though the heat and humidity slowed him to a time over five minutes outside his best and he was exactly 50sec ahead of the

Canadian, Arturo Huerta, who set his own unusual record by becoming the first Mexican-born athlete to win a Commonwealth medal! In the evening the finals were at 100 for men and women, men's steeplechase and discus, and women's 5000, and there was also the completion of the heptathlon. Denise Lewis, the defending champion in the heptathlon, had won the European title in Budapest less than a month before, and although she was never seriously pressed by any of her opponents in Kuala Lumpur she put together another 6,500-plus score, which included a 15.09 shot-putt on the first day and a 6.52 long jump and 51.22 javelin throw on the second.

The men's 100 was of such a high standard that Dwain Chambers, of England, ran 10.18 and did not get through the semi-finals, while Matthew Shirvington set an Australian record of 10.03 in the final and did not get a medal. The winner was the muscular Ato Boldon, of Trinidad, running in his characteristic splay-footed manner and winning his country's first gold medal for 32 years. Boldon had been bronze-medallist at both 100 and 200 at the 1996 Olympics, and his first names of "Ato Jabari" come from the Yoruba language of Nigeria and translate as "Brilliant Leader". His time was a scintillating 9.88 - which only he beat at non-altitude during the year - and behind him Frankie Fredericks finished in 2nd place for the ninth time in a major championship. Obadele Thompson, who had won the World Cup 100 six days earlier in 9.87, was 3rd, Shirvington 4th, and the new European champion, Darren Campbell, 5th in 10.08. The women's race, lacking Merlene Ottey again, was not in the same class, though Chandra Sturrup, of the Bahamas, did run 11.06. There were 60,000 spectators in the stadium, while another 13,000 were watching Malaysia play Canada at hockey less than a quarter-of-a-mile away on the far side of the vast Bukit Jalil Sports Complex, and there were 6,000 more at the neighbouring swimming arena.

The absence of some of the best Kenyans in the steeplechase was purely academic. John Kosgei, a 3:34.09 performer at 1500, outsprinted the World record-holder, Bernard Barmasai, for the gold and 19-year-old Kipkirui Misoi was 3rd, which meant that Kenya had now won 14 of the 21 medals on offer in the seven Games steeplechase races they had contested. The women's 5000, replacing the 3000, disappointingly attracted only eight runners and the winning time was not remotely in international class, but it was an oddly compulsive race with Australia's

Kate Anderson the unexpected winner and Andrea Whitcombe making up an enormous amount of leeway in the last couple of laps to give England the silver. The day's other gold medal was won in the discus and marked a unique double for 37-year-old US-based Bob Weir, who had been the Games hammer champion 16 years before. It was also the first win ever achieved by a Briton in the discus event at World, Olympic, European or Commonwealth level.

The decathlon was completed on Friday 18 September with two athletes of rare talent among the participants: in 1994 Jagan Hames, of Australia, had won the World junior high-jump title and Du'aine Ladejo had been European 400 metres champion (and Commonwealth silver-medallist). Hames led from early on the first day, and though his high jump of 2.19 was obviously exceptional he showed consistent form throughout to set a national record of 8,490. Ladejo ran 10.47 for the 100 and a storming 46.12 for 400 but lacked strength and technique in the throws. The champion of 1986 and 1990, Michael Smith, was in 3rd place.

The day's finals were at 400, triple jump and hammer for men, and 400, 400 hurdles and shot for women. In the men's 400 Iwan Thomas completed a Herculean task with his victory in 44.52, having also won the European Championships and World Cup finals. The tall, long-striding, sandy-haired Thomas had switched from BMX cycle-racing as a teenager and started his running career at 1500 metres, making his first major impression at 400 in the 1994 Commonwealth Games when he set a Welsh record of 45.98 in the semi-finals. Behind Thomas and his English rival, Mark Richardson, the bronze medal was taken by the slight and elegant Asian champion from Sri Lanka, Sugath Thilakaratne, who had broken 46 sec in his heat, quarter-final and semi-final and whose final time of 44.64 would have won gold at every previous Commonwealth Games except 1990. Jamaica's experienced Sandie Richards, who had already run in 17 major championship finals, won the women's 400 and beat Cathy Freeman's Games record in the process, with Allison Curbishley setting a Scottish record in 2nd place after taking advice from Sally Gunnell. Freeman, who had won the 1997 World title ahead of Richards, was injured and unable to run in Kuala Lumpur.

Jonathan Edwards was also suffering problems and missed the Games to undergo an operation on his heel, but the former World junior

243

champion, Larry Achike, proved an able substitute for England in the triple jump with a winning leap of 17.10. In an otherwise unexceptional hammer contest Michael Jones, also of England, whose training was carried out in a friendly farmer's field, got the silver after placing 4th in both 1986 and 1994. There was bound to be a record in the women's shot because Judy Oakes only needed to step into the circle for her first-round throw to register her sixth Games appearance in 20 years, and that effort of 18.50 was quite sufficient to win her third title by a very wide margin from the 1990 champion, Myrtle Augee, though Oakes actually threw further in round three (18.83). At the age of 40 she thus became the oldest woman to win a Commonwealth Games title, while between them she and Augee had now won six of the nine medals on offer in the event since 1986, but there was promise shown by the next generation as the bronze medal went to an 18-year-old South African, Veronica Abrahamse. In the 400 hurdles Barbados achieved their first Commonwealth gold through London-born Andrea Blackett, who was not a particularly fluent hurdler but was so quick between the barriers that her time of 53.91 was well inside Sally Gunnell's Games record. Gowry Retchakan, the 38-year-old silver-medallist for England, had first competed internationally for Sri Lanka, and she was coached by the octogenarian Empire mile champion of 60 years earlier, Jim Alford. Karlene Haughton, the bronze-medal winner for Canada, had run for Jamaica in the 1994 400 hurdles final. Worryingly, only seven athletes entered the event.

The first full day of finals was on Saturday 19 September: 200, 800, 5000, 400 hurdles and high jump for men; 200, 800, 10km walk, pole vault, long jump and javelin for women. The early-morning walk was thought to hold out the realistic prospect of a first Malaysian athletics medal for Yuan Yu Fang, formerly of China, and she duly went off with the favoured Australians, Kerry Saxby-Junna (the 1990 and 1994 champion) and Jane Saville, but after a warning by the judges the Malaysian paid no heed to her coach's pleas to slow down and she was disqualified. Saville, who had been 2nd in the World Junior Championships 5km in 1992, went on to win by half-a-minute, as Dr Lisa Kehler (nee Langford) collected a second bronze medal in a UK record time of 45:03. The post-race discussion between Yuan Yu Fang and her team officials was strained, to say the least.

With Ato Boldon and Frankie Fredericks having caught an early flight to compete in Tokyo, and Obadele Thompson withdrawing, the 200 was dominated by the home countries. Though there was only a two-hour break after the semi-finals Julian Golding, the European Championships bronze-medallist whose coach was the joint 1982 Commonwealth 200 champion, Mike McFarlane, won the gold in a personal best 20.18 and Christian Malcolm, the 19-year-old World junior 100/200 champion, broke the Welsh record with 20.29 in 2nd place. Behind these two mightily promising aspirants to Linford Christie's place of honour in athletics history was John Regis, whose first major championship appearance had been in last position in the 1986 final and who was now taking the bronze. No Freeman or Ottey in the women's race, nor Mary Onyali (who was in Tokyo), but still a win for an Olympic gold-medallist ... an Olympic gold-medallist at hockey, that is. It was only after the Atlanta Games that Nova Peris-Kneebone, like Cathy Freeman an aborigine, decided to take up athletics seriously at the age of 25 and she came to Kuala Lumpur merely as a relay reserve. Then Freeman's indisposition opened up a place for her and in true Cinderella style she won in a personal best time, though her team-mate, Melinda Gainsford-Taylor, was clearly slowed by injury when leading in the straight.

Both finals at 800 were cracking races. Six of the eight men were from Africa and the other two were English. The Kenyans were 19-year-old Japheth Kimutai, who was the African champion and had run an astonishing 1:42.76 to head the World rankings, and Kennedy Ngetich (also known, rather confusingly, by the name of Kimwetich), whose best time was only marginally slower at 1:43.03. Ngetich/Kimwetich led the first lap in a wildly extravagant 48.55, but the strategy presumably worked as planned because Kimutai came through in beautifully relaxed fashion to win from the South Africans, Hezekiel Sepeng (his third silver medal in a major championship) and Johan Botha (setting a personal best). The English duo of Andy Hart and Brad Donkin suffered, as always, by comparison with Coe, Cram and Ovett, but both of them also ran their fastest times. The women's 800 lineup intriguingly included the former champion, Diane Modahl (nee Edwards), back in competition in the Games after eight years but still in legal confrontation with the British athletics authorities over drug-testing procedures, and Maria Mutola, who had first appeared as a 15-year-old at the Seoul Olympics of 1988, had won World titles indoors and out, had held every Mozambique national record from 200 metres to 3000, and was now getting a further unexpected medal opportunity following the acceptance of her country into the Commonwealth. The race itself had an air of inevitability about it: Mutola had broken Modahl's Games record in the heats and led all the way in the final to improve the record further to 1:57.60, with her cousin, Tina Paulino, 2nd and Modahl very commendably getting close to her personal best set back in 1990 to take the bronze medal.

The defending champion at 400 hurdles, Samuel Matete, bye-passed Kuala Lumpur to run in Tokyo. He won there in 48.34 and he had also won the World Cup event at altitude in 48.08, but success in the Commonwealth final would have been by no means assured. Dinsdale Morgan, a graduate of Pittsburgh State University, in the USA, who had placed 3rd in the World Cup in 48.40, broke Matete's Games record with 48.28. It was Jamaica's first Games win in an event which had now shared out titles between 10 different countries over the years, and noteworthy among the other placings was Victor Houston's Barbados record of 49.21. His previous efforts at the Games had been rather more protracted. He had placed 12th in the decathlon in Victoria.

In those 1994 Games a Kenyan teenager had rushed off on a suicidal sub-58sec first lap of the 10,000. Here, in Kuala Lumpur, he cannily saved a similar effort until the penultimate lap of the 5000 and led home a 1-2-3 for his country. But then Daniel Komen had picked up a few ideas and gained a lot in ability in the intervening four years, having won the World title and set World records at 3000 and 5000, and he was not at all stretched in a time which was strangely predictable. Komen ran 13:22.57, and six of the eight Commonwealth finals at 5000 had now been won in the 13:22-to-13:25 range, leaving Ben Jipcho's record from 1974 unchallenged once again. Komen's team-mates, Tom Nyariki and 17-year-old Richard Limo, were the other medallists.

The women's field-event finals varied markedly in standard. The pole vault, introduced at these Games, was won by the World record-holder and one-time star of The Flying Fruit Bats circus act, Emma George, at a modest height for her of 4.20, and there was an encouraging entry here of 15 athletes from eight countries. The women's long jump went to

England's Joanne Wise, but the distance was only 6.63 and the loss of Fiona May was sorely felt. The Derby-born junior World champion of 1988 had won the Commonwealth bronze in 1990, but after marriage to the Italian pole vaulter, Gianni Iapichino, opted to compete for Italy and had gone on to win the World title in 1995 and Olympic and World silver in 1996 and 1997. Louise McPaul, whose first international competition had been as a heptathlete, retained her javelin title at 66.96, but her London-born team-mate, Joanna Stone, had to pull out with injury suffered in winning the World Cup event eight days earlier with an Oceania record of 69.85.

The men's high jump was not the tense affair of previous years, but it did provide the opportunity for Dalton Grant, competing in his 14th major championship final, to win gold. It was England's first win in the event in the Games and Grant's first outdoor title, though he had been European champion indoors in 1994. He had previously finished 7th, 2nd and 5th in the Commonwealth Games. The defending champion, Tim Forsyth, was less than fully fit and lost 2nd place on countback to Grant's 20-year-old team-mate, Ben Challenger, with Khemraj Naiko, of Mauritius, who had been last in the 1994 final, only just missing a medal in clearing a national record 2.28.

With the athletics events unusually scheduled to finish on a Monday, the men's and women's marathons took place on the morning of Sunday 20 September, and none of the competitors would have been at all unhappy when they awoke well before dawn and drew back their curtains to find that it had been raining and the roads were wet and the air fresh and cool. The 25 men started at 7 a.m. and they were followed by 11 women at 7.15. Without South Africa's Olympic champion, Josia Thugwane, or any of the 14 Kenyans who had run faster than 2:09 within the preceding 18 months, it seemed as if Australia might provide the winner even though 1994 champion, Steve Moneghetti, had opted for the 10,000 in Malaysia, as they were fielding Sean Quilty and Pat Carroll, who had placed 2nd and 5th respectively in Victoria. But then the majority of the runners were Africans, and mostly unknown quantities, so it was something of a lottery trying to pick out a potential champion as the field set off from the ornate city-centre square at Dataran Merdeka to cover a serpentine course which doubled back and forth round the largely deserted streets.

Despite the rain and the early hour the temperature soon rose and the pace was never quick. The leader for more than half the race was Kenyan-born, but it was David Taylor, running for England, who had thrown down the gauntlet and for a while it seemed as though he might cause a major surprise, but on the undulating stretch in the last 10km it was an African trio who broke away and 30-year-old Thabiso Moqhali won Lesotho's first Commonwealth gold. He had apparently made his marathon debut at the age of 11, and it was actually his fourth appearance in the Games, though anyone could have been forgiven for not realising this, as he had failed to finish the 10,000 in 1994, was 10th in the marathon in 1990 (though in a time which was faster than he ran in Kuala Lumpur) and 14th at 5000 in 1986. It has to be said that the general standard of the race was modest, but that did not worry his jubilant supporters, led by the Lesotho team's Chef de Mission, Kennetha Hlasa, who had run the Commonwealth marathon himself in 1978 and 1986. "This victory is so important for our country," Mr Hlasa enthused. "Maybe he'll become an idol for people to look up to."

The women's race inevitably developed into something of a procession with such a small number of runners, and at the finish there was almost 10 minutes between 1st place and 6th, but the winning margin was only 24sec as Heather Turland, a 38-year-old with four children ranging in ages from 10 to 16, won from her Australian colleague, Lisa Dick. Only Judy Oakes in the shot two days earlier had ever won a Games title for women at a greater age, and Mrs Turland's success was all the more remarkable for the fact that earlier in the year she had suffered a broken leg when she was hit by a motorcyle while training in Rome, but despite wearing a plaster cast for a month had kept fit by swimming. The bronze medal went to Elizabeth Mongudhi, the only woman in the Namibian team, whose name could also be found buried in the small print of the 1994 Games results - 13th at 3000. Gillian Horovitz, 43, took 4th place for England 19 years after setting a British record, and it's a pity that more spectators did not turn out on this marathon morning to cheer on such valiant competitors as 39-year-old Hugh Marsden, from the Falkland Islands, who came last by more than 17 minutes in the men's race (having also been last in Victoria four years earlier), and Swaziland's Julie Cory, who eventually completed the women's course over three-quarters of an hour after the winner.

The Sunday evening schedule comprised finals of the men's 110 hurdles, pole vault and long jump, and the women's 10,000 and high jump. Without Colin Jackson the hurdles looked to be between three men: his perennial runner-up, England's Tony Jarrett, 2nd in 1990 and 1994; Australia's Kyle Vander-Kuyp, 5th and 6th in those same finals; and Steve Brown, representing Trinidad & Tobago and an ex-US citizen who had missed selection for the 1996 Olympics by only 7/100ths of a second. As it happens none of them were close to their best form and the result was primarily of sentimental value with Jarrett overcoming his jangling nerves to win a gold medal at last after six silvers and three bronzes in hurdles and relay finals at various championships. Both Brown and the South African bronze-medallist, Shaun Bownes, set national records. The women's 10,000 was nothing like the spectacle it had been in the past, and it was really notable only for the fact that Esther Wanjiru became Kenya's first woman champion in a Commonwealth Games event. Wanjiru, like a number of other young Kenyans, had followed the example of Douglas Wakiihuri in going to Japan to live, train and race.

It could not actually be claimed of the pole-vault winner, Riaan Botha, that he had progressed from last to 1st in successive Games because in Victoria he had failed his opening height and therefore was not placed at all, but his gold medal in 1998 was all the more meritorious for that. The silver originally went to New Zealand's Denis Petushinskiy, a former Russian national champion and 6th in the 1993 World Championships, but he subsequently tested positive for the steroid, stanozolol, and he was disqualified. This ruling had at least one pleasurable side-effect in that it gave Mauritius its first Games medal as Kersley Gardenne was elevated from 4th to 3rd place. Australians took the top two places in the long jump through Peter Burge and "Jumping Jai" Taurima, both of them clearing 8.22, and the women's discus was won in immaculate style by the World champion from New Zealand, Beatrice Faumuina, ahead of the 1990 Games gold-medallist, Lisa-Marie Vizaniari. As in the men's high jump, the defending champion from Australia in the women's event - in this case, Alison Inverarity - was beaten into 3rd place, in what was a low-key contest won by the 20-year-old South African, Hestrie Storbeck.

The closing day of competition, Monday 21 September, began with the 50km walk at first light, followed by a compact two-and-a-half hours of track & field competition in the late afternoon. The walkers set off at 7 a.m. on a 19-lap trek round the Lake Titiwangsa circuit, which to the uninitiated might seem to be a rather tedious affair. Yet however esoteric an activity race-walking might be, there's no doubting the athleticism of its leading exponents because with a winning time of around the four-hour mark, depending on conditions, the leaders would be moving at a speed in excess of 8 m.p.h. The amended rules for race-walking now required that the lead leg should be locked at the knee, rather than that one foot should always be in contact with the ground, and controversial as this refinement is there is no question but that the event requires enormous powers of pace-judgment and technical accomplishment.

Quite what went wrong for Craig Barrett is something that maybe even he could not properly answer. The fact is that Barrett, at 26 a seasoned competitor from New Zealand who had placed 13th in the 1997 World Championships 50km with a time of 3:56:30 and 8th in the 1994 Commonwealth 30km, led by some six minutes with only a kilometre to go and was striding out purposefully towards certain gold when without warning his legs gave way and he slumped to the side of the road. He tried several times to regain his feet, only to fall back on the grass verge, and was eventually lifted on to a stretcher and taken by ambulance to the finish and onward to hospital to be treated for dehydration, reviving memories of Jim Peters's collapse in the 1954 Empire marathon. Unquestionably, the oppressive heat and humidity of approaching midday had taken its toll. Meanwhile, the totally unheralded Malaysian, Govindaswamy Saravanan, who was so little known that even the official programme listed him only as "Saravanan", had appeared in sight and to the increasing frenzy of the local spectators crossed the line an easy winner. With his fulsome moustache and his decidedly bashful demeanour, he had something of a Chaplin-esque air about him, but whatever the circumstances it was a famous victory - the first in athletics for Malaysia, whose previous Games successes had all been in weight-lifting and badminton - and it was a pity that he did not get the opportunity for a victory lap in the National Stadium. His gold medal and a new Malaysian record earned Saravanan a Government cash prize of 83,000 Ringits (about £14,000), and Barrett recovered well enough after treatment to be back in competition early in 1999 and break his national record in the World Cup.

Australia, England, Jamaica, Kenya and South Africa were all title-winners later in the day. Marius Corbett, the South African who had so surprisingly won the World javelin title in 1997 from Steve Backley, repeated the feat with another huge throw, and Backley's eternal England companion, Mick Hill, placed 3rd after three successive silver medals. The men's shot was won by another South African, Burger Lambrechts, ahead of silver for the Cypriot, Michalis Louca, whose brother had competed in the event in the Commonwealth Games and whose father still held the national record from 1975. Bronze-medallist Shaun Pickering also came from an athletics dynasty: his late father, Ron, an outstanding coach and then TV commentator, and his mother, Jean (nee Desforges), a double bronze-medallist in the 1954 Vancouver Games and European long-jump champion. The World indoor record-holder, Ashia Hansen, made a belated return from injury to win the triple jump with her one valid effort, and there was a pleasing silver medal for Francoise Mbango, the debutante from the West African republic of Cameroon. No Michelle Freeman to defend her 100 hurdles title, but the win went to Jamaica, anyway, as Gillian Russell ran a World-class time of 12.70.

Both 1500 titles were won by Kenyans. The diminutive Laban Rotich, whose positively frail physique belies his strength and speed, followed the lead of his team-mate, John Kibowen, through two moderate laps of 61 apiece and then a much faster one close to 58 (presumably all carefully planned beforehand), and won with considerable ease. Jackline Maranga, the wife of 5000 silver-medallist Tom Nyariki, triumphed by only a slightly less margin, and in both cases English runners took the silver. John Mayock joined Jerry Cornes, Kip Keino, Filbert Bayi, John Walker and Steve Cram as a double medal winner in the Games at the mile or 1500 metres, which is pretty select company, and Kelly Holmes did as well as could possibly have been hoped for after an Achilles tendon operation earlier in the year to finish a commendably close runner-up. Maranga's win meant that Kenyan athletes had taken gold in seven of the nine track races for men and women at 800 metres or further.

Canada, with only Glenroy Gilbert from their team which had won the last three World and Olympic titles, were beaten in the 4 x 100 by the youthful English quartet in a Games record time of 38.20. At 4 x 400 Jamaica won for the first time since 1962 with England 2nd and a spirited

251

Welsh team, including hurdler Paul Gray and sprinter Doug Turner in support of Jamie Baulch and Iwan Thomas, setting a national record of 3:01.86 to earn the bronze medals. Australia won both women's relays, with the 100 bronze-medallist, Tania Van Heer, who had been born in Sri Lanka, leading off at 4 x 100 and running an impressive solitary 50.6 anchor leg at 4 x 400. Then the speeches began, the flags were lowered, the music and the fireworks resounded into the night sky, and another Commonwealth Games was over.

Despite the absence of so many star athletes, the standard of performances in many events in Kuala Lumpur had been high, even if in some others it was distinctly ordinary. Whatever their intrinsic value, the enduring merit of the Games as a showcase for the talented athletes of some of the smaller nations was self-evident: gold medals for men from Lesotho and Malaysia and for women from the Bahamas, Barbados, Kenya and Mozambique, and other medals for Cameroon, Cyprus, Mauritius, Namibia, Sri Lanka, Zambia and Zimbabwe. It's always difficult to compare different Games, with the events held in varying weather conditions and circumstances, but the bare statistics told an interesting story. A study of the 6th-place performances in each event at the Games of 1990, 1994 and 1998 should give an indication of quality in depth, and this shows that the 1998 Games were better in 16 events (10 for men, six for women), the 1994 Games better in 15 (five for men, 10 for women), and the 1990 Games were better in nine (seven for men, two for women). A more subjective judgment would surely be that no people had ever embraced the Games more enthusiastically than the Malaysians, and they turned up in their tens of thousands for the athletics, the hockey and the rugby-union sevens tournament, or simply to stroll wonderingly round the forecourts of the Bukit Jalil sports complex.

The facilities were marvellous, among the best in the World, and the welcome for everyone was genuinely hospitable. Among numerous acts of kindness and generosity that were personally experienced, I cite one as a typical example. Leaving the remote cycle road-racing finish one day, and looking for some way to get back to the Games press centre, I heard a shout from a passing motorist. He stopped, asked me where I was going, and said he'd take me there. I got in the car and he said, "Don't you know who I am?" I apologised for the fact that I didn't, and he explained, "I'm the policeman who gave you directions to the course yesterday. I recognised you, but I'm off duty today. So you wouldn't have known me without my uniform!" The 1998 Games in Kuala Lumpur were going to be a very hard act for Manchester to follow in 2002.

RESULTS 1998

MEN

100 METRES (17 Sep): 1 Ato Boldon (Tri) 9.88, 2 Frankie Fredericks (Nam) 9.96, 3 Obadele Thompson (Bar) 10.00, 4 Matthew Shirvington (Aus) 10.03, 5 Darren Campbell (Eng) 10.08, 6 Eric Nkansah-Appiah (Gha) 10.18, 7 Chris Donaldson (NZ) 10.19, 8 Marlon Devonish (Eng) 10.22.

200 METRES (19 Sep): 1 Julian Golding (Eng) 20.18, 2 Christian Malcolm (Wal) 20.29, 3 John Regis (Eng) 20.40, 4 Anninos Marcoullides (Cyp) 20.43, 5 Darryl Wohlsen (Aus) 20.48, 6 Matthew Shirvington (Aus) 20.53, 7 Chris Donaldson (NZ) 20.62, 8 Dougie Walker (Sco) 20.69.

400 METRES (18 Sep): 1 Iwan Thomas (Wal) 44.52, 2 Mark Richardson (Eng) 44.60, 3 Sugath Thilakaratne (SriL) 44.64, 4 Jamie Baulch (Wal) 45.30, 5 Arnaud Malherbe (SA) 45.45, 6 Greg Haughton (Jam) 45.49, 7 Davian Clarke (Jam) 45.55, 8 Kennedy Ochieng (Ken) 45.56.

800 METRES (19 Sep): 1 Japheth Kimutai (Ken) 1:43.82, 2 Hezekiel Sepeng (SA) 1:44.44, 3 Johan Botha (SA) 1:44.57, 4 Crispen Mutakanyi (Zim) 1:45.18, 5 Andy Hart (Eng) 1:45.71, 6 Brad Donkin (Eng) 1:46.86, 7 Savieri Ngidhi (Zim) 1:46.97, 8 Kennedy Ngetich (Ken) 1:48.13.

1500 METRES (21 Sep): 1 Laban Rotich (Ken) 3:39.49, 2 John Mayock (Eng) 3:40.46, 3 Anthony Whiteman (Eng) 3:40.70, 4 John Kibowen (Ken) 3:42.71, 5 Kevin McKay (Eng) 3:43.22, 6 Hamish Christensen (NZ) 3:43.93, 7 Stephen Agar (Can) 3:44.17, 8 Terrance Armstrong (Ber) 3:44.57, 9 Christian Stephenson (Wal) 3:44.82, 10 Steve Green (Jam) 3:45.66.

5000 METRES (19 Sep): 1 Daniel Komen (Ken) 13:22.57, 2 Tom Nyariki (Ken) 13:28.09, 3 Richard Limo (Ken) 13:37.42, 4 Karl Keska (Eng) 13:40.24, 5 Keith Cullen (Eng) 13:44.69, 6 Lee Troop (Aus) 13:56.32, 7 Kris Bowditch (Eng) 14:02.36, 8 Allan Bunce (NZ) 14:02.98, 9 John Morapedi (SA) 14:06.47, 10 Shadrack Hoff (SA) 14:19.35, 11 Richard Mavuso (SA) 14:28.96. Did not finish - Jason Bunston (Can), Reinhold Iita (Nam), Godfrey Nyombi (Uga). Shaun Creighton (Aus) qualified but did not start.

10,000 METRES (16 Sep): 1 Simon Maina (Ken) 28:10.00, 2 William Kalya (Ken) 29:01.68, 3 Steve Moneghetti (Aus) 29:02.76, 4 Tsunaki Kalamore (SA) 29:05.80, 5 Dermot Donnelly (NI) 29:05.96, 6 Abel Chimukoko (Zim) 29:10.53, 7 Lee Troop (Aus) 29:34.23, 8 Makhosonke Fika (SA) 29:46.41, 9 Glynn Tromans (Eng) 30:04.95, 10 Jumanne Boko Turway (Tan) 30:46.37, 11 Gustaf Hendricks (Nam) 30:56.83, 12 Ramachandran Murusamy (Mal) 31:45.79.

3000 METRES STEEPLECHASE (17 Sep): 1 John Kosgei (Ken) 8:15.34, 2 Bernard Barmasai (Ken) 8:15.37, 3 Kipkirui Misoi (Ken) 8:18.24, 4 Joel Bourgeois (Can) 8:34.50, 5 Chris Unthank (Aus) 8:37.24, 6 Christian Stephenson (Wal) 8:42.95, 7 Ben Whitby (Eng) 8:44.24, 8 Craig Wheeler (Eng) 8:57.29, 9 N. Shanmuganathan (Mal) 8:59.10. Did not finish - Spencer Duval (Eng).

MARATHON (20 Sep): 1 Thabiso Moqhali (Les) 2:19:15, 2 Simon Bisiligitwa (Tan) 2:19:42, 3 Andea Geway Suja (Tan) 2:19:50, 4 David Taylor (Eng) 2:20:30, 5 Frank Pooe (SA) 2:21:12, 6 Julius Kimutai (Ken) 2:21:57, 7 Pat Carroll (Aus) 2:22:14, 8 Thabiso Ralekhetla (Les) 2:22:47, 9 Mpakeletsa Sephali (Les) 2:22:57, 10 Keith Anderson (Eng) 2:23:07, 11 Sean Quilty (Aus) 2:24:43, 12 Elphas Sabelo Ginindza (Swa) 2:24:53, 13 John Mwathiwa (Mlw) 2:25:27, 14 Benson Muriuki (Ken) 2:26:22, 15 Dale Rixon (Wal) 2:26:50, 16, 16 Mluleki Nobanda (SA) 2:28:47, 17 Steve Brace (Wal) 2:29:21, 18 Phil Costley (NZ) 2:29:39, 19 Joseph Tjitunga (Nam) 2:30:30, 20 Benedict Ballantyne (StV) 2:30:44, 21 Billy Burns (Eng) 2:31:16, 22 Hugh Marsden (Fal) 2:48:54. Did not finish - Dave Cavers (Sco), Simon Mphulanyane (SA), Nicholas Ongeri (Ken).

20 KILOMETRES WALK (17 Sep): 1 Nick A'Hern (Aus) 1:24:59, 2 Arturo Huerta (Can) 1:25:49, 3 Nathan Deakes (Aus) 1:26:06, 4 Darrell Stone (Eng) 1:26:37, 5 David Rotich (Ken) 1:26:57, 6 Teoh Boon Lim (Mal) 1:27:47, 7 Martin Bell (Sco) 1:28:20, 8 Julius Sawe (Ken) 1:29:23, 9 Narinder Singh (Mal) 1:30:13, 10 Chris Maddocks (Eng) 1:30:21, 11 Tim Berrett (Can) 1:31:19, 12 Andi Drake (Eng) 1:32:04, 13 Steve Partington (IoM) 1:32:15, 14 Brent Vallance (Aus) 1:36:29, 15 Abdul Rahman Shahruhaizy (Mal) 1:36:32, 16 Dip Chand (Fij) 1:52:47, 17 Pradeep Chand (Fij) 2:03:38.

50 KILOMETRES WALK (21 Sep): 1 Govindaswamy Saravanan (Mal) 4:10:05, 2 Duane Cousins (Aus) 4:10:30, 3 Dominic McGrath (Aus) 4:12:50, 4 Steve Hollier (Eng) 4:18:41, 5 Mark Easton (Eng) 4:22:23, 6 Graham White (Sco) 4:30:17, 7 Kannian Pushparajan (Mal) 4:31:22, 8 Chris Cheeseman (Eng) 4:38:36, 9 Thiru Kumaran (Mal) 4:44:33, 10 Tony Sargisson (NZ) 4:45:04. Did not finish - Craig Barrett (NZ), Tim Berrett (Can), Dion Russell (Aus).

110 METRES HURDLES (20 Sep): 1 Tony Jarrett (Eng) 13.47, 2 Steve Brown (Tri) 13.48, 3 Shaun Bownes (SA) 13.53, 4 Paul Gray (Wal) 13.62, 5 Kyle Vander-Kuyp (Aus) 13.67, 6 Andy Tulloch (Eng) 13.67, 7 Greg Hines (Jam) 13.85, 8 Ross Baillie (Sco) 13.85.

400 METRES HURDLES (19 Sep): 1 Dinsdale Morgan (Jam) 48.28, 2 Rohan Robinson (Aus) 48.99, 3 Ken Harnden (Zim) 49.06, 4 Zid Abou Hamed (Aus) 49.11, 5 Victor Houston (Bar) 49.21, 6 Kemel Thompson (Jam) 49.81, 7 Erick Keter (Ken) 49.98, 8 Wayne Whyte (Jam) 51.10.

4 x 100 METRES RELAY (21 Sep): 1 England (Dwain Chambers, Marlon Devonish, Julian Golding, Darren Campbell) 38.20, 2 Canada (Brad McCuaig, Glenroy Gilbert, O'Brian Gibbons, Trevino Betty) 38.46, 3 Australia (Gavin Hunter, Darryl Wohlsen, Steve Brimacombe, Matthew Shirvington) 38.69, 4 Wales (Kevin Williams, Doug Turner, Christian Malcolm, Jamie Henthorn) 38.73, 5 Cameroon (Benjamin Sirimou, Serge Bengono, Dalle Delor, Claude Toukene) 39.29, 6 Sierra Leone (Francis Keita, Joslyn Thomas, Josephus Thomas, Sanusi Turay) 39.79, 7 Ghana (Braimah Tanko, Leo Myles-Mills, Azziz Zakari, Eric Nkansah-Appiah) 40.00, 8 Mauritius (David Victoire, Barnabe Jolicoeur, Stephane Buckland, Eric Milazar) 42.70. Jason Gardener (England) ran the leadoff leg and Rod Zuyderwyk (Australia) the anchor leg in the heats in place of Golding and Brimacombe respectively. Note: Joslyn and Josephus Thomas were 27-year-old twin brothers.

4 x 400 METRES RELAY (21 Sep): 1 Jamaica (Michael McDonald, Roxbert Martin, Greg Haughton, Davian Clarke) 2:59.03, 2 England (Paul Slythe, Solomon Wariso, Mark Hylton, Mark Richardson) 3:00.82, 3 Wales (Paul Gray, Jamie Baulch, Doug Turner, Iwan Thomas) 3:01.86, 4 South Africa (Adriaan Botha, Johan Botha, Hezekiel Sepeng, Arnaud Malherbe) 3:02.21, 5 Australia (Michael Hazel, Brad Jamieson, Casey Vincent, Pat Dwyer) 3:02.96, 6 Zimbabwe (Jeffrey Maswanhise, Philip Mukomana, Savieri Ngidhi, Ken Harnden) 3:03.02, 7 Sri Lanka (Rohan Handunpurage, Rathna Vellasamy, Ranga Suminda Menis, Sugath Thilakaratne) 3:04.11, 8 Canada (Shane Niemi, Monte Raymond, Alexandre Marchand, Donald Bruno) 3:04.84. Sean Baldock, Jared Deacon (both England), Matthew Elias (Wales) and Marcus la Grange (South Africa) ran in the heats.

HIGH JUMP (19 Sep): 1 Dalton Grant (Eng) 2.31, 2 Ben Challenger (Eng) 2.28, 3 Tim Forsyth (Aus) 2.28, 4 Khemraj Naiko (Mau) 2.28, 5 Brendan Reilly (Eng) 2.24, 6 Gavin Lendis (SA) 2.24, 7 Loo Kum Zee (Mal) 2.20, 8 Mike Ponikvar (Can) 2.20, 9 Mike Caza (Can) 2.10, 10 Nathan Sua-Mene (WS) 2.05, 11 Ronan

Kane (Ber) 2.05, 12 Karl Scatliffe (BVI) 2.05, 13 Lorima Vunisa (Fij) 2.00, 14 Robert Elder (Fij) 2.00.

POLE VAULT (20 Sep): 1 Riaan Botha (SA) 5.60, 2 Paul Burgess (Aus) 5.50, 3 Kersley Gardenne (Mau) 5.35, 4 Matt Belsham (Eng) 5.25, 5 Kevin Hughes (Eng) 5.15, 6 Marcus Popp (Can) 5.05, 7 Neil Young (NI) 4.80. Ian Tullett (Eng) failed at opening height. Denis Petushinskiy (NZ), originally 2nd at 5.55, disqualified after a positive drugs test.

LONG JUMP (20 Sep): 1 Peter Burge (Aus) 8.22, 2 Jai Taurima (Aus) 8.22, 3 Wendell Williams (Tri) 7.95, 4 Shane Hair (Aus) 7.82, 5 Mark Awere (Gha) 7.73, 6 Chris Wright (Bah) 7.70, 7 Steve Phillips (Eng) 7.64, 8 Chris Davidson (Eng) 7.62, 9 Stephan Louw (Nam) 7.46, 10 Zaki Sadri (Mal) 7.23, 11 Rich Duncan (Can) 7.19, 12 Keita Cline (BVI) 7.10.

TRIPLE JUMP (18 Sep): 1 Larry Achike (Eng) 17.10, 2 Andrew Owusu (Gha) 17.03, 3 Remmy Limo (Ken) 16.89, 4 Julian Golley (Eng) 16.83, 5 Ndabazihle Mdhlongwa (Zim) 16.51, 6 Gable Garenamotse (Bot) 16.05, 7 Femi Akinsanya (Eng) 16.02, 8 Zaki Sadri (Mal) 15.49, 9 Paul Nioze (Sey) 15.83, 10 Dane Gasper (StL) 15.27, 11 Chai Song Lip (Mal) 14.86.

SHOT (21 Sep): 1 Burger Lambrechts (SA) 20.01, 2 Michalis Louca (Cyp) 19.52, 3 Shaun Pickering (Wal) 19.33, 4 Clay Cross (Aus) 19.16, 5 Janus Robberts (SA) 19.15, 6 Aaron Neighbour (Aus) 18.77, 7 Justin Anlezark (Aus) 18.49, 8 Ian Winchester (NZ) 18.35, 9 Steph Hayward (Sco) 16.89, 10 Mark Proctor (Eng) 16.78, 11 Jason Tunks (Can) 16.73, 12 Mark Edwards (Eng) 16.59, 13 Ghufran Hussain (Pak) 16.34, 14 Soalla Bell (SL) 14.87.

DISCUS (17 Sep): 1 Bob Weir (Eng) 64.42, 2 Frantz Kruger (SA) 63.93, 3 Jason Tunks (Can) 62.22, 4 Glen Smith (Eng) 60.49, 5 Ian Winchester (NZ) 60.06, 6 Frits Potgieter (SA) 59.01, 7 Lee Newman (Eng) 56.28, 8 Perris Wilkins (Eng) 55.39, 9 Eric Forshaw (Can) 53.50, 10 Robert McNabb (CkI) 43.11, 11 Koo Wan Siong (Mal) 43.06.

HAMMER (18 Sep): 1 Stuart Rendell (Aus) 74.71, 2 Michael Jones (Eng) 74.02, 3 Chris Harmse (SA) 72.83, 4 Paul Head (Eng) 70.36, 5 David Smith (Eng) 69.77, 6 Phil Jensen (NZ) 69.63, 7 John Stoikos (Can) 65.07, 8 Steve Whyte (Sco) 61.57, 9 Joseph Tolbize (Mau) 55.37, 10 Brentt Jones (Nor) 53.80, 11 Tee Kue Wong (Mal) 53.06. Note: David Smith is not the David Smith who placed 1st in 1986 and 2nd in 1990, although both originated from the same city of Hull!

JAVELIN (21 Sep): 1 Marius Corbett (SA) 88.75, 2 Steve Backley (Eng) 87.38, 3 Mick Hill (Eng) 83.80, 4 Mark Roberson (Eng) 80.98, 5 Andrew Currey (Aus) 80.05, 6 Diggory Brooke (NZ) 75.55, 7 James Goulding (Fij) 73.68, 8 Nigel Bevan (Wal) 73.06, 9 Erin Bevans (Can) 72.37, 10 Adrian Hatcher (Aus) 68.99, 11 Yazid Imran (Mal) 62.49.

DECATHLON (17-18 Sep): 1 Jagan Hames (Aus) 8,490 (10.77, 7.64, 14.73, 2.19, 49.67, 14.07, 46.40, 5.00, 64.67, 5:02.68), 2 Scott Ferrier (Aus) 8,307 (10.84, 7.59, 13.34, 2.13, 48.25, 14.20, 43.99, 5.10, 58.95, 4:55.64), 3 Michael Smith (Can) 8,143 (11.23, 7.17, 18.03, 2.01, 50.38, 14.77, 47.89, 4.60, 66.87, 5:00.61), 4 Doug Pirini (NZ) 8,007, 5 Peter Banks (Aus) 7,859, 6 Mike Nolan (Can) 7,703, 7 Du'aine Ladejo (Eng) 7,632, 8 Dominic Johnson (StL) 7,586, 9 Alexis Sharp (Sco) 7,542, 10 Jamie Quarry (Sco) 7,482, 11 Simon Poelman (NZ) 7,425, 12 Georgios Andreou (Cyp) 7,297. Did not finish - Rafer Joseph (Eng), Levard Missick (TCI), Barry Thomas (Eng).

WOMEN

100 METRES (17 Sep): 1 Chandra Sturrup (Bah) 11.06, 2 Philomena Mensah (Can) 11.19, 3 Tania Van Heer (Aus) 11.29, 4 Lauren Hewitt (Aus) 11.37, 5 Vida Nsiah (Gha) 11.39, 6 Nova Peris-Kneebone (Aus) 11.41, 7 Joice Maduaka (Eng) 11.50, 8 Leonie Mani (Cam) 11.63.

200 METRES (19 Sep): 1 Nova Peris-Kneebone (Aus) 22.77, 2 Juliet Campbell (Jam) 22.79, 3 Lauren Hewitt (Aus) 22.83, 4 Melinda Gainsford-Taylor (Aus) 23.04, 5 Heide Seyerling (SA) 23.07, 6 Vida Nsiah (Gha) 23.17, 7 Philomena Mensah (Can) 23.38, 8 Monica Twum (Gha) 23.73. Note: Gainsford-Taylor nee Gainsford.

400 METRES (18 Sep): 1 Sandie Richards (Jam) 50.18, 2 Allison Curbishley (Sco) 50.71, 3 Donna Fraser (Eng) 51.01, 4 Damayanthi Darsha (SriL) 51.06, 5 Lee Naylor (Aus) 52.15, 6 Veronica Bawuah (Gha) 52.70, 7 Melissa Straker (Bar) 52.84, 8 Ladonna Antoine (Can) 52.93.

800 METRES (19 Sep): 1 Maria Mutola (Moz) 1:57.60, 2 Tina Paulino (Moz) 1:58.39, 3 Diane Modahl (Eng) 1:58.81, 4 Mardrea Hyman (Jam) 1:59.71, 5 Julia Sakara (Zim) 2:00.60, 6 Tamsyn Lewis (Aus) 2:01.71, 7 Lwiza John (Tan) 2:01.92, 8 Gladys Wamuyu (Ken) 2:02.74. Note: Modahl nee Edwards; Tamsyn Lewis was the daughter of Greg Lewis, 5th at 100 and 200 and 1st at 4 x 100 in 1974.

1500 METRES (21 Sep): 1 Jackline Maranga (Ken) 4:05.27, 2 Kelly Holmes (Eng) 4:06.10, 3 Julia Sakara (Zim) 4:07.82, 4 Naomi Mugo (Ken) 4:07.95, 5 Cindy O'Krane (Can) 4:08.88, 6 Amanda Crowe (NI) 4:10.68, 7 Leah Pells (Can) 4:10.71, 8 Toni Hodgkinson (NZ) 4:10.94, 9 Helen Pattinson (Eng) 4:12.61, 10 Lynn Gibson (Eng) 4:13.35, 11 Mandy Giblin (Aus) 4:20.15, 12 Sarah Howell (Can) 4:29.68. Note: Jackline Maranga was the wife of Tom Nyariki, 2nd at 5000.

5000METRES (17 Sep): 1 Kate Anderson (Aus) 15:52.74, 2 Andrea Whitcombe (Eng) 15:56.85, 3 Samukeliso Moyo (Zam) 15:57.57, 4 Restituta Joseph (Tan) 15:59.15, 5 Sarah Young (Eng) 15:59.79, 6 Hawa Hussein (Tan) 16:01.25, 7 Anne Cross (Aus) 16:14.98. Did not finish - Kathy Butler (Can). Note: Anne Cross was the sister of Margaret Leaney, 5th at 1500m in 1994.

10,000 METRES (20 Sep): 1 Esther Wanjiru (Ken) 33:40.13, 2 Kylie Risk (Aus) 33:42.11, 3 Clare Fearnley (Aus) 33:52.13, 4 Vikki McPherson (Sco) 34:05.11, 5 Margaret Okayo (Ken) 34:27.39, 6 Sarah Bentley (Eng) 34:40.65, 7 Hayley Nash (Wal) 35:20.14, 8 Angela Joiner (Eng) 35:22.80, 9 Sally Goldsmith (Eng) 36:02.11.

MARATHON (20 SEP): 1 Heather Turland (Aus) 2:41:24, 2 Lisa Dick (Aus) 2:41:48, 3 Elizabeth Mongudhi (Nam) 2:43:28, 4 Gillian Horovitz (Eng) 2:46:58, 5 Leanne McPhillips (NZ) 2:49:36, 6 Danielle Sanderson (Eng) 2:50:54, 7 Sarah Mahlangu (SA) 2:59:38, 8 Nthamane Malepa (Les) 3:02:14, 9 Julie Cory (Swa) 3:28:45. Did not finish - Carol Galea (Mlt), Matsepo Sephooa (Les).

10 KILOMETRES WALK (19 Sep): 1 Jane Saville (Aus) 43:57, 2 Kerry Saxby-Junna (Aus) 44:27, 3 Lisa Kehler (Eng) 45:03, 4 Janice McCaffrey (Can) 46:36, 5 Annastasia Raj (Mal) 46:41, 6 Carolyn Partington (IoM) 48:09, 7 Vicky Lupton (Eng) 48:27, 8 Kim Braznell (Eng) 51:15, 9 Monica Okumu (Ken) 51:56, 10 Karen Neale (IoM) 52:25, 11 Angela Keogh (Nor) 55:00. Disqualified - Cheng Tong Lean (Mal), Yuan Yu Fang (Mal),

100 METRES HURDLES (21 Sep):1 Gillian Russell (Jam) 12.70, 2 Sriyani Kulawansa (SriL) 12.95, 3 Katie Anderson (Can) 13.04, 4 Lesley Tashlin (Can) 13.11, 5 Bridgette Foster (Jam) 13.19, 6 Keri Maddox (Eng) 13.30, 7 Debbie Edwards (Aus) 13.49. Disqualified - Corien Botha (SA).

400 METRES HURDLES (18 Sep): 1 Andrea Blackett (Bar) 53.91, 2 Gowry Retchakan (Eng) 55.25, 3 Karlene Haughton (Can) 55.53, 4 Keri Maddox (Eng) 56.38, 5 Natasha Danvers (Eng) 56.39, 6 Vicki Jamison (NI) 56.62, 7 Mary Kapalu (Van) 59.87. 7 competed.

4 x 100 METRES RELAY (21 Sep): 1 Australia (Tania Van Heer, Lauren Hewitt, Nova Peris-Kneebone, Sharon Cripps) 43.39, 2 Jamaica (Donette Brown, Juliet Campbell, Gillian Russell, Bridgette Foster) 43.49, 3 England (Marcia Richardson, Donna Fraser, Simmone Jacobs, Joice Maduaka) 43.69, 4 Ghana (Mavis Akoto, Monica Twum, Veronica Bawuah, Vida Nsiah) 43.81, 5 Canada (Katie Anderson, Tarama Perry, Philomena Mensah, Martha Adusei) 44.23, 6 Cameroon (Anne Moury, Mireille Nguimbo, Claudine Komgang, Leonie Mani) 45.26. 6 teams competed.

4 x 400 METRES RELAY (21 Sep): 1 Australia (Susan Andrews, Tamsyn Lewis, Lee Naylor, Tania Van Heer) 3:27.28, 2 England (Michelle Thomas, Michelle Pierre, Vicky Day, Donna Fraser) 3:29.28, 3 Canada (Karlene Haughton, Diane Cummins, Ladonna Antoine, Foy Williams) 3:29.97, 4 Jamaica ((Jacqueline Gayle, Keisha Downer, Mardrea Hyman, Allison Beckford) 3:34.74, 5 Cameroon (Claudine Komgang, Stepheni Zonga, Mireille Nguimbo, Leonie Mani) 3:35.50, 6 Uganda (Mary Apio, Grace Birungi, Veronica Wabukawo, Justine Bayigga) 3:36.33. Did not finish - Barbados (Andrea Blackett, Sherline Williams, Joanne Durant, Melissa Straker), Malaysia (P.Kuganeswari, Krishnan Soloseeni, N. Manimagalay, Govindasamy Shanti). Karlene Haughton was 7th for Jamaica in the 400 hurdles in 1994.

HIGH JUMP (20 Sep): 1 Hestrie Storbeck (SA) 1.91, 2 Jo Jennings (Eng) 1.91, 3 Alison Inverarity (Aus) 1.88, 4= Lisa Bruty (Aus) & Michelle Dunkley (Eng) 1.88, 6 Nicole Forrester (Can) 1.85, 7 Susan Jones (Eng) 1.85, 8 Julie Crane (Wal) 1.80, 9 Karen Beautle (Jam) 1.75.

POLE VAULT (19 Sep): 1 Emma George (Aus) 4.20, 2 Elmarie Gerryts (SA) 4.15, 3 Trisha Bernier (Can) 4.15, 4 Janine Whitlock (Eng) 4.10, 5 Rachel Dacy (Aus) 4.00, 6 Jenny Dryburgh (NZ) 3.90, 7= Melina Hamilton (NZ), Cassandra Kelly (NZ) & Tracey Shepherd (Aus) 3.90, 10 Anna Fitidou (Cyp) 3.80, 11 Rhian Clarke (Wal) 3.80, 12 Paula Wilson (Eng) 3.70, 13 Becky Chambers (Can) 3.60, 14= Emma Hornby (Eng) & Alison Murray-Jessee (Sco) 3.50.

LONG JUMP (19 Sep); 1 Jo Wise (Eng) 6.63, Jackie Edwards (Bah) 6.59, 3 Nicole Boegman (Aus) 6.58, 4 Lacena Golding (Jam) 6.57, 5 Tracy Joseph (Eng) 6.35, 6 Chantal Brunner (NZ) 6.35, 7 Frith Maunder (NZ) 6.20, 8 Alice Falaiye (Can) 6.13, 9 Siulolo Liku (Ton) 6.12, 10 Francoise Mbango (Cam) 6.11, 11 Vanessa Monar-Enweani (Can) 6.05, 12 Tsoseletso Nkala (Bot) 5.81. Note: Tracy Joseph, nee Goddard, was 1st in the 4 x 400 relay at the 1994 Games and was the wife of Rafer Joseph, who competed in the decathlon; Vanessa Monar-Enweani was the wife of Cyprian Enweani, 6th at 200 and 5th at 4 x 100 in 1990.

TRIPLE JUMP (21 Sep): 1 Ashia Hansen (Eng) 14.32, 2 Francoise Mbango (Cam) 13.95, 3 Connie Henry (Eng) 13.94, 4 Natasha Gibson (Tri) 13.78, 5 Michelle Griffith (Eng) 13.77, 6 Michelle Hastick (Can) 13.64. 6 competed.

SHOT (18 Sep): 1 Judy Oakes (Eng) 18.83, 2 Myrtle Augee (Eng) 17.16, 3 Veronica Abrahamse (SA) 16.52, 4 Beatrice Faumuina (NZ) 16.41, 5 Tania Lutton-Senior (NZ) 16.03, 6 Helen Toussis (Aus) 15.65, 7 Maggie Lynes (Eng) 15.18, 8 Natalia Brown (Jam) 12.45.

DISCUS (20 Sep): 1 Beatrice Faumuina (NZ)_65.92, 2 Lisa-Marie Vizaniari (Aus) 62.14, 3 Alison Lever (Aus) 59.90, 4 Shelley Drew (Eng) 56.13, 5 Jackie McKernan (NI) 55.16, 6 Philippa Roles (Wal) 54.10, 7 Emma Merry (Eng) 52.32, 8 Tracy Axten (Eng) 51.58, 9 Michelle Fournier (Can) 45.49, 10 Caroline Fournier (Mau) 45.13, 11 Natalia Brown (Jam) 41.35.

HAMMER (16 Sep): 1 Debbie Sosimenko (Aus) 66.56, 2 Lorraine Shaw (Eng) 62.66, 3 Caroline Wittrin (Can) 61.77, 4 Karyne Perkins (Aus) 60.65, 5 Denise Passmore (Aus) 59.10, 6 Caroline Fournier (Mau) 59.02, 7 Lyn Sprules (Eng) 59.01, 8 Michelle Fournier (Can) 57.78, 9 Patti Pilsner-Steinke (Can) 52.59, 10 Tasha Williams (NZ) 56.21, 11 Rachael Beverley (Eng) 55.34, 12 Sarah Moore (Wal) 47.79.

JAVELIN (19 Sep): 1 Louise McPaul (Aus) 66.96, 2 Karen Martin (Eng) 57.82, 3 Kirsty Morrison (Eng) 56.34, 4 Lorna Jackson (Sco) 52.97, 5 Shelley Holroyd (Eng) 50.64, 6 Iloai Suaniu (WS) 43.51, 7 Lindy Leveaux (Sey) 42.94. 7 competed.

HEPTATHLON (16-17 Sep): 1 Denise Lewis (Eng) 6,513 (13.77, 1.82, 15.09, 24.47, 6.52, 51.22, 2:21.90), 2 Jane Jamieson (Aus) 6,354 (13.89, 1.82, 14.36, 24.67, 6.28, 48.14, 2:17.24, 3 Joanne Henry (NZ) 6,096 (14.15, 1.79, 14.09, 24.87, 6.18, 43.27, 2:18.85), 4 Catherine Bond-Mills (Can) 5,875, 5 Kerry Jury (Eng) 5,892, 6 Marsha Mark (Tri) 5,529, 7 Pauline Richards (Sco) 5,456, 8 Clova Court (Eng) 5,420, 9 Candace Blades (Blz) 3,323. Did not finish - Caroline Kola (Ken).

Statistical Notes

THE LEADING MEDALLISTS

A total of 29 athletes have won five or more medals:
(G: gold, S: silver, B: bronze)

9
Raelene Boyle (Aus) 1970-82
G 100, G 200, G 4 x 100 1970; G 100, G 200, G 4 x 100 1974; S 100 1978; G 400, S 4 x 400 1982

8
Denise Robertson - Boyd (Aus) 1974-82
B 100, S 200, G 4 x 100 1974; B 100, G 200, B 4 x 100, S 4 x 400 1978; S 4 x 400 1982

7
Marjorie Jackson - Nelson (Aus) 1950-54
G 100, G 220, G 440R, G 660R 1950; G 100, G 220, G 4 x 110 1954
Valerie Sloper -Young (NZ) 1958-74
G SP, B DT 1958; G SP, G DT 1962; G SP, G DT 1966; S SP 1974
Kathy Smallwood - Cook (Eng) 1978-86
G 4 x 100 1978; S 200, G 4 x 100 1982; S 200, B 400, G 4 x 100, S 4 x 400 1986
Angela Taylor - Issajenko (Can) 1982-86
G 100, B 200, S 4 x 100, G 4 x 400 1982; B 100, G 200, S 4 x 100 1986
Debbie Flintoff - King (Aus) 1982-90
G 400h, S 4 x 400 1982; G 400, G 400h, B 4 x 400 1986; S 400h, S 4 x 400 1990

6
Hendrik "Harry" Hart (SA) 1930-34
G SP, G DT, B JT 1930; G SP, G DT, S JT 1934
Don Quarrie (Jam) 1970-78
G 100, G 200, G 4 x 100 1970; G 100, G 200 1974; G 100 1978
Gael Mulhall - Martin (Aus) 1978-86
G SP, S DT 1978; S SP, S DT 1982; G SP, G DT 1986

Judy Oakes (Eng) 1978-98
B SP 1978; G SP 1982; S SP 1986; S SP 1990; G SP 1994; G SP 1998
Allan Wells (Sco)1978-82
S 100, G 200, G 4 x 100 1978; G 100, G= 200, B 4 x 100 1982
Sally Gunnell (Eng) 1986-94
G 100h 1986; S 100h, G 400h, G 4 x 400 1990; G 400h, G 4 x 400 1994

5

Aileen Meagher (Can) 1934-38
S 220, S 440R, G 660R 1934; S 440R, B 660R 1938
Decima Norman (Aus) 1938
G 100, G 220, G 440R, G 660R, G LJ
Shirley Strickland - de la Hunty (Aus) 1950
S 100, S 220, G 80h, G 440R, G 660R
Yvette Williams (NZ) 1950-54
G LJ, S JT 1950; G LJ, G SP, G DT 1954
Keith Gardner (Jam) 1954-58
G 120h 1954; G 100, S 220, G 120h, B 4 x 440 1958
George Kerr (Jam) 1958-66
B 4 x 440 1958; G 440, S 880, G 4 x 440 1962; B 880 1966
Les Mills (NZ) 1958-70
S DT 1958, S SP, G DT 1966; B SP, S DT 1970
Pam Kilborn - Ryan (Aus) 1962-70
G 80h, G LJ 1962; G 80h, G 4 x 110 1966; G 100h 1970
Jean Roberts (Aus) 1962-74
S SP 1962; S DT 1966; B SP, S DT 1970; B SP 1974
Ed Roberts (Tri) 1966-70
B 100, S 220, G 4 x 440 1966; S 200, S 4 x 400 1970
Charles Asati (Ken) 1970-74
B 200, G 400, G 4 x 400 1974; G 400, G 4 x 400 1974
Sonia Lannaman (Eng) 1974-82
S 4 x 100 1974; G 100, S 200, G 4 x 100 1974; G 4 x 100 1982
Cameron Sharp (Sco) 1978-86
G 4 x 100 1978; B 100, B 200, B 4 x 100 1982; B 4 x 100 1986
Ben Johnson (Can) 1982-86
S 100, S 4 x 100 1982; G 100, B 200, G 4 x 100 1986
Merlene Ottey (Jam) 1982-90
S 100, G 200, B 4 x 100 1982; G 100, G 200 1990
Paula Thomas - Dunn (Eng) 1986-94
S 100, G 4 x 100 1986; S 4 x 100 1990; B 100, B 4 x 100 1994

* Inevitably, it is the short-distance runners who dominate the medals table with at least two individual events and a relay usually available to them at each Games. So of the 29 athletes who have won five or more medals 22 have done so in a combination of short-distance individual and relay events. All but one of the remaining seven are throwers - though the great New Zealand all-rounder, Yvette Williams, also won two long-jump medals - and the only athlete to figure in the list with medals in a track race further than 400 metres or 440 yards is the Jamaican, George Kerr. England's Judy Oakes, in the shot, has no less than three claims to distinction: as the only athlete to have won all medals in a single event; as the only one to have won medals over a 20-year period; and as the oldest woman to have won a gold medal. Three athletes won medals both before and after the Second World War: Tom Lavery (South Africa) at 120 yards hurdles in 1938 and 1950; Keith Pardon (Australia) in the hammer in 1938 and 1950; and Dorothy Odam-Tyler in the high jump in 1938, 1950 and 1954.

* At least 100 of the medal-winners were born in countries other than the ones which they represented at the Games, and remarkably almost half of that total - 48, to be precise - were gold-medallists. Jamaica has made the most significant contribution with 21 medallists for other countries, including a list of 14 champions which makes highly impressive reading: For Canada - Yvonne Saunders 1974, Milt Ottey 1982-86, Angela Taylor-Issajenko 1982-86, Charmaine Crooks 1982-86, Molly Killingbeck 1982-86, Ben Johnson 1986, Atlee Mahorn 1986, Donovan Bailey 1994. For England - Roy Mitchell 1978, Lorna Boothe 1978, Bev Goddard-Callender 1978, Tessa Sanderson 1978-86-90, Judy Livermore-Simpson 1986, Linford Christie 1990-94.

* Nine gold-medallists were born outside the Commonwealth: Anna Pazera-Bocson (Australia) 1958, in Poland; George Puce (Canada) 1970, in Latvia; Judy Vernon (England) 1974 and Ashia Hansen (England) 1990, both in the USA; Carmen Ionesco (Canada) 1978 and Daniela Costian (Australia) 1994, both in Rumania; Bruno Pauletto (Canada) 1978, in Italy; Werner Reiterer (Australia) 1994, in Austria; and Bruny Surin (Canada) 1990-94, in Haiti.

* No athletes specialising in middle-distance or long-distance events or in any of the jumps have won five or more medals, and it is therefore worth noting the following among those who have won four medals:

Jack Metcalfe (Aus) 1934-38 - B LJ, G TJ 1934; G TJ, B JT 1938
Brian Oliver (Aus) 1950-54 - G TJ 1950; B 4 x 110, B 4 x 440, B TJ 1954
Suzanne Allday (Eng) 1954 62   S DT 1954; S SP, G DT 1958; B SP 1962
Dave Power (Aus) 1958-62 - G 6m, G Mar 1958; S 6m, S Mar 1962
Ron Clarke (Aus) 1962-70 - S 3m 1962; S 3m, S 6m 1966; S 10,000 1970
Howard Payne (Eng) 1962-74 - G HT 1962; G HT 1966; G HT 1970; S HT 1974
Mike Bull (NI) 1966-74 - S PV 1966; G PV 1970; S PV 1974, G Dec 1974
Kip Keino (Ken) 1966-70 - G 1m, G 3m 1966; G 1500, B 5000 1970
Mary Peters (NI) 1966-74 - S SP 1966; G SP, G Pen 1970; G Pen 1974
Brendan Foster (Eng) 1970-78 - B 1500 1970; S 5000 1974; B 500, G 10,000 1978
Ben Jipcho (Ken) 1970-74 - S SC 1970; B 1500, G 5000, G SC 1974
Daley Thompson (Eng) 1978-86 - G Dec 1978; G Dec 1982; S 4 x 100, G Dec 1986
Jane Flemming (Aus) 1986-94 - S Hep 1986; G LJ, G Hep 1990; S Hep 1994
Myrtle Augee (Eng) 1986-98 - B SP 1986; G SP 1990; S SP 1994; S SP 1998
Mick Hill (Eng) 1986-98 - S JT 1986; S JT 1990; S JT 1994; B JT 1998
Steve Moneghetti (Aus) 1986-98 - B Mar 1986; S Mar 1990; G Mar 1994; B 10,000 1998

THE LEADING GOLD MEDALLISTS

A total of 38 athletes have won three or more gold medals. Details are not repeated below for those athletes who already appear in the list of leading medallists above.

7

Marjorie Jackson - Nelson (Aus)
Raelene Boyle (Aus)

6

Don Quarrie (Jam)

5

Decima Norman (Aus)
Valerie Sloper - Young (NZ)
Pam Kilborn - Ryan (Aus)
Sally Gunnell (Eng)

4

Hendrik "Harry" Hart (SA)
Yvette Williams (NZ)
Charles Asati (Ken)
Allan Wells (Sco)

3

Lord Burghley (Eng) 1930 - 120h, 440h, 4 x 440
Arthur Sweeney (Eng) 1934 - 100, 220, 4 x 110
Eileen Hiscock (Eng) 1934 - 100, 220, 440R
John Loaring (Can) 1938 - 440h, 4 x 110, 4 x 440
John Treloar (Aus) 1950 - 100, 220, 4 x 110
Shirley Strickland - de la Hunty (Aus)
Keith Gardner (Jam)
Dorothy Hyman (Eng) 1958-62 - 4 x 110 1958; 100, 220 1962
Howard Payne (Eng)
Kip Keino (Ken)
Dianne Burge (Aus) 1966 - 100, 220, 4 x 110
Jenny Lamy (Aus) 1966-74 - 4 x 110 1966; 4 x 100 1970; 4 x 100 1974

Mary Peters (NI)
Daley Thompson (Eng)
Gael Martin - Mulhall (Aus)
Sonia Lannaman (Eng)
Tessa Sanderson (Eng) 1978-90 - JT 1978; JT 1986; JT 1990
Kathy Smallwood - Cook (Eng)
Steve Cram (Eng) 1982-86 - 1500 1982; 800, 1500 1986
Mark McKoy (Can) 1982-86 - 110h 1982; 110h, 4 x 100 1986
Judy Oakes (Eng)
Merlene Ottey (Jam)
Debbie Flintoff - King (Aus)
Kirsty McDermott - Wade (Wal) 1982-86 - G 800 1982, G 800, G 1500 1986
Angela Taylor - Issajenko (Can)
Angela Chalmers (Can) 1990-94 - 1500 1990; 1500, 3000 1994
Cathy Freeman (Aus) 1990-94 - 4 x 100 1990; 200, 400 1994

THE YOUNGEST AND OLDEST MEDALLISTS

The oldest gold-medallists:
Men - Jack Holden (Eng) Marathon 1950, aged 42 years 335 days
Women - Judy Oakes (Eng) SP 1998, aged 40 years 216 days

The youngest gold-medallists:
Men - Sam Richardson (Can) LJ 1934, aged 16 years 263 days
Women - Debbie Brill (Can) HJ 1970, aged 17 years 137 days (Brill, incidentally, was still competing in 1999 at the age of 46, and cleared her own height of 1.75, only three centimetres below her winning performance in 1970!)

The oldest medallists:
Men - Jack Holden (Eng) as above
Women - Rosemary Payne (Sco) S DT 1974, aged 40 years 252 days (The former Mrs Payne, now Rosemary Chrimes, won a World veterans' discus title in 1999 with a World best performance in the 65-and-over age group of 33.27)

The youngest medallists:
Men - Sam Richardson (Can) as above
Women - Sabina Chebichi (Ken) B 800 1974, aged 14 (or possibly 15)

OLYMPIC AND WORLD CHAMPIONS

A total of 55 athletes who have won gold medals at the Commonwealth Games have also won gold medals at the Olympic Games (to 1996) or World Championships. They are listed below in chronological order, according to when they won their first Commonweath title, and the events referred to are at the Olympic Games unless otherwise indicated.

1930
Lord Burghley (Eng) 400h 1928
Tom Hampson (Eng) 800 1932
Percy Williams (Can) 100, 200 1928

1934
Jack Lovelock (NZ) 1500 1936
Godfrey Rampling (Eng) 4 x 400 1936

1938
Bill Roberts (Eng) 4 x 400 1936

1950
Marjorie Jackson-Nelson (Aus) 100, 200 1952
Shirley Strickland-de la Hunty (Aus) 80h 1952; 80h, 4 x 100 1956
Yvette Williams (NZ) LJ 1952

1958
Herb Elliott (Aus) 1500 1960
Murray Halberg (NZ) 5000 1960
Betty Cuthbert (Aus) 100, 200, 4 x 100 1956; 400 1964

1962
Peter Snell (NZ) 800 1960; 800, 1500 1964

1966
Lynn Davies (Wal) LJ 1964
David Hemery (Eng) 400h 1968

Kip Keino (Ken) 1500 1968; SC 1972
Naftali Temu (Ken) 10,000 1968
Mary Bignal-Rand (Eng) LJ 1964

1970
Charles Asati (Ken) 4 x 400 1972
Hezekiah Nyamau (Ken) 4 x 400 1972
Robert Ouko (Ken) 4 x 400 1972
Don Quarrie (Jam) 200 1976
Julius Sang (Ken) 4 x 400 1972
Mary Peters (NI) Pen 1972

1978
Daley Thompson (Eng) Dec 1980; Dec 1984; WCh - Dec 1983
Allan Wells (Sco) 100 1980
Tessa Sanderson (Eng) JT 1984

1982
Steve Cram (Eng) WCh - 1500 1983
Rob de Castella (Aus) WCh - Mar 1983
Julius Korir (Ken) SC 1984
Mark McKoy (Can) 110h 1992
Debbie Flintoff-King (Aus) 400h 1988
Glynis Nunn-Cearns (Aus) Hep 1984
Merlene Ottey (Jam) WCh - 4 x 100 1991; 200 1993; 200 1995

1986
Kriss Akabusi (Eng) WCh - 4 x 400 1991
Roger Black (Eng) WCh - 4 x 400 1991
Linford Christie (Eng) 100 1992; WCh - 100 1993
Colin Jackson (Wal) WCh - 110h 1993, 110h 1999
Steve Ovett (Eng) 800 1980
Sally Gunnell (Eng) 400h 1992; WCh - 400h 1993
Liz Lynch-McColgan (Sco) WCh - 10,000 1991

1990
Julius Kariuki (Ken) SC 1988
John Regis (Eng) WCh - 4 x 400 1991
Douglas Wakiihuri (Ken) WCh - Mar 1987
Cathy Freeman (Aus) WCh - 400 1997, 400 1999

1994
Donovan Bailey (Can) 100, 4 x 100 1996; WCh - 100, 4 x 100 1995; 4 x 100 1997
Carlton Chambers (Can) 4 x 100 1996 (ht only); WCh - 4 x 100 1997 (ht only)
Frankie Fredericks (Nam) WCh - 200 1993
Glenroy Gilbert (Can) 4 x 100 1996; WCh - 4 x 100 1997
Samuel Matete (Zam) WCh - 400h 1991

1998
Ato Boldon (Tri) WCh - 200 1997
Daniel Komen (Ken) WCh - 5000 1997
Maria Mutola (Moz) WCh - 800 1993
Nova Peris-Kneebone (Aus) Hockey 1996 !
Chandra Sturrup (Bah) WCh 4 x 100 1999